FORMATION

Popular Music History
Series Editor: Alyn Shipton, Royal Academy of Music, London.

This series publishes books that extend the field of popular music studies, examine the lives and careers of key musicians, interrogate histories of genres, focus on previously neglected forms, or engage in the formative history of popular music styles.

Published

An Unholy Row: Jazz in Britain and its Audience, 1945–1960
Dave Gelly

Being Prez: The Life and Music of Lester Young
Dave Gelly

Bill Russell and the New Orleans Jazz Revival
Ray Smith and Mike Pointon

Chasin' the Bird: The Life and Legacy of Charlie Parker
Brian Priestley

Desperado: An Autobiography
Tomasz Stanko with Rafał Księżyk, translated by Halina Maria Boniszewska

Eberhard Weber: A German Jazz Story
Eberhard Weber, translated by Heidi Kirk

Handful of Keys: Conversations with Thirty Jazz Pianists
Alyn Shipton

Hear My Train A Comin': The Songs of Jimi Hendrix
Kevin Le Gendre

Hidden Man: My Many Musical Lives
John Altman

Ivor Cutler: A Life Outside the Sitting Room
Bruce Lindsay

Jazz Me Blues: The Autobiography of Chris Barber
Chris Barber with Alyn Shipton

Jazz Visions: Lennie Tristano and His Legacy
Peter Ind

Keith Jarrett: A Biography
Wolfgang Sandner, translated by Chris Jarrett

Komeda: A Private Life in Jazz
Magdalena Grzebalkowska, translated by Halina Maria Boniszewska

Lee Morgan: His Life, Music and Culture
Tom Perchard

Lionel Richie: Hello
Sharon Davis

Mosaics: The Life and Works of Graham Collier
Duncan Heining

Mr P.C.: The Life and Music of Paul Chambers
Rob Palmer

Out of the Long Dark: The Life of Ian Carr
Alyn Shipton

Rufus Wainwright
Katherine Williams

Scouse Pop
Paul Skillen

Soul Unsung: Reflections on the Band in Black Popular Music
Kevin Le Gendre

The Godfather of British Jazz: The Life and Music of Stan Tracey
Clark Tracey

The History of European Jazz: The Music, Musicians and Audience in Context
Edited by Francesco Martinelli

The Last Miles: The Music of Miles Davis, 1980–1991
George Cole

The Long Shadow of the Little Giant (second edition): The Life, Work and Legacy of Tubby Hayes
Simon Spillett

The Ultimate Guide to Great Reggae: The Complete Story of Reggae Told through its Greatest Songs, Famous and Forgotten
Michael Garnice

This is Bop: Jon Hendricks and the Art of Vocal Jazz
Peter Jones

This is Hip: The Life of Mark Murphy
Peter Jones

Trad Dads, Dirty Boppers and Free Fusioneers: A History of British Jazz, 1960–1975
Duncan Heining

Two Bold Singermen and the English Folk Revival: The Lives, Song Traditions and Legacies of Sam Larner and Harry Cox
Bruce Lindsay

Vinyl Ventures: My Fifty Years at Rounder Records
Bill Nowlin

Formation

Building a Personal Canon, Part I

Brad Mehldau

SHEFFIELD uk   BRISTOL ct

Published by Equinox Publishing Ltd.

UK: Office 415, The Workstation, 15 Paternoster Row, Sheffield, South Yorkshire S1 2BX
USA: ISD, 70 Enterprise Drive, Bristol, CT 06010

www.equinoxpub.com

First published 2023

British Library Cataloguing-in-Publication Data
A catalogue record for this book is available from the British Library.

ISBN-13   978 1 80050 313 7 (hardback)
           978 1 80050 326 7 (ePDF)
           978 1 80050 420 2 (ePub)

Library of Congress Cataloging-in-Publication Data
Names: Mehldau, Brad, author.
Title: Formation : building a personal canon, part I / Brad Mehldau.
Description: Sheffield, South Yorkshire ; Bristol, CT : Equinox Publishing
    Ltd, 2023. | Series: Popular music history | Includes index. | Summary:
    "As an innovative and constantly inventive jazz pianist, Brad Mehldau
    has attracted a sizable following over the years, one that has grown to
    expect a singular, intense experience from his performances. With
    Formation, Brad seeks to extend that experience to the page, by sharing
    some of the deeply personal elements of his life, and how these came
    together for him to become the musician and person that he is today. For
    the first time, he offers an in-depth look at how he came to understand
    his adoption, survive sexual abuse, and overcome heroin addiction"--
    Provided by publisher.
Identifiers: LCCN 2022044820 (print) | LCCN 2022044821 (ebook) | ISBN
    9781800503137 (hardback) | ISBN 9781800503267 (pdf)
Subjects: LCSH: Mehldau, Brad. | Pianists--United States--Biography. | Jazz
    musicians--United States--Biography. | Jazz--History and criticism. |
    LCGFT: Autobiographies.
Classification: LCC ML417.M48 A3 2023 (print) | LCC ML417.M48 (ebook) |
    DDC 781.65092 [B]--dc23/eng/20220927
LC record available at https://lccn.loc.gov/2022044820
LC ebook record available at https://lccn.loc.gov/2022044821

Typeset by Witchwood Production House Ltd
Printed and bound by CPI Group (UK) Ltd, Croydon, CR0 4YY

For Bill, James, Kevin, and all the angels.

Bildung: (German) formation, development, education

Contents

List of Illustrations

Preface
Saying Goodbye to Your Story

Canons are commonly for everyone. Their compilers aspire to universality. I propose a personal canon: this is the music that rose to the top for me. Here is how and why. I do not endeavor to list a formal concrete canon here. Instead, I will show how one came into being, specifically my own musical canon, and how that process played out in tandem with my development as a jazz musician throughout the first twenty-six years of my life. In a second book that is under way, I will focus more directly on the canon itself.

In this first book, though, I've taken a cue from the Bildungsroman genre, inaugurated in Goethe's *Wilhelm Meister's Apprenticeship*. This kind of novel – Bildungsroman is German for "formation-novel" – tells the story of a young person and how they grow into maturity. When that maturity is reached, the novel is finished. The apprenticeship is a period of gestation. The formative experiences I describe here are those that shaped me as a musician. I do not wish to imply that, when this story is finished, the development stopped. Yet it has only become possible to take stock of this growth half a lifetime later, in an effort to find meaning in the events.

The book is twofold. As a jazz pianist, I've tried to illustrate a picture of what the music felt like in the late 1980s and first half of the '90s in New York. I hope to have sketched how a particular ethos came into being, one that included myself as well as contemporaries and friends of mine. In addition, though, I tell a more personal story here, as a way of saying goodbye to it, as a path towards healing. Perhaps there will be something in it that folds into your own story as a reader.

Music heals through its storytelling – when one hears one's own story in it. Music mediated, guided, and shaped my *Bildung*. As long as I can remember, from the earliest memories, it unfolded as a narrative, and had intimate kinship with the novels I began to discover in adolescence. I will show how literature – like the Bildungsromans I mentioned, other novels and short stories, and literary and musical commentators and theorists from both left and right

– informed not just the musical canon but also how I came to understand myself. To borrow a term from a great teacher, Thich Nhat Hanh, literature and music "inter-are."

Along the way, I will also explain how the personal experiences and musical development shaped a politics – not just an affiliation, but more how I began to understand my role in society, personally and as a performing artist. I will confirm the truism that the personal is political, and that therefore, in my view, the artist/performer's output is always political, intentionally or not.

This opens up an inquiry which hovers over everything else, one that addresses the "why and how" questions I began to ask during my *Bildung*: Why did I become a jazz musician? How do I live as one? These questions probe the broader meaning behind the vocation. The answers remain provisional, but by my lights that's as it should be. I follow Rilke's admonishment not to seek closure but rather to "live the questions now." This may seem inconsistent in a Bildungsroman, which would properly end with resolution for its protagonist. Yet there was a resolution, of a kind, as the period I write about drew to a close. It was a resolve to keep on asking those questions, because they were the ones worth asking; and to find, if not definitively final answers, then a series of helpful ones along the way, open to further revision.

That resolve has remained. As a musician and as a human being, there is a never-ending mediation between the dull dead end of some sterile, unsatisfying conclusion and the exhausting vortex of endless rumination. Both are crippling. During the time I write about, I began to look for something onto which I could hold fast, something absolute and unshakeable that did not so much answer those questions succinctly, but rather, drove me to ask them. Caring about all those thorny *Bildung* questions in the first place hinged on the hope that there were answers. Even if I would never find them, I could collect clues.

Hope – the hope that I finally found again after the crisis I experienced, was necessary for my survival. Without it, there was no will to carry on. You, the reader, may understand hope in less all-or-nothing-at-all terms – perhaps simply as a force that drives your vision forward and gets you out of bed every morning to face daily strife, or just a principle of optimism you operate on with varying degrees of success. Or maybe you will find an echo in a crisis of your own that you've weathered or are still experiencing. I venture to say, in any case, that we all need hope.

That hope, in turn, is buttressed by some kind of belief that there is a meaning and order more generally. You seek evidence of that because it gives you purpose, and a sense of purpose gives you the will to persevere. That seeking, though, is driven by a deeper need – a fathomless thirst for kindness and mercy: for Love. The meaning and order are an empty husk without it. If you tie your own teleological belief to that love, then you might find someone or something you call God. There are many ways and words to describe that relationship, but in this book I share my own experience – my initial apprehension of that presence in early confrontations with the sublime, a continuing search for a workable understanding of all that and how it played into the music I made, and finally, as the book closes, God's grace as I experienced it, directly. That experience, more than any formulation or words to name it, is all that matters in the end. All ideas fall away in that moment.

I have found a maxim. It is one of those maxims that can never be met in perfection, but to which one can aspire: you have to be willing to let go of your own story about yourself completely, to drop your whole idea of who you thought you were. That means everything you don't like about yourself but also everything you cling to because you don't know who you would be without it. The story is what's tying you down. It has stopped working. When you know this to be true, it is not an intellectual realization. You feel it in your core.

This arrival can be exhilarating. There is an open expanse before you, an identity waiting to be formed. You begin to tell another story about yourself – perhaps even one about how you used to be locked in an old storyline but are now finally free from it. And then, a decade or two later, this story in turn is no longer viable.

Saying goodbye to your story can be painful as well. You're parting from something you loved, even as it was holding you back. There's grieving in that. You need hope to move forward, but it should be a hope that serves you, reinforced by an honest appraisal of what has and hasn't worked in the past, as a map for the future. False hope, on the other hand, is rooted in blind desire. It may even be desire for salvation, but it still dulls your perception, locking you in ignorance, beckoning you into a happy fantasy of the future based on an unhappy fantasy of the past, stealing away the richness of the present. If I catch myself hanging on to a hope that no longer serves me, valorizing it, it may be time to let it go.

Saying goodbye happens in as many ways as there are stories for each one of us. Often there's the grieving, but it can also be more like cutting something out of your insides with a knife. You have to walk right into the fear and face it directly. It's a fear of losing your identity. Who will you become? Or it's like climbing a mountain with only a little flashlight, all alone. The mountain gets steeper as you ascend, and the top is covered by clouds. You push forward, even when you think you can't anymore. You need faith for that.

There is a kind of faith that is not blind. It is based on knowing what has worked for you in the past, and trusting that some version of it may work in the present. That demands self-knowledge. It involves having a nuanced and honest story to tell about yourself, for your own well-being, one that is nevertheless open to revision at all times. You aspire to self-honesty, even if you don't achieve it perfectly. You don't try to snuff out what remains in you from your past. It's very rare that we truly make a clean break with anything, after all. There is always residue. Our past experiences melt into our present ones and condition them. To be aware of this affords us grace and direction during difficult times when we say, "Why am I stuck here again?"

I'd like to thank all the teachers who guided me on my *Bildung*. Some of them will be mentioned here, others not. They were all indispensable. If I have forgotten any, it is merely a slip of memory and I apologize to them in spirit. Many of them are mentioned in the story that follows. They are here in rough chronological order, in separate categories, first musical:

Throughout childhood and adolescence: Mel Subulkin; Ruth Hurwitz; Lee Callahan; Ray Cavissino; Haig Shaverdian; Peter Cassino; all of my teachers at Merrywood in Lenox, Massachusetts, including Andrews Sill, my piano teacher and chamber music coach there; drummer Larry DiNatale, who gave tenor saxophonist Joel Frahm and me our first real jazz gig, every Wednesday night at the 880 Club in Hartford; Bill Stanley; and all of the chamber music teachers at Apple Hill in Keene, New Hampshire.

Upon arriving in New York City, the list is long, and begins with teachers at the New School for Social Research Jazz Department. Firstly, my private piano teachers Junior Mance, Kenny Werner, and Fred Hersch, in chronological order. Kenny and Fred also taught classes that combined theory, composition, and motivic analysis. There was classical music history professor Henry Miller, early jazz history with Phil Schaap, a class taught by Loren Schoenberg that focused on Brahms' Third and Fourth Symphonies, big-band arranging with Kirk Nurock, ear-training teacher Aydın Esen, and Latin jazz with Andy Gonzáles. And I sat in on some exhilarating funk workshop classes with drummer Bernard Purdie. There was trumpet player Cecil Bridgewater and drummer Joe Chambers who led my ensemble classes. Drummer Jimmy Cobb taught rhythmic development in my first year, which was a high point during all my time at The New School. I wish to thank the Eubie Blake Foundation for giving me a scholarship to attend there. Finally, there was Arnie Lawrence, whom I describe below. The New School, in its ethos, was largely Arnie's vision, and he welcomed me there with open arms.

There are detailed descriptions of drug and alcohol abuse in this book. I want to stress that, although I describe the pleasure of using them, I hope I will have shown that they were a mistaken path, one that injured me and almost took my life. They are a part of my story. I do not know why I survived when close friends of mine did not. Perhaps because of this, I feel an obligation to tell that story honestly. Drugs and alcohol were painkillers which only caused more pain, and I want to underline: *they offered no insights musically, in the least.* The late great bassist Charlie Haden, whom I also thank here as an important guide and support near the end of my *Bildung*, put it succinctly in a conversation I had with him once: "Bird did not play great because of heroin. He played great *in spite* of heroin. And just imagine *how much more he could have done* if he had not been an addict." One thing is certain. He shouldn't have died that young. In considering his drug use, it is important to remember that Charlie Parker was an unqualified genius. Nobody else was like Bird.

In my case, playing on heroin worked in a sense, but I was on autopilot. It was what I already had, and I wasn't building from that any further. Real creative flourishing only began after I got clean.

I must thank Jorge Rossy for remembering much more than I ever could have on my own, about the Brooklyn scene I describe in the section "Park Slope and Carroll Gardens – meeting points." He helped me sketch that significant time for all of us. Additional thanks go to Larry Grenadier for sharing his early journey into the music, Joshua Redman for helping remember how I came into his band, Spike Wilner for his account of Smalls's humble beginnings, David Sánchez for recounting my time with his band, and Matt Pierson for his perspective as A&R at Warner Jazz when he signed Joshua Redman and we recorded *MoodSwing*.

I'd like to thank John, the older brother of Bill, my dear friend and a friend to many, who was taken from us at a young age, for giving his family's blessing to write about him below. This book is dedicated to Bill and two other close friends I lost, whom I also write about below, James and Kevin.

Finally, I'd like to thank my family: Fleurine, Eden, Ruby, and Damien. They began the next chapter of my life after the *Bildung* I write about here. I could have never imagined when I was a young person what a rich chapter that would be. My gratitude for their love and the lessons they've taught me is immeasurable.

Several names have been changed in this book to respect the privacy of the people I write about.

I

Tom Sawyer

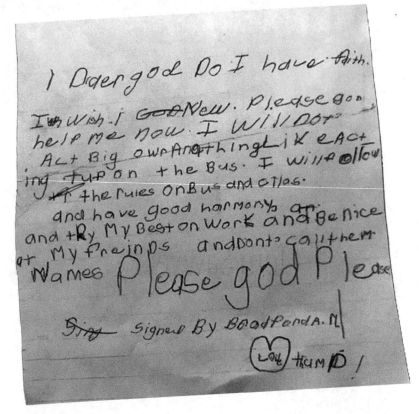

Letter, circa 1976 (six years old)

Dear God,

Do I have faith. I wish I knew. Please God help me now. I will not act big or anything like acting tough on the bus. I will follow the rules on [the] bus and [at] class, and have good harmony, and try my best on work and be nice at my friends and don't call them names. Please God Please.

Signed by Bradford A.M.

Love thump! (?)

Seeing Cain the first time

When I was eight years old, in third grade at Memorial Elementary School in Bedford, New Hampshire, there was this one kid, a couple years older, in fifth grade. I never knew him and forget his name now. I was drawn to him and watched him secretly. He had eyes that were so blue they were almost gray, thin and squinting, and I imagined he had blood from some rugged, faraway Eastern place I had seen in *National Geographic* – maybe the steppes of Siberia or Mongolia. Yet there was that sandy, washed-out blond hair. He was from somewhere *else*. That much was certain. His gaze was slightly downwards most of the time, just below your eye level, but not out of any shame – more out of disdain for everyone else, except sometimes when he suddenly looked upwards at me with his eyes only, not raising his head. If I didn't turn away, he would hold his gaze towards me for a moment and then look back down again, uninterested.

He was a loner. The other kids made fun of him. He would never say anything. He didn't cry or show any emotion. I wasn't sure why they were picking on him. He wasn't ungainly; he didn't talk funny. He didn't talk much at all. Maybe that was why they were mean to him – they didn't trust his silence. Kids were like that, running on animal instinct. To me he looked cool, kind of rugged, like the tough kid I would have liked to be – me, with my bifocals and Dickie trousers. He always had on the same pair of Wrangler jeans.

One winter day on the playground, this loudmouth fourth-grader had been taunting him for most of recess. Some other kids were giggling – not just the boys but girls as well, which made it even worse. Then: all of the sudden, he stepped forward and knocked the wind out of the loudmouth – a fast knuckle punch right between his ribs. The kid went down on his knees, trying to breathe. Then he started to sniffle and cry in spurts, the snot dripping out of his nose and freezing onto his upper lip like it did on those cold New England days.

A crowd of us gathered around the two – the one crying and the one standing over him silently. I remember feeling scared of that fifth-grade loner, scared of the way he came out of nowhere with that punch. There was no hesitation in it and, after he did it, he showed no remorse, only calm resolution. At the same time, I understood him. I understood how he was always alone. I already felt that burden. I wasn't with those other kids – I didn't want to be. But I didn't really *want* to be alone, the way it seemed he truly did. So there was this mixture of fear and recognition. The yoking of those two primal emotions was my first, foundational meeting with what I came to understand as The Sublime.

Through the crowd, another kid stepped forward – a sixth-grader, a real alpha-type, a shotcaller on the playground. He decided quickly that the loner was wrong for hitting the kid, and had to be punished. The other kids lined up dumbly behind him and yelled insults at him. The alpha bruiser pushed the loner once on the chest. He lurched back, but stayed on his feet. He made no move to strike back. The teacher on recess duty was already on her way. She broke it up and it was all over.

I sided with the loner, and felt no sympathy for the loudmouth who received his fierce, unexpected punch. The loner, it seemed to me, was the real victim, because the whole group fell in line with the ringleader. It was betrayal by the tribe. He was attacked by the group, not just by the loudmouth. That seemed much crueler than what he had done, and the sixth-grader alpha kid was nothing but a big windbag by my lights, with his John Wayne act. I still felt fear of the loner. He had my sympathy, though, and, more importantly: my admiration.

I never became friends with him. As I went along in life, these kinds of people were models for me, but I never entered into a direct exchange with them. In fact, I came to realize that I didn't have much in common with them. They were out of the tribe. I was straddled somewhere between outside and in. I was never quite ready to make the break, and I guess I didn't really want to. Besides, you don't actually choose your tribe – it chooses you, just as it casts you out.

The error I made was in my conflicted perception of the loner: if he was really so strong, if he could really roam in his own solitude so freely, without all of us, then he was no victim. Yet I projected that quality onto him. Unwittingly, I had made a model for myself. I would valorize my own sense of victimhood in the years to come, always trying to be a real outsider like him, never quite succeeding.

Dream music

Some of my earliest memories are musical, from age four when my family lived in Roswell, Georgia. My mother and I would sit at the Sohmer spinet piano from my father's childhood home in Bay Bridge, Brooklyn. It was the piano I played and practiced on until I left for New York at age eighteen. She would play nursery rhymes for me, and then I would imitate her. I could quickly repeat what she played, and enjoyed the game. My mother found the two most important piano teachers of my childhood and spent many hours taking me to and from lessons, fostering my musical growth in those early years.

The following year in 1975, when I was five, we moved to Bedford, New Hampshire, and lived there for the next five years. I began piano lessons soon after with a man my mom found named Mel Subulkin. Mr. Subulkin had a weekly gig at a hotel restaurant in Manchester, the small city next to Bedford, and my parents took me to see him there a few times. He backed up a singer, and they played hits from that time like "This Masquerade" or "Isn't She Lovely." I looked up to him. He played a Yamaha CP80 electric grand on that gig – an instrument whose timbre colored much of the pop music that entranced me in the next several years.

We began with method books in those first lessons – simple things for kids designed to teach how to read music, fingering, etc. – and then started to work from songbooks of popular hits from the day. He would teach me how to embellish what was on the page by adding ornamentation. We took this approach with songs like Barry Manilow's "Mandy," "If" from Bread, or the theme from the popular TV show *Love Boat*. I started to develop likes and dislikes: the Barry Manilow and *Love Boat* were okay but sounded a little like the soap operas I saw on TV sometimes – syrupy, a little glib. "If" had something deeper, though, in both its sadness and dreamy happiness. Mr. Subulkin was the first model of someone being spontaneously creative at the piano. He put the idea in my head early on that you could make stuff up and music wasn't strictly about reading notes on the page. This was the embryonic beginning of improvisation for me, aged seven.

Bedford was a sleepy, small town. The steeple of our Presbyterian church was the highest edifice. It had a few days of national fame every four years during the Republican primaries. New Hampshire was a big zone for Republican presidential hopefuls who wanted to give their pitch and present themselves as authentically libertarian – "Live Free or Die," like the license plate says. Bedford, in the Republican myth, was a small town full of regular scrappy, no-nonsense folks, laconic Northerners shaped by snow and ice, hardy types who didn't need the government telling them what to do. All the news outlets would set up camp there, and the politicians would show up and campaign to the townspeople, while the camera angled on their silent, frowning faces, listening to the jargon.

Our cousins had a beach house in Hampton Beach, NH, and that's where I am, aged five

Celebrating my eighth birthday

That year, George H.W. Bush came through Bedford, the first time he ran for president in 1979 and lost to Reagan. He gave a short speech one evening in the auditorium of my elementary school and my family went. There were probably no more than a hundred of us there, and he took some questions at the end of his talk. A couple of kids got to ask questions. One asked him what he would do about nuclear bombs, and was the world going to blow up. The question was met with sad, pinched smiles from the adults and platitudes from Bush ("There are no easy answers to these tough questions . . .").

The previous Thanksgiving – we celebrated every year in Haverhill, Massachusetts with my cousins on my Dad's side of the family – I had been listening to a conversation between my father and my Uncle George, talking about the "Russians." They were going back and forth a bit with some mumbo jumbo I didn't understand – something about a "cold war," whatever kind of war that would be, and then, all of a sudden, Uncle George said to my dad, "Yes, but Craig, what about the Russians? *What do we do about the Russians?*" My Dad was stumped and didn't have an answer. I was impressed. So I had my question ready for Bush. I was going to ask him, "*What about the Russians?*" I had no idea why the Russians were worthy of concern, but it sounded cool and advanced when my dad and my uncle were talking about it. I wanted to sound important like that for Bush. (He didn't call on me that night.)

My first memorable strong connections to music were through the clock radio in my bedroom in Bedford. I got it for Christmas when I was seven years old, and I listened to the hits of that period. As I didn't have a record player yet – that came a year later – I would hear a particular song, fall for it, then simply wait around until it was played again. I would try to catch it when we were in the car, when I was allowed to sit in the front seat and choose the station. The other place I would hear those songs was coming from the lifeguard's transistor radio at our public swimming pool, where I spent many days in the summers of 1976–79. I got lost in them. I can still smell the chlorine and feel the hot cement and the warm sun when I hear those songs from that time. I can feel the sweet anticipation in my belly as they begin.

I hear them now, and they're like a good dream I'm recalling. There's a sad kind of feeling of something that's gone, but there's an ache of happy yen all mixed up in it. There's something that I can never get back, but here's the thing: maybe I never had it. The first time I heard it, it was *already* like a dream – it was already beckoning me to somewhere that was better than here. The music showed me that place, but I could never really enter into it. So when I go and try to make music every time, I'm trying to crawl back into that dream. Even though I can't, echoes of it remain everywhere in this world of action, and experiences add more colors to it, and soften or sharpen the hues that are already there.

The dream and reality stand apart, but they're wrapped into each other at the same time. Music is not so much the gift itself, but the slow, endless unwrapping of it, and a hint of what might be under the wrapping. What lies there is the Absolute: God. He is infinite; I am not. Music is both the expression of my finitude, and its consolation. I walk towards God in an asymptotic line, never quite meeting him directly. Yet there is evidence of this absolute, abiding presence here and now, in the music, every experience that informs that music, and every experience it informs in turn, in a perpetual exchange.

In the summer of 1977, "Dreams" from Fleetwood Mac's *Rumours* was playing all the time at the swimming pool. It became my own dream: Stevie Nicks's voice, the harmony, the steady, grounding groove of the band. I was still there with everyone at the pool, but it had taken me away in head, heart, and body.

Thunder only happens when it's rainin'
Players only love you when they're playin'
Say women, they will come and they will go
When the rain washes you clean, you'll know

Hits from the Steve Miller Band's *Fly Like an Eagle* were all over the radio. "Rock'n Me" was ecstasy for me. When a song felt so good and was so simple like that, the message was: you don't have to change anything right now. Whatever was going on at that pool, it all froze in place as he sang, in a moment of perfection.

And I know that it's true that the things that I do
Will come back to me in my sweet time

I'd look around, at the lifeguards, at the other kids and the adults, and I'd be filled by this sense of excitement about how good everything could be, and how beautiful it already was, when it was shot through with that soundtrack. It imbued everyone and everything in front of my eyes with grace and some quiet, unknown purpose. As soon as the song was over, the dream left, until the next one came on. And it went on and on like that. In particular songs, that dream feeling was more pronounced. The dream was the *subject* of the music, or so it felt. I began to call that Dream Music. "Dreams" and "Fly Like an Eagle" itself were potent, bewitching examples.

"Sara," from Fleetwood Mac's next album *Tusk*, was another. There was Stevie Nicks again, sounding far away and maternal all at once, calling me, like a siren, into some eternal womb.

Wait a minute baby
Stay with me awhile
Said you'd give me light
But you never told me about the fire

In all of these songs, it was the harmony that wove the spell, like the undulating guitar under the lyrics of Boston's "More Than a Feeling."

I looked out this morning and the sun was gone
Turned on some music to start my day
I lost myself in a familiar song
I closed my eyes and I slipped away

Hotel California from the Eagles was full of dreams. In "Life in the Fast Lane," the Eagles told a story I didn't quite understand, yet it made me want to join them. When I was seven and would listen to that song, I always heard them singing "*bike* in the fast lane." We would hear it on car rides to our cousins in Haverhill. I'd turn and gaze out the window, and would imagine myself speeding easily past all of the other cars in the breakdown lane of the highway, pedaling my 1976 Schwinn Bicentennial Sting-Ray at supersonic speed, kicked back on the banana seat. Right alongside me was Joe Walsh riding a Harley with a suicide clutch. It was dangerous freedom, and I felt that in the song even before I grasped what it was about – the high-rolling life of rock'n'roll, and the toll it took.

"New Kid in Town" from the same record was the first example I had of a song that could go from carefree to troubled in a split second: When the harmony abruptly dropped into a minor key at the chorus, and Glenn Frey sang, "Johnny come lately / The new kid in town," it made me sad but I had to hear it again. The sudden change of mood, the unexpected trauma in the song, hit like a visceral punch. It was just as much a physical feeling as anything else, and I began to understand that music had a way of connecting emotion and physical sensation. These kinds of emotional/physical rips were jarring, and I started to seek them out, addictively. My family made regular trips to Boston, an hour ride from Bedford, where my father, an eye doctor, would attend ophthalmology conferences, and we would spend the day at Faneuil Hall Marketplace, the Boston Aquarium and the Museum of Science. We'd often eat dinner before riding home at an Italian restaurant called Florence's in the North End of Boston with a jukebox, and "New Kid in Town" was the favorite song on it for both my mom and me. We'd play it every time we were there.

On those car rides, I heard my first classical music. We had one cassette of Rudolf Serkin playing Beethoven's Fourth and Fifth Piano Concertos, with Eugene Ormandy and the Philadelphia Orchestra, and another one with him playing the "Moonlight," "Pathétique" and "Appassionata" Sonatas. The heroic style of Beethoven's middle period was my first model for classical music, and Serkin was the first model for a classical pianist.

Billy Joel's *Glass Houses* came out right before the summer we moved to West Hartford in 1980 and the first tune I heard from him was one of its hits, "You May Be Right." It was rock'n'roll piano, and I wanted to embody that. I didn't understand much about the lyrics on "You May Be Right" except that he was being sarcastic, and was kind of pissed off and cracking jokes at the same time. I dug that. Billy Joel's music became bigger for me in the next few years, as I started acquiring his earlier records, working my way backwards chronologically: *52nd Street*, *The Stranger*, *Turnstiles*, *Streetlife Serenade*, and of course *Piano Man*. His music moved well past the normative harmony of much rock'n'roll, and on *The Stranger* I heard my first jazz soloing: the wistful solo from alto saxophonist Phil Woods on "Just the Way You Are," and trumpeter Freddie Hubbard's scintillating contribution on "Zanzibar."

All those records laid a big imprint on me as a musician in terms of harmony and melody alike but, perhaps even more importantly, their storytelling. There was an arc to the songs, a journey in just a few minutes that went someplace far and took you back to where you started, having gained an insight, like in "Scenes from an Italian Restaurant" from *The Stranger*. Songs like that one, "Streetlife Serenader" or "Captain Jack" had a melancholy and nostalgia which I identified with instinctively. When it reached its end, it seemed like the song itself already yearned to go back in time to its own beginning. Yet that longing was already at the start. It was that perpetual longing, longing for the dream, the first dream. Everything built off that.

There was an early simpatico with "adult" emotions. I know I'm not the only one to experience that in my youth. I had as of yet no personal identification with the stories Billy Joel was telling, the ones that rode on that wave of nostalgia and sadness. "Scenes from an Italian Restaurant" was a story about idealistic love that fizzled out, told wistfully years later, looking back; "Streetlife Serenader" brought humanity to busking musicians, trying to play for anyone who would listen; "Captain Jack" was about someone eerily close to whom I would become fifteen or so years later – a young failure, back living at home with my parents:

> Saturday night and you're still hangin' around
> Tired of living in your one-horse town
> You'd like to find a little hole in the ground
> For awhile

I was still far away from all the regret and disillusionment those songs described. Yet there was a catharsis listening to them – they brought some pain that was already directly before me, laid it at my feet, and I looked it in the eye. That is what music could do, and it could heal me that way. Years later, hearing those songs, they do exactly the same thing, now that I've gone through some of the experiences Billy Joel shared in his music. When I got under the trauma I had as a young person, I realized that the songs were already providing me relief, even if they didn't correspond to my life then. Or maybe it's a chicken–egg thing: we carry these heavy feelings with us already – they're waiting to be discovered and then confirmed when we confront sadness through an actual event. All I can say is, thank God for music, as a means to name something difficult that was already inside me. Music is not as much a discovery of something outside of yourself. It's about coming to know yourself truly – the things locked inside you.

Lonely music

Sensations of a pleasurable nature have nothing inherently impelling about them, whereas unpleasurable ones have it in the highest degree. The latter impel towards change, towards discharge, and that is why we interpret unpleasure as implying a heightening and pleasure as a lowering of energetic cathexis.

Sigmund Freud, *The Ego and the Id*

I'll go out on a limb and speak for artists in general and not just the ones in my musical neck of the woods. I won't even categorize them, except to say that artists make things from their own discreet world of dreams, sometimes finely wrought and breakable, sometimes grand and sturdy. For whatever reason, you decide to accept the invitation into their small/big world. It affects you, and finds its way into your own dreams.

It's a common understanding that artists transmit something that's brimming at the surface of their emotions, and then becomes lucid enough to fall out as a cohesive creation. Take sadness and heartache, loss and grieving. You feel it in their work, and you think: they're in touch with that. And if you choose to speculate on the person who made it, you envision them as someone entrenched in sorrow, enough so to bring it forth. Their work, you reason, is a cathartic coming-to-terms with difficult emotions.

Yes and no. If every new creation was an act of self-reparation, artists would perish from the grief between those atoning moments, in the heaviness of the long wait. Artists are stronger than they often admit. For, in order to craft something that embodies trauma, cancelled hope and vanishing dreams, they have to step outside or above all that misery, to a degree. This is not an orderly "process" in the normal sense of a means to an end. The idea of a succinct "end" is conciliatory, but no more than a wish. There is a catharsis, but it is never final, because art is never final. It comes to a provisional end at some point – we leave the club, concert hall, gallery or theater; we close the book, and return soon enough to what's waiting for us.

When you are an artist, you make an agreement with yourself, consciously or not, to never completely relinquish the overwrought moment of cathexis – that condensed millisecond before the discharge of grief. You hold some in reserve. There is no tidy inner-peace and resolution, acceptance of "what happened," and the ability to "reflect" on it in the artwork. Yet you persevere, along with everyone else. This is why we may see someone who outwardly is functioning and thriving, all the while making something that looks or sounds like breaking down and crashing.

This implies a dual personality – the artist dips into trauma when they're at work, and then switches back to quotidian repose when it's time for a break. Yet it's not so different from what everyone experiences – provisional resolution, but some store of grief that never quite leaves. If there is an artistic temperament, it is a predisposition – or "talent," if you want a more flattering word – for keeping the trauma close by and working with it, with relative ease, even with welcome. Pulling one's hair out in the dark of night, drinking bottles of whiskey, shooting heroin, leading ruinous lives – these clichés are not unique to artists, nor necessary for their success. Artists achieve their work *in spite* of these actions, just as Charlie Haden put it to me. Like anyone else, they either survive and potentially grow from their injuries or succumb to them.

It may be magical thinking, but I understand the cathexis to already lie within us, before the actual moment of injury. This is why at a young age we hear music that describes misery, and already feel kinship with it, the way I did with "Captain Jack" and other songs. I would daresay that that foreshadowing experience is part of art's dæmonic attraction. It calls us to future trauma. Yet the catharsis – the way out – lies within us as well. Cathexis/catharsis is unfolding in every moment; it's just that we feel it more acutely in the heightened sneeze of some definitive event. Not just every emotion, but every moment of confusion, of gnosis, of love and hate, of walking away from God and walking back towards him, is already there.

"Captain Jack," "Billy the Kid," and of course "Piano Man" were Billy Joel songs that I heard on AM radio, which was a back channel to other Dream Music, from Jim Croce, Gordon Lightfoot, Harry Chapin, Cat Stevens, and other singer-songwriters. They told stories that were models for the one I began to tell about myself. AM radio was like a heaven where songs went, and stayed there forever. I'd hear them on those highway rides at night, coming home from Boston.

I'd see the Mack trucks passing by, and I fantasized that that was my gig – driving alone through the night. I loved the idea that there was a sleeper above and you could pull over in a rest stop and go to bed. You'd have your favorite book, favorite stuffed animal, and a little nite light.

The other job I wanted to have was working in the tollbooth. Whenever we stopped and paid the toll, I'd try to look at the people working there. It was their own private world, a small enclosed space between them and the travelers. The only people they saw were people in cars paying the toll for a brief moment – then they were gone, speeding away, never to be seen again. What a strange job that must have been – to have a life like that, behind glass, and this endless series of momentary connections with people going somewhere, somewhere they wanted to be, not here where you were. You were in between, in a highway place where nobody ever stopped for long. But you got to *stay* there; you were frozen while they moved. I embraced the idea of that kind of loneliness. It seemed like sanctuary.

Out on the highway itself, though, loneliness had sadness and an ache of fear under it. You'd open the window for a moment and feel the cold wind and darkness rush in. I was with my parents and sister in the car, but I was already far away from them and everyone else. Supertramp's *Breakfast in America* came out in 1979 and, when I heard "Take the Long Way Home," it didn't matter who I was with in reality. With that song, I was alone, riding through the night, right from the opening introduction with its world-weary harmonica.

> When lonely days turn to lonely nights
> You take a trip to the city lights
> And take the long way home
> Take the long way home
>
> You never see what you wanna see
> Forever playing to the gallery
> You take the long way home
> Take the long way home

It was exactly where I'd be a few years later in my twenties: trying to quit but still strung out on heroin, living back in West Hartford with my parents, driving the two-hour car ride into New York City to do a few gigs and get validated, never finding what I wanted, driving back home alone through the night. I already knew how that felt – not the experience, but the feeling – when I was a kid.

Absorbing more music in the following years, I discovered that loneliness had lots of hues, and they weren't all pitch dark. It could be mysterious and finely wrought, like in Jon & Vangelis's "The Friends of Dr. Cairo," or like an empty landscape in Dire Straits' "Telegraph Road." It might be majestic and tragic in David Bowie's "Space Oddity," or quirky and remote in Thomas Dolby's "One of Our Submarines."

It was Pink Floyd who raised loneliness into something harrowing. *The Wall* was released at the end of 1979, and it was a big deal. Even before getting it, just through the singles I heard on the radio, it seemed like something important and forbidden all at once, an adult experience that was off limits for me, but one I wanted – like the R-rated movies I couldn't go to yet. I begged my mother for almost a year and finally got it for my tenth birthday on August 23, 1980, just a few days before we moved to West Hartford. Her reluctance to bring it into our home was based on the popular radio hit from the record "Another Brick in the Wall (Part 2)," yet I suspect it wasn't simply on account of its call-to-arms refrain (*We don't need no education . . .*). It had more to do with a quality I remember her calling "creepy" in their music.

Indeed, she was describing what attracted me to it like a lonely siren. It was the real despair in that song, just under the children's cockney chorus, the disco-in-peanut-butter groove from drummer Nick Mason, the bluesy guitar work from David Gilmour and the distinctive vocal style of Roger Waters – low-pitched, a little gravelly, with a large shadow of some past trauma and a portent of more to come. It was far more serious than anything else I heard, not kid stuff. Many musicians with whom I've spoken, recounting the early stage in their *Bildung*, mention these introductions to works that might have seemed too dark for their age – or too gnomic, too intellectual, too carnal, etc. Yet, as with me, they were harbingers of actual experiences they would come to have. You wanted to know those experiences already, to sneak past your parents and peek behind the curtain. Can music predict one's future? I believe so, in a fashion.

I knew some other anthems of insurrection like Alice Cooper's "School's Out" or Cheap Trick's "Elo Kiddies" – rock'n'roll straight down the middle, with a dose of anarchic glee and, in the case of the Cheap Trick, something wild, with real ecstasy. But "Another Brick in the Wall (Part 2)" still expressed the solitary experience of its protagonist, Pink, and, if it grabbed any feeling I already knew, it was alienation. I just didn't have that name for it yet.

I began to make a distinction between "public" music that told of a shared experience, and this other kind of "private" music. "Another Brick in the Wall (Part 2)," the most well-known hit from the record, was told in the plural first-person "we." Yet it was an exception. Elsewhere on the record, Pink wasn't standing up with any mob in solidarity; he was apart from everyone. After all, other people were terrifying on *The Wall* – in their condemnation of Pink, or their outright violence, like in "The Trial" or "Run Like Hell." When Pink spoke to the public in "In the Flesh" (part 2) he inverted the roles, stoking one's fears with fascist cruelty. It was all in self-protection, though, and he was describing something I would carry out later, in my own more muted manner. I'd lock myself out from others in that fear, into a cage of anger and loneliness. The loneliness of "Nobody's Home" had a bit of consoling humor; but "Is There Anybody Out There?" seemed to come from a room where the door was nailed shut – there was just a little crack where all that sad, beautiful music from David Gilmour's acoustic guitar seeped through to us. It was almost too much to listen to. "Hey You" was someone trying to push the door open a little, and ultimately failing.

If songs from Fleetwood Mac and the Steve Miller Band had the quality of a dream, Pink Floyd introduced a scary subgenre: Bad Dream Music. "Goodbye Blue Sky" started in a wistful/happy childhood place with wordless singing, almost a lullaby, and in the next moment turned into a nightmare of wartime terror. It was a sudden switch-up like in "New Kid in Town," but the polarities were much further apart, and they took place in an interior place that was closed off from everyone and everything else. When you listened to *The Wall*, you agreed to set foot in there and have the door shut behind you for its duration.

Loneliness found me again like an old friend in different clothes when I started to build a personal canon of jazz. It was there in Billie Holiday's sad/smiling way of singing "I Can't Believe That You're in Love With Me." There was often a quiet irony in her delivery of those happy pop tunes of her day, and, in this case, she was signaling: *It's too good to be true.* Herbie Hancock's "Little One" on Miles Davis's *E.S.P.*, full of pastel woe, met my loneliness, as did Kenny Dorham's trumpet-crying on "Escapade" from Joe Henderson's *Our Thing*. When I began to play jazz myself, loneliness was a twofold companion: not only the affliction but the way out as well, through the catharsis of playing instead of merely listening.

Loneliness traced through Brahms' music, like in the early Ballade #4 in B Major, Opus 10 which I studied with my next piano teacher, Ms. Hurwitz. Brahms showed more than anyone how you can make a major chord sound impossibly sad. Schubert, his predecessor, had a long pedigree of noble loneliness, in music like the second *Andante Sostenuto* movement of his last Piano Sonata, or just about any song in *Winterreise*.

Later on, other singers and songwriters made solitude palpable even if I didn't understand their words at first. Léo Ferré and Jacques Brel were masters of *chanson* – lonely, weathered Prosperos, singing songs like "La mémoire et la mer" or "La ville s'endormait" from their shipwrecked islands. They could actually cry and sing at the same time, and so could Chico Buarque on a song of parting like "Trocando em Miúdos." There was so much music that spoke to my loneliness . . . all of it both confirmed it and consoled it. It was music to listen to in the tollbooth.

West Hartford

New England is often thought of as a uniform collection of states, with certain associations – founding fathers, Ivy League schools, Waspy old money, the ivory-tower liberalism of Martha's Vineyard. But Bedford, New Hampshire and West Hartford, Connecticut, where we next moved, were two very different places to grow up, and the juxtaposition of the two made an impression on me.

My family moved to West Hartford in 1980 at the end of the summer, right before eighth grade started for my sister and fifth grade for me. I had just turned ten. The move was exciting for us but difficult. I can still feel the butterflies in my stomach walking to that first day of school. We moved so that my dad could start a joint ophthalmology practice with his old friend from medical school, Bernie. Uncle Bernie (as we called him), his wife Rita and their two kids were our idea of West Hartford before we moved there – we visited them a lot before we arrived from New Hampshire. My folks and them became friends in New York City, where we lived while my father and Bernie finished their residency at Cornell when my sister and I were little – I have no memory of that time.

Bernie and Rita had a group of friends that largely comprised of couples like themselves – a Jewish husband and a Scandinavian wife. The wives had met each other through a social club. I have no recollection of anyone European living in Bedford, and there was exactly one Jewish person in our whole elementary school: a girl named Sarah in my first-grade class who told the class about Hanukkah during the holiday season and brought the menorah to show-and-tell.

My parents' new social group in West Hartford exposed me to much more cultural variety than the more homogenous Bedford, although still no people of color. For the most part, that would wait until my move to New York City after high school. Rita was from Norway and spoke with a cool accent. Bernie drove a strange car called a Saab which looked like it was from the future and sounded like an airplane. They ate cheese from France, bought Deutsche Grammophon albums, read the *New York Times*, and went to see strange, sad movies made by someone named Ingmar Bergman. They gave dinner parties in the summer where they served a cold soup that tasted like V8 juice and which I always thought was called *gestapo*; imagine that: cold soup. They had a swimming pool, and sometimes Rita and the other women would swim topless. I would steal looks at their breasts: milky, secret treasures in the soft evening light, a promise of something in the future. It was all new to my sister and me. The only other culture that we had been exposed to, with the exception of trips to Boston and one vacation in New York City, was my grandfather's farm in Ohio – even more rural than New Hampshire.

My first day of fifth grade at Bugbee Elementary School sucked. I remember it now: the rumbling in my stomach, the weak, nervous feeling. I remember the scratchy new Levi's corduroys I had just gotten for the new school year, the unfamiliarity of the surroundings, and how everything smelled different: the cafeteria, the hallways, the classroom. My mom had arranged that I would go to a kid's house down the street, who would then walk with me the rest of the way to school, but I got lost on the way to his house. I went home and my mom explained the route again, and the second time I made it there. His name was Silas and we quickly become friends that year.

On the walk together we were largely silent, the way kids can be when they first meet each other; small talk comes later in adulthood. The friendships that last for me have always been built on that sacred silence, no matter how uncomfortable it is initially. In a short time, there was a path ahead and we entered. "Bugbee Path," Silas explained. "You can ride your bike on it. That's what I do," he continued, implying that I was holding him up walking with him on his first day of school, which was true. There was nothing like this in Bedford, where paths were cut long ago and passed through woods in people's backyards, and were interspersed with stone walls people said were built by the Indians before the Pilgrims got there. This path was paved, and I could see it was a straight shoot the whole way, opening up at the end, maybe half a mile down. Bugbee. What would it be like?

We walked a ways and there was another path that shot off to the right, this one unpaved, wooded. In the next few months, I would begin to explore it on my own, on the way back from school. It was fun to walk on, just wide enough, and full of tree roots popping out that you had to watch for so as not to trip. Further in, you came to an incline, and there was a necessary hop over a little stream. After a rain or snow, it filled up and was surrounded by mud; you needed a wider jump to the other side for risk of landing in it.

Next you came into a clearing with tall trees and moguls of dirt – bike jumps. Cool. In Bedford, the older kids had fashioned them out of stacked plywood right on the road and would cajole us into lying down in a line, sometimes up to four. Adults would drive by in the cars and look out their windows with disapproval. They would gather speed on their bikes and make the jump over us. The kid at the end always risked getting landed on right on his stomach. What would have happened, I always wondered – would he puke out his guts, or worse? It never happened.

On the other side of the clearing was a vertical drop with mysterious trees ascending out of it; all the trees there were large and majestic. The whole area possessed mystery from that first moment I saw it. At the bottom of the drop I saw a wide brook, interlaid with little islands where more, smaller trees grew. We would play games there, Silas and I, each giving his island a name, like a territory. Further up, I saw the back of the school, separated by a gate. There was a crawl space dug out, just large enough for a kid to fit under if they wanted to take a detour to enter the schoolyard. To the right another path continued, and you came to a wooden bridge, one side facing the school, the other facing those miniature islands. You crossed out onto a cul-de-sac and were now on the street that bordered mine. It was a quicker, less scenic route to Bugbee, and when I took it I went through my backyard to shave off even more time, skipping over a small barbed-wire fence into the adjacent backyard of the old woman who lived behind us.

That whole wooded area behind Bugbee alongside the bike path remains frozen in my mind. There are many memories there. The following summer after fifth grade, I got a dirt bike for my eleventh birthday – a "Mongoose" with a shiny chrome frame. I would make jumps with Silas and Peter, another new friend from Bugbee, both from my classroom. A few years later, I wound up in those woods at the height of my first solitary trip on LSD, freshman year in high school, taking it all in, the colors sharper, the trees more mysterious. There were hangs – sophomore through senior year with my buddy Dave, smoking weed and drinking grain alcohol in the cold November air, riding out the afternoon in conversation or silence. Every year thereafter I would return, and, to this day, every time I visit, all those memories hold. I walk through, consolidating them, shoring them up once more.

Silas and I arrived at Bugbee and entered the fifth-grade classroom. Our teacher was Mr. Mazzie; he introduced me, saying that I had just moved from New Hampshire. At recess I hung back, but some kids approached me and we talked a bit. On that first day, I heard an expression I had never heard before in Bedford: *loser.* "He's a real loser." "She's a total loser." I didn't get it at first. I asked a boy what it meant, to be a loser. "Is it like, you lose a game, in sports?" I ventured. That's all I could come up with.

He just looked at me and rolled his eyes, shaking his head, saying, "You are *such* a loser."

I started to understand that if you were a loser it meant you were being held in contempt for just being who you were, and that you were unworthy of respect. There was no immediate fix for that, because the judgment was all-encompassing. It seemed that there was a consensus on who was a loser: lots of kids would chime in together, calling one kid a loser. All of that – the derision itself, and the ganging-up into a group – was not yet part of my direct experience. It felt like these kids who were my age were not really kids. Any time I acted like a kid – acted silly or goofy, say – they called me a loser. The problem was: I didn't know what else to be – I didn't know how to fit in and be something else than what I was. What I didn't realize then was that neither did they.

The main difference between West Hartford and Bedford was this idea in West Hartford that there was something better out there – something cooler, something less loser-like – and that someone like me wasn't privy to that. West Hartford had more money, it had more cool stores and restaurants, but the kids back in Bedford were more content with what they had.

Bedford was less wealthy than West Hartford and, perhaps because of that, less materialistic. Even though the Republicans would go on television during the primaries and cynically co-opt New Hampshire-style libertarianism as their own phoney virtue, there was something to it in actuality. It had to do with the actual social fabric. In Bedford, there was a view of others that was less weighted by the desire for prestige more characteristic of West Hartford. As I went along in the coming years, I appreciated Bedford in a different light.

There were cliques at Bugbee as well, also new to me, although really only two: the jocks, who were good at playing soccer and lacrosse, and were good in gym; and the nerds: kids like me who wore glasses, read Ray Bradbury stories, would soon go on to play Dungeons & Dragons, and were always picked last for teams in gym. The jocks called us "losers" and that was that. I joined the nerds and became friends with them. They were nice; there was nothing tricky about them, and we had similar interests.

Until I reached junior year of high school, age sixteen, I hardly came across any kid my age in West Hartford who was *integrated*. You were one thing. In high school, the social groups splintered into more varieties, and each one took on more nuanced characteristics. The jocks were still there, but, as they entered the arena of team sports, they carried a heftier weight. Their tribe glued itself together more strongly than the others, in the rituals of hazing and regularity of practice and games. Nerds were still there, but they had stature now: everyone knew they were going to do something important with their lives when they got out of high school, or at least worthy of respect. There were burnouts, deadheads and gearheads alike, and of course the drama club crowd. Yet there were only a few people who didn't fit some category, or could easily move between them. They were usually quiet types, flying low. It was only in junior year that we all started mixing together more, shedding our cliquey personas a bit.

Ricky

There was one kid who started on me almost as soon as I arrived at Bugbee: Ricky. Uniquely, he neither hung with the jocks nor the nerds. He was in a tough spot because he called us nerds "losers," so we were reluctant to seek his company. But the jocks didn't want to hang out with him either. He seemed like he was alone but was always talking to everybody. In retrospect, Ricky was actually someone who was already integrated – he was really himself, even as he suffered for it. And what was the designation he got at the point? He was in his own solo category for the jocks: "weird."

Ricky may have sought me out as a kind of self-therapy, like kids do – find the one who is even more of an outsider than you and then pick on them. I wore glasses from the time I was four years old until I was thirteen. Ricky called me a loser all the time, and then it was "four-eyes." It would happen in French class – for the few minutes before the teacher arrived, he would go on and on like that. It really messed me up, mostly because I didn't get where the venom was coming from – what did I do? Why was he trying to make me feel so bad? The other kids would just watch, smiling, waiting for me to cry.

I never cried, but I never really knew what to say back to Ricky. Obviously, he didn't wear glasses like me, he didn't actually look "weird" even if the jocks called him that, he didn't talk funny, and he didn't smell bad. So I sat there for a couple of months, silent, until one day, out of nowhere – I wasn't planning it or anything – my snappy comeback flew out of my mouth:

"Jew."

The room was silent; everyone waited. Finally, Ricky said, very seriously, *"Did you just call me a Jew?"* I said nothing, already regretting it.

"Nobody calls me a Jew. Fight on Bugbee Hill after school today." Then he was off, and some of the jocks in the class were already chanting, "Fight! Fight! Fight!"

Later, after lunch, another kid delivered a folded note to me. I opened it, and it said, *"YOU ARE DEAD AFTER SCHOOL."* It was unsigned and written in red magic marker, very dramatic. It seemed silly, but I was nervous. Ricky was no bigger than me, though, and I couldn't back down. After school, we headed out to the hill. "Bugbee Hill," as it was called, was at the back of the school behind the parking lot and basketball court, and was a pretty good sledding hill in the winter. It wasn't that big, but on that day it felt like a long climb up to the top; two gladiators, trudging slowly up, with all of the kids gathered there, watching, some of them beckoning us.

"Kick his ass, Ricky! He can't call you a Jew!" That was from another Jewish kid, a big tall guy in the sixth grade. I had really fucked up. What was I thinking? I had heard Ricky talking about Hebrew School with other kids who went. Nobody in my family had ever used a slur like that; it certainly wasn't learned behavior. I was trying to hurt Ricky back – I was trying to use some secret weapon that would instantly cancel out all the times he had called me four-eyes or loser. I knew that it was really, really bad to call someone a Jew, at least with the kind of derogatory tone I'd given it. I knew about Hitler and the Holocaust. So maybe I wanted to try on some of that evil for a minute and see if it had an effect. It was a disaster.

I took the first swing and aimed for Ricky's face but kind of missed and hit his forehead. Still, it connected and threw him off – he wasn't expecting it. He punched me in the arm, grabbed me and we were on the ground. Then I pinned Ricky and was on top of him, punching him in the face. He taunted me while I hit him: "You're just slapping me." It's true that I wasn't punching him hard – I didn't have the hatred required to really try to smash his face with my fist. I heard yelling around us and everyone crowded in and it was a blur of adrenalin, anger, and mostly fear.

And then – it was sadness. I felt so sad. I got up off of Ricky and couldn't hold back anymore. I started crying. I turned and walked away and was crying my eyes out, sobbing, just being the loser kid from Bedford and letting it all hang out, because the whole thing was so awful, the way all the kids wanted us to beat each other up and the way no one there was on my side. I felt alone and the world seemed like a shitty place and I just wanted to go home but then I couldn't go home and tell my parents about it because they would be horrified if they knew I called someone a Jew like that. So I had to get the cry out and walk a little and let my eyes get normal again and not all puffy. It was a rough afternoon.

With my crybaby routine, Ricky of course declared himself the winner, and, well, he was, because he was more of a hard-ass on the hill – he didn't break down and cry. The last thing I saw as I walked away was Ricky jubilantly shaking his fists in the air, yelling to everyone, "I won! I won!"

Ricky taunted me for a few days after that, but then, strangely, he let me be. And then it passed. I started fitting in a little more in West Hartford as the school year went along. Kids found out that I could play the piano and I wasn't just some clueless loser anymore. It wasn't easy, but I began to find my way.

Meanwhile, I made an important discovery. Out of all the kids in the school, Ricky, my recent tormentor, was the one other kid who could make music! He played drums, and he was good. I heard him playing a rock beat in orchestra class and a bunch of kids were watching. When Ricky played drums, his whole personality changed – he was really sure of himself. That's kind of how I felt when I played piano: I felt like I wasn't just acting cool; I really *was* cool. Maybe Ricky wasn't a jerk after all. I kept noticing how he got picked on by the jocks, and I felt bad for him.

My first year in West Hartford passed, and sixth grade rolled around. I began playing drums in the wind ensemble, something I would continue to do through eighth grade, where I got to play mallet percussion instruments like the xylophone and vibes, and timpani as well. The band met for class in the auditorium. Ricky must have heard me playing piano there a few times after class, and one day he came up to me and said, "Do you know 'You Really Got Me'?" Sure I knew it – the Kinks original and the more recent cover by Van Halen. Could I play it? Sure.

Some kids gathered around us and we started playing it together easily. I got goosebumps when Ricky's thrashing rock beat lit up the simple riff I played. The kids were quiet watching us, impressed. A few months later, we played in the auditorium for a talent show and they screamed and hooted for us. Kim, the girl I had a crush on already in Mr. Mazzie's class, a quiet beauty with sleepy eyes, looked at me for the first time and half-smiled. I blissed out for days, recounting that dreamy gaze.

And so the Rolling Pebbles were born.

I think the name was Ricky's mom's idea. Anyhow, it stuck for a while, at least. Later iterations of the band, which was always Ricky and I at the core, had other names. My favorite band name we had, later in seventh grade, was Prophets of the Void – prophets, Ricky's older brother was quick to point out, of absolutely nothing. The Rolling Pebbles played school functions – talent shows, class picnics, that sort of thing – and we performed a lot in Ricky's basement. Ricky's mom would lure kids from the neighborhood in with chips and punch and we'd play our whole repertoire in under an hour.

It was almost all covers. At first we didn't sing: we just played the themes. It worked pretty well. Our next big score after the Kinks was a medley of hits from the biggest record of that moment, *Freeze-Frame* from the J. Geils Band: the title track, "Centerfold," and "Rage in the Cage." It was a tripartite slam. All we had to do was play the hooks and the kids went crazy.

We did have one strong original. Ricky wrote the lyrics and I wrote the music. It was called "Don't Know Who She Is." Ricky sang, with real feeling:

> Walkin' down lonely across the street
> Lookin' for someone that you'd like to meet
>
> I just don't know who she is . . .
> I just don't know who she is . . .

That's all I can remember. After those verses and choruses, which were in a slow rock feel *à la* "The Weight" from The Band, we morphed into a double-time jam over the chords to the guitar solo in Lynyrd Skynyrd's "Freebird." It was our boldest effort. Looking back, the lyrics seem just right. Having had 0% experience with girls at that point, we really did not know who "she" was.

Ms. Hurwitz

Shortly after we moved to West Hartford, my mom found a woman named Ruth Hurwitz to continue with my piano lessons. I studied with her for the next four years. Ms. Hurwitz's background was classical; she trained at Juilliard and had a career as a concert artist before she had children. From the first lesson with her, everything changed. She started me on real classical piano repertoire, which until that point I had never played. At that first lesson she assigned me Bach's first Two Part Invention, Chopin's early Nocturne in E♭ Major, Opus 9, #2, and the first movement of Beethoven's Piano Sonata #1 in F Minor.

From there we moved around. There was more Bach, Beethoven and Chopin, and also Mozart sonatas, Brahms *Klavierstücke* and Bartok *Mikrokosmos*. Later came some of the warhorses like Chopin's first Ballade in G Minor, and also two of Debussy's preludes. Brahms was my favorite and Bach pissed me off then – it was just too damn hard. There was no place to hide. I came around eventually to Bach and he still provides endless edification and nothing short of spiritual nourishment. Beethoven was and is the model for a paradoxical creator, one with a certain willful inspiration. Brahms gives solace and consolation. The Three Bs as they're called – I'm a happy member of that cliché.

Ms. Hurwitz taught me all twelve major, harmonic minor, and melodic minor scales with the correct fingerings. We worked on each one for a few weeks until I had it. We would break up the rhythms in different ways – first evenly, then dotted, then in triplet patterns. In this way, you could expose the difficult parts of each scale in terms of fingering. The goal was to get up to sixteenth notes at 160 bpm on the metronome. We also worked arpeggios and some of the Hanon and Czerny exercises.

Through all of this, Ms. Hurwitz taught me good technique at the piano, and its application in the context of the actual repertoire. Until that point I had never given much thought to technique; whatever I was doing was mostly intuitive. I hadn't considered the idea that there might be a "right" way to position your fingers on the keys, a right amount of curvature in your fingers as you played. She taught me how cross the thumb under the other fingers in such a way that the desired dynamics, rhythm, and articulation of the phrase were not compromised. This kind of stuff is basic, but it never gets easy in the sense that it can always be better. I've always enjoyed the anecdote from Rudolf Serkin: he continued to practice the C major scale (with only white keys) throughout his life, saying that it was the most difficult of all of them. I think he meant that it is the most honest – it will show you and anyone else listening exactly where your technique is at, like having a straight, long shot with no angle on the pool table.

Ms. Hurwitz taught me correct technique from her own perspective and I did not question it. I respected and trusted her as my teacher, absolutely. I feel very fortunate to have studied with her. The technique she taught me at the piano when I was ten years old is essentially the technique that I have now. I have never had any physical problems like tendonitis that come about from playing the wrong way (knock on wood), and I have her to thank for that. I've never met another pianist who has good technique without having had a good teacher for that at some point. Good technique for me means achieving maximum expression with the least amount of extraneous physical effort.

She had me keep a daily log of how many minutes I practiced. The goal was one hour a day. The responsibility and accountability to someone else about whether or not I was practicing instilled a work ethic which I retain today. In retrospect, the move to West Hartford at age ten was ideal for my musical development. I was passionate about music. I knew already that I was going to be involved with it for the rest of my life, but I was not studious. More often than not, I didn't achieve the one-hour daily goal of practice, and hovered on average around forty-five minutes. Ms. Hurwitz and my mother, though, found the right balance of admonishment and encouragement. There were only a few times I remember feeling shameful from being reprimanded; and from Ms. Hurwitz, very importantly, I felt love behind that reprimand, so the hurt was good hurt, and it passed quickly. A good teacher is a lot of things, but the most important thing a teacher can give to their students is that love. The best teacher has a simple, strong desire to see a student grow and blossom, above anything else.

I became more serious about music and started to develop a trait that I think is indispensable for any musician: the desire to excel and demonstrably kick ass at something, which takes self-discipline. Later, with no guiding teacher, the accountability became self-accountability.

Upon entering through the front door of Ms. Hurwitz's old house, you went to a waiting room where you'd sit if another student wasn't done yet. My mom would drop me off and pick me up, sometimes staying for part of the lesson, listening in. In the main room, there was a New York Steinway B, the classic mid-sized grand which in my opinion is still the most beautiful-sounding of all their pianos, and the one I own today. There was also a Steinway upright on the other wall, on which she might demonstrate something, or else it was used for the two-piano music that was sometimes played. That was a gorgeous-sounding piano as well.

Ms. Hurwitz held recitals every few months at her house where she taught, and all of her students would perform. The audience comprised the other students and family members, seated in several rows of fold-up chairs. The boys dressed up in ties, jackets, and saddle shoes, and the girls wore dresses. She would call us all up by name, one by one, announcing the pieces we were going to play. After it was over, there were cookies, Breyer's vanilla ice cream and punch. It all seems quaint looking back, but I remember the nervousness

I felt before playing, waiting for my turn – butterflies in the stomach, sweaty hands, trembling – the whole bit. I also remember the thrill of finishing the performance and the applause. All of us kids would hang around together in a mixture of pride and relief. These were some of my first experiences performing for other people. Without knowing it then, I was hooked already.

The mark

Early on in that first year in West Hartford, our teacher Mr. Mazzie gave the fifth-grade class an interesting assignment. It was only October, the beginning of our second month living there. I had not distinguished myself to any of my classmates and had won no friends as of yet. I was still a nameless "loser" for the most part. The assignment was a family tree. We were supposed to go home and ask our parents to tell us everything they knew about their grandparents, their great-grandparents, and so on, as far back as they knew. Then we'd make a tree of it on poster board and get artsy-craftsy with magic markers – the names, where they came from, whatever you find out: When did they come over to America? Did they arrive at Ellis Island?

Mr. Mazzie introduced the assignment with a class discussion. He went around asking all of us, Where does your family originally come from? Kids had different answers. Maria was Puerto Rican and her parents had come to Hartford the year before she was born; Waspy Todd, one of the jocks, bragged that his ancestors came over on the *Mayflower*; a Jewish kid explained that he was "Ashkenazy" and had Polish blood, and when his great grandparents arrived at Ellis Island, the customs officer shortened their name to the one he had now so it would be easier to pronounce in English.

Wasn't it great, Mr. Mazzie cooed, that we could all be so different? But in our differences we shared something strong: our common pride in our origins, in what made us unique, what made us who we were! Those differences, he concluded, were exactly what unified us, what made us Americans! It was a big happy melting pot!

Everybody had a cool story and there was recognition all around. There were even giggling exchanges between the jocks and the nerds. Mr. Mazzie settled down the giddy anarchy; it was my turn. "And what about you, Brad? Do you know where you are from?"

"Well," I said, "I can't really say about myself. I'm adopted." The class was silent.

Mr. Mazzie said, "Oh, I see! That's very interesting. Well, no problem. You can just do like everyone else for the assignment, and ask your mom and dad to tell you about their family tree." I nodded. No fun jokes or communion with the other kids followed, just some stares. I was outside the melting pot, left on the countertop.

"Do like everyone else," yet, not *be* like everyone else. I would use my mom and dad's family trees – not mine. I didn't have one. It was the first time I put that together. Being adopted wasn't having another story to tell. It was having no story. I didn't know anything about my birth parents. There was nothing to report. I was a cipher.

I had never given it that much thought until right then. I knew why I was different, but it hadn't come up like that in a class. However my parents had told me that I was adopted, it was so early on that I don't remember the actual event of them telling me; I only remember that I knew at a certain point. That point was from my earliest memories, when I was four years old and we lived in Roswell – I remember only the knowing.

I thought that my sister and I were lucky, because our adoptive mom and dad – the ones who raised and nurtured us – loved us. If someone adopted me, I reasoned, there was no question that they wanted me. They sought me out. On the other hand, there was this unanswered question: Why did those other people give me away? Didn't they want me? After that day in Mr. Mazzie's class, I developed a suspicion that I was looked upon differently – I was inferior, I was outside of something. The exchange with Mr. Mazzie in front of the other kids felt like being exposed. I felt shame. At that point, it was just a feeling, as of yet unrecognized and unnamed. Without realizing it then, it started a story I had about myself as an outsider.

Early on in Hermann Hesse's Bildungsroman, *Demian*, the mysterious title character recounts the biblical story of Cain to the protagonist Sinclair: after Cain killed his brother Abel, God banished him from the tribe, and gave him a mark. The Bible tells that God placed the mark on him to protect him from being killed as he wandered. The protection was also a curse, ensuring that he would live out his days as an outsider. Demian had another take on Cain and his mark:

> Here was a man with something in his face that frightened the others. They didn't dare lay hands on him; he impressed them, he and his children. We can guess – no, we can be quite certain – that it was not a mark on his forehead like a postmark – life is hardly ever as clear and straightforward as that. It is much more likely that he struck people as faintly sinister, perhaps a little more intellect and boldness in his look than people were used to. This man was powerful: you would approach him only with awe. He had a "sign." You could explain this any way you wished. And people always want what is agreeable to them and puts them in the right. They were afraid of Cain's children: they bore a "sign." So they did not interpret the sign for what it was – a mark of distinction – but as its opposite. They said, "Those fellows with the sign, they're a strange lot" – and indeed they were. People with courage and character always seem sinister to the rest. It was a scandal that a breed of fearless and sinister people ran about freely, so they attached a nickname and myth to these people to get even with them, to make up for the many times they had felt afraid – do you get it?

When I read that in my early twenties, I thought, this is brilliant! The "sign" that I wore was a mark of distinction. Instead of shame, I could feel special – even superior. I would apply this kind of reverse reading to selected parts of my story – being adopted, homosexual feelings and experiences, being sexually perpetrated in high school, becoming a drug addict. Instead of feeling shame, all of that would give me this special mark, the mark of a romantic transgressor, a cool outlaw. I could then discard that old story I had about myself – a story that was saddled in Old Testament shame. As I charged forward and began the life of an addict, I embraced this belief. Much later I realized that I had traded one bad story for another one. But the outsider model, the one with the cool mark, held dominion throughout my *Bildung*.

Prog

In 1981, the first summer after we moved to West Hartford, my family was on vacation visiting my grandfather on our annual trip to his farm in Ottawa, Ohio. That's when I heard Rush's "Tom Sawyer" for the first time.

> No his mind is not for rent
> To any god or government
> He knows changes aren't permanent
> But change is

It was just starting to hit the radio. My dad and I were driving to the grocery store in Toledo and it came on in the car. It rocked hard, so I was in there right away – I related that hardness to AC/DC, Led Zeppelin, Black Sabbath, and Van Halen, who were all in my ear already. But it was completely different. There was some different kind of harmony going on. I wouldn't have been able to specifically articulate what was special about it, but it was dreamy. "Tom Sawyer" was Dream Music of a different order: it was in the dream, but just at the moment before waking, when everything collides together and time congeals back into an awakened state. I got lucky and we heard it again in the car, on the way back from the shopping. I heard that it was a band called Rush, from their new record, *Moving Pictures*, and I was hooked. I couldn't stop thinking about that song for the rest of the vacation and every time we went in the car I would try to find it on the radio.

With "Tom Sawyer," Rush gave me an unapologetic Cain-figure: a badassed kid around my age, recast into their song. And, although I didn't grasp the lyrics right away, they also pushed open a door of political awareness, just a crack. Rush's brand of Ayn Randian individuality made an impression. In high school, characters like Howard Roark from her novel *Fountainhead*, or John Gault from *Atlas Shrugged* were further Cain models.

Rush immediately became the biggest thing for me as a daily listener of music for a good chunk of time. I bought or begged for their records, and, by the time their next record, *Signals*, came out, I had everything of theirs up to that point. I saw them in concert with my father on their *Signals* tour at the Hartford Civic Center and it blew me away – a power trio to the highest degree who could rock with fire and sweep you away into that dreamy place, in equal measure.

"Subdivisions" from *Signals* was the first song I learned and played that used the odd time signature of 7/4. It planted the seed of all things "seven" in my brain and I followed up much later, exploring that rhythmic meter in the jazz format with my trio. Much of occidental music is rhythmically written and felt in continuous groups of two, three, or four beats. Other rhythmic groupings – like five, seven, nine, or eleven – often turn up in much music from other sources, but are not the norm in jazz, pop/rock and Western classical music – the three broad genres that I allude to most often in this book, only because they are the three I am personally most steeped in as a listener and a musician. Now, "odd" rhythmic meters, as they are sometimes called, do indeed crop up in those genres: composers began to use them in the twentieth century, jazz musicians like Dave Brubeck popularized them, and they show up with some regularity in progressive rock. For me, the portal into odd meters was Rush.

"Subdivisions" was one of two vocal features I had in the Rolling Pebbles. The other one was The Who's "Behind Blue Eyes." I went for the thoughtful stuff and left the more hard-edged vocals to Ricky; already at that age I was too self-conscious to be a rock star. It would have never worked for me.

I definitely fantasized about it, though, and, looking at Rush, I wanted to be every one of those three guys in that band. I did a lot of air-guitaring to Alex Lifeson: for instance to his blistering, sculpted solos on "Freewill" or "The Trees," and, of course, "Tom Sawyer" itself. Geddy Lee's bass lines were killing as well, and a big part of Rush was his innovative synth work – it gave an extra dimension to their sound. Really, though, it was most often Neil Peart that I idolized. He pushed against the boundaries of rock drumming, stretching them further. He raised the level of virtuosity in his field, single-handedly. He was a new model for me in that regard, regardless of the fact that he played a different instrument. Before Neil Peart, virtuosity to me meant the recordings of the classical pianists Ms. Hurwitz gave me to listen to, or the ones my parents had at home: Vladimir Horowitz playing Rachmaninoff, Rudolf Serkin playing Beethoven, Arthur Rubinstein playing Chopin, Glenn Gould playing Bach. After Neil Peart, my idea of virtuosity extended to rock musicians. When I heard Oscar Peterson a year later, it then included jazz musicians.

Virtuosity must never be made light of and should not be condemned as something useless "for its own sake," as we read often in pejorative music reviews. When we hear this grievance about a performance or recording, often the problem is that, on the contrary, virtuosity was *lacking* – the player was aspiring to it but didn't reach it, or tried to give the impression that they had it but didn't really. Virtuosity is not playing fast but sloppily; nor is it playing with precision but with little dynamic variation. What makes virtuosity inspire titters and dropped jaws from the audience is when difficult musical feats are pulled off with élan. Undoubtedly, virtuosity implies power on the one hand, but one mustn't forget that it depends on absolute control and strict attention to detail as well. Most of all, it comes alive only when combined with an expressively compelling viewpoint on the musical material. It is a power that is bridled and kept reined in, displayed only when it is needed. Virtuosity can indeed be with all the bells and whistles, but just as often, to gloss on Theodore Roosevelt's phrase, it may mean speaking softly and carrying a big stick.

Being inspired by a virtuoso display is also frequently the way into playing music for a young person. An eleven-year-old kid, when they hear Chopin, is probably not listening for the subtle logic of the voice-leading that winds under the melody, nor the deep formal integrity of a Beethoven sonata, or the hidden anagrammatic message of love that Brahms is sending Clara Schumann in a chamber piece. The child certainly hears the virtuosic passages, though, and invariably wants to play them. Why? Because it's cool, because it is a way of impressing others: the teacher, the parents, siblings, peers who study with the same teacher, other friends. Why else would a kid slog through such difficult music – for edification? That comes later. The initial desire to excel in music, versus just playing passably well, is rooted in the ego (as is the desire for edification, but in a sublimated way). One wants to distinguish oneself from others, and gains that distinction immediately through a virtuoso display.

Neil Peart inspired me so much that I just had to try to play the drums. I began lessons at Bugbee, learning how to hold the sticks, and learning some rudimentary stuff on the snare – the flam, the paradiddle, the double-stroke roll, that kind of stuff. As I mentioned, I played in the school wind ensemble for the next three years, in sixth, seventh, and eighth grades. It was always a blast to play in the marching band during the Memorial Day Parade through West Hartford Center, leading the band with the snares in the drum corps. I played all the pitched percussion for the wind ensemble as well: the vibes, bells, marimba and timpani.

Eventually, air-drumming was not enough for me when I listened to Rush and Neil Peart at home, and the snare lesson once a week at school was just a tease in terms of getting to play the instrument. A drum set was not forthcoming, so I built one. God bless my parents and sister, who had to hear me. I was not directly in their midst, though. In West Hartford, we had a basement, and that's where it went. The "drum set" was put together mostly from cookie tins that were turned upside down. They really weren't very resonant at all because I taped them onto three pieces of plywood which surrounded me on the floor where I kneeled. Each had its own character nevertheless, and the sound changed the more I pounded on them. There were also a few bigger tins with plastic tops which I placed right side up with the plastic top on. They gave a warmer, lower sound, like a muted tom-tom. They worked until I banged them too hard and the plastic tore.

I drummed along with Rush on the stereo that my sister and I had down there, and anything that came up on MTV. In those beginning days of long-by-gone MTV, the cable television channel had only a small collection of videos, and, if you watched for even an hour, you might see the same one again, like the Canadian band Chilliwack's "My Girl (Gone, Gone, Gone)" ("Gone gone gone she been gone so long . . ."). There was also a segment every now and then called "Closet Classics," where they played old video footage of stuff from the '60s, and you could see things like Jimi Hendrix at Monterey Pop Festival,

Santana at Woodstock, and darker footage as well from the Rolling Stones' disastrous concert at the Altamont Speedway Free Festival. That for me was a peek into another turbulent, romantic time, much more exciting than the Reaganite '80s.

The drumming-along with Rush was big for my musical development. I was getting exposed to the complex rhythmic stuff that Neil Peart was doing, and, by trying to play along with it, I was *feeling* it as well, feeling how it rocked, feeling how pleasurable it can be in your body to make a rhythm. The pleasure of rhythm: that is so often the spark that begins a musical performance or listening session. We hear the stuff that makes our body feel good, and, if we're musicians, we try to imitate so that we can generate that feeling ourselves. That's how we learn how to groove: by exposure and osmosis.

During my first few years in West Hartford, the cellar was a refuge for me. It was an escape place – it was underground and private. My sister and I had a tacit agreement: neither of us would come down there if the other one was there. We never had an argument about how we would share the cellar; we just never shared it. She had her fantasy world down there and I had mine. She was all about dancing and pretending to be the singer – Pat Benatar, Donna Summer, and others. I was drumming, pretending to be in some band.

The basement in West Hartford was strange. It was a refuge to find solace in, but it could also be scary – a place to run out of, in panic. That depended on which way the fantasy was veering, whether towards good or evil. Our second year in West Hartford, my parents went out to a dinner party and my sister and I watched *The Exorcist* in a rebroadcast on TV. When the poor girl was possessed by the devil, she talked in a menacing man's voice that was not hers, her head spun around all directions, and she vomited on the priest. I was filled with terror, and the images burned into my brain. For a couple of years after that, I would imagine that she would be in the cellar with me at times, behind my back. I would leave, and, as I ascended the stairs, I felt her behind me, chasing me in her puke-covered nightgown, taunting me. I would race out and slam the door behind me.

Fantasy, as a literary genre, was connected to my love for Rush. Rush had big designs on records like *Hemispheres* and *A Farewell to Kings*. They were going for the epic sweep, telling a story in different parts, taking you on a journey far away, and then returning you home. It corresponded to the fantasy books I was reading then, particularly those of Madeleine L'Engle, C.S. Lewis, and Stephen R. Donaldson. Those books all shared a similar storytelling device. Their protagonists, such as Thomas Covenant in Donaldson's books, or the children in Lewis's *Chronicles of Narnia* and Madeleine L'Engle's books in the *Wrinkle in Time* trilogy, would begin at home in the real world in the present time, but would then leave that world and reappear in another world. These were worlds full of magic and wonder, but also danger and dread. It was far more intense than the one they had temporarily left behind, with richer glory and adventure, greater tragedy and loss. When the characters came back from that faraway land, after months had passed, fighting evil lords, falling in love and whatnot, almost no time had elapsed in our world here.

That narrative conceit of suspended time in our world while time passes in an alternative world was connected to dreams. When we dream, we enter a world where other things are possible – we can taste ecstasy not available to us when we're awake, and we might also confront something more terrifying than anything in this realm. A dream can span a long time. Days and months can pass easily in a dream, and we even sense their passing, yet, when we wake up, very little time has elapsed; sometimes the dream was only ten minutes in real time, as in morning dreams after we've hit the snooze button the first time.

Rush's music was related to fantasy stories and dreams for me. Songs like "Jacob's Ladder" from *Permanent Waves* gave me the same feeling of suspending time and traveling to some place far away. When I listened to their music, it could be for twenty minutes or so – one side of an LP – but it felt like I had traveled long and far. I discovered other earlier progressive rock after Rush, working my way back to bands like Yes on records like *Fragile* and *Close to the Edge*, and Gentle Giant on *The Power and the Glory* and *Octopus*. Progressive rock had a great impact on me and was my gateway from rock to other kinds of music, mainly jazz and classical. I related the expansive strain I found later to large-scale jazz suites and classical music – whether John Coltrane's *A Love Supreme* or Beethoven's *Eroica* Symphony – to my earlier experience of prog rock.

Here are my personal prog rock criteria. You can't join the prog club without some credentials. Not every prog tune has to have all of the qualities on the list below, but it will have at least one of these characteristics. One could, for example, consider two exemplary songs from the genre: "Starship Trooper" by Yes, and "Xanadu" by Rush. Taken together, they represent two "generations" of prog rock: Yes, an early crucial band, and Rush, a band that expanded on prog's large aspirations in its next generation. Both songs contain all of the criteria below.

1. **A longer song with a grander design than the two- to four-minute schema favored by pop/rock music.** Expect at least five minutes, usually six minutes or more. It could be analogous to a jazz suite in design, or even symphonic in scope, with several separate songs operating like "movements," as in Rush's "Cygnus X-1, Book II: Hemispheres."

2. **Unique sections within that longer song that contrast with each other.** These sections are quite different from those that we find in so many songs that adhere to simpler binary and ternary forms, whether they are nineteenth-century lieder, Tin Pan Alley or later pop songs. Prog rock songs do not make transitions with the trademark cohesiveness of a verse, chorus, and bridge. A new section radically changes the character of the music. Often it sounds like a new song. Thus the

oversized aspect of prog. Its impulse extends to a form of expression that is greater than the frame associated with its genre.

3. **In the story of the song, a dichotomy, like we find in fantasy literature, between a place that is here and now, and a place that is far from here and now.** The various moods and the shape of the song will be informed by that dichotomy. The deeper, more authentic and alluring world is something that we discover in the song, with the band – we travel there together. This sense of travel is important: we do not simply begin in some faraway world; we have to get there first. In this way, we feel the distance.

4. **The lyrics likewise often have a gnostic quality.** There is a poverty of knowledge in the visible here-and-now world. The knowledge lies distant and hidden, and we must travel to find it. It is revealed to us. What does our gnosis award us – what lies at the end of the prog rock journey? There is the promise of ecstasy and perfection, of union, reparation, utopia. We are allowed to taste that for a moment. Once we have a taste on our tongue, we want to find our way back to that other place.

5. **A certain amount of virtuosity from the band members.** There is respect for the *craft* of music making. The mystique of prog is related to its virtuosity, and makes it opposite in character to punk rock, which in some respects was a reaction against the proto-prog gestures of bands like Led Zeppelin. Prog rock is played by competent and often brilliant musicians; punk rock can be played by people with very limited knowledge of their instruments or of music more generally. Think of the well-known joke that a punk group needed a bass player for the band, so the guitarist asked his buddy to join who had never played an instrument prior. Then think of Geddy Lee.

There is a long-standing, grouchy polemic in rock music – To Punk or To Prog? In the same way that the Wagner and Brahms debate went to the heart of what it meant to be a German Romantic composer after Beethoven, and the Coltrane versus Sonny Rollins debate went to the heart of what it meant to be a modern jazz saxophonist after Charlie Parker, the punk–prog binary goes to the heart of what it means to rock after Led Zeppelin, as I'll argue later. It is serious business.

Or is it? Is the subject even worthy of a polemic? What could possibly be wrong with *being able to play your instrument really well*? Nothing, it would seem, yet prog rock gets dissed afresh by every new generation of hipsters who come along, keen on making a joke out of it. Scorn for prog, though, stems partially from this next criterion:

6. **Earnestness.** Classic prog is unapologetically earnest. Here are some verses from Rush's "Closer to the Heart":

> And the men who hold high places
> Must be the ones to start
> To mold a new reality
> Closer To The Heart.

And then later:

> Philosophers and ploughmen
> Each must know his part
> To sow a new mentality
> Closer To The Heart.

Rush was invoking a past/future complete with ploughmen. It might be some place like medieval England or an imaginary Hobbit-like land. The formalized cadences like "And the men who hold high places" call to mind a decree being read somewhere a long time ago, established by a good king. It sounds feudal. It's not that Rush was endorsing old-school feudalism. Rather, they were calling for higher-ups in our own time to lead the way in terms of becoming "closer to the heart," which I take to mean more loving, more aware of our human brother- and sisterhood. It's part Enlightenment ode, part Love Thy Neighbor, in the form of a rock song.

A punk band like the Sex Pistols did the inverse. They invoked the present-day vestige of feudalism in their society and spat on it, nihilistically:

> God Save The Queen her fascist regime
> It made you a moron a potential H bomb
> God Save The Queen she ain't no human being
> There is no future in England's dreaming
> Don't be told what you want don't be told what you need
> There's no future no future no future for you

"God Save the Queen" and "Closer to the Heart" were both released and made it on the charts in 1977, and their opposing outlooks were two very different options for a rock listener to get behind. As I went along, I was strongly attracted to groups like Romeo Void and the Violent Femmes – bands that were not punk per se, but took something of its attitude into their aesthetic.

Prog rock has a moral code, and it is much like the one we find in those fantasy novels. There is a constant struggle between good and evil with ancient origins. There is a sharp division between right and wrong, never any doubt about the righteousness of the good side or the malevolence of the dark side. There is less account for the slippage between good and evil.

Classic prog songs often transmit an uplifting message in their lyrics. What they do not express is a certain kind of happy nihilism, if one may say that, one that is central to a whole other huge cross-section of rock'n'roll, including the punk of the Sex Pistols, but also any number of bands I heard on my clock radio – bands like the Rolling Stones, Cheap Trick or AC/DC. All of these performers are often sending out a message in their songs that boils down to: *Fuck Everything!* That is often a celebratory gesture, not glum or defeatist. It is liberating because it is free from virtue, and freedom from virtue is a big part of what rock'n'roll is all about. Prog's stance might seem the antithesis of that, but for me it's not. It's just another way of rocking – earnestly. After all, punk is childlike as well, or teenage-like at least; it's immature to just say "fuck everything" indefinitely, and never suit up and do something constructive in society. In my own wanderings, I've found grown-up proggers a happier bunch than grown-up punkers. They seem to age better.

A protracted song length, differing sections within the song, the attempt to represent distance in time and space, Gnostic searching, respect for craft, a high premium on virtuosity, unapologetic earnestness: These proggish characterstics rubbed off on me unconsciously, or I sought to embody them consciously. Prog was a formative influence.

Hate

Seventh grade was my first year at King Philip Middle School. I had some friends like Ricky who had come over from Bugbee, and would meet some new ones in the next few years who would change my life. I had a rough time with a few guys who bullied me regularly. One memorable time, though, I was a bully myself to a guy who would wind back into my life in young adulthood – James, or Jamie as he was called then. He was taunted mercilessly because he was overweight. I wasn't friends with him then, but we would become close years later after high school. One day in gym class, we were running laps. I don't know what got into me but, as he was lugging along, I passed by him and shoved him – nothing but malice on my part, out of nowhere. Not really hard, but not friendly at all. He looked at me and said nothing, resigned – this kind of thing happened to him all day at school. In retrospect, I think I was just going along with what I saw everybody else doing. I still feel shame when I think about that.

This other kid, Rob, saw me, and ran behind me. "Hey, Mehldau, what are you doing? Why'd you push him?" He was angry and aggressive. He was egging for a fight. Plenty of other times he had bullied James and any number of kids, but now all the sudden he was feeling righteous. He was kind of a dimwit and didn't have much going for him except brute strength. He kept at me. "You can't say that to him. Fight after gym class!" Rob's chest-thumping had caught on with the other boys and, by the time we were in the locker room, everyone was chanting, "Fight! Fight! Fight!" I didn't want to fight, and Rob kept on saying, "Take off your glasses!" He had some gunslinging code of honor that he wouldn't punch me with my glasses on. So I kept them on and got shoved against a locker a couple times. I did nothing in return and he stopped after a while.

A few weeks later, I was walking home and a school bus pulled up to the stop light where I was. I looked up and saw Rob on the bus. All of the windows were open, and I heard someone count, "1 . . . 2 . . . 3 . . ." Then most of the bus screamed at the top of their lungs, "Brad is a loooo-ser!" My stomach sank. I looked at Rob, smiling dumbly from the bus window, and walked off the sidewalk, right up alongside his window. I collected the biggest loogie I could on my tongue, and then spat upwards. It landed on his face and lap through the window. The bus was silent. As it drove away, he screamed back at me, "You're dead, Mehldau!" I felt alone, shaking, seeing only black. But this time, unlike with Rick on Bugbee Hill, I didn't cry. I had hardened. Some part of me was triumphant, I suppose. I had thrown that idiot hatred back at him, and it felt good. When we showed up the next day at school, he threatened me a bit, but then left me alone. I had stood my ground, but the taste of revenge was gone and all that was left was the bile, fear of further retribution, and disgust.

I was bullied regularly throughout seventh grade by another guy and his lackey, who tagged along with him. They'd wait outside after school and put me in a headlock or throw me against a wall. I wasn't the only one. This guy distinguished himself as being a fighter, and not much else. As with Rob, I didn't fight back. Resentment and hatred began to build up in me, though. For years, I would have fantasies of throwing him on the ground and kicking him in the face repeatedly, stepping on his blood-covered face, along with others like him later in high school. These kinds of fantasies were utterly useless as a musician and as a person more generally, I'm certain. Nothing poetic or illuminating ever came out of them. There was no catharsis, only cathexis. Resentment, in itself, is worth shit artistically. Yet I was so full of it, already then, that I'm surprised it didn't swallow me up completely.

I have this memory from very early on. It's me sitting on the swing set in Bedford, alone, probably around age eight. I can hear all my neighborhood friends playing a few doors down, laughing and happy. But I'm sitting there, hunched on the swing, full of anger. The thing is, I can't even remember what I was so upset about. I just remember that feeling, of wanting to be alone yet not really wanting to be alone, yet being too angry to go back to my friends. It's the same feeling I would have for years to come: black, black, black; upset by something, too proud to admit it, alone in a shithole. But it was *my* shithole. There was all this sadness and loneliness right under the anger. Through my twenties, the anger calcified into bitterness towards people – contempt, judgment, a kind of early-onset misanthropy. And there was self-loathing, the feeling of being an emotional cripple.

Because those feelings and negative thoughts were there in the early memory, but not the actual event that led me to them, I often wondered: maybe *there was no event*, or it was negligible in reality. Maybe this is just the way I am, I thought; maybe my resentment was there early on, before anything particularly traumatic happened to me. Maybe I'm just wound up like that, and all of this trying to find the right story – trying to get to the root of why I am the way I am, why I became a drug addict, why I suffered so much, blah blah blah – is just subterfuge, to avoid the real story, which is that I was the true asshole all along. I wasn't traumatized by some earlier event. I just got pricked easy.

To look at your life that way is to wipe away any excuse for your wrongdoings. The story becomes one of undiluted, direct self-loathing and pity. It then becomes easier to evade accountability as well. You can simply say: "I'm just a piece of shit, all the way to the core." And you can use that as an excuse to fuck everything up, as I started to in high school. It won't take away the dejection, though. Negative experiences shaped my behavior and world-view, but I was also prone to that blackness; it was in my make-up. Either way, the question becomes: how do you play the hand you've been dealt?

The dragon

> ... As a kind of terror, the sublime crushes us into admiring submission; it thus resembles a coercive rather than a consensual power, engaging our respect but not, as with beauty, our love.
>
> Terry Eagleton, *The Ideology of the Aesthetic*

Rush's music took me on a journey, but it started in my bedroom. My bedroom, with my stereo and headphones, and posters of Rush and Pink Floyd, was actually two very different things. It was the portal to the other world, like the wardrobe closet in the C.S. Lewis books, but also a kind of womb – an insulated chamber that protected me from everything banal and shitty that was outside of its walls in the real, day-to-day world, like the bullies at King Philip.

It was escapism. Other musical discoveries that came soon after – my discovery of Jimi Hendrix and Coltrane's music – were quite different: they threw me out of that womb, onto a street somewhere far from home. Later, I realized that Coltrane was also an escape. An escape to something that seemed *more* real. An escape from everything that seemed hollow and fake.

Ms. Hurwitz ran a summer camp called Merrywood, and that's where I discovered Coltrane and Hendrix, and much else. I attended there three summers in a row, from 1981 to 1983, age ten to twelve. We called it "music camp." There were some fun typical camp activities – a day trip to a state park, a hike up a mountain trail, volleyball, movies, – but the main focus was music making. Merrywood was located in the Berkshire Mountains in Western Massachusetts, just a mile or so from Tanglewood, where the Boston Symphony Orchestra takes up residence every summer. Top-tier classical musicians would come from around the world to perform there, and several times a week during those summers we could go hear orchestral and chamber music, solo and vocal recitals. It was the opportunity of a lifetime. I was ten years old and was hearing Leonard Bernstein and Seiji Ozawa conducting in the big shed, or titans like Emanuel Ax and Yo-Yo Ma at the beginning of their careers, playing chamber music in the smaller shed.

The attendees at Merrywood, aged ten through eighteen, got to study and perform chamber music, play in an orchestra (we pianists would supplement the orchestra time with four-hands piano), have private lessons, and generally live and breathe music for several weeks. The instructors were mostly graduate classical music students in their twenties. They would also play and perform together and inspire us kids in turn. Everyone who was there wanted to be there and the connecting thread was a love for music.

Those three summers at Merrywood were magical. They were an escape from cramped suburban West Hartford, into something lucid with a beating heart. I found friends who spoke my language – music. The young adults who taught us were at turns brilliant, crazy, and often fascinating. Some of them were bigger nerds than anyone I had ever met, but their nerdiness was clever, confounding, even exalted. Others were cooler rebels or transgressors, noble misfits in their middle twenties who would play chamber music with some kind of super-intelligence, light years ahead of where we were. There was this passion in their playing, one I wasn't privy to as of yet, when all of those teachers performed in the weekly recitals they gave for us. I surmised then it had something to do with sex and love, as I watched some of them pairing up over the weeks and sneaking off for walks together in the woods surrounding the camp. When they played Brahms together, they looked and sounded like they were at turns in pain and lost in some crazy joy.

They were my models. I knew even more that this world of music was mine, even as I knew it was a small world. That small world was just what I wanted and needed, though. Merrywood was a refuge for me. It made me know that there was a place for me, with these people. I rarely lapsed into my unhappy Cain act in my three summers at Merrywood. I was part of the tribe, no matter what. I was on the inside, finally.

Indeed, in my third and final summer at Merrywood, I played a new role for the first time: Cain, the leader of his own tribe. I wasn't just on the inside, I was in the center of what was happening with the kids there, and often steered the ship among us, instigating insurrection at times. It was strange, how there were these two people inside of me, one afraid and alone, and one self-assured and among my peers. The dichotomy would play out in my musical output – the retracting inward, and the displaying outward.

Merrywood was the locus for many important firsts in my life, most of them in my third and final summer there – exposure to new music, like Mendelssohn's Piano Trio #1 which I got to play the first movement of, but also my first joint smoked, first sexual experiences, my first girlfriend and then first experience of being dumped, and some friendships that affected and shaped me for years to come. It subsequently became a primary site in my memory.

It was Eden right before the fall: you've walked towards the tree, taken the fruit into your hand and bit into it, but still haven't swallowed. It's the time in your life that's the most mysterious and fertile, because the taste of transgression is just on your tongue, but you're still innocent, so what you experience is just another kind of happy radiance. As a musician, you'll try to walk back to that tipping point for the rest of your life and never find it, but, in all the attempts, you can claim what's rightfully yours – you can stitch that all together into a picture of what that was and show it to everyone else, saying: that time may be gone now, but that's still *me*.

In order for creation to take place, there must be a prior destruction; a space must be cleared in which to begin again. Where there was unity and repose, now there is flux and disarray. Nothing is ever like it was again, and while there is shock and even pain, there is also the possibility of rich new experience. The shattering for me – the beautiful/destructive rupture – took place in my third summer at Merrywood when I was twelve. Before that summer, I wore glasses, played classical music, listened to Billy Joel and Styx, and hung out with brainy, well-behaved kids. I wasn't particularly well behaved myself, but was far from being a difficult kid. I didn't rebel so much and wasn't a lot of trouble.

After that summer, entering eighth grade, I was a different person: the glasses went that winter; my vision had gradually corrected itself to the point where I didn't need the prescription anymore. The glasses had been a burden – I was always swallowing all that "four-eyes" stuff from other kids. So I was free from what I had perceived as a geeky identity, at least visually. I started trying – and repeatedly failing – to grow my hair long (it always curled up when it got longer and looked stupid). Billy Joel, Styx, and even Rush were out for the time being. Jimi Hendrix, Crosby, Stills, Nash & Young and the Grateful Dead were in. The Vietnam War and the hippie movement fascinated me, and I wished I could have lived then. The '80s seemed like a kid's clown show compared to the '60s.

I began smoking cigarettes, smoking pot when I could find it, and stealing booze from my parents' liquor cabinet. I started to run with some new friends who were always getting into trouble. In one sense it was one typical enough version of teenage troublemaking, but for me it arrived a little early and it was a complete break from the person I had just been. What had happened? I'm not exactly sure, but it had to do with some awakening that had taken place the previous summer at Merrywood.

The change in me that summer I turned thirteen was not simply a negative one. It was the beginning of discovery. I was developing a hunger for new sensations and experiences, and becoming a sensualist; my preference was for the strong, intense variety, the kind that knocked the wind out of you for a moment. Around that time I read a story by Tolstoy which described a practice of the Russian Cossacks in battle. If a horse became wounded, the rider would cut a vein with his sword close to the throat. The bleeding horse was then spurred to greater speeds by its own mortal fear. The cruelty made sense to me. You had to feel alive above all else, and one way was to get closer to death for a moment.

During my third and last summer at Merrywood, Louis, one of my cabin mates who was a year older than me, turned me on to the John Coltrane Quartet with McCoy Tyner, Jimmy Garrison, and Elvin Jones. He had a cassette of that unparalleled band playing "My Favorite Things." It was a live version that lasted over twenty minutes. (Years later, I deduced that it must have been a 1965 live recording from a club called The Half Note in New York City. It was a radio broadcast that floated around for years as a bootleg on cassette, and was finally released officially in 2005.) Louis was from New York City, and it seemed like all the kids who were from New York City were on to the hippest music – not so much new music, but older music from before any of us were born. Moreover, they lived in a cultural Mecca I could only dream about for the time being. Whereas I was getting to hear Bernstein at Tanglewood conduct for the first time, they talked casually about taking the 1 train a few stops to go hear him regularly with *his* orchestra at Lincoln Center– the New York Philharmonic. They were exposed to all that music through their parents, and then brought it on cassettes to Merrywood. Back home in suburbia my friends were listening to the Police and Van Halen; these New York City kids were listening to Coltrane and Mahler.

My first time hearing Coltrane's music was an initiation, and it was ceremonial, like an Indian sweat lodge. The cabins were hot during the day, and usually we would just stay outside during those hours when the sun peaked and find some shade. But Louis and I went into the cabin, and we shut the door and kept the windows shut. We sweated and listened to the Coltrane Quartet for about half an hour on his cassette player. When we emerged again from the cabin, I was changed. Sometimes music can do that to you. It raised the bar for my expectation as to what music could be. The intensity of the Coltrane was something I chased thereafter as a listener. Later on, when I became a jazz musician, it was the ideal when I played. The idea was to change someone's perspective – really, to change their life – through your playing. If you failed, and you might fail most of the time, the effort itself was noble.

Through my other cabin mate, Joe, who was a piano player like me, a year older, I discovered Jimi Hendrix. We listened in particular to the live album, *Band of Gypsys*. I had never heard a riff as badassed as the one on "Who Knows," with bassist Billy Cox and drummer Buddy Miles supplying the groove. It sounded like Hendrix was just swinging his dick across the whole audience at the Fillmore East, slapping them into submission. It was "Machine Gun," though, with Hendrix's guitar solo, that took me somewhere else and just dumped me there. I was lost after that solo – it seemed to carry the grief of the world on it. It showed me a grief I hadn't even known existed. Hendrix's music was raw. Coltrane was also raw, yet with a complexity that I immediately sensed, but which completely baffled me. It came on like some magic system of hieroglyphics.

The Coltrane and Hendrix that summer registered as pleasure, but a new, destabilizing kind. Something felt dangerous about their music. It made me tremble and feel weak in my stomach. It came from somewhere far from the safety of my surroundings, and had great power. My initial reaction to it was fear – fear of that power, of its ability to crush me emotionally. Yet, as with my sublime encounter with the loner kid in Bedford, there was recognition and identification. The music, however vast and fathomless, was a mirror for my own soul, laid bare. Whereas the sublime meeting with the loner kid was a one-off, hearing Coltrane and Hendrix gave me an appetite. I began to think of that appetite as a dragon, one that awoke that last summer at Merrywood. It had a hunger for stronger, destablizing sensations, not only musical ones. In my twenties, the dragon almost killed me. Fear of a sublime object was fear of my own obliteration. Yet the dragon was attracted to it – attracted to death.

In my first year at King Philip I had been an unhappy Cain – still the loser kid with glasses, with the bullies to contend with. In that last summer at Merrywood that followed it, I found my tribe once more. After the summer, a chapter of childhood was closed. Upon returning to West Hartford and starting eighth grade, I began to move even further and further towards an outsider role, away from the safe center.

The outsider artist

> The artist must be unhuman, extra-human; he must stand in a queer aloof
> relationship to our humanity; only so is he in a position, I ought to say only
> so would he be tempted, to represent it, to present it, to portray it to good
> effect. The very gift of style, of form and expression, is nothing else than
> this cool and fastidious attitude towards humanity; you might say there
> has to be this impoverishment and devastation as a preliminary condition.
> For sound natural feeling, say what you like, has no taste.
>
> Thomas Mann, *Tonio Kröger*

> One is slowly led along to write a book and this looked good, no trou-
> ble with the cast at all and that's half the battle when you can find your
> characters.
>
> William Burroughs, *The Adding Machine*

I was the outsider on the school lot in West Hartford, but a dissatisfied one –
disappointed in the dumb mob of kids with their groupthink, resolved to cast
them off, but feeling untethered: could I really go it alone? What became of
that kid in Bedford, the one I sided with, who hit the other kid? He was truly
alone. If I only partially identified with the nerdy kids and scorned the ones
who fitted in, I still worshipped that valiant warrior. He was an outlaw like Tom
Sawyer and I'd discover him in a musician like John Coltrane – someone who
disregarded the old ideas about beauty and, because of that, found something
new and raw, like a big wall that reached toward the sun. If you could surmount
that wall and descend its other side without perishing, you could walk away
from the whole rabble, once and for all, and find beauty on your own terms.
The noble loner kid from Bedford was someone who I couldn't be in real life,
but I could try to achieve his grace as a musician, like Coltrane had done.

In high school, I began to discover him in the authors I read. He wasn't
a mere outcast, in some moral struggle with himself. Whatever his morality
was, it wasn't one you could discern. You couldn't find him if you looked.
He was great like Dostoevsky or Shakespeare, in the way they were invisible
in their own authorial creations. You never knew where Dostoevsky came
down on in *The Brothers Karamozov* – was he a real believer like Alyosha,
or a contrarian atheist like his brother Ivan? *The Merchant of Venice* used an
anti-Semitic myth to tell its story, yet Shylock was no one-dimensional villain-
ous character: he had humanity and the reader sympathized with him. In that
dual portrayal, Shakespeare effectively revealed nothing of himself.

That kind of literary achievement became a model, not for the kind of
music I would make but for the kind of artist I wanted to be. As I reasoned, an
artist could be a true outsider like the kid I admired in Bedford, through their
own undetectability within their creations. It was the beginning of elitism,

one that grew like a plant out of the mud of isolation. I figured: if I'm already apart from everyone, why not make it work for me?

In that last summer at Merrywood when I heard Coltrane and Hendrix for the first time, just short of thirteen years old, I met Caleb. Caleb seemed cooler than anyone I had ever known. He was from Brooklyn Heights and seemed to know about everything, even though he was a year younger than me. He was knowledgeable about classical music, and privy to the greater cultural world that surrounded it more generally, the one outside of West Hartford, which suddenly seemed provincial and small upon meeting him. We quickly became close.

Caleb was funny and quick, but at the same time he was mysterious and had this gravity about him. Early on after meeting him, he told me that his mother had died. There was a weight that he carried about that, but it was subtle, like a quiet perseverance, and, for me, it made him more beautiful. The kind of feeling that I had for Caleb – feeling like someone's sadness was beautiful – was new. Although I had had crushes on girls already for a couple of years, this was altogether different.

"Feeling like someone else's sadness was beautiful." It could be the description of a certain type of artist but, in another way, it sounds like the description of someone so self-involved that he forgot to actually care about that other person. Welcome to the artistic temperament, or at least my version of it during my *Bildung*. Aestheticize everything, good and bad – especially bad, because the bad, painful stuff is more striking, more noble, particularly that of your friends. They were the closest to you, so you could really draw on all that in detail. You could almost begin to wear it yourself, in a fashion – but not quite. You didn't actually want to suffer; you just wanted it vicariously, to try it on and nestle in its contours.

Something was beginning in those years that would remain a constant. There was a strong, almost instinctive tendency to objectify other people I admired. Caleb represented a desired state of grace that I couldn't reach. I envied his humor and intelligence – the way he could be gentle and mocking at the same time with his campmates; I was jealous of the weight he carried; I wanted to be quietly sad like he was sometimes, and project that to the world. His life was so much richer than mine, it seemed – his cosmopolitan smarts, the heaviness of his mother's death, his easy, graceful way. And he was beautiful, with curly brown hair, a few freckles, and twinkling eyes that squinted when he smiled – an angel from Brooklyn Heights. As I raised him up, I lowered in my own stature.

It was the beginning of a certain folly that would continue through my adolescence. When you objectify someone, you are effectively distancing yourself from the real person, even as you feel exactly the opposite. Your feelings cease to reflect your deeper truth, for the time being. With Caleb, my crush was self-reflexive. It was all wrapped up in who I wanted to be myself.

But don't most devotions – the ones that course through us urgently most often when we're young, the ones we remember forever – begin from one or another fairy tale in our heads? We start out by filling the lens with other material born independently of our object, from our own imagination. It's our imagination, at least in the beginning, that makes our ardor for that other person burn so brightly. Like the poet said:

> For all that beauty that doth cover thee
> Is but the seemly raiment of my heart

My feeling for Caleb was strong, and I might have called it love. For all the genuine friendship we had, though, my pining for him was a backhanded form of narcissism. I started to realize how that worked years later, after it had played out a few more times. A particular kind of friend could represent everything that I wanted to be, regardless of who he really was. Why have to confront the sloppy reality of someone else, with all the work that entails? Better to build him up and beautify him in your head. This would be the pattern for similar types of crushes in the years to come.

That summer at Merrywood, I had my first sexual experience with a girl, in the attic of the main house, with Erika, who was one year older than me. The exciting polarity between us, the way we danced around each other for a bit, and then our first fumbling, electric contact in that cramped room – it just all flowed together perfectly, like one of the Brahms Intermezzos I was playing then. We went out with each other for three enchanted weeks, stealing away to the attic a few more times, or just sitting together outside in the evening and holding hands, right up until curfew. My desire for Caleb was completely different. I already sensed, without articulating it, that there was something disingenuous about my feeling. I was taking something I liked about him that was real, stealing it for my own gratification, and then feeding it like a plant. Yet how could a feeling, itself, be dishonest? That was always the question for me in the years to come. What was *real* in what I was feeling?

In my twenties I began to make connections between desire and art, and how they might play out in my own music. Artists and musicians, I figured, should at least try to create something *better* than what is around them – something more compelling, something worth the price of admission. How did that work, though, with the novelists I admired? They seemed to draw their works out of themselves, yet they picked up fodder for their creations from their outward surroundings. As artists, they were of the world, yet not of it – hyper-attuned to it yet disavowing it in the same breath, all in the aim of transcending it for their own selfish reward. They were constantly watching other people and things, grabbing only the parts they liked, and leaving the rest – the banal, the dumb, the unredeemable – behind and unused, like a discarded carcass. Selfish, that – contemptible, really! They were takers, only out for themselves. At worst, they were a species of monster – like a troll waiting under the bridge, ready to gobble up someone else's authenticity, mercilessly dismembering them.

Were novelists truly calculating and heartless, as Thomas Mann suggested? As much as I loved fiction, it seemed wrong or at least questionable how some of my favorite authors ransacked the lives of those close to them to come up with material for their books. The writers who I was drawn to in high school, like Jack Kerouac, did it openly, but I suspected that there was a similar theft at play in other authors I was reading, albeit more covert, like John Updike in his *Rabbit* novels, or Philip Roth in books like *Portnoy's Complaint* and *Goodbye, Columbus*. The danger for these novelists, I presumed, was that they might inadvertently wind up empathizing more with the characters of their own creation than the real people they were based on. Then they would be egoists, because, after all, those characters, no matter how lifelike they are, were still just extensions of themselves. That was the judgment I had begun to make against myself, with Caleb and others that followed him.

Any good relationship between people involves empathy. You're able to sit in someone else's shoes when you pay attention to who they really are, not merely imagine what they represent. What I felt for Caleb was complicated. I was his friend and did my part as such, holding his sadness with him. These moments – we would sit quietly, apart from others, and say nothing – were sacred for me. At the same time, I put him on a pedestal in such a way that there was unevenness between us. And, when that happens, you forfeit some degree of empathy, because you are not meeting that person at eye level any-more. The nature of your exchange becomes more selfish, less fraternal – you want that person to fulfill the role that you have made for them, and you are fixated on that idea, rather than the one is actually there before you.

I came to regard myself as a taker with other friends later on, one who tried to co-opt traits in them that I desired, traits that were authentically theirs – their beauty, which was often confoundingly connected to their chasteness; their ease with others, which I lacked; their quiet resolve; their unaffected humility. I steadily began to loathe myself for this spurious pursuit. I did not allow myself to express the affection I had for them, for fear of their rejection or outright scorn. If I could have done that, *I* could have been authentic, come what may.

That trepidation was informed by my experience with Caleb. After that last six weeks at Merrywood, I went with him to their summer house in Litchfield County, Connecticut for a week. There, we spontaneously began an exchange of pleasure, one that meant more for me than it did him, wrapped up as it was in my asymmetrical, rose-colored admiration towards him. I was in delight – I had won the prize of his closeness, in that giving and receiving. He ended it suddenly though, prohibiting it further, calling my hesitant efforts to intensify our shared gratification futile, with some joking sarcasm and derision. I gave no outward reaction beyond quiet compliance. Underneath, I felt the sting of his disapproval, and the sorrow of that permanent interruption. Where he had welcomed me, suddenly there was brusqueness. I perceived his superiority in his condescending mockery towards me; in myself, I saw an inferior, snubbed character, one left wanting something no longer permitted.

Was I truly "stealing" Caleb's beauty, or anyone else's later on? And, if I was, could any redemptive good come out of it? There could indeed: music could convey the beauty of my object in all its steady radiance, even as it traced the insurmountable distance between it and myself. It all went back to that first apprehension I had in childhood, that music was something dreamed and, as such, one could never fully enter it.

I found a vindicating model for the outsider artist in Thomas Mann's *Tonio Kröger* and *Death in Venice* in my early twenties. They described me in the high-culture Germanophile context I was fetishizing then. I felt that I was being honest with myself in my identification with their protagonist writers, but the honesty was only to a point. My earnestness stretched too far as I idealized myself into the figure I wanted to be – someone like Mann who could wax about his own dejection and raise it into something with teeth.

Tonio Kröger was about an outsider – specifically, a writer-outsider. Already in his youth, making embryonic attempts at verse, Kröger realized that his elitism was conflicted. It was suffused with an inverted aversion towards himself, towards his own sophomoric poetry. He considered his classmates.

> On the one hand, Consul Kröger's son found their attitude both cheap and silly, and despised his schoolmates and his masters as well, and in his turn (with extraordinary penetration) saw through and disliked their personal weaknesses and bad breeding. But then, on the other hand, he himself felt his verse-making extravagant and out of place and to a certain extent agreed with those who considered it an unpleasing occupation.

He felt contempt for his peers, yet was already not satisfied with the alternative he had found in writing. He lacked access to something they had. Observing them, he mused:

> To be able to walk like that, one must be stupid; then one was loved, then one was lovable.

He would have been fine with being stupid! He was marked, though, like Cain:

> "You can disguise yourself, you can dress up like an attaché or a lieutenant of the guard on leave; you hardly need to give a glance or speak a word before everyone knows you are not a human being, but something else: something queer, different, inimical."

His fate was to love his dumb objects from a distance and, with his gift, sublimate and transform that love into something beautiful for others. That strategy paid off for the writer, bringing him prestige:

It sharpened his eyes and made him see through the large words which puff out the bosoms of mankind; it opened for him men's souls and his own ...

The price was relinquishment of true union with anyone he objectified. They saw his mark.

And then, with knowledge, its torment and its arrogance, came solitude; because he could not endure the blithe and innocent with their darkened understanding, while they in turn were troubled by the sign on his brow.

Years later, in middle age, Kröger finds himself once more on the outside, observing the dancing, dumb crowd, the beautiful ones. All the same elements are at play, as they were in his youth – there is that familiar exhilaration that comes from standing on the perimeter of the action, not quite in it. It is tempered, though, by years of loneliness.

He was exhausted with jealousy, worn out with the gaiety in which he had had no part. Just the same, just the same as it had always been . . . Yes all was as it had been, and he too was happy, just as he had been. For his heart was alive. But between that past and this present what had happened to make him become that which he now was? Icy desolation, solitude: mind, and art, forsooth!

He is still apart, and the only consolation, the only thing showing for his sacrifice, is the strong writing he produced – a cold comfort.

To put it more prosaically, regardless of his stature as a writer, Tonio's ability to love someone and give himself over to their love is all screwed up. How much of this complex character came from Thomas Mann's own life-experience? Mann's view of the artist as outsider was surely conditioned by his own suppressed homosexual desire. Tonio's love for his simple, handsome childhood friend Hans as the book begins could be read as merely platonic infatuation, but there is no doubting the erotic nature of Gustav von Aschenbach's love for the boy Tadzio in *Death in Venice*, written eight years later. We know it had an autobiographical source, a vacation Mann took in Venice, where he became entranced with the youth he would later use as a model for Tadzio.

An artist-outsider in the vein of Mann, one who never fully relinquishes his pining to come inside with everyone else, could nevertheless achieve poetic justice. I took note: through the strength of his strong creation, he would finally graduate from his outsider role in society, but then immediately skip a grade, walking right past the insiders he addressed. He would become a paragon for them – once more on the outside, but speaking, majestically, *for* them. All of this made me think back to my own graduation from outside status to rock star on a much less exalted, kid-sized scale – to that first musical meeting with Ricky in the music room in West Hartford. I had been an outsider, a loser from Bedford, New Hampshire. Then Ricky and I had that impromptu jam on the Kinks tune, and *voilà* – I was someone cool.

Did Mann believe that he must also maintain ironic distance from his characters, like Tonio Kröger and von Aschenbach did? Did he suppose there was some universality in his artistic aloofness, or was he just being even more aloof – writing aloofly about a writer who writes aloofly about unperturbed breeders? I surmise the truth was somewhere in between. Mann's project was self-redemption through irony. In real life, he wanted to forgive himself for not being aloof enough. Reading his diaries, it's not hard to sense that he keenly recognized a conflict in how he lived his own life, as he wouldn't permit himself what he wanted. In this sense, he was not at all detached from his characters.

He knew, though, the power of authorial distance. Just by continuously retracting from his self-styled protagonists, he could find a shared identity with them as they folded back into his own life – for they retracted as well in their storied actions. He could thus redeem himself from his own painful inner contradiction in a self-forgiving act that would partially erase it. Mann was not the only model for me as an artist, but he was the quintessential model for a particular kind of one in the Romantic vein, one inaugurated by Goethe in *The Sorrows of Young Werther* and *Faust*. His protagonists personified a credo: *live* for art's sake; don't just make art for art's sake. In art alone you will find salvation, even if you have to abdicate your real-life connection to the beautiful people you come across.

Yet perhaps that dictum was just so much self-protection. After all, it wasn't as if you had chosen your lot as an outsider, artist or not. You didn't walk away from the others. You were forsaken, or at least that's what it felt like. You wanted their camaraderie, and maybe even courtship, more than anything. It was your damned acute self-awareness that restricted you from real communion, like an allergy. The writer-protagonists Kröger and von Aschenbach lived outside of what they wrote about. Neither was awarded direct experience of the episodes they dreamt up, yearned for, and envied others for having. Yet they could write about beauty and grace more lucidly than the others who were directly embodying those qualities.

If, as Mann's protagonist Kröger maintained, the writer must "fastidiously" bracket himself out from his characters so as to make them strong and enduring to the reader, then, by Mann's own logic, so must he too remain aloof from Tonio, regarding his creation coolly. Kröger and von Aschenbach were self-referential though – highly cultured, creative men like Mann himself, tortured by their own sensuality, unaccepting of its nature. This sensuality, mediated through the intellect and only partially sublimated, is a subtext that runs through the two novellas, and more diabolically in the later novel *Dr. Faustus*. Mann could not fully accept the kind of desire he sketched, for it was anything but detached. It was *mushy*, or so I read it then – unmanly, cloying.

Whether or not Mann saw himself like that, I think that he strategized even more to distance himself from his own sensual impulses, even as he wrote about them, or, really, *by* writing about them. Kröger and von Aschenbach are most authentic as characters when they are most pathetic in their pining.

To cover all the possibilities, it might be, following the logic of this distance, that Mann was truly aloof, that he really didn't care or sympathize with Tonio at all. If that were the case, he would have succeeded in real life the task he charged the fictional writer Tonio Kröger, and could have wrapped the whole thing up in a self-congratulatory win. But this would mean bracketing out what we know about Mann: Kröger and von Aschenbach seemed to be versions of a guy a lot like himself.

No, perhaps true distance would be achieved by distancing himself not from Tonio but from Tonio's stated criterion of distance *in itself*, and thus allow himself vulnerable, intimate proximity with his character. We would expect Mann to live by the credo he assigns to Kröger. Now, though, he could have his cake and eat it too: he could drop all that fastidiousness and let it all hang out for us, but this disclosure would itself be an ironic act, partially obscured. It was a qualified victory. This act of self-redemption through his writing could then also be an act of self-forgiving. I suspect that Mann could best redeem himself – come back to himself, and finally be at provisional peace with himself – with the tool he knew best, irony. Otherwise, he would have been buried under the weight of his own serious self-regard, a mere sentimentalist with nothing to show except the disclosure itself.

Mann, it seemed, would begin to show me his naked self, but then would retreat, holding me at bay. His authorial stance was appealing and discomfiting all at once. I saw something of myself in him, recognized its merit, and also its weakness.

Redeeming yourself with the thing that led you away from yourself – it seemed a sleek gambit. Mann was instructive, and from him I retained this conviction: your outsider status as an artist can buy you universality, if you express it succinctly, with subtlety. In my own music, I was the outsider, trying to pry his way back in – or, in other cases, being confined inside, trying to break out again.

Longy

There was a coda to Merrywood in eighth grade, one more opportunity to congregate with the classical tribe, at Longy School of Music in Cambridge, Boston, a short walk from the Harvard campus. The all-day program at Longy was for ages eight through eighteen. Every Saturday, four of us kids would carpool together every week from Connecticut with our mothers rotating the driving duty, starting the journey at 6:00 in the morning to arrive for the first class there at 9:00.

That was solfège, which I strongly disliked. I couldn't see its utility. Why learn only the diatonic scale, and then paste it onto all twelve keys, avoiding the inevitable necessity of learning all of them, with all their respective sharps and flats? What's more, you had to sing all that silly do-re-mi stuff, like those bratty von Trapp kids in *The Sound of Music*.

I understood the logic behind it. All of the other kids in the class were aged eight to ten, and I was the lone thirteen-year-old. They were starting with solfège as a grounding form of ear training, to develop a sense of pitch and the relation between scale intervals. I had already learned those pitch relations as the notes themselves in the various tonalities. Now I had to backtrack and learn something that I didn't need. Ear training was not necessary for me, because I had perfect pitch, and had no problem naming intervals.

I could have been cocky about that innate skill, in itself. The problem was that I was not quick at matching the pitch with its respective solfège name, not just because it was new to me but because that kind of dot-connecting cognitive skill was never my strong point. I struggled slowly when I was called to read a passage out of the study book, and all the munchkins would giggle. It was the first example of something I'd experience as I went along in my musical training. I had already achieved the pedagogic goal of some particular instruction in my own manner, but then was obliged to struggle on another path towards it, one which seemed superfluous. Although unpleasant, it instilled a lesson. Some things may come naturally to you as a musician, but others don't at all, and might never.

Next was a lesson accompanying Scott Yoo, who was then a young violin prodigy. Later he would go on to become a conductor, leading his own chamber orchestra, Metamorphosen, and conducting the orchestral music from my record *Highway Rider* when we took it on the road. Scott was already accomplished then, at age eleven, and very disciplined. I was right at that age where I was really starting to slack off with everything, so I did not learn my part well on the piece we were working on – Beethoven's glorious "Spring" Sonata – and was not prepared. I regret that. The renowned violinist and teacher Roman Totenberg was instructing.

Lunchtime was my favorite part of the day. We had an hour to ourselves, and I'd walk to Harvard Square along the campus, sometimes with Scott tagging along, but mostly alone, spending a lot of time in The Coop, which had a sizable classical record store alongside an art shop which sold reprints of famous pieces. I discovered a lot of stuff just leafing through there and, whenever I had some spare money, I'd buy an LP or a print from Dalí or Kandinsky to put on my wall back home in West Hartford.

Cambridge was appealing to me, because it felt like it was occupied by my tribe, which was only partly true. On the one hand, the atmosphere of Longy, with its quirky, brilliant professors and talented kids, was as close as you could get to Merrywood. As in Merrywood, I was attracted to that and identified with it, embodying it in solidarity with them. There was again validation. Yet, on the other hand, I was already moving away from all of that – starting to smoke weed and drink, hanging out with different kinds of friends, listening to different music, and pushing back against everything in general, including the safe haven that a place like Merrywood or Longy could offer me. Sometimes I walked into the Harvard campus to peer more closely at the students on its storied grounds as they walked in quick, purposeful strides, creating their destinies. I was already certain that I would never have membership of that group.

Importantly, at Longy, I had my first jazz instruction, and it stuck with me. The jazz pianist Peter Cassino taught us an introductory class in jazz. I was the only one there out of five of us pianists who had a bit of knowledge about jazz, and I soaked up everything he showed us. We all had to transcribe something from Coltrane's classic record *Blue Train*, and he assigned me a chorus of Curtis Fuller's trombone solo on "Moment's Notice." It was daunting but exciting. I realized I had a knack for that, and took studious pleasure in the task. This was the kind of ear training I liked. I saw the real utility in that kind of exercise soon enough, as a means to an improvisatory end. Once I had the solo transcribed, I read it back and plugged it into the corresponding network of chords that underpinned it. Then, pieces of it would fall out of my own attempts at improvisation. First transcribe, then copy verbatim, then assimilate. This was the approach I would take in the following several years in high school, transcribing solos from Bird, Coltrane, pianists McCoy Tyner, Bud Powell, Red Garland, Wynton Kelly, and others.

Dylan

Dream about Dylan. He was fourteen, his age from that time, and I was my adult age of thirty, but still in the high-school setting with him – the setting where so many of these dreams take place. They always involve a few things going on at once that could not coincide with each other in reality. Although I am an adult in the dream, I have still not graduated from high school. In some of the dreams I go to high school and then go home to my wife and children, like other people go to work. It seems plausible somehow in the dream, though not normal. There is always a feeling of unease – I know that it is not right that I am still in high school, yet there I am.

In this dream, there was some kind of town fair going on outside at our high school, with lots of people buying food and milling around. Dylan was there and when I saw him I felt happiness and fear at the same time. I didn't know how he would treat me. He looked great – beautiful even. His hair was jet black like always but he was taller than I had remembered. He put his arm around my shoulder tightly, compelling me to do the same, in a fraternal gesture. Then he began to lead me on a walk. He told me that Ed and him were okay with everything that had happened between us three at the end of that summer, but now he had to be careful and maybe hide out because he could get in trouble for what we had just done now. It seemed like he and I had stolen something – maybe school property.

We walked through the crowd and got to the edge of the school grounds. The dream shifted, and it was now a regular school day. I said, "We should definitely be careful now because you could get double-busted for leaving school grounds." Even though I was also still in school in the dream, it seemed like he was the one in more danger of getting in trouble, like he was more culpable for whatever had happened. Or perhaps I had some leverage because of my adult status. Now, I felt more like the adult I was in real life, yet was still addled by what had happened between us back then – self-reflexive, aware of my abnormality, of the strangeness of my own perspective, yet still entrapped by it, still held by the rich mix of fear and rapture that the dream gave off.

Dylan said something like, "It's all right; I won't get busted." Now it was only he that remained in high school, and all I had were my connections to him emotionally. For the moment at least, I was not in danger of receiving the punishment. It seemed like he was the potential fall guy. This was a new type of role for him in my dreams – a victim of sorts, but a heroic one, taking one for the team, for Ed, him, and I. Still, I felt distance from him, and the old shame and fear – fear of rejection, my old, first fear, with so many faces. I wasn't sure if he really liked me anymore, but welcomed his contact and outward show of affection. Why did I still give him and Ed so much power? Why did what happened with them have such dominion over my memory? I wondered it then as I dreamed, feeling butterflies from Dylan's imagined touch on my shoulder.

We walked together and exited the school grounds, and came upon a strange sight. It was a huge hearse parked across the street from the school. It was a striking vehicle. It had two floors like one of those double-decker buses in London, and was completely made of glass, so you could see everything inside. The interior looked more like a room, the top floor at least. There was red carpet, and several unusual musical instruments there on display. They were all golden, and clearly were artifacts of another time and place – maybe Greek antiquity. There was no coffin, and thus no proof that this was indeed a hearse, yet somehow in the dream I knew that it was. Dylan seemed to know as well. His demeanor changed. He lost his confidence and grew quiet and still. A dark shadow seemed to pass over his face, and I felt fear for him – instead of fear of him. Then I woke up.

My first clear thought upon awakening was, "Is Dylan dead?" It wouldn't have been the first time that I felt as if I got a message from a dead person in my dreams, nor the last. Those kinds of dreams were always filled with deep sadness. This dream was different, though – more mysterious, sad but not inconsolable, like a clue to something I didn't yet know.

After that transformative summer at Merrywood, I met Dylan in the beginning of eighth grade, aged thirteen, and we were close friends immediately. The friendship was intense and it ended as quickly as it began. Ed, one year older, was already his friend, and the three of us hung out together a lot. Ed was always getting into fights, which unsettled me. I didn't know how to fight and didn't want to, so I'd hang back, and then worry that he judged me for not having his back. We did different, riskier stuff together: we'd push Dylan's mom's car out of their driveway in the middle of the night and go joyriding through a back country road in the neighboring town of Farmington, turning the headlights off. We'd steal beer and liquor, and smoke weed when we could find it, which was still infrequent then. I instigated as much of that as they did – at that point, I sought out anything that was transgressive. We spent a lot of time at Park Lane Pizza in their neighborhood, huddled in one of the booths, nursing Cokes, chain-smoking Marlboro Reds, playing Asteroids. I took Dylan along with my family to Nantucket for a week's vacation there. It was mostly nothing but fun with them that summer, until the last week.

Dylan and I hung out practically every day that summer, and, at a certain point, we started being sexual together. At first, I liked what we did. But I was also on the fence, because I didn't want to be a "fag." It was 1983. I was homophobic – not aggressively, but inwardly, like many boys my age were then.

Dylan was different from me. On the outside, to everyone else, he was this macho, scruffy dude, thin and kind of a runt, and he probably put on the gruff act as self-protection. But when we were alone in his attic or bedroom on those afternoons that summer, he gave himself over to me and the tough act went away. He wanted to go further than I did. After a couple weeks, I stopped what we were doing. I didn't say why, or say much at all – I just ignored him if he would try to begin something. I didn't know why I didn't want sex with him any more than I knew why I wanted it in the first place, a few weeks earlier.

Ed and Dylan lived on the other side of West Hartford from me. My neighborhood was relatively wealthy, with families of doctors, lawyers, and insurance execs who worked in Hartford. Theirs was more blue-collar. The friends I had up until that point were timid sexually for the most part, and of course it was all new at that age. Not so with Dylan and Ed. That summer I knew them, they might have sex with each other, get dressed, and then go get into a fight or vandalize a building. Yet Ed in particular was vehemently homophobic, which confounded me. The vandalizing, the joyriding, the stealing: they were all things that were in opposition to someone else – an authority. Ed's aggressive hatred towards anything that smacked of gay, though, was in opposition to himself. It didn't add up. That kind of pent-up, conflicted stance is well known, but I had no playbook for it then.

One night in the last days of summer vacation before my first year of high school, just after my fourteenth birthday, both Dylan and Ed were sleeping over at my house. My parents were asleep and we had been stealing booze from their liquor cabinet for a while. We'd take some nips from one bottle and then replace it with water, then go on to the next bottle – gin, schnapps, vodka, Bailey's, rum, crème de menthe – you name it. After a short while, it was just me drinking. The next day I was dry-heaving into the evening.

But I was having a great time that night. The other guys were drinking less, and wanted to screw around. Every time I came back, they had fewer clothes on, and were finally naked. I was more interested in the booze. I was put off that they were doing that in my bedroom, with my parents right down the hall. I wasn't into it, the three of us like that. The times with Dylan had been intimate. I didn't feel anything towards Ed.

I went downstairs to pilfer some more liquor, and, when I came back in my room, Dylan and Ed were having full sex, with Ed on the receiving end. That was something I had never seen, and it seemed dirty to me. Ed was way into it, though. It was strange. If anything, Ed was always even more of a macho guy than Dylan – a year and grade older than us at fifteen, muscular, strong, getting in fights all the time, talking shit to everybody, with a real mean look in his eyes. But here he was now, not just taking it from Dylan, but demanding it imploringly: "Oh yeah, man. Give it to me in my ass. I really need it," with that same mean voice he would use when he was about to fight someone – all hoarse, like Mr. T from *The A-Team*. It was so incongruous with the Ed I had known up until then, and yet – it wasn't. It was just a different side of him, and he was showing it to me. I looked at skinny Dylan behind him, winking and smiling at me, like it was all a joke.

Freshman year of high school started a week after that. When I saw Ed and Dylan in the hallway, I went up to them, but they were cold – they didn't have too much to say to me. Skip ahead a few days, and they were downright hostile: "Fuck off," "Get lost," that sort of stuff. What had happened? I didn't get it at first. Next, Ed, in particular, started with a whole spree of name-calling – fag this, fag that, fucking faggot blah blah blah, and really aggressive. Then it was, "I'm gonna kick your ass, faggot." Then pushing me against the wall in the stairwell, following me around, spoiling for a fight. Dylan followed him dumbly. I tried to get his attention, but he was gone – he wouldn't look at me. I called him on the phone after school and he wouldn't pick up, and then they started prank-calling me, with more of the name-calling and threats before hanging up.

What had happened was clear enough: Ed was ashamed of what he had done and what I had seen, and wanted to turn the tables on me. I intuited that but, because he knew that I had been sexual with Dylan that summer, I couldn't simply say, "It's not true; I'm not a fag." My shame about Caleb's rejection the previous summer redoubled. But Caleb and I remained friends. Ed and Dylan were now shunning me, aggressively.

It was all I could do for the first three months of high school to avoid a fight with Ed. The last one I had been in was with Ricky on Bugbee Hill and I didn't want a repeat of that. So I never fought back. I retreated whenever he shoved me in the stairwell as best I could. I guess the main reason was plain fear, because there was something in Ed's eyes like blind hate, like he wouldn't stop until one of us was dead. I could see it. He wasn't just wound up; something in him had switched. I didn't get outwardly angry. I just got sad and scared, like a pit in my gut. I wanted to disappear, not fight back. It was a feeling I would relive throughout my *Bildung*. I was an unhappy Cain again – banished from a tribe, a tribe of three. I had broken a sexual covenant with them, by not participating in their ritual.

That all happened in the first weeks of freshman year at high school, which was already a new, uneasy environment. There was no one I felt I could talk to about that. In the next few months, I was starting to find my turf and my tribe "out back" as we called it, where kids were allowed to smoke. I discovered graffiti written on the brick wall there in white chalk: *Brad is a fag*. My stomach sank. I felt what would become my old friend: shame.

The only thing that bugged me about Ed's bottom routine was that he and Dylan did that around me, on my bed no less. Otherwise I didn't care one way or the other. As for Dylan, that really hurt. I didn't just lose a friend; my best buddy turned into an enemy from one day to the next. Was it because I had already rejected him by stopping the sex between the two of us? Did he want to get back at me? Was that why he went along with Ed's homophobic freak-out? Or was he just following Ed blindly, maybe because Ed was a year older and had seniority, or out of loyalty because he knew Ed longer than me? With Ed, who knows? Maybe if I had taken him like Dylan had, we might have had some communion of sorts, and then he wouldn't have bullied me at all. It's like you'd fuck someone to cement your friendship. I saw that play out with some ostensibly straight guys later when I got to New York.

When Dylan was done with Ed, he got off my bed and looked at me. "All yours." I just laughed and drank some more; I didn't want it. In the years that followed, though, I would play out the episode with a different ending, one in which I was able to give Ed what he wanted, like Dylan had. In that way, I imagined, what followed would have been avoided.

Another guy from Dylan and Ed's neighborhood was Darren. He was really a sadist, worse than them in some ways. For the most part he was dumb as a brick, but he had an ability to verbally strip you down for the sheer pleasure of it. His dad probably did that to him every morning before he went to school. He was another one like Ed who really prided himself on fighting. With all of those guys I never stood up for myself because I just didn't want to get my ass beat. Why didn't I just fight back once, even if I would have gotten whipped? I wonder even now.

At some point in that freshman year, Ed must have told Darren his self-protective version of that night the previous summer: that I was the queer and not him. In any case, just when Ed was starting to let up in my following sophomore year, all of a sudden I had to contend with Darren. For a good while, Darren made me an object of his hatred, with a pet project – to goad me into a fight. He would approach me at lunchtime. The time I remember most clearly, I was outside the lunchroom, but not out back where I usually went. It was an area where other students congregated – good students with a future ahead of them. I was sitting on steps with an old friend of mine from King Philip, the kind I used to hang with – gentle, glasses, kind. It felt safe to be around kids like that, even though I never hung out with any of them anymore since after I came back from Merrywood. But now, since Darren was on me, I was retreating back into their company during lunch, not going out back in an effort to avoid him. Still, he eventually found me there as well, and approached me.

"Hey, Mehldau. What's your fucking problem? You're a pussy, right? That's what I heard from Ed. He tells me you're a big pussy. Are you a pussy? Are you a little cocksucker?" He spoke the words sharply with a half-smile, glaring downwards, standing over me. Darren was actually handsome, even if he was a raging dipshit. He had good cheekbones and curly locks that he grew out a bit, mullet notwithstanding, and his lips kind of pouted all the time. He always wore tight Levi's and a cheap belt, one of those kinds you bought at the headshop in the mall, with a buckle made of fake brass and a band's insignia on it – I think it was Whitesnake, or some other cock-rock band. Every time I walked behind him in the hallway at school I noticed that the back of his jeans rode up the crack of his ass a little, like a gay guy might wear them. But I never revenge-fucked him in fantasies later on. When I had hung out with Darren a few times that summer before high school with Dylan and Ed, I noticed something about him: mixed in with the odor of cigarette butts, he smelled a little like shit – like a kid who had worn the same dirty underwear for a few days, like a kid who never learned how to wipe his ass.

He squatted down so he was face to face with me. I breathed in the Winstons on his breath and that stale shit smell. "What's up? Ed told me some stuff. You're just a little faggot, right?" Darren wasn't the brightest bulb. His taunting approach lacked in variation – repeated, menacing questions on one theme, all the more effective in their dull redundancy. It was boilerplate bullying technique, and it worked. He was pounding me down, making me smaller and smaller, filled to the brim with shame and fear. For years later, well into my twenties, I would reimagine this scene.

[replay – Darren:]

I stand up and meet his gaze. He always leaned right up into my face and now I lean back into him. He takes a step back. I speak: "Okay man. You want a fight? I'll give it to you. But first I'm gonna tell you about Ed, about what happened with him, Dylan, and me. And then after that if you want to fight we can do it, okay?"

His visage changes. The menacing smile drops into something like confusion for a short moment. Then his eyes squint, and he returns to his role:

"Alright, you fucking poof. Let's go!" He stands up.

"After school," I return.

"Why, chickenshit? Let's go now – out back!"

I step up to him again: "You've got no life. You're a white trash piece of shit. But I don't want to go and get suspended behind your baby games. Today, after school, in the parking lot across the street from out back. There under the trees. Just you and me."

He pushes me back with his two hands in my chest, but my feet stay on the ground. "After school today," he mutters. "You're fucking dead."

When school's out we trudge across the lawn out back and cross the street. I said to be alone but he's brought a few of his lackey friends. We walk behind some trees into a clearing.

"What the fuck have you got to say before I kick your ass?" He's up close, a couple inches from me.

"It was this past summer, a week before school started," I begin. "Ed and Dylan were at my house. Ed took it up the ass from Dylan like a little

bitch – yelling the whole time: 'Oh yeah man, give it to me. I need that
cock in my ass!' What do you think of that, you dumb shit? He turned the
tables on me because he was afraid of being found out as a queer. What
do you think now of your buddy Ed?"

Darren is silent, looking at me quizzically. Before he can react, I step
back and punch him directly in the eye. He's startled. Then I kick him
sideways in the knee with the heel of my Doc Marten and break the joint.
He lurches backwards. I punch him upwards in the chin, and then once
more in his nose, in rapid succession. (As I fantasize this, I experience a
pleasurable retraction in the groin: an inverted anti-erection of sweet,
imagined revenge. Sex and violence push up against each other, knocking
around in the bile of my gut.)

He's on the ground. I push him flat so he's lying on his back. There's
blood coming out of his nose and his eye is swollen and half-shut. I've
broken him. He lies still, looking at me dimly. I open my trousers and
take out my dick. The urine flows easily and I start to piss onto his face.
It stings on the fresh wounds and he smarts, tightening up. With my left
foot, I open his jaw and continue pissing. It collects in his mouth and he
coughs and spits. His friends start to move in, ready to attack. I pull out
the stiletto I bought in the mall and snap it open, brandishing it; they step
back. They can only witness their friend's shame. I zip up, and before I
leave, I kick Darren once more hard in the ribs, breaking a few of them,
and finally lean down to spit into his mouth. He burps up a bubble of
blood onto his jean jacket.

With the loss of Dylan's friendship, Ed's rampage, and Darren's act the following year, sex with guys became tied with intimidation and shame. I wanted
to take back the power I lost with Ed. I wanted reprisal against Darren. It was
also something unresolved and unfinished – a broken intimacy. I wanted to
mend it. I wanted to have my friend Dylan back.

After a grueling couple months the beginning of freshman year, Ed let
up and stopped seeking me out, as long as I avoided him. Dylan seemed to
disappear. But one day I was walking home after school and saw him a little
ways ahead of me on North Main Street, trudging and smoking. He should
have been taking the bus but I guess he missed it. He was alone. I didn't wait.
I caught up with him, calling him. "Hey man! What's up?" I was sarcastic,
smiling. "All alone without Ed, huh?"

He looked at me then looked back straight ahead, and kept on walking,
faster now. "Who's the fag now? Maybe it's you." I continued. The taunting
came easily enough. It was driven by the brick of hurt I had from him ditching
me as a friend. Underneath that was fear, though. My heart was beating fast,
like it had a few years back in the fight with Ricky. But, whereas Ricky had
picked on me, now I was the tormentor. It wasn't a role I knew. How would
it play out? Would he strike back with his fists, right there on the sidewalk?

Further underneath that fear was sorrow. I still wanted him back as a friend even if I thought I didn't right then, and I felt that even as I tried to tear him down.

Dylan tried to smile back the menacing smile I was giving him, but I saw the sadness. I knew then he wouldn't fight. He kept on walking fast. I can still see his expression, his lips trembling a little, eyes downcast. Finally I let him alone. He walked on and I trailed back, putting distance between us. I felt vindicated, but only briefly. For years afterwards, I had remorse not only for pouncing back like that, but also for pushing him away earlier that summer. Even if I hadn't meant to hurt him, I thought, I shouldn't have done that. Then all of this wouldn't have happened. All of that recast itself into experiences in the years to come. It was like with Ed, but it went much deeper. I should have let Dylan do what he wanted. I should have let him go the whole way, even if I didn't want it then.

The first few months of high school were hard for me, and I felt like I couldn't tell anyone about what had happened with them. So I walked around and kept it inside. I was out of Eden; grace was gone. However negative it was, though, the knowledge of good and evil would gestate and then give birth in the music I made later. Pain is fertile.

[replay – Dylan:]

I catch up to him. "Hey man! What's up?" My voice is kind now. He looks up with that silent fear and keeps on walking. I put my hand on his shoulder. He snaps back, pushing me away on the chest. I take it on, deflecting it. "Don't worry. Let's just walk." I'm reassuring. He looks down and I see his tears. "It's okay," I say quietly. He says nothing, but his walking slows and I stay with him. We're silent now and approach Bishop's Corner, the shopping area on the north side of West Hartford – the cushier side, close to where I lived. Dylan and Ed lived on the south side of town, close to the Hartford line.

"Let's go to Westmoor," I say. Westmoor Park was just a ways from the Corner, over and down a sloping hill, across from our church on Flagg Road – a road among others that traversed to and from dreams and memories thereafter. It had a petting zoo as you entered, and then big, open lawns. As you walked farther in, there were woods you'd reach by crossing a little bridge over a shallow stream. We walk the lawn and head into the woods, through some trees into a sheltered clearing where I'd get high with Ricky and others. Ricky lived beside the park and you could cut through his backyard right into it.

The last time alone with Dylan that previous summer, I stopped him when he tried to kiss me. Now we're face to face again. With ease, I bring his face to mine and finally kiss him the way he had wanted, stroking his black hair. I've made it right. We're best friends again, and we'll stay that way from now on. We have a secret bond, but one without shame. It's quiet and sacred.

Musical religion

You don't choose your religion. It chooses you. If you think you can choose who or what to worship, you're still window shopping. You're a tourist. Later, you might become a traveler if you keep at it. If you're lucky, you'll prodigally find your way home. But if that home is the Absolute, what makes you think you'll ever get there by your own lights? And, even if you disavow that absolute, it will surround you all the more. You'll see it everywhere obliquely, confounding you. You'll move away from it and back right into it. You'll fear it deep inside your gut, like it would annihilate you. Yet, if you surrender and fall into it, it's where you'll finally find grace. All those demons: they were just angels in disguise.

It's the same with your tribe – they'll find you just as they'll shun you. You can't pass freely through their gate, and, if you think you're walking out of that gate by your own volition, you're wrong. You were quietly banished. Yet, wherever you go next, you'll never be alone, even if you wanted to be, even if you hide yourself like some ascetic. Like the old poet said: no man is an island.

Before I had a name for it, I was already thinking about the music I loved, the music that stuck with me, as a canon. I had been listening to as much music as I could up through eighth grade, beginning from those first years in Bedford on the clock radio. It had been a solitary pleasure in Bedford, a self-indoctrination. Upon moving to West Hartford, that started to change. Now there was a new source in addition to the radio to discover music: older brothers of my friends, grumpy guides who dutifully turned us on to their music because someone had done that for them. They'd permit us into their room sporadically, revealing their LPs. In some cases, these were lovingly arranged in alphabetical order; in others, they were strewn across the floor, out of their jackets.

Mostly laconic and not given to florid set-ups before the needle hit the vinyl, these elder siblings would dispatch a few phrases: "Check this out," "Good one." In that way they preserved the mystery of the music and allowed us to draw our own initial conclusions, which was best. They knew their role – a shepherd mostly, rarely didactic. You might get a reprimanding judgment in the form of a sneering reply if they didn't approve, or just an eye-roll and a long sigh.

You'd hear a variety of stuff that you missed because you were still a little kid a few years earlier: the Econoline rock of Bob Seger, early Doobie Brothers or Grand Funk Railroad; the ur-metal of early Black Sabbath, the half-prog of Kansas, or the one-man genre of Zappa. Importantly, they introduced you to a key dichotomy, the mouth of many rivers: the Stones and the Beatles. You weren't ready yet, but they planted the seed. An occasional soft-rock outlier from Ambrosia, Pure Prairie League or Climax Blues Band surfaced in the pile, and, since it didn't go with everything else, you asked about it. He'd look briefly at the record and just ignore the question. You surmised there was a backstory, probably something with a girl.

When I got to high school, something changed. The music you listened to may have been a private pleasure, but it was also a shared experience and a public statement. Your choices announced a proclamation to your peers and adversaries alike. You were putting your flag down. Still, the music had called you, not the other way around. In fact, you hadn't made the choice. You were born in its country already. Each individual in high school was forming his or her personal canon, but it was helped along by their tribe, as they'd turn each other on to new music, or share it together in an after-school ritual act.

I quickly found my place the first day of Hall High School out back. There was a metal sculpture which you could hoist yourself up and sit on, in the middle of the lawn. The older, more established smokers would gather there in small cliques and look tough. The deadhead types would sit and loll around the lawn. On the concrete by the double doors that led back into the cafeteria were the younger ones, hanging back, or loners.

Just in that tobacco-fueled microcosm alone, there were several different musical identities I observed during the years 1984–1988, each with corresponding attributes.

"Classic" metalhead: Iron Maiden, Judas Priest, Black Sabbath, AC/DC, Motörhead. Favorite classes: metal shop, wood shop. Maybe on hockey team, otherwise non-athletic, but you have the feeling he could kill you casually. Drives: muscle car. Demeanor: quiet, a little scary – like the character of Linderman in *My Bodyguard*. Basically harmless, often kind on the inside. Might drive you home from school in his Mustang silently, leaving you at the corner of your street: "That's it. Far as I go." Age: upper-classman. Smokes: Marlboro Reds.

New metalhead/cock-rocker: (Darren) Def Leppard, Guns N' Roses, Metallica, Megadeth, Mötley Crüe, Poison, Ratt, Whitesnake. Favorite classes: metal shop, wood shop. Drives: muscle car. Demeanor: loud, homophobic, caustic. Mad at father, father often alcoholic rager. Always picking fights. Age: sophomore or junior. Smokes: Winstons.

"Classic" deadhead/latter-day hippie: A Cain, secure in his singularity. In addition to the Grateful Dead, has done excavation work, uncovering music of a prior generation: Little Feat, Hot Tuna, The Band, Country Joe & the Fish, Big Brother & the Holding Company, Canned Heat, Crosby, Stills, Nash & Young, Traffic, as well as a baptismal dip into Dylan. Favorite subject: unpredictable. Often mental aptitude is high: could be brilliant at physics; could be leading role in Drama Club play, but then loses it because he doesn't show up for rehearsals. Few and far between – only two or three in a school of 600 students, because many have left already for the open road. Possesses trippy wisdom. Often from old money and pushing back against that. Age: senior. Smokes: Camel unfiltered or Old Golds, cloves, or rolls his own Drums. Naturally flexible and often adept at sports, might have been a star pitcher in little league back in seventh grade but would never go out for a team now. Drinks cranberry juice and grain alcohol out of a leather flask after school while he plays ultimate frisbee with other deadheads and jocks alike; stands in hacky sack circles with all of them during lunch break. He is like that. For all his flux, he's one of a handful who's already integrated, moving freely between tribes with an invisible passport. Has older girlfriend he met at a Dead show; they bonded instantly to "Fire on the Mountain," tripping on purple microdots. Is one of only a few at school who goes directly into the North End of Hartford to score the big ounce of sensimilla from a Jamaican guy there named Les, with no trepidation.

Bullshit twerp "deadhead": Got into the Dead when they entered high school. Doesn't know any other music from that time. A year ago, might have been listening to Cyndi Lauper or REO Speedwagon, or simply nothing. Now all of a sudden is into the Dead for some reason. Wears tie-dyes all the time. Favorite class: humanities. Age: freshman or sophomore. Smokes: Camel Lights only out back or at parties. If female, a classic deadhead may deflower her and then dismiss her, haughtily.

Sexy classic-rock babe: Aerosmith, Led Zeppelin, Heart, Fleetwood Mac, Bad Company, Blue Öyster Cult, Thin Lizzy, Tom Petty & the Heartbreakers, the Eagles. Was into Journey until eighth grade but has grown out of them. Junior or senior. Jean jackets, feathered hair, lots of make-up, world-weary at age sixteen. Dreamy and beautiful, but tough. Intimidating to younger guys; unapproachable. Usually has a boyfriend who is older, out of high school. Smokes Marlboro Light 100s, maybe menthol. Favorite class: couldn't be bothered, but maintains a steady C+ average.

Glammer wildcard: Bowie, Bowie, and Bowie as the underlying constant thread. Assortment of other stuff from glam, New Wave, punk and hardcore: Violent Femmes, the Cure, Echo & the Bunnymen, New Order, Madness, the English Beat, Depeche Mode, Level 42, the B-52's, Talking Heads, Roxy Music. On the face of it, the least dogmatic about genre, yet in a way also the biggest snob of all. These are the people who go on to become rock critics. They affect an ironic superiority over the other tribes, yet remain tethered to their own. Whether male or female, wears blazer with shoulder pads. Favorite class: art or drama. All ages, pretends to smoke Dunhills or Parliaments, not inhaling.

Hardcore/punk heretic: Mohawk, junior or senior. Expatriated or banished outright from either Glammer or one of the Metalhead tribes. Black Flag, Ramones, Sex Pistols, the Clash, Dead Kennedys. Arrestingly open-minded if you hang with them in a listening session, like a glammer without the smug hubris – will give anything a listen on principle before dismissing it. Favorite class: art. Smokes: Marlboro Reds.

Jock straddler: Junior or senior. On the football team, but not *of* it. Bums a smoke out back once a day during lunch. Acid-washed jeans, tight and cuffed up, Puma sneakers, white starched T-shirt. Van Halen, but only starting from their more recent poppier release, *1984*. Had an epiphany to Eddie's virtu-osic Oberheim display on "Jump." Later will compare it to "classical" music. Springsteen, but only *Born in the U.S.A.* At the school dance, led the varsity football team in rigid, choreographed steps to "Glory Days." Only later in life will confront the New Jersey gravitas of earlier Boss on records like *Greetings from Asbury Park, N.J.* or *Born to Run*, through which he will read back his own Tri-State area *Bildung* with the sharpness of passed time, cathartically. Actually a cool guy – not down with the bullying antics and hazing of his teammates. Favorite class: phys ed.

Knowledgeable British classic-rock dude: Another excavator, with a broad spectrum – the Byrds, The Who, Led Zeppelin, the Beatles, the Stones, Eric Clapton, the Kinks, the Zombies – but also early, grounding prog like Yes, King Crimson and Emerson, Lake & Palmer; perhaps even pre-disco Bee Gees. Upperclassman. A reasonable if pompous type; often quite intelligent and talks a lot at parties: for instance, taking you hostage while listening to the trippy jam in the middle of Led Zeppelin's "Whole Lotta Love." "Robert Plant was using his voice like an instrument – an *IN-STRU-MENT!* No one did that before him! Listen! – *Lis-ten!*" [Grabs your shoulder, squeezing it painfully.] Favorite class: civics. Does not smoke tobacco but smokes a lot of pot and does coke which he will not share with you.

Pink Floyd loner: Pink Floyd, yes, but: cursory or no knowledge of band's earlier work with Syd Barrett; it all starts from *The Dark Side of the Moon* and stops at *The Wall* – not much use for groundbreaking albums like *The Piper at the Gates of Dawn*, the brilliant *Meddle*, or the latter elegiac *The Final Cut*. Little or no interest in other bands. Depressive type, waiting for Saturday midnight movies to go see Alan Parker's *The Wall* alone. Mostly invisible to others; social interaction is limited. Pink Floyd's songs are conduits for com-munication: instead of talking directly to a girl he likes, a Pink Floyd Loner may play "Wish You Were Here" on a boom box while standing ten feet away from her, smoking, adapting a tough/lonely expression. Smokes: Marlboro Lights.

Looking back, it strikes me that everything out back was white music-wise. It was the larger tribe I was born into in the white suburban America of the 1980s. At Hall High, I listened to jazz only with my one friend in the same grade, tenor saxophonist Joel Frahm, who would join me in New York City a few years later. We were mostly a two-man tribe, or three when Ricky joined us, and we'd wait a few years to join a much larger one.

The thing about all these groups in high school is that they couldn't relate and sometimes had real antipathy toward each other. The metalheads loathed the deadheads; the deadheads just shook their heads sadly back; their only exchange was selling drugs to each other. The British classic rockers had no time for the glammers. By their lights, Bowie was melodramatic and over-wrought – a "God-awful small affair" indeed. The new metalhead/cock-rock-ers pronounced everything besides their music and the ur-metal that had preceded it quite simply, as "fucking gay." Could something as seemingly abstract as musical taste engender such exclusivity and antagonism?

Someone might say that musical taste is merely a symptom, not a cause. Other factors like social background, or upbringing, determine it. That works the other way around as well, though. Music gives people a sense of purpose. It gives a shape to their longing, a vessel to fill with their pain and fear, an identity. It gives them a dictum they follow with their actions. Music acts on our emotions and bodies, and we are never the same after we hear it.

Where was my identity in all that exclusivity? I had my prejudices, for sure. I couldn't use hairbands. I didn't like anything teenybopper, which then was stuff like Rick Springfield or Bryan Adams. I dug the single "Don't You (For-get About Me)" from Simple Minds that year as it played at the end of *The Breakfast Club* – a strong emblem of a time and our place in it – but, on the whole, I had an aversion to those kinds of bands. As I saw it then, they had emasculated rock'n'roll by neutering the guitars and building the whole sound around synths. There was no real backbeat or strut in the drums either, which were often electronic. All of the guys seemed to be whining, wearing all that synthetic fabric. And all that frowning, fretting, and posing. But now I go back and there's strong stuff there – enduring songwriting and lyrics from bands like Tears For Fears, really strong musicianship from individual players, like bassists John Taylor from Duran Duran or Mark King from Level 42.

There was nevertheless a lot not to like in the '80s, and for me it all boiled down to gated reverb on a snare drum – the sound of Phil Collins and it seemed like just about every other band for several years. Most of them were new acts, but there were also established ones who had produced warm, son-ically appealing records only ten years earlier: Stevie Winwood, formerly of Traffic and Blind Faith; Nancy and Ann Wilson from Heart; Bruce Spring-steen; Aerosmith. And now they were making records with that goddamned snare that sounded like diet soda. The songwriting was still there like on their older stuff, but it was hard to get past the sonics.

I had some pet peeves, but for the most part I loved a wide range of stuff: Jimi Hendrix, Pink Floyd, prog rock bands like Gentle Giant and Yes, Led Zep, or the sophisticated funk, gnomic lyrics and harmonic complexity of Steely Dan. Most importantly, I was at the beginning of a love affair with jazz. Clas-sical music discovery on a deeper level would come later in college; hip-hop would as well, but was in its natal stage and for the time being not on my radar. Jazz took center stage for the next several years, but I never stopped digging all the other music. It didn't get replaced by jazz, it just got shoved to the side for a while. I always thought that, if you truly love some particular music – if it affected and changed your life the way rock'n'roll did mine – how could you just disavow it? How could you strike it off your personal canon? So, amidst all the clans that first year at Hall High, I was a chameleon or, some might have said, a traitor, in terms of musical allegiances:

Classic rock admirer/occasional metalhead/junior deadhead/latter-day hippie/scared of cock-rockers/closeted bisexual glammer/half-hearted Pink Floyd loner/British classic-rock neophyte/lover of the three Bs/jazz initiate: Freshman. Smokes: Old Golds or sometimes Camel unfiltered, trying to imitate older latter-day hippie. Hangs back from the group like a Pink Floyd loner some of the time, but other times jumps into the fray and sits with the deadheads and classic rockers easily enough, finding his way, maybe sneaking off campus with them on lunch break to smoke a quick joint. Bemused by the glammers but not truly scornful. A bit scared of the old-school metalheads. Not talking about jazz or classical music too much – don't bother to share it with anyone. Loves all the music because it's where he finds solace. It's where his home is. Doesn't quite feel like he's in any one of those tribes. There's another tribe that awaits him. He's dreaming of it.

Scripture

The first day of school out back, I sighted Billy, one of only two senior dead-head/latter-day hippies at Hall High, smoking clove cigarettes in his kaftan, barefoot. Over the next few weeks, I inched towards him, fawning, taking off my shoes as well, trying to imitate him. He accepted me, tousling my hair. Billy was less an eye-level friend that year and more a mentor, leading me on what yoga practitioners call the "left-handed path." He scored me my first acid, we hung out with his beautiful deadhead girlfriend who was already out of school, ate pomegranates and drank grain punch, tripped on mushrooms together and went on hikes.

In the case of "Tangled Up in Blue," Bob Dylan's story-song from *Blood on the Tracks*, I was hanging out with Billy one afternoon in his bedroom and he simply wrote down all the verses from memory in a fervent blue streak on a couple sheets of lined paper, while I waited curiously. It took about half an hour, and then he handed them to me, with silent mystery. I read them first and then listened to the song, in that order. Billy's message was simple: *Lyrics*, man. Dylan's *lyrics*. It was a gift in the form of a lesson, from a senior to a freshman; from an arhat – or so I saw him – to an aspirant.

"Tangled Up in Blue" spanned a chunk of life over seven lucid verses. It covered so much, but there was one ever-present character in Dylan's story. A woman, *that* woman, the one who held him under her spell. She was in everything else, already emulsified into every place he went before he arrived there, awaiting him. Even as she confounded him, she drove him forward like some teleological beacon. She was more than a muse. She was his Goddess – he built up a religion around her mystery and grace, in the scripture of his songwriting. He chased her and would catch up to her for a spell, but he never possessed her. She possessed him.

The song was a cycle that began and ended with her. She changed and took on different faces. At times it seemed like he was meeting her for the first time. Other times it seemed like he knew her already and they were reuniting, or some mixture of both. Was she a composite of several different women? It didn't matter. It made her even more tangible, because you knew, you just knew, that she was conjured into a song from the rapture and turmoil of his own experience. She was real, and he made her even more real in the song, for all of us.

In the first verse, she was there as someone he knew already – they had already parted ways. He had already lost her. The prelapsarian moment of their first meeting had passed before the song began, and now he walked a road outside her Eden.

> Early one mornin' the sun was shinin'
> I was layin' in bed

> Wondrin' if she'd changed at all
> If her hair was still red

Dylan condenses so much – time, space, feeling, and flux – in only a few lines. In the second stanza, he tells of their first alliance and abrupt fissure:

> She was married when we first met
> Soon to be divorced
> I helped her out of a jam I guess
> But I used a little too much force
> We drove that car as far as we could
> Abandoned it out west
> Split up on a dark sad night
> Both agreeing it was best
> She turned around to look at me
> As I was walkin' away
> I heard her say over my shoulder
> We'll meet again some day
> On the avenue
> Tangled up in blue

The lyrics convey distance, and it's an American kind of distance, traversing a large, kaleidoscopic landscape. In the next verse, he's alone, rambling through its regions. She is far away now, but always right in front of his vision:

> I had a job in the Great North Woods
> Working as a cook for a spell
> But I never did like it all that much
> And one day the ax just fell
> So I drifted down to New Orleans
> Where I was looking for to be employed
> Workin' for a while on a fishin' boat
> Right outside of Delacroix
> But all the while I was alone
> The past was close behind
> I seen a lot of women
> But she never escaped my mind
> And I just grew
> Tangled up in blue

At the time Billy introduced me to the song, I was under the spell of Jack Kerouac, Henry Miller, and William Burroughs. I had stayed in touch with my older cabin mate Joe from Merrywood, and he guided me to books and music in a letter exchange, telling me to read Kerouac's *On the Road* and Burroughs's *Naked Lunch*. I read the Kerouac the first month of freshman year. As soon as I finished it, I wanted to leave home right then and there, to set out on the open road like he had, tasting all the locales he described – not just the big iconic cities like New York (I would start there, I figured) but also romantically forlorn locales like Laredo, Texas, where he hunkered in with his benny-addled friends Old Bull Lee and his wife Jane – his depiction of real-life William and Joan Burroughs. When Dylan sang about the Great North Woods or Delacroix, it did the same thing that Kerouac did. It announced the possibility of a future filled with pathos and radiance, with equal parts of solitude and connection, always in the context of lucid discovery. I would be a traveler like them, rambling with others in temporary tribes, all of us just sojourners, never staying for long; all with our own backstory, tangled up in our own kind of blue. I would come out of the tollbooth of childhood and finally drive the long highway.

It seemed to me that the America that Dylan and the Beats sang and wrote about was fading away or already gone. There was certainly no evidence of it in West Hartford. I had caught a whiff of its traces in New York City two years earlier with Caleb. During that visit to their summer house in Litch-field County, his dad drove us into Manhattan for a day trip and Caleb and I went off on our own. He showed me around the West Village neighborhood where I'd live ten years later. We saw the Village Vanguard, where musicians like John Coltrane and Bill Evans had broken new ground. We walked down along Christopher Street, past the Stonewall Inn where the gay liberation movement began. We crossed 6th Avenue and walked towards Washington Square Park, where Joni Mitchell, Allen Ginsberg, Dylan, and others con-vened. I remember the smell of the neighborhood as we ascended from the A train station at 6th Avenue and 3rd Street – fried dough, garlic and roasted meat from the street vendors, cigarette and weed smoke, car exhaust and sweat, all mixed together. It was like a drug. All of that would become part of my direct experience in the years to come, when I would move to Jones Street one block west.

Yet I sensed that there was already something storied to its famous locales, that it was already a funky museum and I was another tourist, sniffing at the vestiges of what it had been. Henry Miller had described other neighbor-hoods of that earlier New York City like the Bowery and Lower East Side in grimy, sensual detail, in his trilogy of *Sexus, Plexus,* and *Nexus.* Burroughs had gone outside of New York like Kerouac, to other bygone places, ones that were more lawless and dangerous, creating his anarchic homosexual version of the Wild West in books like *The Wild Boys* and *The Western Lands.* As with Dylan's landscape, I wondered how much of that more dangerous, alluring kind of American experience was still available, if any. Caleb and I had walked by used book stores and record shops along Bleecker Street and I saw old copies of Kerouac and used, out-of-print Coltrane Impulse records asking a high price. I thought, it already happened – I missed that.

I surmised that Dylan and the Beats saw back then that it was fading already, and their words and music were elegiac, trying to bottle up some of that vital energy, and bear witness to the night-time air rushing into a boxcar from the plains outside, before they were paved over and filled with big-box stores; or some of that hallucinogenic, frenzied noise of a big city in full tilt, before it congealed into conglomerate sterility. I would try my hand at musical elegy later, on my first solo record, *Elegiac Cycle*. As I went along, I discovered that everything was always fading, and that kind of elegiac impulse was essentially a Romantic one that traced back to the Industrial Revolution, with its poetic cris de cœur from Wordsworth, Blake, and others. The Beats and Dylan were following suit.

I turned other friends onto "Tangled Up in Blue" later, and they passed it on, all of us paying it forward. Friends and music – it wasn't clear where the one ended and the other began. You listened to what someone had to say about a band because you liked that person and what he or she was about. It was a kind of campaigning, but essentially benevolent, without any disguised motive. Someone wanted to win you over to their side and dig the band as much they did, so you could share that gnosis; so you could just look at each other, and that was enough – you knew that the other one knew. When someone turned me on to their music, I welcomed their biased, loving take on it – often in a running commentary as we listened, a set-up ahead of time, or an impassioned appraisal afterwards. I did the same in return. Sometimes there was nothing to say. Words muffled the meaning instead of clarifying it.

Music was an important part of almost every significant friendship or relationship I had during adolescence, throughout my *Bildung*. It was how you connected with someone on deeper grounds. It was how you achieved solidarity. Deeper than sex? People go on about how art is a sublimation of our desire. But you could flip that around as well, and say that sex is a more outward expression of music – music, bewitching and expressive, an elusive, sacred portal to deeper friendship and love. For it wasn't just that you listened to music with friends who "had the same interests" as you did. In some instances you literally picked friends *because* they liked the same music as you did – and if they liked the wrong music, that could be a deal-breaker.

There was solidarity through music, but solidarity implies its flipside, exclusion, of those not in your tribe. In that first year of high school, I learned a socio-musical lesson: to respect and allow for the utter partisan quality of musical appreciation of friends and even adversaries, in the form of disdain that they had for music that wasn't theirs, while continuing to stay open to new input myself. I sympathized with that partisan urge and felt it some myself even as I tempered it. I understood that, if you define yourself through a set of characteristics – some things that you love – then you also define yourself in opposition to other things, and set yourself against them, at least initially.

Teen jazz snobs

The most biased, snobby, and self-satisfied music lovers in high school, even more than the glam kids, were a handful of upperclassmen in the jazz big band. I say that with complete affection thinking back on them. They were a phenomenon unto themselves. When I was a freshman, three or four of them would periodically descend on me in a practice room, where I'd be jamming on some tune, noodling around: "Mehldau, when are you going to quit listening to Pat Metheny and Weather Report and start listening to some *Bird?* And some *Monk?*"

"Yeah, Mehldau's just slacking. You know what he did last week?"

"What?"

"He went and saw the *Grateful Dead.*"

"Oh come on – cut the crap. Mehldau – you gotta be kidding me. You *what?*"

"Yeah, well what do you expect? He's just hanging out with all those burnouts out back, probably smoking weed. Mehldau, are you smoking weed?"

"Sure he is. Look at him – he's high right now!"

"Man, we should kick his ass right here."

"Pathetic. Mehldau – get into the shed and start working on 'All the Things You Are.' Listen to some *Bird*! The Grateful Dead . . . Jesus."

"Yeah, Mehldau. Don't be a burnout."

"Don't be a loser, Mehldau."

There was that West Hartford word "loser" again. In this context, you were a loser if you didn't check out Bird and Monk – lazy, incurious, ignorant. By this time in high school, I was into being a rebel so, when those older guys chided me like that, I didn't give them any satisfaction of a humble promise to check out Bird and Monk. Yet it worked. Bird bit me right away, easily seducing me. Monk's music didn't enter at first listen, but I stuck with him because they talked about him with such imperious reverence. By age sixteen, when I discovered the live record with Trane at the Five Spot, there was no turning back. "Trinkle, Tinkle" offered the wildest, most unbridled essay I had heard from Trane yet. You could hear that it had something to do with the opening melody of Monk's composition itself – dizzying, supersonic, ahead of anything else I had known. Also, their performance together of "Monk's Mood" shot through me: there was a mixture of lucidity and tenderness in Monk's composition and Trane's rendering of the melody. It was so personal.

In high school I related to the deadheads, jazz snobs, and British classic rockers alike. The political was personal – the political conviction (or ambivalence) was connected to the broad personal musical aesthetic. Perhaps that big-tent sentiment went deeper. I wanted to play both sides of the fence. I had one set of friends that was in the "burnout" group in middle school and high school, which covered most everybody out back, and another that wasn't.

Often, my burnout friends were the proletarians – from the other side of town with a blue-collar background. The others, like me, were from wealthier families. Both groups of friends had contempt for the other, and sometimes it was a diplomatic balancing act hanging out with all of them.

I had both heterosexual and homosexual feelings and didn't like the idea that anyone would label me in that regard, especially in the hurtful way Ed and Dylan had. All of these factors combined into an rudimentary politics that would congeal later: a strong, often strident belief in the right to privacy, in keeping the government out of one's personal life; yet just as strong a belief that the government had the responsibility to lift everyone up, not just a select group; and, because of my own relative privilege, a certain idealism about how all those well-meaning sentiments could co-exist in practice.

Hall High School was known for its highly prized big band. Families even moved to West Hartford if their kids showed musical talent, with hopes that they could participate in it. You had to audition for it as a class, Jazz Band 1, and, if you didn't make it, there was Jazz Band 2, which, for a high-school-level band, was not bad at all. Jazz Band 1 took first place in the national competitions held at Berklee College of Music in Boston for years on end. The band was known all over the country, and its director Bill Stanley was revered and feared by all of us before we even arrived at Hall.

We heard about Mr. Stanley already at King Philip in seventh and eighth grade from Haig Shahverdian, the jazz-band director there. He was a very good teacher and band director, but of a different mold, and didn't use Mr. Stanley's ego-crushing tactics. He prepped us regularly, though, telling us what to expect, and what Mr. Stanley would and wouldn't abide.

The teen jazz snobs, two or three years ahead of us, had gone through a ritual of hazing in the band themselves, and when we arrived, they subjected us to it in turn. That sometimes abusive karmic transference from upperclassmen to freshman and sophomore recruits was a well-rehearsed cliché in the football or swim team, but in the jazz band it was strange to me. It didn't fit with the idea of jazz I was forming. It didn't seem to have much to do with Coltrane. Joel Frahm had moved from Wisconsin just before the beginning of our sophomore year and made it into the band. Some of the guys in the sax section were just brutal to Joel – sadistic, really. Ricky was second drummer to an upperclassman who had the seat already for two years. The three of us would jam regularly after high school in the band room. Those were joyful hours of mutual discovery.

Mr. Stanley came from a Southern Baptist background, and had more than a little Old Testament brimstone in his manner. He taught mostly through intimidation, like a drill sergeant. In his appraisal, we started the school year from absolute musical depravity, without a clue, and it was his job to whip and chisel us in the months to come. He had an instruction that he loved to repeat to us: "*Aspire to mediocrity*." The irony was funny enough, but he wasn't really joking. He had charisma, though: you wanted him to like you by default, if only for the reason that he doled out so much criticism and very few compliments.

The parents of the students in the band and rest of the school faculty tolerated Mr. Stanley, and to some extent put him on a pedestal, because he got results. The ensemble playing he summoned from the different sections, the intonation, the phrasing, the attention to dynamics – it was all quite an achievement for a high-school band. The national accolades were the proof in the pudding, so the adults held their noses when they got a whiff of his cruel tactics. What the band didn't have was any sense of swing or swagger. Our feel was stiff and corny.

Every year in the early spring, there was the Hall High Pops'n'Jazz show. It was a huge event for all involved, not just the jazz band, but the jazz choir, dancers, and tech crew, some forty students in all. It was more than that, though: it was a point of pride for the school, and for West Hartford more generally. It ran for five evening performances that were two-and-a-half hours long, with three sets, costume and light changes, and moving stages, all calibrated and executed with glitzy élan. The show was Vegas style – the purple tuxedos and ruffled shirts we had to wear could have come from Wayne Newton's closet. For one week prior, there were daily dress rehearsals that ran into late evening after school. It didn't matter whatever else was going on in your life, academically or otherwise – you would show up for every one and stay through the end, or you were out.

Truth be told, a good chunk of the audience showed up solely for the jazz dancers – I mean the whistling teenaged boys who didn't care a rat's ass about jazz or any of it, and the more quietly leering middle-aged men. The dancers were a hand-picked group of twelve or so girls, many of them from the cheerleading team, with gymnastic bodies and apple-pie seductiveness. Their routines were in the vein of the Rockettes with some modern dance thrown in, all in slinky, revealing outfits. During those long rehearsals, Mr. Stanley would sometimes dress someone down in front of everyone else, shaming them. One time I remember he called out one of the dancers and ripped into her, criticizing her steps harshly in front of all of us, reducing her to quiet tears.

In the 1980s things were different, for sure. There was another teacher involved in Pops'n'Jazz during that time in charge of the choreography, lighting, and tech crew. During our senior year, he had sex with one of the dancers. The summer after I graduated, he and his wife were gone without a trace. We had all heard about it, and word was the father of the girl had run him out of town. Nobody talked about it much after that except in snickering whispers. That's how it was done back then.

Mr. Stanley respected me to a point. Along with Joel and Ricky, I was playing improvised jazz. A lot of the repertoire of the big band was Sammy Nestico stuff in the great tradition of Count Basie. We delivered swingless, rigid performances, but did the music some justice in terms of execution. The Bird, Miles, and Coltrane that Joel and I were checking out was not as much on Mr. Stanley's radar, but he was impressed with our ability to improvise, and sensed our fledgling feeling for swing, the blues, and some beginning bebop vocabulary.

I was rebellious, not so much through open rudeness, but more through cocky negligence. I'd show up late to rehearsals, or forget my music and try to ad-lib my way through it. Often I showed up high. One time I came to an evening rehearsal directly from one of those ultimate frisbee games with Billy, juiced up on grain punch to the point where I couldn't play, and he threw me out with a disgusted hiss.

Our worst showdown, he and I, happened at the graduation ceremony for the class ahead of me, at the end of my junior year. I was to accompany one of the jazz singers as part of the ceremony. I don't remember now what the song was: most likely something patriotic. I didn't know exactly when it would be, so I was hanging around in the school waiting, close to the double doors by the band room which opened to the outdoor stage. At some point, it seemed like a good idea to walk to another set of doors and step out to smoke the remainder of a joint, followed by a cigarette. As I strolled back, pleasantly baked, I tried to listen for what was going on in the ceremony. It was absolutely silent — what was up with that? Suddenly one of the other students burst in. "Mehldau, you moron, get out there – she's waiting for on stage already for more than a minute!" My stomach sank. I raced out, my shirt untucked, stoned. There was a deafening silence, followed by snickers and groans from the audience in the school lawn, which numbered probably at least 500, among them all the proud parents of the graduates, their extended families, the football team, town eldermen, you name it. The poor girl had tears in her eyes. We did the song.

I trudged back into the building with remorse and embarassment. I heard the doors open again behind me, and turned around to see Mr. Stanley running towards me in a rage. Before I had time to say anything, he grabbed me by the chest and threw me hard back against the lockers next to the band room. "You goddamned, stupid piece of *shit!*" he growled, holding me there, poking his meaty fingers once more in my chest for good measure. He stepped back, glared at me a few more moments, and walked away brusquely. What was it about my chest, that all these guys liked to put their hands on it so much, and then throw me against a wall – starting with the bullies in seventh grade, then Ed, and now Mr. Stanley? Did I have a sign on me that said, "Grab and push"?

The next year, my senior and final one at Hall, the Jazz Band made the trip to Berklee once more to participate in the national high-school big-band competition. I took the award that night for "Best Improviser." Mr. Stanley came and sat in the seat next to me. He was smiling but it wasn't relaxed. I think he felt pride for me, for what I had achieved with him and the other students the last four years. But I was too resentful to share it with him because of how he had slammed me against the wall the year before. He said something forced like, "Well, you really did it tonight." I forced a half-smile but couldn't find anything to say, and he got up and returned to the front of the bus.

Mr. Stanley wasn't so much an influence on me going forward as a musician as he was a character-builder. He was sound in his judgment if not his unbridled anger. I was disrespectful in my negligence, not just to him, but to that poor girl and all the attendees at the graduation, and to the other kids in the band when I showed up late or without my music. Even though it wasn't conscious, I was already feeling like I could get away with stuff because of my talent. He let me know: you may get away with disrespecting others in the short term, but it will catch up with you, and someone else will throw you against that wall in one way or another. It was a lesson that took a long time to learn. When Joshua Redman fired me out of necessity because of my heroin use a few years later, I had to learn it some more. (He didn't throw me against any wall.)

Cain goes to work

My first real job was the summer I turned fourteen. It was at a tobacco farm in the neighboring town of Avon. They hired kids under sixteen and paid them just under minimum wage. I was practically the only white kid there and felt like I stuck out right away. It was all in my head, in retrospect. No one was paying particular attention to me. Mostly, it was Puerto Rican families bussed in from Hartford, with the grandparents, parents, and children all out there together, where the temperature could get as high as 110°F under the nets. The work was tough enough. The first day there, I didn't know what I was in for. I wanted to wear shorts but had none that fit, so I showed up in a bathing suit that was too small. We began loading bales of tobacco leaves onto a truck. I immediately got cuts all up my legs and was bleeding from the little scrapes. The guy in charge was a big dude who spoke only a little English. He looked at me and joked with his friends, calling me a *maricón* to the other workers, who laughed. A few days later, my mom was on the phone with her sister and my uncle from Cuba, and I asked him what the word meant. He explained that it was a derogatory gay term.

That kind of run-of-the-mill hazing at the workplace – it stopped there, and they didn't treat me unfairly the two months I worked there – became so much more for me than it really was. I replayed the scene for months, imagining his contempt for me, and the derision of the other workers' laughter. I felt like a white-boy wimp, and didn't want to go back the next day. I kicked myself over and over again for wearing that damned bathing suit. Most likely, the whole thing wasn't that menacing, and they were having a laugh at the rookie. But I took these things so heavily because I already felt different.

The next paycheck I earned was the following summer, canvassing for the West Hartford voters' registrar. I had to knock on doors and find out who was living where, if the information was up to date, and, if not, correct it. Two weeks into the job, I got a real surly type who was just coming home from work. "What do you want?" he growled. I explained my gig. He responded, "Get off my yard!" Really nothing horrible but, again, I recalled the episode over and over in my head, feeling both fear and anger towards the guy.

It was always: "This person doesn't *like* me." That was such a big deal. I would see other people who didn't get fazed by that kind of rejection – other students at school, for example – and I envied them. Everything seemed easier for them. Why couldn't I just let stuff roll off my back? This was the beginning of self-loathing. The next tier is meta-loathing: when you just loathe yourself for loathing yourself so much. It's so self-referential, you just want to turn it off. When you find your first drug or drink, you're hooked from the gate. It feels like what you've needed all along. It takes away that shitty feeling and you finally have the last laugh – fuck 'em all! You don't know it then, but you're just getting started on a much longer journey of self-hatred.

When I turned sixteen and could earn minimum wage, I got a job at Papa Gino's in Bishop's Corner. It was a pizzeria with all the usual grill stuff – cheese steaks, pita pockets, meatball grinders. I started out on "dining room" like everyone else, cleaning tables, mopping the floors, bathrooms. Next, I graduated to the grill. I was slow and not good at it. After a couple weeks, I sent out an order with undercooked sausage. When it came back from an angry customer – I could have given her parasites from the raw pork – Tom, the manager, came back to me at the grill and said, "Buddy, why don't you head back out to the dining room." Meanwhile, this other guy I knew pretty well from school, Jeremy, started working there after I had been there a few months already. In no time, he had graduated up through grill to the coveted, highest spot: flipping pies. And I was still at first base, scrubbing urinals.

One Sunday morning, Tom had the whole staff gather before opening for a morale-building get-together. He went around introducing everyone by their name, and with each he had a funny anecdote and maybe a nickname for them. There were lots of laughs. When it came to me, Tom got visibly awkward. He had nothing funny to say. "Brad's new here and we're just getting to know him." There was a pause and he moved on. What the fuck? Jeremy was newer than I was and Tom was hamming it up about him like they were old friends. Where was my joke? He couldn't even think of one.

It was the teenaged iteration of Mr. Mazzie's class with the adoption. Everyone was joshing around, bonding, and, when my turn came, everything got shitty and quiet. The question became: was I truly marked like Cain? Or was it all in my head? Or was it a self-fulfilling kind of negative feedback loop, in which I was afraid of being marked – so I drew the mark on myself out of fear? Perhaps, I thought, Tom sensed my discomfort and felt aversion for me *because* of it.

That kind of low self-esteem was offset by the fact that I started getting gigs. Guys from the Hartford area were calling me to play with them for wedding receptions, office parties, and the like around Connecticut. I could make as much as $150 for the weddings, which was more than what I made in two weeks part-time at Papa Gino's. That was pretty cool, and I was quiet about it – I didn't get cocky. So there was a duel aspect to being an outsider. It could be painful, shameful, and even humiliating. Or it could be gratifying, righteous, and pleasing. In the one scenario, my ego was bruised; in the other, it was right-sized.

The "club dates" as we called them on the East Coast – elsewhere they're called "socials"– gave me an early view into male middle-aged jazz musicians not always behaving great. A lot of them were doing coke and slurping up drinks at the open bar throughout the gigs. They would talk shit about their sexual prowess, take their wedding bands off, and ogle the women at the parties, which seemed lame. It was fun and kind of surreal though to get high and do coke with people my parents' age. Some of them felt guilty but I quietly pushed them on, saying it was fine. If I brought the weed, they would

Joel and I in 1985, during the 880 days

never turn it down. It was like getting paid to party – a hell of a lot more fun than Papa Gino's. What was not to like?

There were gigs with singers, and they were another ball of wax, much more high-stress. I learned how to play tunes in whatever key the singer requested, on the spot, and I started to build up a repertoire. By the time I got to New York City a few years later, I had a good head start with a collection of "standards" under my belt. These were Tin Pan Alley songs like "What Is This Thing Called Love?," or "Night and Day," which you were expected to know and be ready to play, to be used as springboards for collective improvisation. This was on-the-job training, and of course I made mistakes. Sometimes the singers were patient, sometimes they were not at all: "Who's this kid you brought along?" Or they would dress me down in front of the audience: "What the hell kind of intro is that? Give me the *key*, damn it – set my shit *up!*"

The ones who hired me for the club dates were people I met and played with at the 880, the jazz club in Hartford where I had my first real gigs – "listening" gigs, where people come for the music, not for something else with the music serving as background entertainment. These were primarily with Larry DiNatale, the first real jazz drummer I played with, in my second year of high school. Larry mentored Joel Frahm and me, and also saxophonist Pat Zimmerli who was two years ahead of us at Hall High. Pat and I worked together years later as well, on *Modern Music* – a record with pianist Kevin Hays, also a Connecticut native, with Pat's compositions and arrangements. Larry gave us a gig every Wednesday night at the 880, playing with us. Often present were Nat Reeves, the stellar bassist who played with Jackie McLean for years, trombonist Steve Davis, studying with McLean at Hartt School of Music in Hartford, and tenor saxophonist Antoine Roney, brother of trumpeter Wallace.

It was an introduction to the jazz hang. Larry smoked these really thin cigarettes and would hold court outside the 880 between sets with Joel, myself, and the other musicians. Joel and I were both juniors at Hall High by then. Joel was a crucial musical peer growing up. He invited me to play duo with him on his record *Don't Explain* in 2004. That date caught some of the spirit of discovery we had when we started out together.

Larry liked to throw rhetorical questions at us. We were very earnest, and he'd try to ruffle us up a bit with "really" questions: "Was Thelonious Monk really that great?" "Do Black guys really swing harder than white guys?" "Could Horace Silver really comp?" "Was Miles really a good trumpet player?" That kind of stuff. He would try to provoke a reaction, and it was partly in fun, but it also got us thinking outside of our boxes. On the bandstand, Larry would often play "easy" with us – not breaking the time up too much, just laying it right down the middle. Other times, though, he would really throw stuff at us, playing aggressively, throwing us off, dropping bombs, all the while glaring at us intently.

It was all provocation, but I learned from Larry that provocation was a musical principle in itself, one that you had to confront if you wanted to play jazz. You had to be able to at least stand your own ground when someone poked you in the music like Larry did; and, if you were on your toes enough and the stars aligned, you might use that poke to your favor – you could answer it back with an even greater provocation. That's when things got interesting. The two greatest bands of the 1960s – the Miles Davis Quintet and the John Coltrane Quartet – *began* from that point of provocation, and then went from there.

The model of a jazz musician that Larry gave me, on and off the bandstand, was attractive because it promised two things I wanted: the transgressive experience I had already been seeking for a few years since returning from Merrywood, and at the same time an experience of integrity and beauty. I wanted to actually *create* that experience and not just be privy to it – to be the person who could do that, like Coltrane and Miles. They were gods, because they could create and destroy, like Yahweh and Krishna – benevolent and crushing all at once. I had tasted dark and strong transgression, but it left me wounded. I needed to heal. In every act of playing, music would open the wound and heal it all at once, cathartically.

The jazz music I discovered and loved in particular at that point was the kind that cut a wound right away, and then left it splayed and open for a while: the Eric Dolphy/Booker Little Quintet playing "Fire Waltz," Mingus's band playing "Praying with Eric," Booker Ervin playing "A Lunar Tune" with Jaki Byard, Richard Davis, and Alan Dawson. They were all just walking all over each other. In my sophomore year during that time, I went to a Ramones show at the Agora Ballroom in Hartford, a club that fit about 600 people, packed in standing. When they started, I took my shoes off, went into the middle of the mosh pit and stayed there for the whole show, getting slammed around by guys with big necks in their twenties and thirties. My feet were bleeding all over at the end of the show. I loved it. It was like someone grabbing your head and throwing it in a sink of ice water, but with a good heart all the while. It woke you up and made you want to live more. It was a baptism.

Larry was a guy in his forties with life experience who hadn't turned square like other adults, and he wasn't the least bit creepy like some of the ones I was intersecting with then. He'd talk with us into the late hours out in the parking lot of the club after the gig. One night we were all outside. Larry was smoking those thin cigarettes, holding court with several of us. Joel and I had been gushing earnestly about all of our favorite players, different records we were discovering, and wonking out about jazz. Larry smoked impatiently, then suddenly turned to me and said, "Brad, let me ask you something. Let's say you're a master chef."

I nodded, waiting.

"If you're a master chef, what do you do when you go home at night, when you're done with work?"

"I don't know," I said. I couldn't imagine.

"Do you think you sit around and read cookbooks all night?" he asked. The tone in his voice suggested no.

"Probably not," I ventured, not understanding.

"Of course not," he confirmed. "A master chef doesn't need to keep reading cookbooks after he's done at work. He goes home and he finds time for something else – he reads other books, or he enjoys music, or films. He's interested in other things."

I was sixteen and I got what he was saying intellectually but my whole being went against it. For me, it seemed like, in order for the master chef to remain a master, he should go home and "shed" some more cooking – he should keep on practicing. He should strive to become even *more* of a master, whatever that might mean. The idea that someone would consciously choose to pursue an interest outside of their most immediate passion was off-putting to me, because I was completely consumed with jazz. I was a new convert, and here was Larry telling me that there was a stage after the one I was in now, where I wouldn't be as passionate about it.

Of course that's not what he was saying. In my greenness, though, I equated passion with single-mindedness and stopped there. I didn't have the breadth of input and experience to realize that the intensity needn't ever diminish. You never have to relinquish the act of edification. As you gain knowledge and experience, you expand outward, continuing to absorb fresh material. Also, you don't ever leave anything completely behind that you've already absorbed. There's real value in retracing a circle you already made, because each time you do that, the context will have changed, depending on what you've absorbed since the last time.

Working off gym class

Senior Year of High School, 1987

I was a horrible student in high school. There were a few classes I got something out of – English class senior year was engaging, and I did well there – but, for the most part, school was a disaster as far as actual work. Now the reckoning was approaching, and there was a good chance I wouldn't graduate. I knew how it worked already from a few friends who were older than me. You participated in the ceremony and were handed an envelope like the rest of the class, but when you opened it up, there was no diploma in there.

I spent four years of high school smoking cannabis through a water pipe, often with Ricky, who had remained my close friend since our rocky beginning at Bugbee Hill. We would do bong hits in one of our parents' station wagons before school ("wake and bake"), then head into our first-period class stoned. During lunch we'd sneak off campus and do more bong hits and, immediately after school, still more. There were solo bong hits before dinner, and finally bong hits before bed. My teen years were spent in a cloud of marijuana.

Usually I got detentions for being late to school, late to class, or skipping gym, and by the last half or so of my senior year I had over 200 of them. A detention meant that you were obliged to stay after school for an hour as a punishment for your infraction and sit quietly in a room, doing work with other detainees. There was no way to serve all of them after school my senior year because I had more detentions than there were days in the school year, and the deal with detentions is that you couldn't graduate from high school without serving all of them.

My guidance counselor and I made an arrangement for me to work off the detentions, pairing up with Ricky, who was in a similar situation, although with not quite as many. We would meet after school with Mark, the janitor, and help him with his work. Mark was really cool, into music like us. We'd smoke a joint with him sometimes before we grabbed the mops, and then talk about bands like Grand Funk Railroad and the Allman Brothers while we worked. After three or four cleaning sessions, Ricky and I eventually blew off Mark, not showing up. He cut us loose. Ricky was going to be all right, but I had still only worked off a portion of my stint. The guidance counselor said tough turkey – you're on your own. I had a chance and blew it.

How did I graduate then? I made a Faustian bargain with Dr. Dunn, the school principal.

My experience with Dr. Dunn might be surprising to my fellow alumni of Hall High School – or might not. Anyone who went to Hall High knew about the men's bathroom stalls. At least a decade before we arrived, Dr. Dunn had ordered that the doors be taken away. The story went that guys had been smoking weed or doing other drugs in the stalls with the doors locked. His solution? Off went the doors! This meant that, if you had to take a dump during school, you did it with no door, at the risk that someone would walk right by you while you were in the middle of taking a shit.

And that's exactly what Dr. Dunn would do. He would hover around the hallways between periods, waiting for some unlucky soul to go into the men's room. If you were in the shitter, he would make his move, walking into the bathroom, right up to the front of the stall, and start having a conversation with you. It never happened to me, but I saw him doing it to another guy once while I was at the urinal – just standing there talking about nothing, looking at the guy while he did his business. You'd have to either sit there and wait it out until he split, or wipe your ass while he watched. I left without finding out.

One deeply crappy aspect of high school for me was gym. I hated it: I hated having to get changed and run around in the middle of the day – it just seemed so pointless. I hated the slogans, I hated playing in teams, I hated the fecal smell of the locker room. So I skipped gym a lot, and flunked it. It was required that you pass gym every year or repeat it so, by the time I got to my senior year, I had earned my own special ring of hell. I had gym three times a day – freshman gym, junior gym, and senior gym. I had made up sophomore gym in my previous junior year, but then flunked junior gym that same year. The teacher said I skipped more than four classes, which made you flunk. She was wrong. I had been careful to cap it at four skips, no more. It was her word against mine though, so I got an F. Her decision shaped my destiny.

Dr. Dunn found out about my situation and pulled some strings, as only the principal could. It was established that I would work off the detentions and the gym credits all at once with him, one on one, so that I could graduate from high school at the end of the year. We would meet in the gym when we had free time – sometimes after school, sometimes on the weekends. Basically, what it amounted to is that I would do some gym-like stuff – run laps around the gym, jump rope, and do some other stupid shit for a while – and he would watch at first. Then he would split, saying, "Keep at it, Brad." When he left I would slip outside the building and smoke a joint or cigarettes and just sit around. I'd circle back after an hour and he'd come back.

The whole thing had been arranged through a back door and I wasn't supposed to tell anyone about it – most of all the gym teacher who had flunked me junior year. So there was this secrecy. Even my parents didn't know what I was doing. I hid it from them. Only a couple of my close friends knew. The second time I went, on a Saturday, I snuck out through a back door of the locker room and met up with my close friend Dave, who was waiting. He kept me company. We just talked shit and smoked bowls to pass the time. We laughed about how weird the whole thing was.

Dr. Dunn came outside all of the sudden and surprised us. He wasn't pissed that we were getting high. He was pissed that I was with my friend. "I told you this was just our arrangement," he said to me quietly. He wanted the whole thing to be just us two. The thing I took out of that was people don't get pissed at what they're supposed to get pissed at. They get pissed at other stuff that they don't want to admit. So the reason not to fuck up wasn't because of what was right or wrong. It was so you didn't give them an opening to get what they really wanted.

Dave shuffled away, not looking up. He was embarrassed by the whole scene – for himself, for me as well. I was embarrassed that he was embarrassed for me. No one else tagged along to the gym sessions again. We had this silent covenant, Dr. Dunn and I, and it would get me my diploma. The shame I felt led to secrecy but, also, the secrecy led to shame. That felt like a reboot of the disaster with Dylan and Ed, which I'd been carrying alone all through high school. Dr. Dunn was way ahead of those guys, though. He was completely in control, completely understated. No threats or violence – just silence and long looks.

Looking back, with only one exception, there was no one else there during our sessions – not in the locker room and showers, the gym, or the weight room. It was like he had clean-swept the place. I'm not sure how he pulled that off. He had a big set of master keys like Mark the janitor, attached to his suit pants all the time, and sometimes the locker room was locked when we entered. That's kind of how I felt anyways – locked from the inside. We were alone.

He'd have me go in the weight room first, and I'd half-heartedly do a few bench presses. He'd stand there right over me, watching with this mixture of contempt and tenderness as I struggled with the barbell. He'd smile and look at me all over, sort of rolling his hips towards me, appraising me. Under that smile was something else that I couldn't name or didn't want to name because it made me uncomfortable. It was something quiet – it was his desire, mixed with his own shame. He still had the power, though. He gave the orders. It felt like we were in some courtship process that I didn't want to be in.

After my first bullshit workout, he suggested it was a good idea for me to take a shower in the locker room. Nobody ever took showers there except the teams after a game. Besides, I hadn't broken a sweat at all. The first time I turned him down and saw that he was disappointed. After I fucked up and got caught getting high with Dave, I felt obligated to do the shower.

In what became a ritual, I'd take off my clothes with him watching. His eyes would get this piercing look, almost like squinting. Then he'd do this back and forth thing – he'd look at me in the eyes and wait until I'd look up at him. Right at the moment I met his gaze, he'd look down at my crotch and hold his eyes there. He wanted me to know he was looking at my dick. He wanted me to know that he *could* look at my dick whenever he wanted.

I'd walk into the large shower stalls and he'd walk right in with me. He gave me some soap and stood as close as he could to me in his tie and jacket without getting water on himself. Sometimes some water splashed on his grey blazer but he didn't care. He talked about dumb stuff like "how's the piano going" and "I saw your father in the pharmacy the other day," that sort of bullshit, and the whole time he just stared between my legs and at my backside when I turned around, then back at my eyes, with this little half-smile and that squint. He spoke more and more quiet as the shower went on, almost whispering. It was always this prosaic nonsense, like a code for something else. He never said anything real. That was my take-home: *Don't say anything real.* Don't say what you're feeling; hide it. That's what the principal does.

This was the arrangement for a while – the obligatory ten or fifteen minutes of gym, and then down to the shower. I knew I had some power over him because he wanted to perv on me like that. So I blew him off a lot and even skipped off completely a few times and didn't come back, because what was he going to do? He wanted me to come back. He knew that he could help me graduate, though – that was his strong card – so I had to go along with him and show up there the next time. It was a tacit negotiation.

One time, someone came into the locker room. It was the gym teacher from my freshman and sophomore year. I was just done in the shower. Dr. Dunn was standing by the towel room. His thing was always to hold off on giving me the towel until after the shower so I'd have to walk naked across the stalls to him while he looked at me. Then I'd go into the towel room where he'd finally get one. The guy walked through, looked at both of us for a moment and turned away. He walked out of there quickly. It was bizarre – wouldn't he greet the principal? Neither of them said anything, so neither did I – more silence. I remember the look in that guy's face. It was a kind of fear, like being in complicity – he didn't have the resolve to do anything.

But resolve for what? I was just taking a shower, after all. Nothing wrong with that. Just us guys.

Then I remembered where I had seen that look on the gym teacher's face another time. It was earlier in the school year. There was this one guy who had some coke, a friend of a friend, and we went up a stairwell behind the cafeteria during lunch. If you went to the top you'd get to a door to the roof. The door was alarmed but right there at the ledge was a spot to do something illegal quickly. Being inside it was not a place to smoke anything, but good for a quick blast of powder with a few buddies – no wind to blow it away. Then back to lunch with a medicine taste in your throat and that tickly rush.

No one would see you unless they decided to walk up there for whatever reason. So the biggest risk was having all the coke out in mid-operation and someone coming up right then. That's what happened. That gym teacher walked up the stairs and stood there halfway up the flight. He looked at us, he looked at the rolled up bill in my buddy's hand, and the three lines of coke on his wallet. He had that same kind of fear look. We looked back at him blankly. Then he turned around and walked back down, out the double doors to the second floor – end of story. We finished the coke quickly. We didn't even high-five or make a joke about the whole thing. We didn't say anything. The whole episode was just weird. It's like the guy was too much of a pussy to bust us right there. I felt bad for him even as I was relieved.

Those are the kind of lessons I learned in high school. Do whatever you want, but do it quietly. And if you see someone else doing something, don't rat them out. That goes for teachers – and principals – as well. If you stay quiet, they'll let you go and fuck off your life all you want. They don't really care if you're snorting coke. They care if you're going to make their day more difficult. So pick your battles, don't make noise, and it'll work out okay for you. There was even a way to do coke in school with a certain propriety.

If you do get caught, though, don't worry too much: you'll find a way to earn it off with not too much pain because most of the ones in charge don't have any backbone anyways. There was a persistent apprehension that everyone is culpable, in one way or another. As time went on, I embraced that culpability; I felt like it was mine and at least I owned it.

Adults had led the way in that regard: Mr. Stanley with his rage, the teacher who had sex with one of the jazz dancers, and Dr. Dunn. Adults could be several things at once, it seemed, and often it didn't add up to an integral whole. They were all breaking the moral guidelines they were supposed to embody, so why shouldn't I?

Larry DiNatale was the mentor with integrity: Larry, the outlier outside of that academic environment. The osmosis he offered through playing with us weekly at the 880, the fervent, provocative talks on the breaks between sets – they were essentially altruistic, with no trace of malevolence. I took note; the bohemian world of jazz was the one for me, for the simple reason that I found real kindness and generosity there. Going forward, my hunch was right. In the years to come, from my older peers like guitarist Peter Bernstein and Jesse Davis, to all the teachers who imparted their knowledge to me, and finally master musicians like Jimmy Cobb who gave me a chance to play with them, there was never an ounce of that icky duplicity, and no abusive words or actions on their part.

I didn't want to run with the lambs. I liked beating a rap. That stance was self-protection, though. It wasn't true, after all, that there was no pain to the earning off: there was pain; it was just deferred. It's like that with some lessons – they sink in long after they're taught. I learned some good lessons as well in high school, but the kind of lessons I'm talking about here were initially detrimental because they weren't explained. They were demonstrated silently. So you'd draw your own conclusions, and sometimes they were way off, or, if they had a certain logic to them, it wasn't particularly comforting: when that guy saw Dr. Dunn and I there, I felt like I had to keep my mouth shut and stand there naked as he walked by, because he had kept his mouth shut for me with the coke. But wait, what was *he* hiding? Well, he was hiding the fact that he had shut his mouth about the coke. It was a series of continuous white lies that ricocheted off of each other.

Isn't that how these things go? *Don't make waves.* Why didn't I say to Dr. Dunn, "I don't need a shower today. If we're done with the gym, I'd rather go home"? It was fear. He had the authority. He decided my fate. In addition to the fear was something that was already in place: low self-worth. I didn't want to displease him. However oily and creepy he was, I wanted him to like me. The violent rejection from Ed and Dylan was still fresh. Maybe this was a way not to fuck up again – to give somebody what he wanted instead of pushing him away.

Every time before the shower, Dr. Dunn would ask if I wanted to take a whirlpool bath to "relax my muscles" or some bullshit. What they called a whirlpool was an old contraption that had probably been in the school since the 1960s, and was nothing but a steel cauldron with a faucet and a rubber house. It was there for sports injuries, apparently, but I never saw anyone use it – not the football team, nobody – in my four years there. I always turned him down, because the idea seemed so stupid and filled me with discomfort. I felt ashamed just thinking about having to climb into that thing.

But the third or fourth time he suggested it I felt pressured and didn't want to displease him. I thought, maybe I can wrap this whole thing up quicker and earn some points with him, so I agreed to it. I remember I also felt kind of guilty, and sorry for him. He wanted it so badly. Finally, though, I was scared.

There was something I hadn't seen in our four years together when I tried to turn him down again – something dark in his face. He had it when he caught me outside with Dave, but here it was stronger. He was angry.

He filled the thing with warm water and I climbed in naked. It felt good enough, like a warm bath does, and I relaxed a bit. Then he started his usual patter about nothing, but while he talked, he took the rubber hose, which was shooting out water quickly, and started aiming it around underwater. Talking more quietly, scanning my body with his eyes, he began to aim the hose right between my legs, eventually just keeping it there, a couple inches from my penis, looking at me like he was trying to see right through me. I spread my legs because at that point it seemed like the right thing to do.

It's like you're just trying to do what the person wants – you're trying to be considerate. And, as fucked up as it is, when you see that you've pleased the person, it feels good, like when you were a kid with your parents. You still care about that shit. One part of you feels good because you did something "right," even as another part is scared because it feels wrong. That's the problem: everything gets all tangled up together. Here was a way to be an obedient high-school student, finally. And for the top dog no less – the principal. But it was all mixed in with this shame and discomfort, and a sense that none of the "good" was real.

When it was time to get out of the bath, I stood up and hovered over him, letting him look for a while. I took my time drying off and putting on my clothes. I was relaxed now and everything was moving slowly. The discomfort being naked had dissolved and I was in a trance. We were both in a trance. It was like some kind of ceremony. He stood there watching me, smiling, his eyes all shiny.

Somewhere in that whole exchange he had finally caught me – he had broken me down so I wasn't uncomfortable anymore. It seemed normal now. The thing is, for four years he had been working me up to this, starting in my freshman year. He would call me down out of class every couple weeks. There was never any real reason. He was just using his authority to get me down there into his office. The door would close and we'd have these chats, and he'd do the thing with his eyes going onto my crotch the whole time, squinting and half-smiling, looking back at my eyes. It didn't feel good, but I didn't have a way I knew to express that. Tell my parents, or my friends? No way – it would be humiliating. I was afraid that my parents would disapprove of me. Why did you have to go to his office all the time in the first place? What did you do wrong? Why are you only telling us this now? I wouldn't have known what to say. Continuing to not tell anyone as time passed compounded the fear in a vicious cycle.

I'd be laughed at by my friends, and even more by people who weren't my friends – every other kid in the school. Because it would get out, it would leak, you could be sure of that. I would be portrayed as a sissy who let that happen to him – a real Class A Loser. There would be a stigma on me for the rest of high school. And then what would happen to him anyways? He hadn't actually touched me. And, even if he had, it was his word against mine: me a burnout pothead with a history of academic failure; him the vaunted principal with decades of public service behind him.

It was that same formulation I had made after being bullied in middle school and then in freshman year by Dylan and Ed: don't be a pussy. And don't be a rat. Just say to yourself, this is normal, and swallow the weird feeling, over and over again. And then one day – it's normal.

Dr. Dunn had the hose blasting water down there for a good minute or two, so, when I stood up from the tub, I was in a state of physical arousal. At that moment, something flipped in me, as I hovered over him, looking down. It didn't last more than ten seconds but it seared into my consciousness indelibly. *I* had the power now, even just for a moment.

It was all about an exchange of power for him. That was how he really got off, with me towering over him like that in the tub, naked and puffed up. He could finally relinquish his own control. I understood what he really wanted finally, behind all the deception. He wanted my dominion over him. He was so obsequious, his eyes watering – a real queen, whispering, his voice trembling a bit as I made my way out of the tub: "Oh, that's very good Brad. Take your time, that's right."

Shape-shifting

For years after, high school was the locus of continuous disquieting dreams. In many of them I was trying to graduate. Sometimes sex would be wrapped into them, or sometimes there was some portent of death, like in the dream of Dylan with the hearse. Trying to keep something alive, trying to kill it at the same time. Invariably, in those dreams, I had fucked up somehow and wasn't going to graduate, and I'd wake up with my heart racing, panicked. There was so much anxiety. I didn't know whether I was actually going to graduate until I opened the diploma, and the whole thing had hinged on pleasing Dr. Dunn. I kept reliving all that into adulthood.

For better or worse, that trauma formed a strong template for my music after I finally got clean. It began to find its way into the playing and writing, slowly but persistently. The pain, the transgression, the excitement and ecstasy, the loneliness, the sadness. The anger, the confusion, and, finally, despair. It was my *Bildung*, my apprenticeship. It's good stuff if you can figure out how to use it. But you don't figure it out, actually. It comes to you when you're ready, in bits. It's how you heal, and maybe you can bring some of that healing to other people.

There was even a certain value to those lessons in duplicity that I learned in high school. Hiding something, or disguising a motive, could be effective in the small-group improvised jazz setting in which I would land a few years later. It could get you out of a bind when someone didn't play how you wanted. You could play some shit that wasn't true to yourself, briefly – to get them to give what you needed. Likewise, you could *not* play certain things and get them to draw back, pull their head out of their ass and listen. That even worked with players you respected, players with whom you had a musical relationship. Because, when you're improvising with others, there's always a point, no matter how good the communication, when someone does something in the music that puts you off. So you could lie to your friends, and it would be all right, just for that moment.

I see it all the time on the bandstand. It's part of the package. A lot of the time the audience is more adept at seeing when someone's lying than the ones playing on the stage. It's not so much that the one who's getting lied to is the last to know. He might *never* know; he might never find out. He'll go home content, feeling like he nailed it. Jazz musicians and their audiences are unique in this generous exoneration of those in their own tribe.

The great pianist and teacher Jaki Byard used to say: "You can't lie." He meant that who you really are would eventually come out in your playing. That's sound. But in a way you can lie, at least temporarily. You can lie to tell another truth. There are small truths and larger truths that hover around them. If I tell you what you want to hear, it could be a lie in that moment. But maybe you're not ready for the truth. You will be, but I can't give you the medicine in one shot. It would tear you down too much. So that little lie to you is my truth right now, because in my heart, where a larger truth resides, I don't want to hurt you. That plays out in the music. I'm certain that people lie to me as well, "telling" me what I want to hear as we play together. It's fine. It's on them to tell the truth in their own time, and on me to hear them when they do. Ideally, you don't need words for that – you do it in the music.

Everybody butters each other up, and, in a way, why not? There was a reason why I held on to the romantic conviction so long that music, and art more generally, should be free from moral obligations. It came from the sense that you could take stuff that was squarely wrong, and make something that was good and whole from it, something that washed away all your sins and sorrow. Redemption. It had to have a little of the bad left in it, though. It had to have that scar across it so you wouldn't forget how it felt when the wound was open.

Putting the trauma aside, the thing that I gleaned later about sexual roles, looking at them detachedly with the fastidious eye of Tonio Kröger, is that they could always be shifting and changing, and thus ironic and surprising – like when macho Ed turned into a happy bottom for Dylan that night, or when I gained the power over Dr. Dunn, switching the tables. Going into my twenties, out of high school, my desire for guys was only partially physical. It was more the game of power; it was that head trip. The one you were with wasn't a partner: he was your adversary, he was the one you had to conquer, and that act of conquering was an act of transgression – you stole his power, or he stole yours. It was a disavowal of intimacy. The rush was the betrayal. The rush was just as much in losing power as it was gaining it. At the same time, though, I wanted that intimacy badly. I wanted to mend a wound through sex. Those were the two narratives.

But that was all way too real, and I wasn't anywhere close to putting it together. So it remained secret – a secret to myself just as much. It came out in the music. I found a shape-shifting, transgressive quality in jazz, where you could improvise your way into another identity at any given moment. You could break the social code; you could rip past a boundary. And instead of creating pain from that rip, you'd make something with beauty. Or maybe you could even reach for the sublime. Beauty was contingent on laws, on finitude, on limitation. The sublime had no laws. Or, you could say, it was its own law, the only law. Riffing on Kant and Freud, Terry Eagleton wrote:

> It is beauty's point of inner fracture, a negation of settled order without which any order would grow inert and wither. The sublime is the anti-social condition of all sociality, the infinitely unrepresentable which spurs us on to yet finer representations, the lawless masculine force which violates yet perpetually renews the feminine enclosure of beauty (*The Ideology of the Aesthetic*).

The sublime I found in jazz was my way out. My sin and shame could reshape itself into a poetic victory – something that would stick. It was a way of getting back at Dr. Dunn for breaking a boundary with me. By taking back the power in the music, I could give something back that wasn't dirty and sad. It was strong and real, even as it was fluid and intractable. Jazz was about breaking the laws of beauty and making your own new law right then and there. At the same time, the blues – central to my experience of jazz – could be an act of self-forgiving. There is nothing to the cliché that the blues are merely dirty. They are the way towards healing. That's the beauty part, the one that holds fast – real beauty with a dusty, rough surface, waiting to be chiseled. But it's chiseled out of something that's non-transient. Beauty and the sublime inter-are.

The shape-shifting of Ed, Dylan, and Dr. Dunn, which had confounded me so much, became a quality I admired in my favorite jazz musicians, when they surprised you and changed their identity from one moment to the next – from all hard and badassed to a sensitive lover, in just a heartbeat. You could go from dominating to passive, from demanding to acquiescent, and then make an about-face, from docile back to menacing. Miles was the ultimate master of that, on records like *In a Silent Way*.

The impulse to shift your creative identity in this way is an erotic one: it springs from that same game of seduction and power. If a musician always wears the same hat, it's boring in the same way as a lover who wants to get off the same way every time. If you listen to the way a jazz musician improvises, you can get some idea of how they make love. All hot and leaving no space? Controlled, intellectual? Sentimental, simpering? The best ones, like Miles, leave space.

Dream of high school. I have not gone to algebra class for a big portion of the year. There are variations on this dream, but the backdrop of looming anxiety is always the same, because I will undoubtedly flunk for too many absences. Yet there is some small hope that, if I catch up with the work, I could still pass. I am looking at the current lesson in the textbook. Since I missed so much, I can't follow it at all. It is like what really happened with algebra and so much else in high school. Everything was okay to begin with, and then I started to lose ground. Ever since then, I've tried to find it back, but always through subterfuge, through one lie or another. In all of these dreams I have hovered vaguely between being in high school and the present day. But, whereas previously I was my adult age physically, here for the first time I am my younger self at that age of seventeen, my senior year. I feel all that original shame and fear, compounded by years of self-hatred and resentment.

I have been told by my teacher to report to Dr. Dunn's office. I feel the old embarrassment as the kids in the class snicker at me just like they did then, for being one of the students in whom he took a "special interest." (I was not the only one.) I leave the class, but, instead of going directly to his office, I wander around, anxious now, avoiding the teacher's order. Then, my name is read over the school intercom and the message is repeated: proceed to Dr. Dunn's office, now. As was then, there is this foreboding that I will not graduate. The hallways get longer as I trudge toward the office. The school now becomes like some run-down hospital, dingy, unwelcoming, and cold. I feel the bile churning in my stomach. I taste it in the dream. It tastes sweet and rotten in my throat.

In the same way that I am finally younger in this dream, instead of straddling the past and adulthood, likewise, the jeopardy of my potential non-graduation is now more immediate. It is not so much that the present is turning back to the past. The past is pursuing the present now, and it might overtake it. That sense of being trapped and alone is in the forefront. I feel the lack of resolve inching its way upwards, until it is a voice that says: "You can't do this. You will fail." I believe more acutely that I am still that ten-year-old loser kid in Mr. Mazzie's fifth-grade classroom compared to everyone else – all those other students who were able to get through and move on with their lives, all those people who weren't held back. I will be stuck here. I'm sure of it.

The math in the dream is the same freshman algebra that confounded me so much that first year of high school when everything started to go wrong for me – the painful split from my friend Dylan, the violent rejection and subsequent bullying from him and Ed that began in the first days of school, and the grooming from Dr. Dunn. I wonder: did my subsequent academic failure in so much of high school have less to do with some kind of deficiency in intelligence, and more with a belief that I was not worthy of any success?

It seems like there is always one more layer to peel. What was it that caused me to seek out Ed and Dylan as friends in the first place? Why did I leave the Eden of my bookish friends, Rush albums, and Ray Bradbury stories after that last summer in Merrywood and go so far away, stepping willfully into insurrection? Indeed, there is always something further back, something earlier to uncover, closer to some initial rupture. But was it something that befell me and cut open a wound, a wound that wouldn't close? Or was it by my own design? Perhaps this whole idea I've had all along about some "rupture" after Merrywood is all wrong. I've built a grand story around it, full of enough pathos to distract me from someone else – a ghost who comes to me in the night when I sleep, hidden to me except in these dreams, where he shows himself in riddles. Is that ghost just simply me, or is it someone else? Surely I had the power of my own volition along the way. I had choices.

When you were slaves of sin, you were free in regard to righteousness. But then what return did you get from the things of which you are now ashamed? The end of those things is death.

When I was a small kid, age three, I saw his hand for a moment just as I woke, that ghost. It's my first memory. We were in a hotel room with pure white walls and a blue carpet, somewhere on a long drive between Georgia and my grandfather's farm in Ohio. I didn't see his face, just that hand. I was terrified – it moved over my face as if to suffocate me, to snuff me out. Who was he? Was he a dream or was he real? Just as much as my God, he has always been with me – hovering close by my shoulder, or bearing his weight fully on it, pushing me down with that gloved hand, spiking me with doubt, holding me back, hindering me from running out of that dark room. Did I take his hand and knowingly walk into ruin? Or was I blind in the dark, lost, thinking he would lead me towards salvation? He has filled me with his peril even as God has given me sanctuary, and those two form a template, a story I will try to tell in music: a story of dark and light, of being lost and alone, of finding God's love again, only to lose my way again, groping around, looking for the exit.

Did that which is good, then, bring death to me? By no means! It was sin, working death in me through what is good, in order that sin might be shown to be sin, and through the commandment might become sinful beyond measure. We know that the law is spiritual, but I am carnal, sold under sin. I do not understand my own actions. *For I do not do what I want, but I do the very thing I hate.*

When I approach Dr. Dunn's office in the dream, as I did so many times for those four years, I do not make it there. In the front corridor of the school by the entrance (I want it to be the exit, where I can walk out, once and for all) I see him standing there waiting for me, smiling. There is no kindness in his smile, only malevolence. I see it naked now in his eyes. He does not wish me well.

For the mind that is set on the flesh is hostile to God; it does not submit to God's law, indeed it cannot; and those who are in the flesh cannot please God.

There are people all around. I sneak into the bathroom and take out a flask from my backpack like I had in those days. I begin to drink the grain punch. I carry it out towards the crowd gathered in front of the office. Dr. Dunn approaches me and sees the flask. He grabs it. This will be my downfall. I pull away as he calls me from behind, menacing now, taking pleasure. "Come back here!" I've been caught; that was my last chance. I start to walk towards the double doors. It is the entrance to the school.

I want it to be the exit. I want so badly to leave all of this, for good. A student approaches me. He is deranged, out of control. He is yelling. He pulls on my arm, trying to hold me back. I see his face. He looks scared; he is out of control. He is trying to keep me from exiting, yelling incoherently in a gargled voice. Who is he? Is he some inside-out version of me, the inner turmoil of that last year? There is the noise of all of the students and teachers – derisive, hateful. I wake up.

Dr. Dunn's smile was evil in the dream, like he was taking pleasure in my failure. Was there any truth to that in real life? Perhaps it was some complex mixture of kindness and craving, of wanting to give and wanting to take. Was there ever any true benevolence in his actions, though, all those years during the trips to his office, or when he led me to the showers or the tub? Success would have barred him a way in – he depended on my academic failure those four years to keep me in his proximity; he needed my weakness. There was always that look in his eyes, that wanting. His smile and his eyes gave two different messages.

II

New York

New tribe

I knew already from that day trip with Caleb when I was twelve that New York City would be my Mecca. Reading Kerouac's *On the Road* along with Henry Miller's *Tropic of Cancer/Tropic of Capricorn* in high school cemented my decision.

The tension that had begun in youth and adolescence – between the jocks and the nerds, between prog and punk, between the jazz band hazers and the burnouts – continued when I came to New York. In my first years there, there were roughly two jazz tribes I ran with, making provisional allegiance to both of them. In one, I did my best to invoke iconic hard bop piano stylists like Red Garland, Wynton Kelly, Bobby Timmons, and Sonny Clark. Then, there was a whole other swath of players my age who wanted another "modern" approach, although, in fact, it was one that had reached its own fruition already in the mid-1960s. In this group, I would channel Herbie Hancock or McCoy Tyner as well as I could, often some mixture of both.

At some point all the influences converged. Looking back, there was always some kind of reconciliation of polarities. It was between that hard bop language and the abstracted harmony that followed it in the '60s. Or, more broadly, it was between the German Romanticism of Schubert, Schumann and Brahms and the Blacker influence of jazz, steeped in the blues feeling and swing. From all that, I found my own approach, which involved a negotiation between those polarities, and finally an emulsification of all of them. It was a sound that would work, ideally, with anyone. I never wanted to be someone who could only play with his own band, or only with the musicians in a particular tribe. I also didn't want to be a pushover or milky hybridist, and was as allergic to those kinds of musicians as my stablemates were. I wanted my shit to cut through, though, for both sides of the fence and all points in between, however much that was possible. I realized that it couldn't and wouldn't – I had already learned that from the high-school tribes. But it was an ideal, one to hold onto.

The fence was just as much inside of me as outside, and I was the one who had to break it. Jazz was cathartic when it helped me achieve that, through a friendly alliance with someone from a different place than me. I refer to a musical exchange, but also those outside the bandstand. A big fence, and one that broke as soon as I got to New York City, was racial. I experienced very little diversity in Bedford and West Hartford, nor at Merrywood during those three summers. Just about everyone was white. The Black American jazz greats to whom I'd been listening through my adolescence were faraway giants, intangible, only known through records, photos, and liner notes. When I came to New York and connected with Black people significantly for the first time, it was through the music. It gave me an opening into a communion with people in a new, larger tribe. My early period in New York City, even as I was getting saddled to alcohol and drug addiction, was a musical thrill ride. Both Bedford and West Hartford were great in their own ways. I had felt love and support from my extended family, friends, and teachers like Ms. Hurwitz. But my life became immeasurably richer when I came to New York City, and it was because of the people I met just as much as the music we made together.

Musically, those first few years I was a people-pleaser to my own detriment, meaning I tried to play what people wanted, and was ruffled if someone didn't dig what I was doing. It's a truism that your greatest flaws are your greatest assets. That people-pleasing stemmed from a fear that could cripple me in other contexts. I put way too much on being liked because I didn't want to be rejected and wanted to fit in. It went back to being adopted – to feeling rejected right from the gate, to feeling different, and probably to some extent to all the bullying and shame I had experienced in high school. I wasn't near to processing all that. When I found something I could shine in, I put that fear to good use. I tried to invite people in and not make them feel different when I played with them, because that's what I wanted for myself. I tried to find common ground. It gave the lie to the Cain story. I wanted to be in the tribe, alas. It felt good when I was. But, whereas the Merrywood tribe was mostly lollipops and roses, the New York jazz tribe was tougher. I was ready, mostly.

I wanted to make the other players feel good on their own turf. I wanted to accept the story they were telling on their own terms. It seemed expedient to take this approach. If you listen back to someone as they're playing with you and acknowledge their ideas continuously, you can break them down slowly, like a wild horse. Before you know it, you're steering the ship. At that point, you can fulfill Demian's promise of Cain, leading your own tribe outside of Eden, wandering somewhere new. They might not even realize you're in charge. Who cares if they do or don't? It's your show. You didn't demand their respect – you earned it.

The New School

In my senior year of high school, while other friends of mine were getting accepted to various colleges, my graduation wasn't guaranteed. Even without that little problem of gym credits, I wouldn't have gotten accepted to any regular college with my grades, which were mostly C's and D's. I wanted to become a musician, but I couldn't just hightail it to New York and live on my own. I needed my parents' financial support, and for that to happen they needed to get behind my dream and not feel like they were throwing me into the woods. Music school was the obvious choice. It offered structure.

Halfway through senior year, my parents and I went to New York for a weekend and auditioned at two schools: Manhattan School of Music and the New School for Social Research. Both had a four-year bachelor program in jazz. We drove in from Connecticut and started uptown at Manhattan School. I was accepted and offered a scholarship after my audition. They told me who my teacher would be the following year. He was a fine pianist but played in a style that did not grab my imagination at the time. I was happy to have been accepted like that, but didn't like the way that was already decided, matter-of-fact.

We headed downtown to the New School next and, upon entering, we met Arnie Lawrence, the alto saxophonist and director of the jazz program. I happily observed Arnie's cottonmouth and squinting, reddened eyes – a fellow viper – and sensed right away that I was in the right place. Manhattan School of Music, in the uptown Ivy League environs of Columbia University, had felt a little like Longy – a place to be further edified. The New School, on the other hand, could be a place to learn, but judging from Arnie, a place to party as well. It was situated downtown just a few blocks from Washington Square Park in the epicenter of Greenwich Village, where I had read about Ginsberg and others congregating. My memory of that visit with Caleb had remained through high school and continued to beckon me back.

Arnie spoke like a hipster, with a few twenty-seven-dollar words thrown in. Neither my parents nor I really knew what he was talking about, as he riffed on about "the jazz vernacular." Next, he took us into a class he was teaching in the auditorium. There was a group of twelve or so students there, walking around the perimeter of the aisles slowly, with a self-conscious bounce and sway in their step. What the hell was this?

"At this school," Arnie began in his half-whispered Brooklyn drawl, "we're trying to focus on the complete vernacular of this music. So to begin with, you have to learn how to walk like a jazz musician. This is a class in jazz walking."

A class in walking? I thought it was crazy, but my kind of crazy – something way off the beaten path from the last four years of high-school academia, which had been mostly a failure. I auditioned for Arnie and a few other of the faculty. They listened and offered me a scholarship for the same amount as Manhattan School had offered. On the trip back to Connecticut, I expressed the desire to go to the New School and, in not much time, my parents agreed to support my wish, by paying the remainder of the tuition and housing the following year. They knew it was the place – Arnie's cottonmouth and the walking class notwithstanding – and went out on a limb for me.

Our trip to New York City spanned a weekend. On Friday evening, we made our way to Sweet Basil, a club that was five blocks down from the Village Vanguard on 7th Avenue South. I would listen to lots of greats there in the coming years, like Art Blakey with some of his last Jazz Messengers bands, and Tommy Flanagan and McCoy Tyner with their trios. That night with my parents there was a stellar band, the cream of the cream: the Timeless All Stars, made up of Harold Land, Curtis Fuller, Bobby Hutcherson, Cedar Walton, Ron Carter, and Billy Higgins. Seeing them live – hearing Billy Higgins's inimitable beat, listening to and watching the way Cedar Walton comped, zoning in on Ron Carter's role in the rhythm section, soaking in Harold Land's tenor style, hearing Bobby Hutcherson's sound and compositions – everything changed right there. The records I had amassed that they had played on had been my gateway into jazz. This live experience was the real issue.

Saturday night we went to Bradley's, the fabled club on University Place that focused on piano. That night was Hank Jones with Red Mitchell on bass. Hank Jones had already put his stamp on me, particularly through his playing on two records: Coleman Hawkins's *The Hawk Flies High* and Cannonball Adderley's *Somethin' Else*. Those records had caught his subtle touch, but they hadn't caught the depth of tone behind it. You had to hear that in a room. I had the same experience soon after arriving in New York the following year hearing Joe Henderson at Fat Tuesdays. I could sense that he generally played softer in volume than other tenor greats, like his contemporary Wayne Shorter, for instance. You could hear it on *The State of the Tenor*, a live trio record from the Village Vanguard he made a few years earlier. Yet, when I heard him live at Fat Tuesdays, his sound filled the whole room, resonating right into the chair I was sitting in. "Soft" wasn't really the right word to describe his playing.

We thanked Hank Jones after the set and my dad took the lead, mentioning that I was an aspiring jazz pianist bent on coming to New York. What did Mr. Jones think about that? Was it wise? The next thing I knew, he sat down at our table and talked with us for about fifteen minutes, asking me questions about my playing. He was all kindness and wished me well, saying: "Come to New York City, by all means – it's the place for you. And look me up when you're here." Years later, I got to play with him in a two-piano duo concert at the Montreal Jazz Festival, and it was a gas, of course. I reminded him of how he had encouraged me early on. Hank Jones was an angel.

I cannot emphasize enough how important for me at that time was that kind of blessing from someone I revered. It would have been enough just to hear him and Red that night, but that benevolence made an impression on me. When I saw the Timeless All Stars the night before, I felt more tangibly what jazz could be through a performance from its highest practitioners. At the same time, I realized how far I was from embodying that. Hank's kindness took the edge off the intimidation I would feel in those exalted environs, and I held onto it as I began to tiptoe around them in the following years. He wasn't alone in that regard. Drummer Jimmy Cobb, in a more laconic way, embodied that, and tenor man Junior Cook did as well, when I got to play a week with him at the Village Gate, courtesy of drummer Joe Farnsworth. Pianist Junior Mance also did, and there were others. They all let me know I was in the tribe, and that was so important. I needed that and they gave it to me. I thank them all here.

The New School was a mixed bag of mostly positive experiences, and some really fabulous ones. At the time I arrived in 1988, it was a grand experiment, only three years into existence. It was Arnie's vision, and he was a musician – a true bohemian. Other folks couldn't abide by that, and eventually felt they had to tighten it up with more structure, to fit into the accredited confines of academia – especially if people were going to throw down a lot of money for the full tuition. Arnie got pushed out.

I began private lessons with Junior Mance my first year there. He was someone I loved as a comper on Dizzy Gillespie's *Have Trumpet, Will Excite* and some Lester Young recordings, and as a leader on his live trio record at the Village Vanguard. When I found out he was teaching, I asked to study with him. I told him I wanted to work on comping. "Comping" is short for accompanying, and refers to the pianist's role supporting the soloist. Every piano player I loved thus far – Red Garland, McCoy Tyner, Wynton Kelly, Tommy Flanagan, Cedar Walton, Bill Evans, Mal Waldron, Sonny Clark, to name a few – had a comping style just as individual as their solo style, and I wanted Junior's insights. Particularly, I wanted to hear what he had to say about comping alongside a guitarist, like he did on Dizzy's record, where he and Les Spann comped at the same time. How do you stay out of each other's way? Junior told me: "There's no fixed method. You listen to each other and it's intuitive."

But – a classic student question – how do I listen intuitively, then? What Junior and I mostly did was play together: him comping for me as I soloed, and then vice versa. That's how I learned. It was exciting, and I was nervous at first. Playing with Junior, I had the experience of being *pulled* into someone else's stronger swing. I would feel that again, playing with Jimmy Cobb and Billy Higgins. It was more often drummers who could do that, but the great jazz players on any instrument, and vocalists as well, will pull you into their feel, through their rhythmic inflection and phrasing, all rooted in swing. Eventually, down the road, I would be able to pull others along as well. That's not something that can be taught with words. It has to be felt and experienced first through playing with someone like Junior, and then the transaction is

Junior Mance, foreground, playing a
duet in 1992 with Lionel Hampton
Photo: Derek Drescher

made. It's more of what I would come to view as a particular kind of jazz
gnosis – unsayable knowledge.

That learning process is also called osmosis, and it continued in a class
with drummer Jimmy Cobb called "Rhythmic Development." We would simply play with Jimmy for more than two hours. I was in heaven. This was the
guy I had listened to for the last four years straight, on records with Miles
Davis, Wynton Kelly, Wes Montgomery, and others. And now I was getting to
feel his swing, and interact with it. Again, I got pulled by it, and it seeped in.

Pianist Fred Hersch taught a composition class. He got me thinking for
the first time about why certain tunes were so great, by breaking down how
they were put together motifically. With a composer like Thelonious Monk,
it wasn't just the outright melody that drew you back to the tune every time.
It was these building blocks within the melody – motifs, as they were called.
They might only be three or four notes long, and Fred showed how they could
drive a whole tune of Monk's. You wouldn't "hear" all that. Rather, you would
sense it unconsciously, and feel that the tune just had some sort of integrity,
even if you didn't know why. Fred gave us a play by play, for instance, of the
motific unfolding in Monk's "I Mean You."

That unfolding wasn't just some abstract phenomenon that you could
forensically break down with the kind of pleasure that one might find in an
elegant math equation. It was a means to a narrative end. Motifs were part of
the way that Monk told his story. I began to think about how that storytelling

Fred Hersch
Photo: Derek Drescher

also played out in jazz improvisation in great soloists like Miles Davis. As I started to develop my own style, I consciously leaned into motific composition and improvisation in equal measure.

Motific development had a long pedigree in Western classical music. In Beethoven's symphonies and sonatas, it became larger-scale, running through multiple movements. Brahms followed his master Beethoven in that regard. Loren Schoenberg taught a class that sparked my love affair with Brahms even more. The first half of the school year we studied Brahms' Third Symphony; the second half, we moved on to his Fourth. Loren cracked those symphonies open for us, connecting all sorts of dots.

At every turn when he uncovered some motific or thematic link, I thought, "Ha! *This* is why Brahms is so great." It was both a revelation and a confirmation at once, just as it had been with Fred listening to Monk. We were studying music that I was already emotionally wedded to, and now I was discovering why. All this formed a conviction that what makes Brahms great is what makes Monk great, and is the same thing that makes Miles great, which is the same thing that makes Beethoven great, and so on. It was the *story* they told, and whether the story was improvised, or composed, or some measure of both, there were concrete reasons for that – things that you could break down with a good teacher.

Pianist Kenny Werner was another important light at the New School my first year there. In his theory class, he presented an approach to building lines in one's solos that was all his own. I won't go into a more specialized technical description of what that was but, suffice to say, I grabbed on to some of the key tenets of Kenny's method, and they seeped in. In a few years, they had codified into something that was part of my approach. The strength in Kenny's teaching was that it was specific and open-ended all at once: there were guidelines rooted in foundational principles of harmony, but they could be applicable to any number of soloistic contexts, in real time.

Other valuable teachers at the New School were Kirk Nurock, who taught an orchestrating and arranging class; ear training with pianist Aydın Esen – much more invigorating than the solfège at Longy – and an exhausting class in jazz history from historian Phil Schaap, whose knowledge, particularly of the first thirty years of jazz, was unparalleled. Bassist Andy González, who was riding high with his brother trumpeter Jerry in their Fort Apache Band, taught the clave rhythm in a similar way as Jimmy Cobb taught swing, by playing with us.

There was ensemble class every week, and my first year we were taught by trumpeter Cecil Bridgewater, who workshopped our tunes with us and showed us how to develop good arrangements. Cecil was a great teacher and we'd get to hear him at the Vanguard playing in Max Roach's band. The great tenor saxophonist Chris Potter arrived at the New School the same year as I, and was in that ensemble as well. Back then, he was playing mostly alto, and just burning it up already – everything was there. Chris came up to New York from South Carolina, where his friend drummer Andy Watson hailed from as well. Andy, or "The Sheriff" as we called him, for the cowboy hat he often wore, came around the same time, and frequently played with us in Jesse Davis's band at Augie's on the Friday- and Saturday-night slots.

For part of the following year, I was in an ensemble taught by the drummer Michael Carvin, whom I knew mostly from some interesting duo records with alto saxophonist Jackie McLean. Michael was an intimidating figure: he was ex-military, and always made you just a little uneasy, although you knew he had a good heart. My third year was a dream: an ensemble led by drummer Joe Chambers, who was on so many records I loved from Wayne Shorter and others. Joe played vibes with us, and we worked on new tunes of his that he was writing. It was a gas.

There were one-off encounters as well with pianists Barry Harris and Walter Davis Jr. in masterclasses they taught – pianists who had been close to the holy grail of Bud Powell and Thelonious Monk, and were still around to transmit some of that to us.

Bebop Nazis

What a partisan, bickering bunch we all were when I arrived in Manhattan, aged eighteen. There were a few guys I played with who weren't even out of high school yet, but were the most valiant defenders of Rome out of all of us, like guitarist William Ash and bassist Ari Roland. They were just kids but already strong players. They knew dozens of tunes already and sat in with the older players at jam sessions with zero trepidation. They would call standards that few others knew, like "East of the Sun" or "Where or When." I had a similar feeling of inferiority on meeting William and Ari as I had years earlier meeting Caleb and Louis at Merrywood, other native New Yorkers who were way ahead of me in their exposure to what I was only just stumbling upon.

"Calling" a tune is what happens at a jam session, like the kind I went to when I first came to New York, the kind that existed long before that, and continue today. Let's say you're at one and you're the pianist. There are three horn players, a bassist and drummer, and you've been called up to play. The trumpet player calls a tune: "Let's play 'Dancing on the Ceiling.'" Everyone else nods in accord, ready to count it off. They look at you. Ughhh . . . How does that go? You might know the beginning . . . But what's the bridge? And there's some sort of coda, right? No – can't risk it. "Sorry . . ." you mutter apologetically, "I'm not solid on that one." Everybody looks down, frowning, quietly judging. God forbid that happens again, or again after that. Eventually, you might simply be shamed off the bandstand. Calling a tune is something between a solicitation – "Let's play this one" – and a challenge: "Can you handle this one – do you even know it?" It was all part of the atmosphere of jam sessions those first few years in New York. There was this tension between congeniality and cut-throat. In those days at least, there were tunes that were off the table, that you simply *couldn't* call, because they were overplayed, like "Stella by Starlight," "On Green Dolphin Street" or "Autumn Leaves." There were also strong tunes that were called too often, ones in vogue at that time, like Tom Harrell's "Sail Away" or Benny Golson's "Stablemates."

Jam sessions seemed to bring out the best and worst in people. You could have never met someone before the moment you were on the bandstand with them, and you already knew they were an asshole just by the way they played. Or you heard them and thought, that person is cool – there's a kindness, a curiosity, an openness. That character assessment through the music worked best if the player had some skill already. If he or she was a beginner, there was an X factor: they might play offensively out of simple ignorance, with the best intentions. Being an asshole didn't mean you couldn't play. You might play proficiently, brilliantly even, but in an antisocial way, with no regard for the other musicians or those listening – you'd solo way too long, leave no space, or play at one loud volume the whole time. There were a whole host of players like that – the ones with the "personality problems," as we called them.

I was more prepared than some of younger players when I arrived in New York, because I had already been working with singers through high school and had learned a fair amount of tunes. Yet there were other ways to get shamed, even if you knew the tune, or, more to the point, you *thought* you knew it. I got corrected more than once. Monk's classic "'Round Midnight" was a prime example. Like many, I knew Miles Davis's iconic version, and played the chords he used. I got strongly frowned upon the first time I did that in New York. Miles's chords were not the ones Monk wrote. "Go check out the original again and then come back – don't do a disservice to Monk." I understood and ultimately agreed with that kind of stricture on principle, but it smarted on its delivery, there on the bandstand with the other musicians and audience.

We jokingly called Ari, William, and other strong players who were mostly still in their teens the "Bebop Nazis." It was harsh, but for me at least it was an affectionate term. I thought it was hip in itself that anyone would be so stridently passionate about Bird. Why not defend something as grand as bebop?

The tenor saxophonist Chris Byars was in that scene, playing regularly in groups with William, Ari, and other strong players like pianists Sacha Perry and Jason Lindner, still in high school. One night at Smalls, the club where a lot of things began for us, Chris called the Gershwin tune "I Got Rhythm" on the jam session. Now that was a head-scratcher on the face of it. The melody was solid enough, but corny, or at least facile compared to something from Bird or Monk. What was his animus?

"I Got Rhythm" itself had long been used purely as a harmonic structure for jazz musicians to cut their teeth on. Lots of famous tunes had been written off of it, by replacing the Gershwin melody with some of the most endearing and ingenious jazz heads. "Heads" are the opening ("head in") and closing ("head out") melodies of jazz tunes that frame the improvisation that takes place in the middle. The head is an expedient means to get you to the solo, and also wrap things up after the solos. It gets the structure of the tune in everyone's ears, audience and musicians alike, before jumping off into the improvisation – and then returns at the end.

Often, musicians will even call the whole tune a "head": "Do you want to play that Bird head?" This designation refers to a certain type of composition like Bird's that, for all its genius, has an almost cursory aspect. The head proper was there to lead you to the "blowing" – the improvised solos that would follow it. In Bird's case, it was no doubt cobbled together from his own inspired improvisations. In this appraisal, the improvisation came first, and the composition came out of the improvisation. (There is another gambit in jazz – the reverse – exemplified by Bird's contemporary, Thelonious Monk. For Monk, the head – his own composition – reigned supreme, and his solos flowed out of it.)

Bird's own "Anthropology" is a representative example of a "rhythm changes" tune, as they came to be called – a jazz head based on the structure of George Gershwin's "I Got Rhythm." Monk's "Rhythm-a-Ning" is another. "Based on the structure" means here, in simple terms, that the head retained everything from the original except for the melody. Bird, Monk, and many others wrote new melodies over Gershwin's structure. That structure then loops repeatedly, but the soloist fashions new melodies over the structure, and the other players follow suit. By "structure" I mean the structure of the "changes" – the chords going by, as they change from one to another. The approach is comparable to an extent to the theme and variations form we find in Western classical music.

"Rhythm changes" for us were something fundamental: a starting point to show where you came down on the music, like at those jam sessions, perhaps playing with people you had never met. The way you soloed on rhythm changes told a lot about you – not least whether you *could* solo convincingly on it, especially at a fast tempo. Would you skate through the changes sloppily? Maybe you could move through them with precision, but no grace and imagination. There was always the promise that someone could find something fresh to say with them. Rhythm changes, like the blues, were fundamental because they connected you to what had come before and offered you the chance to build on that. They were common ground.

They were often counted off at ridiculously fast tempos – we called them "Bird tempos" because on the records we listened to, he was the only one who could play anything coherent at that speed – in the neighborhood of 360 quarter-note beats per minute clocked on a metronome. It was up to drummer Max Roach to keep the whole thing from falling apart, by slamming the downbeat periodically with the bass drum.

There was one exception: pianist Bud Powell. If you slowed down the performance to half speed, his ideas would still be deep and durable. The other players, no matter how strong, could not execute their lines with the same quality at those tempos. Bud stood apart. He was the only one in that first wave of bebop who could play *freely* like Bird, at any tempo. Other players in Bird's inner circle played brilliantly, but did not have that freedom and invention – it sounded like they had worked ahead of time to achieve what they were playing, especially on those up-tempos, and there was a limited amount of material. With Bird and Bud, it was different. When they improvised, they weren't working anymore – they were speaking with grace.

On its procedural surface, Bird's new language was one of "licks" – phrases that could be copied and pasted into different places. On a rhythm changes, you could play a lick in one section of a tune and then play it with some adjustments again in another part of the tune. Yet, if someone described you as merely a lick player, it was pejorative: you were *only* copying and pasting, arbitrarily, with no invention. The idea was to move past the assemblage of licks that you had learned from Bird, and really improvise, inspired by the nuts and bolts of Bird's syntax. He had found a fusion of melody and harmony that was more realized than what had come before. You could hear all of the harmony in his line, but his line was still a strong melody in its own right, not a mere tracing of harmony through arpeggiation.

It was that kind of syntax, and not the licks that came out of it, that may have led people to compare Bird to Bach: not Bach the unparalleled contrapuntalist but Bach as one who could embody melody and harmony already in one single horizontal voice. Sonny Rollins also reached that fusion in his inspired playing – everything was there already in the line. It may be why he didn't concern himself with piano players so much through the years. He didn't need them.

The rhythm changes heads that were born out of Gershwin's original "I Got Rhythm" had a classic thirty-two-bar "AABA" structure, split into four eight-bar sections: one thing, the same thing again, something else (the "bridge"), then the first thing again. This was the schema of a bunch of great standards that everyone played. Part of its appeal was that, in spite of a lot of harmonic flux that took place within it, the structure was square and therefore easy enough.

But hold on a minute: the original "I Got Rhythm" wasn't thirty-two bars – it was thirty-four! This – either a quibble or of tantamount importance – was the point Chris wanted to make when he called the Gershwin original that night, and not another rhythm changes head like one of Bird's. Gershwin the melodist was as deep as they come, but "I Got Rhythm," at first glance, was trite in comparison to his other masterpieces. There was this tiny coda of two bars, though – a "tag" as jazz musicians call it. That little tag, in fact, gave Gershwin's original essay an irony that poked fun at itself one last time, and elevated it into a classic in its own right. He achieved something similar with the tag on "Nice Work if You Can Get It." Jazz musicians, in writing rhythm changes, had simply ignored his tag. Chris was making the same kind of point that someone else had made to me about playing the changes to Monk's "'Round Midnight": learn the original.

The way that played out in the jam session that night was precarious to say the least. Most of us, myself included, had no prior knowledge of those extra two bars. If you were playing the tune at a blistering tempo, as was the case that night, those extra two bars could throw people off the rails when they soloed. As usual, there were several horn players lined up to solo. Some remembered them, others forgot they were there, hiccupping at the end of each chorus. Someone else turned the two bars into four in error. Yet another soloist didn't hear their lapse in the moment, and then realized they were two bars ahead of the rhythm section much later, somewhere in the bridge. Worst of all was the poor soul who still hadn't gathered the thirty-four-bar state of affairs, and turned around at the end of every chorus, scowling and pissed off at the rhythm section, thinking it was their slip-up. They were judged as a double-douchebag – dimwitted and haughty all at once. Chris smiled sardonically.

Peter Bernstein (right) in 1986 with Jimmy Raney (left) and Attila Zoller (center)

Photo: Collection of Peter Bernstein

His tacit point resonated with a lot of us, butthurt or not: if you're going to play a song in its original form, really play the song. Don't bullshit on the melody and harmony, and, in this case, don't bullshit the form. Even if the melody was of secondary importance to you, you should play it correctly. If you can, learn the lyrics. This was the approach of guitarist Peter Bernstein, whom I met at the New School and began playing with soon after arriving in New York. Pete, two years my senior, could often be found in those days at the New York Public Library main branch by Bryant Park, looking for the original sheet music of some particular tune he wanted to learn. Or, he grabbed tunes he had never heard of from songwriters he already knew, like Irving Berlin, Gershwin, Vernon Duke, or Jerome Kern, to see if they spoke to him. You had to go to the source – whatever was published first. Pete and I went on to play with John Webber on bass and Jimmy Cobb on drums in a quartet we called Cobb's Mob. It is the band on Pete's 1994 Criss Cross Jazz release, *Somethin's Burnin'*. Playing in that ensemble was an early high point for me.

Honing in on the melody like Pete did allowed me to focus on melody more generally, as a means to an expressive end in its own right. Now, the Bebop Nazis were polemically opposed to most anything except for the classic bop they tried to match in their own playing, and a few innovative stylists like Don Byas and Lucky Thompson who bridged bop with the language of swing players who came before Bird. They took issue with everything post-bebop for different reasons, depending on the nature of the infraction. In the case of the many Coltrane devotees coming to the jam sessions where we all gathered, they were deemed as lacking melody. Coltrane, when he broke into maturity, began to build his solos out of harmonic configurations, as opposed to more immediately recognizable melodies. The tried-and-true way to solo was to begin from melody, because melody told the story – that was how the thinking went.

Yet Coltrane played some of the most soaring melodies in all of jazz, and mere bebop licks in themselves didn't tell much of a story either. The lesson I got from hanging out with the Bebop Nazis, and at the same time listening fervently to Coltrane, was to look past licks and patterns alike. Tell a story, yes, but don't get caught up in one particular way to do that. Coltrane often *arrived* at his melodies, emerging from a maelstrom of tempestuous, mathematical abstraction, and they were all the more exalted because of that. The general principle was to change your gambit the moment it was becoming stale or contrived. Bird had invented a new bebop language, but, at the drop of a dime, could play straight blues like no one else. Herbie Hancock would play the most sophisticated harmony, and then, in the next moment, slip into greasy funk, all within one solo. The greatest lights could do it all, and they did, constantly toggling between approaches.

It may sound obvious that you should play a melody correctly, but how many people will know if it's correct or not? In the case of classical music, there were written scores, based on some kind of urtext. In jazz though, almost none of us had consulted the original published sheet music of these tunes we played. The canon for us was more a performative one. Often, there was a steady decline in accuracy, in a game of Telephone that played out over the decades. We knew the tunes everyone called the most – "Stella by Starlight," or "All the Things You Are" for example – from records, from bands, from musicians who then improvised over those songs. Often, but not always, it was the improvisation we fell in love with first, and then maybe we grew to like the tune as well. We learned many of these songs so we could improvise on them, perhaps even without hearing a recorded version, but just from each other.

What I gathered from Pete and a few others was: all well and good, but find the urtext, if there is one. There was something of value in that search. When you looked at the original sheet music for some of those Tin Pan Alley tunes, you could often discover nuggets of gold – harmony that was in fact more interesting than the accepted changes everyone played at the jam sessions.

I grew into Pete's sentiment, paying more attention to the songs themselves. There was a feeling among some of us that songs from the 1920s–'40s were deeper than most of the pop music going on in the present day. This was striking, if you thought about it. We were not merely jumping back a generation, say, to the pop music of our parents. These songs were the music of our grandparents. So, when one of us said that music was better then, they were also saying that it was better than all of the great pop music that came after that, which was still before we were born! I may have affected that attitude now and then, but I never believed it. It was apples and oranges.

When you took the time to check out the lyrics to a lot of the Tin Pan Alley songs we were playing, you realized that many of them were hyper-Romantic. If there was a problem with that repertoire, it was its tendency towards sentimental or saccharine emotions. It was never that it was lacking in romance. For us, "burnout" lacked romance. Burnout was the term for the high-energy, muscular way of playing that was popular in other circles, and was a big attraction to a lot of young players then. Most of them didn't have much use for "pretty tunes," as we called them without irony, and they favored a stable of blowing vehicles from the early-1960s period of jazz, like Herbie Hancock's "One Finger Snap," Wayne Shorter's "E.S.P.," or Joe Henderson's "Inner Urge."

We were more focused on the romance. The idea was, even if you played "Just One of Those Things" by Cole Porter at a blistering tempo, the way Bird had, you could still play romantically. The chords would speed by, but you could let that melody soar, just like the lyrics instructed you to do:

> It was just one of those things
> Just one of those crazy old things
> A trip to the moon on gossamer wings
> Just one of those things . . .

Bird himself, or course, was one of the great Romantics – all you had to do was listen to him play a ballad like "Laura" or "Embraceable You." He was one of the best ballad players jazz ever had.

Besides exploring the original sheet music, another important way of learning a tune was by listening to a singer, to hear how those lyrics aligned with the melody. It couldn't be just any singer, though. As great as Billie Holiday was, she was not the one to look to for the original melody – a lot of her genius was in the way she took the words and often simply made a whole new melody, one that made you forget about the original one if you knew it already. She was composing, really, and Tin Pan Alley songs were her set of paints. No, better to turn to Ella Fitzgerald or Frank Sinatra, or even a crooner more in the easy-listening realm like Jack Jones. They might stretch the melody the second time through, as they took the tune home, but the first time through almost always adhered to the original. What's more, they had spotless diction, so you could hear the words clearly.

Coltrane killed jazz

Many of us were in our late teens but playing the part of elder statesmen, even dressing the part. Suspenders and tweed were prevalent, and some would keep that look at all times of the day, not just on the bandstand. A lot of the guys had a studied sourness. Everything going on around us, everything that wasn't what we were doing, was "jive" – not valid, not authentic. That was a favorite word of ours, a blanket condemnation of lots of other jazz. It's still a good word now and then, when used with precision.

We took lessons from Barry Harris in this regard, because, in showing how righteous bebop melody and harmony was, he implied that much of everything else was not. Barry Harris was the patron saint of bebop piano, one of the musicians who was still around from the early second wave that immediately followed Bird and Bud. He had a way of teaching that was unparalleled. He taught masterclasses at the New School, University of the Streets in the East Village, and other places. A group of Barry's acolytes would show up at every one. These were events.

It was easy enough to learn Bird's licks. Many of us had already been transcribing Bird's solos onto paper already, and there was even a shortcut available, something called the *Charlie Parker Omnibook*, with several of his solos already transcribed. I had done quite a bit of transcribing of Bird and Bud, and it was a great way to dive into their melodic vocabulary and start getting it under my fingers in various keys. Barry widened the lens for us, though, connecting those melodies to the harmony underneath them. It was theory but also a model for praxis – he demonstrated it on the piano. Barry would teach, and then you'd go hear him later that night at Bradley's. You dug it like you already had, but you began to understand why, and then you dug it even more.

He had built on Bud's harmony and melodic phrasing. It informed his own playing, and, when he taught, he would hold you to it – there were do's and don'ts. It was a complete aesthetic. This was a strong example: Yes, you had to learn vocabulary, but you wanted to also learn what made it great. It was how you developed a personal aesthetic; it was how you might become a stylist in your own right, with your own calling card. Going forward, if you decided to drop one of those do's or don'ts, or supplant it with another, you could justify your reason. That justification wasn't necessarily for anyone else, although it might play out in one or another polemical quarrel. It was a step towards further self-knowledge. Vladimir Horowitz expressed the same idea in a different context, saying that, in order to move beyond mere virtuosic display, you have to learn how to be a virtuoso first. He meant that if you don't *own* something first, then you can't rightfully discard it – you never had it to begin with.

The most refined, most elder, most withering sourpuss whom we all feared and loved, the one we tried to imitate in vain, was the great alto saxophonist

Lou Donaldson. Lou was from the hard bop generation and had been on some of the legendary records we prized, so the first time I was even close to him my temperature was up. This was the guy who was in the front line with trumpeter Clifford Brown on Art Blakey's *A Night at Birdland* (Volumes 1 and 2). Lou had what we wanted: not just the bebop language, but a real romanticism in his expression, like his reading of the melody on a ballad like "If I Had You" from Volume 2, with his heart right on his sleeve.

Yet Lou could have had a second career as a comedic roaster. Really, he was nothing but kind. He would come down to our fledgling gigs and listen to us try to play the music he had played decades before us, and he stuck around. With Lou, as with Barry, the sourness wasn't truly sour, because it was coupled with a big heart. We felt that. It was incredibly important to have someone like Lou at your gig – intimidating and inspiring all at once. You knew how scathing Lou's criticism was of most everything, apart from Bird, Bud, and a few others. Everyone has their favorite Lou phrases; mine is when he was talking about a band he had just seen at Sweet Basil called The Leaders, led by tenor player Chico Freeman, son of the great Chicago tenor stylist Von Freeman.

"The Leaders? . . . I'd sure hate to see the followers!"

These roasts were ingenious in their timing, delivered in Lou's hipster cadence, with his characteristic high voice, and in the deadpan way they fell out, devoid of mercy, with just a touch of a smile. Yet I was often hesitant to laugh. Most of the people Lou dissed were further along in the game than I might ever get – they had been out there and were respected by their peers and audience alike. Their music had touched people, myself included. But not Lou. It was Lou who introduced the idea that a whole *period* of jazz could be bullshit, with no exceptions. One night, he came to Augie's to see Peter Bernstein, Larry Goldings on his organ set-up, and Bill Stewart on drums. Augie's was a bar uptown where a lot of things happened for all of us early on. I'll talk about the scene there later. After the set, Lou was holding court with all of us, and without warning, made a statement of biblical weight:

"I got news for you. Coltrane *killed jazz*."

I was shaken, but I took it in because it was Lou saying it. It was where he was coming from, from his generation. There was this beautiful, melodic thing that Bird had brought, full of fire but also romance. He was witness to that as it happened and went on to draw from it in his own playing. When Coltrane came along, he seemed to dismantle all that, willfully. From my perspective, it was simple: Coltrane had made something new for jazz. I loved it as much as the earlier stuff; it was another case of apples and oranges. Compared to Lou, though, I was a time-traveling tourist. I was perusing through these different periods of jazz, digging on all of them, but I hadn't ever *lived* through any of them. Chronology was irrelevant to me in the sense that it was all way before me. For Lou, chronology was everything: Coltrane came along, and bebop was effectively over. Coltrane may not have killed jazz, but he killed Lou's jazz.

The Goons

The Bebop Nazis pooh-poohed even hard bop, taking their cue from Barry Harris and Lou Donaldson in their disdain for most everything besides Bird, Bud Powell, and a few others. "Hard bop" was the term that arose for a lot of the great jazz that started in the early fifties, first with musicians like Horace Silver and the early Jazz Messengers formations, as well as Miles Davis and his groups. It continued to dominate for the next decade or so, in artists like Hank Mobley and Lee Morgan, even as Coltrane and others started to push into new areas. Hard bop codified Bird's approach and simplified it to an extent, adding a good dose of funkiness in the mix. In players and composers like pianist Bobby Timmons, a great influence on me, there was a feeling of church and blues mixed together.

There was another tribe who held hard bop as the acme, lionizing its representative players much in the same way as the Bebop Nazis did with Bird and co., aiming for its style. They were the Goons. I met them my second year in New York City. They included musicians like tenor saxophonist Eric Alexander, trumpeters Jim Rotundi and Joe Magnarelli, drummer Joe Farnsworth, and Joe's brothers, trombonist John and baritone saxophonist James. It was bassist Mike Zisman, if I remember, who coined the name "Goons" with some self-irony, being a contented member himself. When I shared an apartment with Mike, Eric, and my girlfriend Sarah a few years later on 2nd Avenue and 5th Street, Mike had a daily regime: "A burger a day, Mehls," he would instruct me. "Gotta do it." That burger ideally came from the Corner Bistro in the West Village, a favorite late-night haunt. The Bistro, a few blocks west of the Village Vanguard, had found the golden mean of juicy and lean on their rotating broiler, and it housed the best jazz jukebox in all of Lower Manhattan. The grill was open until 2:00 am. It was the meeting place for all of us after a gig.

I loved the way all of them played and was happy to find them, feeling like: here are guys who listened to the same records I did. I could hear it directly in their playing. Now, there were the Goons, and there were their straddlers, like Peter Bernstein, bassist John Webber, and others. I fell in with the latter. We loved playing with them but stayed just short of drinking the Kool-Aid. With the Goons, the classic hard bop of the late 1950s and early '60s was more than a musical style. It was a way of life. They had encyclopedic knowledge of many albums, especially those from the golden age of Blue Note Records. On the top of the heap was Art Blakey and the Jazz Messengers, particularly in the period of several years that produced records like *The Big Beat* and *Caravan*.

The Messengers were the analogous hard bop embodiment of that muscular, hyper-masculine atmosphere of the sports teams at Hall High, the one that spilled over into the hazing teen jazz snobs. But, whereas in high school it had been a turn-off, in the Messengers, it made for compelling expression, full of crackling fire. Freddie Hubbard was intimidating like a varsity upperclassman;

Cedar Walton was comping dependably, just behind the line of scrimmage; Art Blakey was yelling at you like a tough coach with his famous press rolls on the snare; Wayne Shorter was the quarterback – the mastermind with the plan, the one with a vision: the composer. Yet there was beauty and integrity behind it all, in tunes from Wayne like "This Is for Albert," in the perfect ensemble playing of "Caravan," and in the sensation of the blues and great swinging feeling that propelled it all, like in Wayne's "The Chess Players."

The fact that the Goons made such strong allegiance with the Jazz Messengers may have partially come out of their own macho identity, but what of it? It was who they really were; it wasn't a put-on. Hanging out with the Goons was great for me, if at times exhausting in its debauchery. I began to reconcile my own resentment and discomfort with a certain type of strong masculinity. That hang-up had grown out of the bullying in middle and high school. Now I was on the team, so to speak.

Joe Farnsworth assigned a nickname to everyone, often a truncation of their last name, Goons and outliers alike – Joe himself was Farns, Peter Bernstein was Berns, Sam Yahel was Ya-Ya, bassist John Webber was Webs, drummer Bill Stewart was Stewie, Eric Alexander was Skippy, I was Mehls, bassist Doug Weiss was Fresh, glossed from beatbox rapper Doug E. Fresh, pianist Jill McCarron was humorously dubbed "J-Mac" – a nickname already taken by the great Jackie McLean – and, at some point, pianist Mike Wilner, another straddler like myself, became Spike, which stuck forever.

Joe in particular was macho; even though he was the youngest brother of five, he was leading the troops, setting the intensity level of the music with his drumming, dropping bombs on us when he felt like it, just like Blakey had done. I dug how he did that in the music, how he threw us off and spurred us on all at once. So, when we came off the bandstand, I kept on liking him and didn't get put off by his sometimes gruff character. It turned out that someone could be intelligent, macho, and talented as hell to boot – who knew. And I could make music with him, jumping in with some of that strong Mars energy. That worked because there was subtlety and care behind it.

It was always the same thing for me as I went on. Something negative from my youth and adolescence had calcified into one or another hang-up. I was able to confront it in the music, square away and reconcile with it, and finally learn how to harness it, shaping it how I pleased. I owned the hang-up in the music first and, when it landed back again in real life, it was steadily freed from its own constraint, transformed into expression. Playing with these guys gave me confidence I couldn't find off the bandstand.

The hang with the Goons was intense. Joe hooked up a regular Sunday-afternoon gig at a sports bar in Midtown East that ran from 2:00 pm into the evening. The deal was: we made next to nothing but got all the free pitchers of Budweiser and Buffalo wings we wanted, and plenty of vodka to knock it all down. We played in a back room, away from the TV in front, where most of the customers stayed, watching whatever game was on. Hardly anyone ever actually came back there to listen to us. It was a free-for-all. We'd drink, playing for hours, all the time eating those wings. When I got back to my apartment and it was only 6:30 in the evening, I had to go to bed, but then I'd wake up at 2:00 am having to piss like something awful, already hungover, with the lingering vinegary aftertaste of the wings. I was "punished," which is how Eric Alexander would have described it.

Two floors up from the apartment with Eric, Mike Zisman, Sarah, and me was another that housed Joe, his brothers James and John, and the great Jimmy Lovelace. Jimmy was one of the deepest drummers I ever got to play with, in a weekly trio gig with Mike on bass at the Metropolitan Grill, a supper club along Union Square, now long gone. He had a swing that was right down the middle – maybe comparable to Art Taylor, but all his own. Whereas Jimmy Cobb and others had pulled me, Lovelace *held* me in place with his beat, gently but absolutely. Jimmy was the oddest match you could have imagined with those guys for a room-mate: in his fifties but looking eternally young, he was a study of mystical calm, with an aura of quiet strangeness. He had a few habits he lived by: he only wore white; he almost never went below Houston Street or above 14th Street except when a gig required it; he took a single tab of acid every Sunday; and took weekly baths in a solution of water and bleach to purify himself.

The players I forged the closest bonds with in those first few years in New York City, ones like Peter Bernstein, Jesse Davis, Jorge Rossy, and Leon Parker, all accepted what I was playing on its own terms. If I played a bit more like McCoy Tyner, and a bit less like Wynton Kelly, or vice versa, they didn't vibe me in the least. They didn't complain or tell me to change what I was doing, and they didn't feel the need to change what they were doing. They had hired me – that was already plenty validation. They accepted the fact that I was a bit of a chameleon at that point, toggling between styles that weren't my own yet. It's the kind of thing you learn as a parent – when your teenager is strident about one viewpoint, and then switches it up a few months later. You listen with patience and don't chastise. Those guys had confidence in me because they had it in themselves. I felt like they were saying, "Don't worry; you've got this." That feeling was really important, because I wasn't always sure I could hang. I was really in my head a lot of the time, especially if I smoked too much weed before we played and it backfired. I'll get to that later.

As for the Goons, even though their taste was not particularly catholic, my jumping back and forth between influences was just fine with them, because they were all ones they liked. McCoy Tyner worked for them because McCoy Tyner wasn't just Coltrane's pianist; he was the guy on great Blue Note records like Hank Mobley's *Straight No Filter*. We all happily referenced the records we loved, sometimes overtly, but more often by channeling a particular feel. If I tried to channel the feel of McCoy Tyner's blistering solo on "Chain Reaction" from *Straight No Filter*, Joe read me and moved into a more

Billy Higgins-like swing, Higgins being the drummer on that date.* For me, it never felt like we were merely aping those greats as a means to an end. It was a way of moving towards my own sound. And, even if I was aping, it was so much fun. We were having this conversation about the music we loved – by playing it, with all our heart.

There was a whole swath of us piano players who were trying to play like Wynton Kelly, the great hard bop pianist who graced so many important records of that era. Sometimes, someone would simply play a whole stretch of one of his solos, transcribed from a beloved record. Normally, that kind of thing would be frowned on, because it went against the principle of improvisation but, here, the fellow piano players who knew the solo as well would give assent and nod in approval. I did this with several choruses of Wynton Kelly's solo on "No Blues" from the Wynton Kelly Trio/Wes Montgomery record *Smokin' at the Half Note*. I still quote from that solo regularly. It's a bedrock of joyous swing, melody and badassed fire all at once. Ditto pianist Bobby Timmons's solo on "Spontaneous Combustion" from *The Cannonball Adderley Quintet in San Francisco*. I wouldn't be who I am without those solos.

We pianists wanted Wynton Kelly's crisp articulation but, more urgently, his *feel*. Your "feel," in jazz parlance, means the way you sit in the swinging rhythmic pulse of the music, or you could say, *where* you sit, which part of the beat you lean into: the front end, the back end, somewhere in between, or maybe a shifting mixture of all of the above. Kelly laid in the back of the beat, and the way he swung was completely unique, and remains so in spite of being imitated by many. I can't hear where he got that feel – I think it was something elemental in him – but you hear lots of pianists who grabbed onto it. Just listen to Herbie Hancock on his early Blue Note records, like *Takin' Off*.

Kelly's comping was influential on Herbie as well. People think of Wynton Kelly as an "inside" player, but he was the first piano player in the small-group jazz setting to comp in a way that wasn't part of the rhythm section grid. He paved the way for the more interactive comping that Herbie Hancock and others would take up after him – jabbing and interspersing stuff between the soloists' phrases, adding punctuation marks. It's a common understanding that Miles called Wynton Kelly in for "Freddie Freeloader" on *Kind of Blue* because he wanted something for that tune that was Blacker – bluesier and more swinging – than what Bill Evans could supply. That may be true, but it's a backhanded diss to Kelly, because his comping was every bit as subtle as that of Bill Evans.

Wynton Kelly dotted his eighth notes quite strongly, and in his own hands the effect was exhilarating; it has that joyous tension and relaxation all at once. It makes you want to move, and if you don't dance outright some part of your body will be squirming happily. Yet in someone else's hands that

---

* I believe the track listing is wrong on that record, and "Chain Reaction" is actually "Soft Impressions," which is listed as the following tune. It only makes sense because the tune is based on the chords of Coltrane's "Impressions."

dotted articulation could sound hokey. Kelly also played straight blues phrases unabashedly and more often than his own model, Bud Powell. He often did that right in the middle of a pretty ballad and made it work, like on "If You Could See Me Now" from Wes Montgomery's *Smokin' at the Half Note*. It was never trite.

Herbie, being Herbie, was able to fold Kelly's influence into his own conception, which was already showing itself on *Takin' Off*. Many players, though, go for Kelly's thing and it doesn't work. It's the sound of a relaxedness that no one else wants – like a guy who wears a muscle shirt when he's a little too overweight to pull it off, and his tits stand out. This kind of unwelcome let-it-all-hang-out feel is a common jazz virus. The other problem is when you've got Kelly's spirit well enough but you're simply not as strong rhythmically, your touch is too soft, or your articulation not as crisp. It's a flabby kind of playing.

Jazz fans and musicians alike complain about the "tightness" of someone's swing feel. Tight playing is certainly a phenomenon, but I don't believe it's due to some incurable lack of hipness, lack of sexual experience, or any of the other clichés one hears. Rigidity of swing is often rooted in lack of self-assurance. That may come from lack of experience and, further, a lack of proper technique. Technique gives one self-assurance because it provides physical relaxation. If you look at a tight player, you'll usually see it in their body language. In any case, I started out corny and tight, and became less so as I gained technique and, with it, relaxation.

Wynton

There was one object of disdain that seemed to be almost universal among all the angry young lion cubs: The Marsalis phenomenon. At Ari's parents' house in the West Village where we hung out sometimes, there was a copy of *Standard Time, Vol. 1* lying around, unceremoniously out of the case, usually on the floor when we came in. Ari and William would play frisbee with it, intentionally missing the catch, letting it hit a wall or table.

Wynton and Branford Marsalis seemed to have just risen out of nowhere, and were suddenly heralded as the biggest thing in jazz since Miles Davis. Wynton was going to save jazz, the story went – but why him? And why did jazz need to be saved? We were resentful of their limelight.

It was partially due to our aesthetic allegiances. In Wynton's playing, we didn't immediately hear any of the trumpet playing we were immersed in – the bop and hard bop of Fats Navarro and Clifford Brown, but also a more understated player like Kenny Dorham, or a one-of-a-kind like Booker Little. In retrospect, Wynton's early records were groundbreaking on their own terms, not in the least for the contributions from the other musicians as well, like drummer Jeff "Tain" Watts and pianist Kenny Kirkland. We just couldn't get with them then. It was wrapped up into the same kind of partisan allegiance I had observed in high school. Now in New York, I had a blind spot, and couldn't see I was caught up in that myself. I avoided checking out Wynton's records.

Other trumpeters like Blue Mitchell, Bill Hardman, or Idrees Sulieman who had never gotten widespread recognition were unsung heroes to us. Or there was someone like Woody Shaw, still on the scene, the most innovative trumpet stylist since the 1960s. Where were all the accolades for him, or anyone else who had been around making records and playing for the last few decades? There was indignation to our partisanship.

I came to realize later that my own indignation, at least, was self-righteous and short-sighted. Wynton cleared a path for a lot of us that wasn't there, and we walked onto it a few years later, starting in the early '90s. The attention that Wynton and Branford received in those years seemed lopsided compared to everyone else, though. There was this feeling that we were obliged to watch them develop whether we wanted to or not. Only a few of us were recording on smaller labels. When Wynton or Branford put a record out, it was billed like the Second Coming.

In spite of his brilliance, we took issue with Wynton being cast as the leader of a "Renaissance." What an insult that term was to all of the great musicians who had been making music for the last twenty years, it seemed to us – musicians like Joe Henderson, Tommy Flanagan, or Shirley Horn. Was that period some kind of dark ages for jazz? Was Wynton qualifiedly better than someone like Barry Harris, we asked, or any of those older heroes of ours who were still around?

The Marsalises' success was not purely on the basis of their music any more than mine was a few years later. Mine was a cliché about a drug addict. They had a better story, one about New Orleans familial authenticity. With the help of good publicists, there was a sudden high visibility in the large media outlets. Wynton did not squander the opportunity, and could back it up in his playing. There was never any doubt in his musical prowess.

In the long run, what he did for jazz was unequivocally positive. He brought it into the view of a largely white public, still under the sway of Ronald Reagan's glib, self-congratulatory conservatism. Jazz already had dignity, but he let a lot more people know about it. One way he did that was by presenting jazz itself as possessing a conservative strain, of which he was the mouthpiece. People heard him, and started to listen to great music to which they hadn't been exposed, music from earlier founders like Duke Ellington and Louis Armstrong. There was a focus on history, on a canon.

The new, broader public Wynton was reaching had no previous passion for jazz. They didn't yet understand, in their *gut*, what he was talking about regarding swing or "the majesty of the blues," at least not in the beginning. A gut love requires falling in love first, and you can't force someone to fall in love. Passion implies an exclusionary love – a personal aesthetic, a viewpoint as to what is good and what is not. As Wynton began taking jazz into venues like Lincoln Center, usually associated with classical music respectability, his performances had a duty-bound quality – duty on the part of the audience, to listen up as he taught them what was what. It is a duty familiar to the "classics" in all arts, be it slogging through *Julius Caesar* in high school, or listening to Beethoven in a music appreciation class. It is the pathway to edification, not necessarily pleasure. The idea is that the two will eventually be linked: once you know why something is great, you will come around to it. But you have to be taught first.

This was valid enough by my lights – it was, after all, the way I had learned a few things in the academic environment of high school, when I wasn't too stoned. Those were things that had put a spark in me even if I didn't care so much then, but, when my head was clearer, I did pursue them further – things about European-based culture, with all those great Dead White Guys. So why not with jazz?

A pedagogic route went against a previous pathway to jazz allegiance for a listener, though: a more gnostic, secret one. It wasn't taught. It was discovered. Jazz had begun as a form of popular music, but then fallen away with the rise of rock'n'roll. For decades it had been something to find on one's own, often independently of peers who listened to pop music. There was a certain pride to that – an elitism, really. If you were listening to Coltrane, you were onto something deeper than pop, and you were part of a small number of initiates. Wynton pushed back on that hipsterish claim, swinging to the other pole: jazz demanded and deserved a properly pedagogic introduction. That caused some musicians, long-time fans and commentators to grouse. The immediate benefactors of the Marsalis mainstream were conservative – entertainers like Harry Connick Jr., who played in a nostalgic style of another era. It went down safe and smooth. Jazz wasn't dangerous anymore. It was similar to what Green Day did to punk rock a decade later.

Wynton's new jazz audience was at Lincoln Center, Kennedy Center, and other performing arts spaces associated with classical music. It expanded into Europe and Japan. This helped all of us because the artistic directors of those large, gilded venues realized that the music he brought had a profundity "worthy" of their audience. There was, of course, a core group of listeners around the world who were already jazz lovers. Much of the audience, though, new to jazz, accepted their duty to learn, because, without a previous aesthetic, they didn't know what they were supposed to be liking.

Wynton's conservatism in those days– fusion was not jazz, free jazz was a mere niche, etc. – played well enough into the zeitgeist of the '80s but, when the '90s started, it wore thin. Perhaps it had partially to do with a broader cultural shift away from conservatism; perhaps it was his didactic approach. One critic I remember at that time named him a "self-appointed expert." Maybe Wynton felt he had to come on strong, or maybe it was simply in his personality. In any case, it worked. He laid the ground for greater recognition of jazz, and his own conservatism, if you will, was an aid in that respect, to the extent that he drew clear lines.

I remember reading Wynton in an interview, talking about jazz education. He was refuting the sentiment that jazz could be whatever you wanted it to be. I paraphrase: he said that, in order to teach something, it has to have an identity. Otherwise, there is no place to begin teaching. He was and still is right, and, a few decades later, most I know concur that Wynton gave jazz a clear identity in a broader forum, outside of its niche, and that ultimately served everyone in the tent, including those who were on the other side.

We didn't see that then because of our resentment, but he was playing the long game. He helped make the whole subject of jazz relevant to a wider public, whether you agreed with him or not. It was in this atmosphere of recognition, however fraught with polemical exchange, that my peers and I entered and began to make our way a few years after Wynton had arrived. Jazz wasn't dead, and it didn't even smell funny, like Zappa had said.

Jazz may have gained wider cultural recognition by the late '80s, but it didn't translate into greater sales for most musicians. There was initially an idealistic expectation that it would, or at least a hope, after Wynton and Branford's success. So, for a period of two or three years, there was a phenomenon of over-signing. Several young musicians who were still getting their shit together were being heralded as "young lions" – itself a rehashed term from the original days of hard bop. They were pushed and got sizable advances from the record companies. There was an inevitable blowback. Their records did not sell, not because people were ignorant but because they weren't exciting records. The zeal to sign young musicians and market them as part of a great renaissance was ineffective, not so much because what they played was not fundamentally popular music, but because their music was not groundbreaking and, often, not on par with the earlier style it was parroting. So, after a glut of mediocre releases with low sales, the big labels backed away from jazz.

Dragon music

When Wynton played, it sounded like he *knew* what he wanted me to hear. It played well into his mission to teach listeners about jazz. That didacticism in the music itself was not available to me; in any case, I did not pursue it. It wasn't that I didn't care what the audience thought. Rather, the music unfolded in such a way that I only knew what I played after it happened. I couldn't lead the audience anymore than to say: go out on a limb with me and let's see where this goes. In some of the musicians I loved the most, there was also a feeling that they didn't know where they would wind up, and that it might all just fall apart at any moment. In fact, my favorite moments were often when the canvas cracked and splintered, and the imperfection rose to the surface. There it was: the bare-assed exposure of a musician's disfigured, true self. Yet that was no simple failure. It was the ambergris in the perfume, the smelly human underbelly beneath the handsome torso. It made the beauty more compelling.

Vulnerability was not a virtue in itself. If someone always conveyed it, it became as insufferable as ceaseless impenetrability. Yet it could invite a listener towards self-forgiveness. Redemption-through-error was part and parcel of the improvisatory aesthetic itself. Beauty was indeed on display in the finished product, but just the endeavor to make beauty, to push past your own handicapped frailty, had beauty.

I could lay my chips on that logic because it seemed to come from a primal, shared experience: When you were young, you had an aspiration. But then you damaged or broke something in your naïve ignorance, for all to see. Someone showed you mercy, though, because that person had once shared your aspiration – they empathized with you – and you had dared to try. Your own failed effort was not only forgiven but it was preserved in the redemption. In musical terms, that meant that, if you fell on your ass on the bandstand in the search for beauty, it wasn't necessarily a negative in the long run.

I found that vulnerable feeling in musicians like Billie Holiday, Lester Young, Booker Little, Wayne Shorter, Chet Baker, and of course Miles. "The Buzzard Song," the opening track of *Porgy and Bess*, Miles's collaboration with arranger Gil Evans playing the music from Gershwin's opera, is a strong example. He delivers the opening doleful melody with such hesitancy. It's so intimate because he has no defensive armor; his playing has this beautiful uncertainty to it. There is a risk in that kind of playing – what if you get burnt, what if you get laughed at? Here, I'm speaking mostly of a masculine phenomenon. As crazy as it sounds, when I arrived in New York, a lot of male aspirants like myself, depending on what they were bringing already from their background, shied away from ballads for that reason.

Miles made it okay for other male musicians to show their ass and not just wag their dick. He was a model they benefited from, because he gave them a safe space for what was already inside of them. Listen to trumpeter Kenny

Dorham's plaintive solo on "Escapade," his own masterful composition on Joe Henderson's Blue Note date, *Our Thing*. You hear doubt and foreboding, even as hope tries to push through. When I hear playing like that, I experience kinship.

Being vulnerable in the music, versus directly communicating it to someone else through words or actions, was appealing for me. My Cain was different, and maybe that was cool to a degree, but he was also secretly unsure. That lack of self-assurance was repellent to me in its outward manifestation socially, and inwardly in the self-loathing monologue going on between my ears. Yet, when I could express vulnerability in music in addition to the confidence that was already there, it gave me a more integrated version of Cain. On the one hand, there was the guy saying, "I've been cast out and I'm not sure who I am." But there was also the guy saying, "This is me – I'm going to pull you over into my tribe: just wait." I was both when I played, even if I couldn't be anytime else.

Miles showed the way. When "The Buzzard Song" breaks into swing after the opening melody, he is unstoppably self-assured. He's flipped the script. It's all the more badassed because we already know who he is on the inside. He catches us off guard. His self-assurance is so much more interesting because we know it's not all there is to him. It's also a surmounting– he is the victor over his own doubt. The doubt he initially expressed becomes more compelling retroactively because we see it was a strong person who doubted. There is still a sense of foreboding, interlaid within the strength.

This deep irony on the emotional level was only achievable by him through initially conveying weakness. That kind of expression was sexual for me when I heard it, sexuality sublimated in music. It was about showing something personal, passively, and then taking charge – all within one performance. I'm not sure if anyone will pull that off again like Miles.

Vulnerably uncertain is not the only way to sound, especially not for trumpet players. Thank God that Freddie Hubbard was Freddie Hubbard through and through. The trumpet can swagger like nothing else. Still, something magic happens when that swagger is tempered by uncertainty. The rub between the two is what makes trumpeter Lee Morgan's music timeless – Lee Morgan, the perfect jazz musician, if there ever was one. The blues was in everything he did, his rhythmic phrasing was always interesting and never locked in a grid. He had more swagger than just about anyone.

Yet in his solos – like on "Chain Reaction" or "Soft Impressions," from Hank Mobley's *Straight No Filter*, or on his own "The Gigolo," from the album of the same name – it was his own *finitude*, and my own, that I heard in his playing. It was the unspoken subject of the music. I don't mean finitude of musical ideas. I mean finitude as our existential condition. Beauty is beauty because beauty is temporary, and beauty is temporary because we are temporary. Our mortality is the birthright that angels can never possess. To seek beauty was to seek an affirmation of life, even as you knew it wouldn't last. While that life pulsed, though, it was absolutely lucid in its strength.

Here was the counterpart to that crushing sublime I had found earlier at Merrywood, hearing Coltrane and Hendrix. Yet it wasn't a mere beautiful foil. Those solos of Morgan were the musical embodiment of the deadly dragon appetite that had awoken in me at Merrywood. In all his breakable vulnerability, Morgan swaggered nevertheless. In a highwire act of improvisation, he played music that expressed the finitude of its own beauty, and the beauty of its own finitude. When I had first heard Coltrane and Hendrix at Merrywood, I apprehended the sublime – a supra-human eternal power that could crush me. Yet there was more to their music. There was this beating heart, this bleating soul-cry.

Morgan and others played Dragon Music. The dragon was elementally strong, breathing fire that could burn you away to nothing. But he was not immortal. Someone or something could still slay him. You cried for him when he bled, even as you were scared of him. You witnessed the sublime – his death, your death – with him, *through* him, through his music.

You'll never be a good comper

I had been playing piano in Jesse Davis's group at Augie's and it was heaven – I felt like a cog in a wheel, comping behind him. He played so rhythmically strong and swinging, and my comping was improving every week, being up there with him. Comping is an indispensable part of being a jazz pianist, unless you only want to play your own music without any other soloists. Even then you should have a handle on it.

The experience with Jesse helped to ease an inferiority complex about comping I had brought to New York. It had started during my first gig at the 880 in Hartford, with Larry DiNatale. Larry told me two or three times: "You're really talented, but you'll never be a good comper." I wasn't then, at age fifteen. Joel Frahm was on the gig with us, and at least he didn't complain too much to me about how I comped behind him. I held onto Larry's words going forward as I arrived in New York, trying to figure out what he had meant, always trying to be good at comping, never really sure. In retrospect, I think that Larry's comment was not flippant. He was sensing something about my personality, and got me aware of how that could play out detrimentally in the music.

I had been trying to people-please as a comper, and my model no doubt came from the musico-social interactions I had in high school, where I would try to come over to someone's side through their music: metalhead? No problem, I'll talk to him about Judas Priest. Stevie Nicks devotee? We can hang out in her basement, and get dreamy together listening to Fleetwood Mac. It had worked well enough in a high-school social setting. But how did that play out in the abstracted sociality of collective jazz improvisation?

I began to learn that instrumentalists and singers often didn't want or need a similar validation from the accompanist. Actually, most of the time, they preferred that you supply your steady support by staying clear of their path, not answering their every idea, but rather laying something down more locked into the bass and drums, even grid-like. If you are constantly trying to interact with every idea they present, you are not really accompanying, properly speaking – you are hijacking their ideas in a sense, and putting the focus on what you're doing instead. It becomes more, "Look at me everyone, I'm so hip and adept at catching the soloist/singer's ideas!" But what it's really saying to the soloist/singer (and the audience) is: "Please like me!" It's overbearing. It feels like one of those people you know who, when in a conversation with you, is constantly affirming what you're saying – "Yeah . . . totally . . . exactly!" – before you've even finished your thought.

My comping complex was rooted in the bad old cloying social insecurity that had seeded in West Hartford – like in Mr. Mazzie's class, or at Papa Gino's. It was that fear of rejection. In the first few years in New York City, I began to excise that quality from my comping. Next, in a familiar self-referential loop,

I feared that the act of excising itself was just so much more people-pleasing. Finally, I began to simply let go a bit and learn through repeated experiences in live situations, through trial and error – what Junior had already instructed. A seed gets planted and then it takes some time to sprout. It sprouted to fruition, I would say, when I joined Joshua Redman's quartet a few years later.

I remembered the guy Jeremy at Papa Gino's who was flipping pies within a few short months while I struggled at the grill. He didn't give a shit – it was 5:45 evening rush hour, the place was packed and customers were eyeing him impatiently. But he was as cool as a cucumber, getting the pizzas in and out of the big oven. Maybe the thing was to just not give a shit with comping as well – not to throw away your taste and sensibility, mind you, but to bring a little of that cavalier pie-flipping thing into it. I started watching this less sensitive kind of comping going on at jam sessions or on gigs, and I didn't always dig it. But I also noticed that other people often did – most importantly, the soloists they were comping behind. So what did it matter what I thought? In building a personal aesthetic it's important to realize it's just that – personal.

The more interactive kind of comping was nevertheless a strong model. The unparalleled master was Herbie Hancock in Miles Davis's 1960s quintet (and also on many Blue Note records, playing as a sideman). When Miles or Wayne soloed, Herbie, with his incredible ears, would hear something in their line in real time. Often it might be an unexpected harmonic turn. Herbie would fuse with it, answering with a very specifically voiced chord that vindicated their idea. At its most inspired, that chord was three-tiered. It acknowledged the bracing audacity of the soloist's note choice – in Miles's case, often a long, held-out note that spanned through several chord changes – by doubling it. Yet it also underpinned that note with other harmony that gave it dimension. Finally, there were a few more lower notes in the chord that welded it to the bottom end of the tonality that Ron Carter supplied. That kind of gambit required a deeply sophisticated understanding of harmony and all its implications, and the ability to call on it in the white heat of someone's solo. If you look at all of Miles's piano players, all of them were at the top of the heap of their contemporaries in terms of harmonic sophistication – Red Garland, Wynton Kelly, Bill Evans – and Herbie pushed the bar higher.

Bill Evans was another role model. We think of Evans most often as a trio innovator. On *Kind of Blue*, though, he inaugurated a coloristic kind of comping, less tethered to the rhythmic pulse, on tunes like "So What" or "Flamenco Sketches." There were other strong instances as well, notably his comping on Oliver Nelson's classic *The Blues and the Abstract Truth*, or his own *Loose Blues*, comping behind Zoot Sims and Jim Hall.

The other approach for comping, just as appealing in terms of its musical results, but perhaps more difficult for me to assimilate into my own expression, was indeed the normative approach, the one that the majority of exemplary piano stylists used. It was not people-pleasing. The idea was to stay with the bass and drums as a supporting team for the soloist. After all, that's why you were part of the rhythm section as a pianist – you didn't have a special title, like "mediator between soloist and rhythm section." In this view, interactive comping was pretentious and unwelcome. Ironically, trying so hard to acknowledge the soloist or singer was rather self-important. You were stealing the soloists' thunder. Instead of validating them, you were taking the wind out of their sails by suggesting they needed finishing touches on their ideas. It might actually interrupt the flow of their story, instead of aiding it. Let them acknowledge themselves. Pianists like Red Garland, Sonny Clark, Cedar Walton, and Mal Waldron were quintessential non-pretentious compers, each in their own inimitable way, and they rubbed off on me.

Jesse did something special, though, when I played with him: he *listened back* to what I was doing, and moved with it. This was, in one light, an altruistic act as a soloist, forgoing his exclusivity as the sole narrator of the story he told. He was feeding *me*, his accompanist, something, and waiting to see what I would give back. It was a wonderful way to play, and I would find it again a few years later with Joshua Redman in his band, who initiated the same thing with me. As a comper, that back and forth exchange is not something you should bring to the table and present to the soloist or singer. You are having a dialogue, yes – but by *their* invitation. They are still the host.

Trivialization

"Getting vibed," as we called it, happened a number of times on the bandstand, in jam sessions, or gigs, and in private sessions as well. It was unpleasant but healthy in a way – like a bracing cold shower for the ego. Once I got beyond the initial butthurt, there was the opportunity to realign and consolidate my own musical convictions, and then either adjust them or stand by them, less defensively. One time, though, was a particular downer, and I subsequently turned it into one of those "I got rejected" stories.

There was another guy our age who had started showing up at Jesse's gig to sit in. One night he was playing with us, and he and I just weren't clicking. When he soloed, whatever I comped put him off. If I played nothing, he would stand there and wait, and then when I played something, he'd stop in mid-phrase, and turn to me quickly. Eventually, without turning around, he yelled, *"Stroll! Stroll!"* That meant to lay out and let him have it, just with the bass and the drums. Fine. The next tune – the same thing – "Stroll!" So I got up in the middle of his solo and pianist Spike Wilner took over, who seemed to fare better. Larry's early words came back: *"You'll never be a good comper!"*

When I got vibed by that guy and walked off the stage, some of the cats hanging out at the bar were shaking their heads sadly at me. I didn't know – were they hearing something in what the guy was playing that I wasn't hip to? It seemed to be mostly chromatic figures, expressed with a certain pensiveness. It sounded "abstract," but from what had it been abstracted? I don't think they knew any more than I did.

There were a number of players on the scene during that time who were obviously indebted to Miles's 1960s band with Wayne Shorter, Herbie Hancock, Ron Carter, and Tony Williams, in terms of how they approached soloing. In that group, Wayne Shorter's writing called for a different approach to soloing than Bird's, in which the composed head had been the outgrowth of a larger bebop language. Like Monk, Wayne inverted that paradigm. Miles, Herbie, Ron Carter, and Wayne himself were obliged to address his writing in their solos, because its tonal implications were new.

Wayne's new music involved harmony that was constantly shifting from one tonality to the next in each chord change, chromatically, so you had to find a new strategy as a soloist, in order to find a way to connect the dots. The language of bebop, which had continued into hard bop for the next decade, would not suffice. You couldn't play Bird licks on a Wayne tune. You hear his shifting chromatic tonality easily on tunes like "E.S.P.," the title track on Miles's album of the same name, or the beautiful waltz-ballad, "Iris," from the same date.

In the writing that began on *E.S.P.* and on Wayne's own canonical records as a leader on Blue Note from the same three-year stretch, he embarked from a modal starting point that Miles had initiated on "So What," and Coltrane was continuing to develop. He then went the next logical step, as we see in hindsight, mixing the various modes and employing other types of scales, like the whole-tone scale in "Juju", the title track from his 1965 Blue Note album. He wrote melodies that crossed through all of that flux, sometimes in obtuse angles, sometimes in soft contours – a gambit not unlike Monk's, but with rich new consequences. Musicians and non-musicians alike often describe Wayne's music in coloristic terms, and in a piece like "Fall" from Miles' *Nefertiti*, one might find a visual analogy in how the modes blur together. The harmony no longer relies on the primary colors of clear tension and resolution, but invokes softer pastels and admixes.

In high school, *E.S.P.* became a huge record for me, along with *Nefertiti*, and several of Wayne's own records, particularly *Juju*, *Adam's Apple*, *Speak No Evil* and *Soothsayer*. Wayne's language informed much of what I began to write a few years later in the first tunes I recorded and released, particularly in a long stream of moody waltzes, among them "At a Loss," "Angst," and "Ron's Place." His writing had already affected many musicians I met and forged bonds with when I came to New York, in terms of the compositional style they were beginning to develop. He was a large presence you couldn't avoid – he became part of the DNA of jazz composition, in a similar way that Coltrane and Bird had as improvisers.

Because Wayne's new harmonic network moved chromatically, often with very little common tonality between each chord change, one result was that the soloistic language of Miles, Herbie, and Wayne became more chromatic. Importantly, that language of that band was an end point just as much as it was a jumping-off point. In Wayne's laboratory of tunes, you could say that harmony reached a saturation point. There was very little wiggle room to create diatonic melodies that flowed through the ever-shifting harmony cohesively, in the way soloists had up until that time. Each one of them had to find their own way, and that's the sound you hear on that string of great Miles records from 1965 to 1968 – the sound of risk and discovery.

Miles, Herbie, and Wayne had *arrived* at that chromatic approach, though, from everything that had come before. The chromaticism in their lines had integrity, because it was directly related to the new composition that Wayne had written. It was interspersed with other soloistic material that pointed to the tune. The music from Miles's band of this period was not a negative abdication of harmonic principles, but a positive inquiry into their further possibility. In its innovation, it posed a challenge for musicians, inviting them to hear harmony in a more nuanced way. In turn, Wayne sophisticated us, the listeners.

What you often heard in the early '90s, though, was a trivialization of the approach of 1960s Miles, in which players would arbitrarily play chromatic figures, willy-nilly. There was no indication that they had absorbed the prior syntax of bebop. Their figures were not an outcome of saturation. They were not an outcome of anything, properly speaking. This kind of playing created only the appearance of depth and abstraction. Furthermore, it seemed an exercise in bad faith, with a faulty, upside-down logic: it was as if an approach that was already three decades old could somehow be reanimated, and now, by aping it, one could be innovative oneself. In the game of jazz, it was play-acting, like trying on your dad's suit that's too big for you.

In any case, it was often deafeningly boring, and both pretentious and childish all at once. When this played out in the venue of "burnout," as the style was called, it was frequently dispatched with a mind-numbing lack of dynamic range. Everything was loud and fast. That kind of energy might be exciting in a climax or scene change within a set, but when it was all you got for ninety minutes, you didn't care at all, and just wanted it to stop. There was a poverty of phrasal variety in these gatherings – mostly iterations on one or two ideas, over and over again. There was zero romance, zero poetry.

Bebop lives

Barry Harris was a model not just because of his mastery of a particular musical language, but because his melodic phrasing was so free within that language. Pianist Tommy Flanagan exemplified that as well. I was fortunate to hear Tommy several times in New York. His playing in the latter years of his career had reached a peak level of refinement, distilled in a beautiful trio setting with bassist George Mraz and great trio drummers like Al Foster or Kenny Washington. There was always all this room in the music, room to breathe. To some, Barry and Tommy may have seemed bent on preserving a style that had passed, but that wasn't true at all. By the time we arrived in New York, they had achieved poetic justice, if you had ears to hear. Bebop, as it was written on walls in the East Village, really *was* the "music of the future." Barry, far from being a throwback, was a Futurist for us.

Barry's teaching style was solidly didactic, but it was more compelling for us at that point than the frontal assault that Wynton was heralding uptown. Wynton advocated a return to authenticity, critiquing the development of jazz, as it began to draw outside influences like rock'n'roll into its expression. It was a global critique, in broad brushstrokes. Yet his music seemed no *freer* as a result. As vital and influential as Wynton was during that time, his music did not convey the mixture of looseness and profundity of any number of older musicians on the scene then. We wanted something we called "between the cracks." Barry and others had it. "Free" had nothing to do with atonality or lack of structure. It was a feeling, not a dictum. It was either there in the music or it wasn't.

Now, of course it's entirely possible to trivialize bebop. It is perhaps more difficult, though, because you can't skimp on addressing the harmony in the same way you can play chromatically all the time, to imitate Miles and Wayne in the '60s, or paste pentatonic figures onto everything willy-nilly, the way Coltrane and McCoy Tyner clones do. Trivialization of bebop is in any case just as rampant as its modal counterpart, and was already, almost immediately after Bird himself was gone. It's no doubt the kind of playing that Zappa had in mind when he remarked that jazz smelled funny.

For myself, the key seemed to be combination, integration, and, finally, assimilation, of these various styles. I wanted to take what was best from each of them – like that openness of bebop phrasing in its best exemplars – and not what was easiest – bebop's most recognizable licks that slide easily enough into a limited context.

Pot paranoia

In my third year in New York City, I started getting sick of marijuana. Pot made me think too much and thinking seemed to screw things up or just bum me out. I settled in on drinking scotch. I ordered Cutty Sark in bars and tried to have it on hand at the apartment, fancying myself like the weathered Wasp who was in the magazine ads, drinking it on rocks on his yacht with a wry, wrinkled smile. Or I'd self-consciously order single malts at the Slaughtered Lamb on the corner of Jones Street where I lived, trying to show off to the regulars. Nobody cared.

Pot had worked for a time. It was already a daily coping mechanism that got me through high school. I rarely smoked it at the 880, though. I had too much respect for Larry. I wanted to have all guns firing for that gig.

I began to smoke on those other first money gigs I got in Connecticut, though – weddings, parties, bar mitzvahs, town fairs. I would share a joint or a few bowls with a pal in the band on the break before the last set. The idea was to put a different slant on everything – perhaps right when I was getting bored with my own playing or with the gig in general. Sometimes the pot really worked. Everything became interesting and I became captivated by the music – captivated, often, simply by the idea of music itself. Everything would suddenly seem rich with possibility, even though in reality it had the same variables as twenty minutes earlier.

In this sense, pot is really a mild hallucinogen, just like it's officially classified. In high school, I had several transformative trips with mescaline, psilocybin, and LSD. There is often a reflective, very intense part of an acid trip that takes place a little over two hours into it – "peaking." The Grateful Dead used to pace their shows so that the "Space" segment would arrive at the audience's collective peak. "Space" was sonic, free of melody, harmony or rhythm. It was a destabilizing trip through the looking glass, full of strangeness. After a time, gradually, with increasing delight from the crowd, they would morph into a song, something joyful but maybe knowing and just a little wistful. You can hear that play out on the transition from "Space" to "Fire on the Mountain" on their classic live album *Dead Set*. In these moments, everyone would dance in ecstasy, at the height of the trip. Questions had been answered, and you began a joyful descent from the peak. It was the promised collective catharsis of a Dead show.

Outside of the Dead context, tripping with friends, I sometimes wound up at the piano at the peak. I would just sit there and play a few notes. I couldn't play actual music – it was just too overwhelming. Instead I would play a C major triad, slowly, repeatedly, and get lost in that for an hour – the way it sounded, the way it felt sensually, but also its implications, what it meant, what it could lead to. It took on huge gravity, and seemed the alpha and omega of all music. There was nothing more to play.

Or, more riskily, I might head solo to the bathroom in whoever's house we were in and shut the door, locking it. I would stand in front of the mirror there. First was a round of mild hallucinations, merely altering my face, but then, ever more contorted, until I began to see other faces, a series of them. They were men, women, young and old, and often I had the feeling they were my ancestors from long ago. A woman from another epoch often showed up, Native American, perhaps Inuit. That could go on for a good half-hour. Sometimes it could go bad, though – the faces became death masks, holding me frozen with their gaze.

Smoking pot could have this quality of making me overwhelmed and frozen up, albeit to a much lesser degree than acid, because I could still function for the most part – you would not want to drive a car on acid. I always felt much more in control driving smoking cannabis than I did drinking, which I regret to say I did then. Thank God I never hurt anyone or myself, or worse. Yet driving while stoned often backfired for the opposite reason. I drove *too* carefully. This driving too carefully is a good metaphor for why pot stopped working for me both socially and on the bandstand.

If you're playing music, particularly improvised music, it's like you're driving. You're looking ahead at the road. You can glance to the side and take in the scenery for a moment, but you don't want to get stuck looking too long. The cannabis, though, inclines one not just to look longer at things, but think about them, and then follow a tangential course to some other thoughts, continuously. Pot paranoia kicks in during situations that normally would be stressful but manageable. When I was stoned, those thoughts could suddenly turn sinister, and I would become paralyzed with fear. I would drive extra carefully, but too carefully, too slowly, not in the intuitive flow of traffic with the other drivers. I would hesitate too much, and then rush forward, nervously. It was a mess.

This used to happen to me when I would drive from West Hartford to Manhattan during my first few years living in the city – I just never learned. I would be in my parents' station wagon and would smoke a joint around midway through the journey. I'd pull off at a highway exit, take some hits, light up a cigarette, and then start the engine again, continuing the journey. There was a fresh outlook. Driving a car was suddenly interesting – epic, downright Kerouacian. I was taken with the experience of traveling the great American landscape in my parents' Chevy, enthralled with it all. I was quite stoned, though, chugging along around 50 mph, in the farthest right lane on the wide, accommodating I-684.

That was fine until I merged onto the Saw Mill Parkway. The Saw Mill is one of several older parkways throughout the Tri-State area. Parkways are a different affair than regular highways, with thinner lanes, closer proximity to nature, and a throwback feeling, like being in the 1950s when most of them were built. There's the Taconic State Parkway which starts just north of the Bronx in Westchester County and continues into the Hudson Valley and the Catskill Mountains, or the Palisades Parkway which hugs the border between New Jersey and New York, with its imposing cliffs along the Hudson River just minutes after coming off the George Washington Bridge from Upper Manhattan. Or there's Merritt Parkway – a link between privileged Connecticut hamlets and the grittier Bronx when it merges into Hutchinson River Parkway.

The Saw Mill after a joint was menacing. It was partially the old road itself, which was not graded well and sloped uneasily, full of twists, turns, and exit and entrance ramps that were little more than the size of a small driveway and sometimes appeared blindly around a turn. All this required more attention and quicker reflexes from the driver than the modern interstates, even without the joint.

Then there was the aggressiveness from other drivers: Westchester County types, speeding along at 70 mph in the thin lanes, racing to their Wall Street gigs in their V8s. And there I was, petrified, trying to maintain 50 mph – completely taken in by everything, *too* taken in, for that is what pot does. It magnifies the *is*-ness of everything. Banal stuff that is always before one's view now shimmers with significance and a feeling of consequence.

The exits alone on the Saw Mill, in that freshly baked state, were worthy of observation and wonder – exits to towns with imposing, British-sounding names like *Hastings-on-Hudson* or *Hawthorne*. They pointed to an intimidating, clubby world behind the woods that lined the parkway. I was an interloper here – the Volvos and BMWs that sped by me were from this world – this was their turf. I was a twenty-year-old doofus in my parents' Chevy wagon, driving alone with my hands clenched on the wheel, catching their scorn when they looked briefly at me, passing by. As I rode, the stream-of-consciousness voice of pot paranoia would be at full throttle, making commentary:

An hour away maybe – what if there's heavy traffic in the Bronx? – What bridge do I take to cross into Manhattan? – What if I go into the South Bronx like I did that one time? – I got stuck and drove around for an hour like an idiot – Willis Avenue Bridge – missed it – Fuck – I shouldn't have smoked that joint – I can't drive – Why is it so much harder for me to drive than everyone else? – Maybe cause you're stoned, Jack – I have to pee – When I'm stoned I can't pee if there's someone standing next to me in the other urinal – Why? – If I take one of these exits, maybe I won't find a bathroom anyway – That happened the last time and I drove around and wasted a half hour and still didn't go – It's just big old houses, not even a gas station – Won't do that again – There was that cop there following me around, mad-dogging me in his stupid cruiser – Couldn't even pull over and pee in the woods because of that fucker – It's like Rambo in First Blood *when the cop takes him across the bridge – He drives him out of town – Rambo gets pissed, he wasn't doing anything wrong – The cop should have left him alone –*

(Light a cigarette with some difficulty, recalling the scene, imagine that you're a Rambo-like figure entering a Westchester town for moment. Heart starts racing from nicotine and lucid Rambo fantasy. Try to calm down and look at road. Then resume thoughts:)

Who are these people driving? – Where do they all come from? – Lots of jazz musicians live around here – I heard that Michael Brecker lives here, and John Scofield – It must be that you grow out of living in the city and then you start a family and move to Westchester if you're a jazz musician – cool – Will I marry? – Will I have kids? – Freaks me out that idea – People with kids are kind of a drag – When they talk to you it's like they're tired – It's like they're sick of telling their kids what to do – They talk in that sing-song voice ho dee hum – I wish I was around for that jazz loft scene in the seventies and early eighties – Fred Hersch told me about that – All those guys like Richie Beirach and Dave Liebman playing "Impressions" all night long in those lofts in SoHo – I bet they did lots of coke – I wish I had that Chick Corea record Three Quartets *on cassette – Why didn't I make a cassette? Brecker is so killing on that – That's some of the best Brecker – Some people get snobby when they discover Joe Henderson and then they turn on Brecker – Stupid – Like all those beboppers at that jam session last week – They were trying to say that Coltrane screwed up jazz – Just young guys trying to sound old – People try to say stuff like it's a done deal like it's finalized – Want to tell them to stop talking – that they don't matter – but that's just me trying to sound final –*

Why do you have to stop liking one thing just because you discover another thing – It's like people who say you either like Brahms or you like Wagner but not both – But hmm that's sort of true because the reason why I like Brahms is kind of the reason I don't like Wagner – Siegfried Idyll is great, though – it sounds like "Stella by Starlight" at that one point – and parts of Tristan – and Parsifal – just too fucking long is all – who wants to sit for four hours or more? – not natural for the body – still would be cool to go to Bayreuth – weird how there's a waiting list for like five years to get in there – Would you really buy tickets for a concert five years in advance? – What if you didn't like Wagner in five years? – What if something came up? – You'd sell the tickets I guess –

(Drive, smoke. Resume:)

Fred is the only guy I know who still has a loft in SoHo now – I wish I had a loft and a Steinway B like him – He's got such a great set-up there – I like his cat, Spike – What does Spike think of that? He's got the same name as Fred's cat – Fred played that Brahms Intermezzo for me last lesson – pretty happening – he plays Brahms behind the beat like

Ashkenazy on that record with Itzhak Perlman – he calls Emanuel Ax "Manny" Ax – Remember Emanuel Ax and Yo-Yo Ma in the small shed at Tanglewood when you were at Merrywood? – Beethoven Cello Sonatas – Want to hear Brahms now, maybe Piano Trio in B Major, that's right here in the car – Where is it – Brahms' first Piano Trio, Opus 8 – He came out stomping – Johnny Brahms – He was like twenty when he wrote that – I'm that old now – Could I write something like that? – Nope – You can tell the guy who wrote the music for Cinema Paradiso *loved that B Major Trio – What's his name? – That's such a sad/happy movie – The end with the music is so sad, maybe it's too sad – Music can be sad but music in movies is sad and kind of clings to you – Maybe that isn't good – Maybe we don't have to feel sad just because it's a feeling expressed through whoever's artistic vision – Maybe I don't want to take that on – I've got enough of that feeling in reserve; don't need more – Yeah, but maybe the music in* Cinema Paradiso *isn't only sad – it's just hitting me that way because the sadness is already inside of me –*

Shit – I'm driving too slowly again; that guy behind me is high-beaming me – Fuck – What's that burning smell – like chemicals? – Shit, the cigarette ash again – That always happens – the wind – Damn, I can't find the ash – It's burning the rug – What evil shit do they put in the rug to make it smell like that when it burns? – Can't look for it and drive at the same time – What will happen? – Would the car actually burn down? – Would the engine explode? – What is it like burning to death? – Probably the worst death – They say freezing to death is comfortable – After a while you don't want to get saved – Your body creates like these opiates – It would be cool if they could synthesize that and you could get high on it, that feeling – but without dying – Burroughs wrote about shooting up different snake venoms –

It was always back and forth – wonderment and pleasure at anything and everything that would sort of spill over itself and turn into insecurity, paranoia, and downright ineptitude, or slide into random speculation. So being on a gig was the same kind of thing. Let's say it was the jam session I had at the former West End Gate up near Columbia's campus a year after I arrived in New York, in addition to its sister club the Village Gate downtown. I hired drummer Joe Farnsworth and bassist John Webber, with whom I felt a real rapport from playing with them in other settings, like with Peter Bernstein. We'd play the first set just trio, we'd play one tune the second set, and then open it up for other players. Joe and I would often go outside and smoke a joint between the first and second set. We'd start the tune, freshly baked, and at first it was great . . .

Man, Joe's feel is so good – I love the sizzle on that ride – He's been checking out some Art Taylor – Could stay grooving like this forever – I'm in it with him, we're locked up – Webber's line – when he stays up high like that walking and then drops down all of the sudden – so swinging – Perfect notes – We're locked – He hears the harmony I'm implying –

But then something would shift – it could be a small trifle, but it would set me off, and I couldn't come back – for, once you descend into pot paranoia, it's near impossible to find your way back to calmness and ease.

Are they rushing? Why is Joe doing that Philly Joe Jones rimshot thing on the four of every bar? Is he trying to tell me something? It feels like they're rushing – but no – that means I'm dragging – Shit – I can't keep up – If it was just a little slower – It's like it's right between two good tempos – Why did I call "September in the Rain"? – I sound corny – My feel is choppy – That lick sounded so stupid – I'm just playing this fake bebop shit – I'm a phony – What the fuck am I doing up here? – My dick is shrinking – Everybody's watching me – They know that I know that they know that it's lame – I'm blushing – Fuck – I wish I could just get up and split –

Just remembering those kinds of nights gives me butterflies in my stomach all over again.

When I was playing these gigs at clubs in front of an audience in my early days in New York, there was usually a certain amount of stress. I was learning on the bandstand. Even though I had great teachers, I learned so much about jazz – about *playing* jazz – through the trial-and-error experience of those gigs. The pressure came partially from not wanting to lay a turd in front of the public, but, perhaps even more, it came from wanting to impress the musicians who had asked me to play with them, just as it had with Larry in Hartford at the 880. They were people like Jesse or Peter, but also musicians like trumpeter Rebecca Franks and alto saxophonist Virginia Mayhew, who had gigs at clubs like the Angry Squire or the 55 Bar. They were my peers but a few years ahead of me in age and experience, and in hiring me they were giving me a break.

I was an established pothead already from high school, and would often be the one to rally the troops between sets to step outside, rolling a fat joint for everyone. This was a force of habit for me from years of pot smoking: a joint went with everything – it just made it all more interesting. But, in the high-pressure environment of that New York jazz scene there in the early 1990s, with everybody trying to outdo each other, everybody trying to be more authentic and badassed than the next guy, the high could turn another direction, and pot paranoia on the bandstand would kick in. It was characterized by a dry mouth, a feeling of weakness in the limbs, butterflies in the stomach, and an unsettling, emasculating retraction in the groin.

My first road gig came about halfway through that year, 1990, with Christopher Hollyday, the alto saxophonist wunderkind who was the same age as me at the New School. I had seen Chris at the 880 when I was in high school and we were both fifteen. He was playing all Bird's stuff, and it was really remarkable how he had that down. His dad took him all around doing gigs everywhere with pick-up rhythm sections. Now he was in New York and was more into Jackie McLean. He was really a fresh-faced kid when he arrived in New York. Peter Bernstein nicknamed him "Goose" because of this funny honking laugh he had.

Chris had a record contract with RCA Novus and invited me to join his band our second year at the New School together, and got me my first date as a sideman on a record of his called *The Natural Moment*. We recorded at Rudy Van Gelder's legendary studio in Hackensack, NJ, where so many records we loved had been recorded, by him. Van Gelder was a grouch that day, and the only words he spoke to me were: "Don't touch anything except the piano – especially not the cheesecloth on the mics!"

Chris and I un-enrolled for a semester, and I went on the road with him, my fellow Goon-straddler bassist John Webber and drummer Ron Savage from Boston where Chris was from. It was a fantastic time for me, often playing five or six nights a week at various clubs around the States and Canada for months at a time. I saw much of my own country for the first time. I began all that touring as one person, musically speaking, and came back another. Yet I only realized that when other friends of mine gave me that feedback – it was one of those phenomena in which you can't see for yourself how you've changed until someone else points it out to you. In broad strokes, I had been playing like McCoy Tyner with some people, like Herbie Hancock with other people, and like Wynton Kelly with others. When I came back, I had merged those influences: I started playing a style that was consistent whomever I played with. I no longer needed to be a chameleon. It was the beginning of my own style.

Hanging with Bill

> Those are people who died, died
> Those are people who died, died
> They were all my friends, and they died
>
> Jim Carroll

Three close buddies of mine – Bill, Kevin, and James – all died in their early twenties, all from a heroin overdose.

Bill was twenty-three when he died. I met him as a student at the New School. He was a guitarist. He came in without much of a jazz vocabulary and in a couple years he had a lot together. He often played with Sam Yahel, who was developing his thing on organ. He was already writing some nice tunes.

In the short but magical time I knew him, my second and third year in New York, we used to kick around together, enjoying that special, unplanned leisure that you can't capture in the same way as you grow older. A typical hang with Bill might start with getting a few "40s" – forty-ounce Budweiser beers in the big bottles – at a deli, usually in the East Village, which was our haunt. The guy at the register would always put them in a paper bag just the right size so you could carry it and drink on the street while you strolled.

We might buy a dime bag of mersh weed on 10th Street between 2nd and 1st Avenues. "Mersh" was short for "commercial," which was itself a vague slang word that referred to a certain "B"-level marijuana. It was cheap; you got more bulk for your money. It had more unsmokable seeds, though, and was all mashed up: the buds of the plants were not intact and you got little pieces of them, or, even worse, sometimes you just got a bag of green powder, as if it all had been put through a meat grinder. Commercial pot was the Chicken McNugget in the hierarchy of marijuana types – it came to you altered from its original form, and you were not sure exactly what you were smoking. The particular dime bag on 10th Street back then had a cherry-like flavor, certainly not natural to the plant. It was as if someone had sprayed Dr Pepper all over the pot. Some other kind of chemical taste was there as well, that made the throat sting. The high was characterized by a dull, droning buzz in the ears.

Bill showed me how to stuff it into a cigar loosened into a funnel shape and smoke blunts. He was a connoisseur of leisure, a teacher of sorts in the art of staying nonplussed by everything and enjoying life for all it had to offer, and a model of laid-back calm for me. We could spend the whole night playing pool or walking around Washington Square Park, watching the hustlers, a lot of times with Sam Yahel. I had a tight friendship with Sam, and three of us were always close by each other with some other guys. Sam was a decent pool player and could play on a real full-sized table, not just bar pool.

I sucked at pool. Bill was better but not up there with Sam. There was one pool hall where we'd play on University Place close to NYU, and another funkier one on 14th around 3rd Avenue. Sometimes, though, Sam took us to a place in Chelsea that was a whole different scene. We almost never actually shot pool ourselves there, and, if we did, we'd take a corner table, out of the fray. Mostly we hovered around and watched the show.

Pool hustlers were everywhere there – guys and girls who would rope someone into playing a set of nine-ball for money by pretending to suck, then snaring them into a game and destroying them. It was a tough gig: courting that person could take hours; and what if they were hustling, pretending to be a mark too? The guys were creepy and the girls were usually beautiful; they all seemed dangerous. I got butterflies when we went in the place.

Other times there were games between established players with no bull-shit. It could be up to $600 for a run to six. It was fascinating to sit and watch that sort of thing, and we could spend hours doing that. That place in Chelsea was open until 5:00 am, and a few times, after a night of rambling around, or maybe after hearing the late set at the Village Gate, we'd go and watch them play until the place closed.

Sam had a strong chess game as well. Often we'd walk into Washington Square Park in the late afternoon before the evening got under way. There were all the chess hustlers there and it was the same idea – they all knew each other and would play along with each other, pulling someone in for a game. They would let somebody win who was actually on the inside – just like a shill in "three-card Monte". But it wasn't really evil because you could already tell they all knew each other anyways. Let them con someone every now and then – it was their choice to sit down and play.

The money was much less – usually no more than $10 a game. A lot of times Raphael D'Lugoff was around. He was another guy like Sam, whose main talent and focus was jazz piano, but had this passion as well for chess. There were also players there who weren't hustlers but might be internation-ally ranked tournament players. Basically, Sam and Raffi played these high-ranked guys for a $5–10 lesson because they almost always lost. I loved the hustlers who would come down from Harlem, though, talking shit all the time while they beat you, slamming down the clock violently after their turn – they were scary and yet funny as hell. I still go to watch them whenever I'm down there in the park. I feel like they're the same guys who were there in 1990 – benevolent ghosts who never age, always there to give you a lesson and dust your ass with good nature.

At night, Bill and I would hit the bars in the East Village and Alphabet City. There was Lucy's across from Tompkins Square Park, also called Ludwiga's. Other favorites were the prosaically named Holiday Cocktail Lounge on St. Mark's between 1st and 2nd, where a large pour of any mid-range liquor was $2; or the International on 1st Avenue. It wasn't as exciting, but there was always Nightbirds on 2nd Avenue and 5th, right below where I lived later with Sarah and the Goons.

Lucy's was our favorite. It was full of NYU girls trying to look tough and skinny androgynous guys their age who looked lost. The jukebox would play stuff like Joy Division or Violent Femmes. There were always lone-dog types in their late twenties or thirties as well – older dudes full of ink and hair gel trying to make a play on those fresh girls and pull them away from the bumbling, navel-gazing guys they were with. The lone dogs would man the pool table, winning round after round, beckoning people for a game, like some sacrificial ritual. The English actor Tim Roth used to hang out solo at Lucy's and played decent pool. He had recently gotten some fame in Quentin Tarantino's *Reservoir Dogs* and everyone wanted to go up and recite lines with him ("Why do *I* have to be Mr. Pink?"), but he put out such a vibe of cool dismissal and badassedness that nobody bothered him except a few daring ones who silently played pool with him.

We'd walk west down Bleecker Street and wind up at the Village Gate. The Gate (now Le Poisson Rouge and a CVS pharmacy) had three floors, and on the ground floor – the "terrace" – there was a good piano player playing six nights a week with a trio or sometimes duo. I watched them there and soaked up everything they were doing with their trios: pianists like Larry Goldings, Kevin Hays, Bill Charlap, Danilo Perez, Bill Carrothers, or Mike LeDonne – guys a few years ahead of me in age and experience. They all made an impact on me, particularly Kevin, Bill Charlap, and Larry. I wanted to play all that sophisticated, slick stuff, and make it swing and feel relaxed the way they did.

Sometimes there were horn players there, maybe from an older generation, like trumpeter Tommy Turrentine, the underrated brother of Stanley, the great tenor saxophone stylist. Tommy was a real grouch and intimidating. I had that hang-up about comping, and, when I watched the confidence that Larry Goldings had behind a tough guy like Tommy, I was impressed. I thought: you have to exude confidence when you're comping; you have to be part of the company and walk upright.

There were older piano masters whom we watched, like my teacher at the time Junior Mance, and also Kirk Lightsey and Herman Foster; we tried to absorb what they were doing. Each one of them was unique in every way: a unique swing feel, a unique touch and sound, unique chord shapes, a unique take on the blues and the way it fit into everything they played, unique tune choices. We watched how they paced their sets – did they start uptown, or build up to a fast tempo a few tunes in? On the ballads, did they go into double time on their solos, or did they really keep it a ballad? We watched the way they did or didn't interact with the audience. We watched how they drank. I watched how they smoked, what brand. The singer/pianist Andy Bey was often at the Gate as well, and he really rubbed off on me – the way he phrased those melodies in his voice, long and drawn-out, holding on to the sweet notes, all the while swinging hard in his comping.

Behind the piano there was a back entrance to the terrace, and you could walk in and stay there, spying on the piano player by peeking through the

Spike Wilner playing at Augie's
Photo: Charles Ruggiero

balusters that framed the back of the stage, trying to grab his technique. We all did that with the masters and the guys a little ahead of us. If one of us was playing, sometimes we'd mess with each other on purpose. Between tunes, you'd clear your throat loudly, standing right behind whoever was playing, and they'd turn around and see you there, and then get distracted, or try to start playing flashier. Sam, Spike Wilner, Larry Goldings, and I did that to each other.

Spike was a big part of our crew. He had an apartment on Bleecker right across the street from the Gate with a baby grand that took up most of a small room full of vinyl, books, and sheet music, and a very fat tabby cat named Phineas named after the great Phineas Newborn. Spike and I were aligned with our listening at that time, sharing the same obsessions. One of them was pianist Red Garland. We would set the metronome at ninety-six – the magic number – and comp for each other on blues for hours, in that Garland zone. As the proprietor of Smalls and Mezzrow, Spike has managed to keep some of that feeling that was there in the Gate and other clubs.

The Gate was a place where a really good piano player who didn't have a huge name could go have a week to play. You could also afford to see those piano players if you didn't have a huge wallet. I remember that in my first year in New York City, Herbie Hancock and Oscar Peterson – two of my idols – were both at the Blue Note, one block up from the Gate, with their trios. The cover for one set of Herbie Hancock was $90 and for Oscar Peterson it was a whopping $120. That was in 1989. I just didn't have that kind of bread, and didn't get to see them that time around. And that's with no hard feelings against those two great, timeless piano players – they should have gotten paid as much, and no less.

There was Bradley's, of course. That was the piano room par excellence – not only Hank Jones and Tommy Flanagan whom I mentioned earlier played there but a host of other greats, including Barry Harris, Kenny Barron, and Cedar Walton. I heard them all at Bradley's, and they all left a strong mark on me through their example. Bradley's itself was not entirely free from jive. It had a clubby crowd, with the pianists holding court, and then a whole bunch of other hangers-on – a lot of them idiots, talking shit all the time, and always going to the bathroom to snort more and more coke. Bradley's had a late set until 2:30 am like the Gate, and there was always a lot of blow around then. These guys would have their Hennessy and draft beer up front at the bar, and then make trips to the bathroom and do a "bump" – a quick snort with a little of the cognac on their nose to add to the rush.

I enjoyed a bump myself back then, although I usually couldn't afford it. Nothing is worse for an evening than cocaine, though. All that fake camaraderie, all that false enthusiasm, all that amped-up nonsense. And then it's 5:00 am and you're all there scraping together enough cash and trying to see if you can wake up what's-his-name for another gram, nobody talking much anymore. It's a nowhere scene. If you decide to go out and do coke for a night, you should just put on a shirt before you leave your front door that says, "I'm a dickhead." Then everyone knows what to expect from you. Often when I went to Bradley's, it seemed like I'd get saddled up at the bar next to some incoherent type who was telling me how I didn't know shit, and how he "saw Coltrane live in 1965" and how there was "nothing happening anymore in jazz," who did a young punk like me think I was, people died for this music, blah blah. Bradley's had its share of belligerent, sociopathic windbags, all of them revved up on that white powder and cognac.

When I was able to find a good spot and listen to the music, though, it was magnificent to be there, and was second only to the Vanguard. A couple times, I sat at the edge of the bar not even two feet from Billy Higgins's sizzle ride cymbal when he played with Cedar Walton and David Williams in that peerless trio. Or the same thing with Ben Riley, playing with Kenny Barron's trio with Buster Williams or Ray Drummond on bass. Those groups were an aesthetic to which I aspired in those years, and remain a strong model. It was the sound of modern jazz for us – quietly cooking, sophisticated, subtle, melodic, egoless playing – all with this huge feeling of swing.

As much as those great pianists influenced and inspired me, the real action for me, the real mystery, was often in watching the drummers. It was the drumming that brought me into jazz. It was drummer Jimmy Cobb's ride cymbal that brought me into "So What" on Miles Davis's *Kind of Blue*. Drummer Art Taylor's ride cymbal locked me into great records from the later half of the '50s, from stylists like Gene Ammons. He put the magic vibe on those Red Garland Trio records and early Coltrane dates on the Prestige label. It was drummer Ed Blackwell who pulled me into Ornette Coleman records and the Eric Dolphy/Booker Little Quintet records. It was drummer Billy Higgins's ride cymbal that hooked me on so many important, great records, most of them on Blue Note: records by Hank Mobley, Lee Morgan, Dexter Gordon, and other greats. It was drummer Elvin Jones who held me in ecstasy on records like *Coltrane Live at Birdland*.

I had been amassing and listening to LPs with those drummers for a good five years, often with Joel Frahm, growing up and becoming a jazz snob in West Hartford during high school. We listened for hours together, afternoons after school, digging that music, letting it seep in. Now I was in New York City, hearing a musician like Billy Higgins live, in person. That transition from hearing a musician on a record from decades earlier, to hearing and seeing that same musician live, here and now, and being so close to them that you could reach out and touch them – that can't be overestimated. I had always wondered: what does it *look* like, when someone swings that hard? I can't put it into words, but it was electrifying, especially with Billy Higgins. There was this poise. He would look to the side most of the time rather than straight ahead in my recollection, somewhere just over his riveted, magical Zildjan K ride cymbal. Often, he turned just his eyes, especially when he punctuated and answered ideas from Cedar Walton. It was grace in action.

The Gate was more relaxed than Bradley's: there wasn't this whole pretentious aura of history bearing down on you there. That vibe never came from the musicians who played at Bradley's. It came from the hangers-on at the bar. The flipside of the Gate, though, was that there wasn't much of a quiet policy at all, and a lot of the times your audience was whoever walked in off the street to have a drink and continue their conversation. I remember one weekend night I played there. Geraldo Rivera, at the height of his cheesy fame, came in for the late set already drunk, flanked by two giggling younger women dressed like they were working. He yelled and laughed at his own jokes through most of the set – quiet ballad no exception – and kept on walking up to the bandstand, belligerent and glib all at once, talking nonsense to us. Nobody did much of anything about it. It was just the vibe of the place, because there was a low cover charge and they had to keep some heads in there, buying drinks. Raphael D'Lugoff, who booked the Gate, was a great guy to give us all a shot – we younger players weren't a big draw by any means – and he paid us quite fairly considering. He understood pianists because he was one of us, and would often play in a duo setting in some of the matinee gigs. Between his support and the people in the audience who were there to listen to the music, the Gate was a great place to be a young jazz musician, and a refuge for one of any age who wasn't commercially big.

Bill and I would take the 1 train up to Augie's at 106th Street and Broadway. Augie's was a college bar haunted mostly by Columbia and Manhattan School

Augie's, 1991
Photo: Charles Ruggiero

of Music students – both campuses were just a few blocks up Broadway. Drummer Leon Parker was the one who started jazz at Augie's. He simply went in there and asked the owner, Augie (or Gus, as he was usually called), if they wanted music there. There was no piano or system so everything had to be brought in, and the band squeezed into the back corner, which became a stage of sorts. A tradition was born and Augie's became an important breeding ground for young musicians during that time. Soon after the great bassist Christian McBride arrived fresh-faced in New York from Philadelphia, Jesse Davis pulled him in for a few gigs with us. Christian had it all together already then, aged eighteen. Augie's closed for a spell and then reopened as Smoke, one of the important New York clubs of today.

There was music at Augie's every night. Leon started with different groups that he led, and often he played with Larry Goldings, Jesse, and Peter Bernstein. Gus was always there, kind of gruff and friendly at the same time, but mostly gruff, and would play chess a lot. There were a few good chess players among the musicians and some of them would play Gus with the clock. I recall that drummer Eric McPherson, who played a lot with Jesse Davis's groups there, and of course Sam Yahel, who had a weekly organ trio slot, could both hang with Gus and beat him if he was drunk.

The band made money mostly from "passing the basket." The band members would alternate with this task, making their way around the room right after the set with a basket, asking for a contribution from the audience. On a good night on the weekend, you could take in as much as $100 a set, but

Saturday night at Augie's, 1988. Jesse Davis's band, with drummer Eric McPherson, a very young Christian McBride on bass, and me on the Fender Rhodes. The first time I heard Christian was that first night I played with him, and he blew me and everyone else away: "Who is this kid from Philadelphia? *Damn!* . . ."

that was high – it was mostly around $40 and if the bar was empty it could be no more than $5 or $10. Gus didn't give us much money on top of the basket pass, and, to be fair, he wasn't being particularly tight-fisted. It was just the economics of the place: it was small, they didn't charge much for drinks, he had to pay a staff, and a lot of the time it wasn't full. On a good weekend night you might walk out of there with eighty bucks, on a bad night as little as fifteen.

Still, Gus was often cheap. One Saturday night, the pianist Tardo Hammer was grousing him from the bar: "Come on, Gus – look at what a full house the band has – everybody buying drinks, making money for the place. Why don't you buy the musicians a round of drinks?" He said it in a loud voice so everyone around the bar could hear it.

Gus sat gazing at the chessboard, not responding. Tardo pestered him some more and we all waited to see whether he would get a reaction. Finally, without even raising his head, Gus pronounced succinctly: "Okay, I'll tell you what: a round of water for the musicians – *no ice!*" It was ruthless but we had to laugh.

A lot of what you got in the basket at Augie's depended on how you passed it. I was horrible at that task when I played there– I was stoned a lot of the time and wouldn't look people in the eye, shuffling up to them and mumbling,

On the Rhodes at Augie's, with
the trusty basket standing by
Photo: Charles Ruggiero

"Would you like to make a contribution to the musicians?" in a soft voice, so as not to bother the conversation at the table. Half of the time I was completely ignored. Other guys like Jesse Davis or drummer Joe Farnsworth were much better at bringing something back for the band. Jesse would use shame effectively, guilt-tripping people if they pretended they didn't see him with the basket: "You know, this music is our *livelihood*. We just played *from our heart and soul* for you." He'd just stare them down until they'd deliver a few dollars. I didn't have the courage to do that. Joe was simply belligerent – "Come on, folks! What's the matter – you didn't like us?" He'd hover over a table, menacingly. It worked. If I came back with only a few singles, sometimes Joe would just send me out again. "Mehls, cut the crap – get back out there and get some more beans in the basket. Come on, Mehls."

Larry Goldings was someone I watched closely as a piano player, but at Augie's he had a monophonic Korg MS-20 and a Yamaha DX7. He played basslines on the synth and used a Hammond organ patch on the DX. This was the humble beginning of Larry Goldings, the jazz organist. He went on to master the real Hammond B-3 organ, and found his own sound on that instrument. Larry quietly gave jazz organ playing an update over the next several years, in particular with what would become a long-standing trio, with Peter Bernstein and drummer Bill Stewart.

Sam Yahel, Bill, myself, and others would go to hear them often. Bill loved Pete's playing and was soaking it all up, Sam was getting inspired by Larry's organ approach, and we all were taken by Bill Stewart, who had a style already at that young age that was all his own: he played with absolute confidence and originality, and the things he was doing with the time and meter were fresh and new. That was a band, those three guys. Every one of them on equal footing, nobody holding anybody else's pants up, each one with a completely distinct voice that blended into the fabric of the trio sound. I remember several nights at Augie's with Bill, Sam, and other musicians, watching them play to a packed house, to a rapt audience. There was that one time Pete just blew us away with his melody and solo on "I Fall in Love Too Easily," playing with such gravity and depth – Bill and I just watched and we were in tears. I got to share all that stuff with Bill, all that music.

Bill was my drinking dog too. He could keep up with me when no one else could and we'd leave people in the dust and keep on going, running the whole night until we would collapse. Then we'd wake up and drink some coffee from the deli and get a couple things done during the day, and by six in the evening we were at it again, hanging out in Washington Square with our Budweiser 40s in paper bags, pondering what the night would bring. I was drinking because I wanted to be somewhere else than where I was, and I wanted to blot out something I was feeling. I didn't want to feel stuff – I felt too much already and wanted to dull it. Bill made me happy, just being around him. He was charismatic and had girls around him a lot of the time and sometimes I felt snubbed because he'd go off with one of them instead of hanging with me. He was solid. You could tell him everything and he wouldn't get phased; he'd have some good advice for you – a sage with a 40 and a blunt. Sometimes he came off a little bit like Sean Penn's Spicoli character in *Fast Times at Ridgemont High* – "Duuuuude!" – but he was really smart and had a sharp sense of humor. When he wanted to he could knock somebody down off a pedestal with a choice phrase. He didn't do that too much, though, because he wasn't mean.

Dream about Bill. I'm hanging out in some place I've never been before. There are a bunch of people there that Bill seems to know, but I don't know who they are. Bill is there, though, and I'm filled with happiness when I see him. A couple of times I have my arm around his shoulder like when we'd pal around the East Village together, and I can feel him again; for a moment it's almost like he was never gone. Since I'm so happy, I'm kind of giddy, and I just keep on talking and telling him stuff. I'm cracking jokes with everyone else there, hamming it up. Bill smiles all the time but he's quieter than I remember. I don't mind that, though, because he's there and that's enough and everything seems all right again. So Bill and I hang out with these people who know me but I don't know their names or who they are. They are kind of like Bill, though – they let me talk and crack jokes, but don't talk.

The time goes by and then I say to Bill that I should get back home; I should get back to the city, and let's go together. When I look back at Bill, he's moved away from me, he's standing apart from me now. He just shakes his head to say, no, he can't go with me. He's still smiling but it's a different kind of smile – not really sad, but like a stern smile. I realize that he can't come back with me and I realize that he can never come back and that I met him in this special place with all these other people like him, just this one time; that he came to me one more time to let me say goodbye to him. But it's too fast and now I don't know what to say, and he's moving farther away from me and he's smiling like that and then –

I wake up and I'm crying. I didn't realize in the dream that he couldn't come back, that it was only one last time. So I spent the whole dream talking shit and being silly. It's just like how I didn't realize when he was alive that I'd have to say goodbye to him, so I never did. He just left. You never really get to say goodbye to people the way you should, not even in your dreams.

Bill wasn't a heroin addict at all. The first time he did it was with me. I wanted to turn him on to it, so I kept asking him to do it, us together. He finally sniffed just a little bit and barfed. Some people use opiates for years and survive, other people use them for a while and then overdose when they get something stronger than they expected. I wished I was there with him the night he overdosed; maybe I could have brought him back. I couldn't shake it, that I pushed him to do it with me, that first time.

After Bill died, we were all shell-shocked, and the next few days were like living through a bad dream, but not waking up. Bill? He was happy; he was strong. There was never any darkness following him around – just light and joy. I felt real grief and loss for the first time in my life.

The day we heard the news, a group us met in a bar together, ordering a few pitchers of draft. Sam, tenor saxophonist and close friend Grant Stewart, a few others close to Bill, Sarah, and I tucked into a corner table in a bar in the West Village. There we were, a little huddled pack, nursing our loss, feeling more than anything else that he was taken away from *us*.

A few days later, our group drove up to Massachusetts outside of Boston where Bill had grown up, for his funeral. When we arrived in the church, it was a huge gathering of people – hundreds, many of them our age. They were all these friends he had from high school. All at the same time, we started crying, really deeply, before the service started. I don't think I had cried like that ever in my life.

When we saw all those other kids, and when we saw Bill's parents and his brother and sister, and all those people from his town, we realized that we weren't the only ones who lost him, that he hadn't only been taken away from us. Besides the grief, I also felt shame – ashamed that I had been selfish about my love for my friend. It's like I didn't deserve him. That's a feeling I had a lot in the following years, even as I couldn't name it: the feeling that I might love other people, but didn't deserve their love back. I knew it wasn't true with Bill but I still felt it.

I put something together about love in that moment – about how you can't keep it for yourself, about how sacred it is, and how conditional it is – not conditional because of our various demands on the other, as the word is usually used, followed by the charge to give love unconditionally. Sure, that was something to shoot for. What I mean, though, is: conditional on how long we'll be here, conditional on death, whenever it comes.

The live sublime

My third year in New York City, aged twenty, the year that Bill and I were close, I moved from St. Mark's Place into a studio apartment on Jones Street in the West Village, smack in the middle of jazz heaven. Surrounding me within several blocks were blue-chip jazz clubs: the Village Vanguard, Sweet Basil, the 55 Bar, the Blue Note, the Village Gate, and Visiones. Bradley's, Fat Tuesdays, Condon's, and the Knitting Factory were only a ten-minute walk away as well.

There was so much great music around me every night. Often, there were tough decisions to make. Pianists Tommy Flanagan, Cedar Walton, Kenny Barron, Barry Harris, and Hank Jones were all titans, at the top of my list. They played regularly at Bradley's in a trio or duo setting for week-long engagements. I watched their touch, their poise at the instrument, their complete relaxation. I listened to their individual timbres, feeling the unique collective swing of each trio – the way the beat bounced around the piano, bass, and drums.

At Sweet Basil, there was a wider range of instrumentation and style. It was the place to see hard bop veterans like Art Farmer or Lou Donaldson, Mal Waldron and Steve Lacy's trance-like duo, and Cecil Taylor's wild Feel Trio. Gil Evans had a Monday-night slot there with his pared-down big band which included all-round keyboardist and arranger Gil Goldstein, a friendly mentoring presence for us early on, and an important teacher for many at the New School. Just up four blocks at the Vanguard, any number of exalted configurations come to mind, like drummer Paul Motian's unrepeatable bass-less trio with Joe Lovano and Bill Frisell. Or there was that week Ed Blackwell played with Don Pullen and George Adams, whose co-led quartet were at the Vanguard regularly. Blackwell's drumming changed everything for me. He showed how you could play in a formally unhinged context, yet create your own shifting grid, one with simplicity and integrity which nevertheless moved easily within the free current of the music. And it felt so good. It had been one thing to hear him do that on those hallmark recordings with the Ornette Coleman Quartet, but the live experience was something else.

The sublime as I experienced it, with its heady duality of recognition and fear, was a *live* sublime in these memorable performances. Blackwell was quietly majestic at the drums: unapproachable, really, in his authority; yet welcoming on some elemental level, like fire coals on a bed of earth. These kinds of visceral impressions did not come from listening to records. The physical immediacy of the musicians made for a far more sensual intake, one that was not only aural/visual. As strange as it sounds, I often felt that I could even *smell* the music. It might be brown liquor: Lou Donaldson's groups, particularly with the joyous addition of Dr. Lonnie Smith on Hammond B-3 organ (and sometimes Peter Bernstein, who had one of his first gigs with an older master playing with Lou), had the bouquet of the Paddy Irish Whiskey I had recently discovered on a tour in Ireland – sweet but not cloying, bracing. Mal Waldron and Steve Lacy were more like Scotch: smokier, and there was also the real smell of smoke that came off Waldron's black tobacco cigarette which remained inexplicably lit for the duration of the set. In Blackwell's case, there was indeed an earth smell to his playing: late summer in a forest, the ground still damp from a recent rain.

Joe Henderson played at Fat Tuesdays, often with the great Al Foster on drums. You could hear trumpeter Harry "Sweets" Edison at Condon's, still in fine form. And every Wednesday night, unless he was on tour, guitarist Mike Stern's trio was playing marathon sets at the 55 Bar practically down the street from my place, usually with electric bassist Jeff Andrews and Adam Nussbaum, whom I knew already from the 880 days in Hartford: a powerful drummer who cracked a whip under me in a few sessions I played with him at the New School. There was a $5 cover charge and you could stay as long as you wanted if you bought two drinks. Most of us were under the legal drinking age of twenty-one, but we never got carded at any of those places in those days, even the baby-faces among us. New York City was much more anarchic then. It all began to change when Rudy Giuliani became mayor in 1994.

Particular sets, like the one with Ed Blackwell the first night I saw him, were one-off transformations for me. I would come out of the club having experienced a musical sensation I didn't know existed an hour-and-a-half earlier. Then I would think: "*That* is the real shit, what just took place. That's what I need to get in my own playing." Maybe that's the reason people become narrow in their taste as they get older – they're chasing that beautiful, incomparable initial rupture, and they want to get back to the thing that broke them free in the first place. You can't.

Those piano players I heard at Bradley's and elsewhere were distinct from each other, but they were all appealing because they had this absolutely relaxed, dancing feeling in their music. I wanted not only to play like that; I wanted to *be* like that. I wanted to carry that coolness with me. I suspected that it had something to do not only with the notes they played but the lives they led. I was projecting, or I wasn't – I think part of what I felt, intuitively, was also their experience outside of the music.

There was this chasm of life between them and me. They were elders but, far from being stuffy or didactic, these elders were *hipper* than I was, not the other way around. There was always that sophistication in their playing, a subtlety that was regal. It demanded your respect, without any words or history lessons. It was all there in the music. Whether they played or whether they stood at the bar fraternizing, they seemed to be free from earthly burdens even as they were solidly on the earth, tasting its fruit with mirth.

I was taking all that in – not just being influenced by the music but also checking out the attitude: the way the musicians carried themselves. Mal Waldron smoked those brown cigarettes while he played in the minimalist approach I had loved on records, building up just one or two ideas for a large span of time, creating a trance with his chugging swing. Billy Higgins had this particular gesture as he answered Cedar's ideas, chopping wood with his fat snare drum – like a shock of energy that snapped through his shoulders and released outwards with a nod of his head. He played with a smile like Buddha – one of delighted bliss, above mere excitement.

They were *in* the music completely, yet they were observing it, manipulating it exactly how they wanted, together as a unit. There was something almost cruel about the casual way they achieved that. How could they not lose themselves in the grandeur of it all? How could they not become entranced by their own creation? That power seemed almost dangerous – like a sword only they could hold. So it brought me a kind of fear beholding it. The live sublime they embodied could be a quiet insurrection – taking my power away as a listener, leaving me whipped, standing by the bar. They achieved it in the music with cold-blooded insouciance, like sipping whiskey, or waiting at a bus stop.

When Cedar Walton would walk off the stage, I might meet his eye before I turned away quickly, not wanting to stare. I was cowed by all those masters, and never approached them. Somewhere in me, though, the music was seeping in. I was going to have that some day. It would settle into me with time and I would speak it with the grace they had. I may have lacked self-confidence in so many areas of my life, but I always knew: that's my terrain, that's within my grasp. Not the way they are doing it – I couldn't do that – but something my own that would come out of it. I just had to stay with the music I loved, and be strong in it. And, even though I didn't want to turn square and get boxed in, I also had to stay loyal to that, and not start playing some candy-assed crap that wasn't real. Looking back, holding to those guidelines was never difficult. It was the rest of my life that was falling apart.

Trio

Shortly after the move to Jones Street, I began playing with drummer Leon Parker and bassist Ugonna Okegwo. I knew Leon already from Augie's, and had worked with him already a number of times with Peter Bernstein, Jesse Davis, and others. Around that time, Jesse used me on his record *Young at Art*, with Pete, Leon, and the late great bassist Dwayne Burno. Dwayne had an uncompromising, compelling approach to bass playing that was all his own, one that many more people should have heard. I was thrilled when Jesse invited me to record with him, and Leon cracked a whip under all of us.

Before we stared playing trio, Leon, Ugonna, and I came together through trombonist Steve Davis, whom I knew from the 880 days in Hartford. "Stevie D," as the Goons quickly dubbed him, had come to New York, and was already playing with what would be Art Blakey's final Jazz Messengers group. Steve had a particular vision for a band: a quintet with tenor saxophonist Mark Turner and himself on the front line, and Ugonna, Leon, and me in the rhythm section. He wrote some beautiful tunes for us, and Mark and I brought in a few. We had a collection of nice gigs he organized, and in a studio we recorded a record's worth of material, which has never been released. Playing with Steve and Mark was a gas: it was a unique front line, the way they were foils for each other.

I felt something with Leon and Ugonna immediately. There was an immediate collective focus. It felt like a strong rhythm section, but also like a trio. Leon was an instigator if there ever was one. His moves weren't arbitrary, though – he had an arranger's eye, and, a bit like Blakey himself, played like the leader, changing the whole scenery in one swoop. It was exciting, but what really attracted me to Leon was his feel. He was tipping in the great tradition of drummers I loved, like Jimmy Cobb, Tony Williams, Louis Hayes, or Joe Chambers – sitting a bit on top of the beat on that ride cymbal, with absolute focus. Everything was consolidated in that cymbal.

Leon had already turned heads at Augie's where he played with no hi-hat. In our trio, he went even further: he played *only* ride cymbal. That's right: nothing else on stage except him and a ride. The bill was: Brad Mehldau, piano; Ugonna Okegwo, bass; Leon Parker, cymbal. I never missed all the other drums. He supplied everything – texture, backbeat, arrangemental kicks, dynamic and timbral variety – with that cymbal. Ugonna had an amazing open-ended energy, with his own kind of percolating articulation on the bass which worked great with Leon's beat, and I loved the way he played under me. Leon and I both brought in some arrangements. The ones of mine foreshadowed the kind of rhythmic strategies I would explore subsequently in the trio format. There was some magic in that first trio, for sure.

I met Mario Rossy and Perico Sambeat my first year at the New School, and Mario introduced me to his younger brother Jorge, who would go on

With Leon and Ugonna at the Village Gate
Photo: Charles Ruggiero

to become a central part of my musical life. They brought me over to Spain, where I spent a fair amount of time during 1992–93 playing in clubs like the Café Central in Madrid, La Cova del Drac and the Jamboree in Barcelona, where the Rossys were from, and Café Del Mar in Castellón, close to Perico's home city of Valencia. The Jamboree has a history, including stints from the great tenor saxophonist Booker Ervin and other expats who traveled through Europe during the '70s and '80s. Two records of that quartet were released on Fresh Sound Records: *New York–Barcelona Crossing*, Volumes. 1 and 2, recorded at the Jamboree. Perico invited me to play on a date of his, *Ademuz*, which combined jazz and flamenco music in a new way. Perico was an influence on me, the way he wrote and led a band.

Jorge, Mario, and I began to play trio as well, and eventually recorded *When I Fall in Love*, in 1993, named for the classic Heyman and Young ballad included on the record. It was a live date, recorded from one night at the La Cova del Drac. La Cova was the favorite club of the Catalonian pianist Tete Montoliu, one of Spain's finest jazz musicians, who came down to sit in that week. One of my most cherished gigs was there a few years later, led by an idol of mine – tenor saxophonist Johnny Griffin – with Mario, Jorge, and I as the rhythm section.

When I Fall in Love would be my first trio record, although it wasn't solely mine. Jorge, Mario, and I were a cooperative; I brought in several tunes, but not all of them. Jorge in particular had lots of ideas as well and organized a lot of the playing situations; we called ourselves the Mehldau–Rossy Trio. Fresh Sound Records, which had been started by Jordi Pujol, had largely been a reissue label, but *When I Fall in Love* was an early product of its "New Talent" series, which focused on younger musicians at the beginning of their careers. In the ensuing years, Pujol went on to record musicians from my generation who grew into influential players: musical peers of mine like Mark Turner, Kurt Rosenwinkel, Ethan Iverson, Chris Cheek, Avishai Cohen, and Seamus Blake, to name just a few. Pujol, like Jerry Teekens at Criss Cross, had good ears, and captured a fertile cross-pollenization that was taking place between New York and Barcelona. Fresh Sound also raised the bar for smaller labels in terms of their visual package: the cover art was often beautiful, reflecting its Barcelona roots and employing artists influenced by Catalonian modernists like Miró. The label had a vibe.

Tunes did not come quickly then. The drink and drugs hampered the creative flow. I had begun to find a compositional voice, though, and it came out on that first trio record, on things like "At a Loss" and "Convalescent." There was also an incipient ballad approach unfolding, like on the title track, with extended piano cadenzas on the front or back end of the tune. The ballad became the emotional climax of the set as I went on playing trio, either placed penultimately or at the very end, and the cadenza in turn became its inner center.

Letting that emotional centerpiece lie at the end of the set, and not the middle, was an idea I took from Mahler, who ended his Third and Ninth Symphonies with slow, climactic final movements. I wanted sharp contrasts between tunes, and looked to the multi-movement symphonic structure of the Beethoven, Brahms, and Mahler to which I was listening. In this way I could achieve the vibrant interaction among the three of us I valued so much, yet still descend into that interiority, and share the loneliness with the public. In those three composers' orchestration, there was a dialectic between public and private music: the whole symphony could be this churning mass of humanity, and then suddenly a solo voice might arise out its fabric, for a scene change with no segue. That jarring effect made sense to me. I could be a Cain leading a tribe, and in the next moment be the kid whispering out from the tollbooth. I was laying down the model for my next long-standing trios: interaction, retraction, and finally reconciliation. I would be among others without trepidation, and alone without despair. In the music, I could integrate all those voices. I was the same person speaking both of them, over the course of a seventy-five-minute set, and, importantly: people seemed to like him.

Jorge brought in an arrangement of "I Didn't Know What Time It Was," in 5/4 time signature, which made it on the record. He had the idea of splitting some of the 5/4 bars into four beats, which had an exciting, destabilizing effect. There was one important conversation I remember we had early on, where he showed me the nuts and bolts of that: fourth-grade fraction stuff really, greatest common denominators. Connecting the arithmetic with the musical application was a game changer for me, though. There was an investigation of odd meters and rhythmic subdivisions taking place in the broader scene, and, as it continued, it blossomed into creative output, becoming an important facet of the music, moving it forward.

Odd meters themselves were not new, but the way many of us were approaching them was. Not surprisingly, the forward motion came from drummers, some of the most important of our generation. Jeff "Tain" Watts was a trailblazing instigator already in Wynton and Branford's groups. Tain had internalized things that Elvin Jones was doing in prior decades. Elvin, it seemed to me, and Tony Williams as well, played unusual subdivisions on the elemental, intuitive level; in any case, it wasn't something you could always notate because it was a little different every time, and came out "between the cracks." Tain brought a new specificity to Elvin's innovation, so, if you carefully studied what he was doing, you might grab some of the numerical nuts and bolts of it. Far from staying there, merely reporting on Elvin, he folded it back into his own playing, and made it breathe in his own new way. This was a feature of our generation. We did a fair amount of fieldwork on what had come before, but the best ones managed to move the music forward. The forward motion was not necessary a revolutionary rupture the way it had been with Coltrane's band. It was more incremental. But it was there, and there was fire to it.

Drummer Bill Stewart, whom we saw regularly at Augie's with Peter Bernstein and Larry Goldings, was another innovator. Pete had a tune called "Jive Coffee" which they played regularly. We all knew it by heart. He had taken the chord structure from the standard "Tea for Two" and placed it in a 5/4 time signature. The melody was signature Pete – he already had his own melodic and harmonic sense then – and Pete and Larry's solos were always killing. The grand slam, though, was at the end of the tune. Pete and Larry would stay on the funky vamp that framed the whole tune, and Bill would unleash a solo that was always breathtaking – inserting and developing ideas over the vamp that were at times complex, at other times quirky and humorous in their bald simplicity, like when he would play something very "square" in 4/4 that would continuously hiccup over the 5/4 barline.

I was inspired by the drum solo gambit in "Jive Coffee" and further developed the approach later on with my trios, writing a more dynamic part for Larry and I to play behind Jorge's solo on "All the Things You Are," giving Jeff Ballard something to dance around and spar with on Nick Drake's "Day Is Done," or interspersing our vamp for him with my own solo, in trading fashion, like on my tune "Fit Cat."

When Pete and Larry held steady on their vamp, Bill could go as crazy as he wanted on his solo, and the listener was invited to still feel the 5/4 meter. I wanted to write and play in that crazy/controlled canvas. These meters became a normative feature in jazz, to the point where some musicians would grouse, "Can't anyone write a tune in four anymore?" Nowadays, talented young musicians eat 5/4 and 7/4 for lunch with ease, and are doing the same kind of exploration/normalization with ever more complex meters.

The 5/4 meter already had a pedigree for decades in one of the most famous jazz tunes ever: "Take Five," by the Dave Brubeck Quartet with Paul Desmond, Eugene Wright, and Joe Morello. The Brubeck group held to the infectious vamp throughout the entire tune, which split the bar into a 3+2 subdivision. What we were trying to achieve was an internalization of that subdivision, whereby we could refer to it less overtly in the soloing, until at moments the subdivision in the bar dissolved, and you could then "float" over the barline freely, just the way Bird could float his beautiful melodies over the barline in 4/4. I was trying to bring the kind of loose phrasing I loved so much from Barry Harris and Tommy Flanagan into this context. Jorge suggested a way to practice this, by taking any classic standard that we loved, placing it in an odd meter, and then try to play the melody with the same laid-back openness that we achieved with ease in the normal meter. That bore some fruit, not just in "I Didn't Know What Time It Was" but also in our performances of "It Might As Well Be Spring," "All the Things You Are," and "Alone Together," all in 7/4.

Another rhythmic strategy that developed among our generation was metric modulation. The idea was to imply a decrease or increase in tempo, yet not actually change how fast the measures and their corresponding harmony went by in the original tempo. The ratio of increase had to be an uneven one: that is, a ratio other than double or half the original. Otherwise, you were simply going into double time or half time, which was nothing unconventional. Often the ratio was a "dotted" 1.5, and you can hear Jorge, Mario, and I working that into the first few choruses of my solo on "Anthropology" on *When I Fall in Love*. This was an approach that had been touched on already in Miles's 1960s quintet, where you could hear Tony Williams and Ron Carter breaking off into a new tempo that was slower but not quite half, on *Live at the Plugged Nickel*. That record was big for just about everyone I was hanging out with at the time. So, again, we were trying to codify and specify something unbridled and off-the-cuff we had heard from those earlier greats.

Jorge and I had played with Mario and made a record with him. We had done a trio tour as well through Spain with bassist Avishai Cohen, and we both liked what he was doing. We were spending a lot of time together, talking about music and, in retrospect, we were honing a shared aesthetic together, through the playing and the conversations. I had gotten a week at the Village Gate to lead a trio. It was the first since the last stint with Leon and Ugonna. I had the plan to hire a few different bass players throughout the six-day run. Mario made two nights; Avishai did one; Ben Wolff, who was playing regularly with pianist Benny Green and would go on shortly to play in Wynton's band, did a night as well; and Larry Grenadier played two. Everyone played really strongly but, with Larry, there was an immediate focus and ease among the three of us. He seemed to know just what we were doing before we even did it, and was right there with us. Importantly, I felt that he always had the bottom end of the music, something I wanted. Yet he was so loose, open, creative, and subtle all at once. Larry was reading back what Jorge and I had already been developing, with no adjustment necessary. The three of us were speaking a fledgling language from the first time we played together.

We went on to become a band proper and recorded several records over the coming years with Matt Pierson, who signed me on Warner Jazz, including a series, *The Art of the Trio*, Volumes 1–5. In whatever way we may have influenced subsequent players has just as much to do with the way Larry and Jorge played as it does me. I think it was really the way we played together as an ensemble that was fresh for the scene. We played as a band. We hadn't made some grand plan to go conquer the world. We thought: we should do this more often; maybe we can get some more gigs? Gigs weren't coming in by the dozens for us at that point. Jorge had connections in Spain, and I was able to find a few things here and there. Things really only started to take off for us after I got clean, but the seed was planted that week at the Gate.

Catch-22

1991
Photo: Charles Ruggiero

I didn't talk about what happened with Dr. Dunn in high school for a while, but it started to spill out after a couple years in NYC, always when I was drinking and my tongue was freed up. I would tell the story at a bar with friends, sardonically, as a dark joke. It was a self-protective story, full of denial. In my presentation, the joke was on Dr. Dunn: "So – this dipshit principal loved to perv on me. But I played him like a bitch, and sleazed out of three years of gym. That's how I graduated from high school!" My friends would laugh along with me, uneasily.

It was a story I told of *me* being in power, and using that power to get away with something – to take a shortcut by transgressive means. It worked well with the guise I wore in my twenties: the Cain routine. But the truth was that I was never in power when it happened. I didn't want to admit it, but he played *me* like a bitch. I hadn't taken any shortcut to graduate. On the contrary, high school was a long road, certainly not all bad, but one that nevertheless began with Ed and Dylan's bullying, and continued with four years of grooming from Dr. Dunn. And who was the person I became in my twenties? I wasn't a Cain-like transgressor. I became a junkie.

I had a low self-image and didn't even know it. But anyone else could have seen it. When I found heroin, it was perfect because it's such a rotten thing to do to yourself – you have to have very low self-worth to go that route. I remember a friend asking me after I was clean: "What kind of pain were you in, where you decided it's okay to stick a needle in your arm?" Indeed. Heroin was the ultimate surrender for me, and part of what I was giving in to was the self-loathing I felt from the earlier experiences, and also the outsider story I had unconsciously already formed, based upon being adopted. Add to that a predisposition towards a dark outlook, one that plagued me more acutely than others, one I had carried around with me as long as I could remember. Depression is the clinical term. I remained undiagnosed, though, throughout those years, and found what felt at first like a magic form of medication. Heroin dissolved the pain and unresolved questions. None of it mattered. *Fuck everyone, fuck everything.*

However cavalier I was about what happened in high school after I left, it confused me. On the one hand, it led to a belief that I must be gay – but not in a self-accepting, healthy way at all. Through all the grooming by Dr. Dunn, I learned that being attractive and receptive to him was a way to gain his favor, and that, by giving him what he wanted, I could achieve success in very concrete terms – I could graduate from high school. I had also received a convoluted message from Ed and Dylan. Precisely as a result of my having turned down the sex with them, they went on a homophobic bullying rampage against me for the first year of high school. It sent an upside-down signal. I could have avoided being bullied by them for being gay, by being gay with them.

Everything commanded me to be gay. Yet, when I came to New York, I had zero success with guys my own age or men older.

My apartment on Jones Street wasn't just close to all those great jazz clubs. I was also in the epicenter of New York City gay culture, just around the corner from Sheridan Square where it all began. Several times, I tried to consummate sex with older men. In retrospect, they were re-enactments of the Dr. Dunn experience. There was a pattern.

To begin, I'd walk across the street to drink at the Slaughtered Lamb on the corner of 4th and Jones, always alone. I had to be at least a little drunk, because otherwise I was too ashamed to try to approach someone or make myself available. This first act was a re-enactment of my initial shame. I created the conditions for it, and then courted it.

When I was sufficiently drunk, I would walk over to one of the gay bars on Christopher Street. I made myself available, and in no time an older guy approached me. After a few more drinks, we would leave the bar and go to his apartment or mine. In this Act II, I had successfully seduced him. Yet now, importantly, unlike with Dr. Dunn, it was on *my* terms. There was that feeling of power over someone, a victory achieved. It was a way to conquer the initial feeling of being weak.

Act III, the final one, was always the same and it was always quick. We would start to have sex but I was never aroused. There was nothing about that person that sparked anything at all – his body, what he was doing. I would try to please him by letting him do what he wanted. The whole thing was strangely altruistic on my part, but demeaning. Then, suddenly, I had had enough. I would break it off abruptly, stand up and get dressed, and get out of there as quick as I could or send him on his way. It always seemed to surprise me as much as it did them. I was caught off guard by my own aversion to the experience every time. A few times, I became aggressive suddenly. I was drunk already, and the guy was thrown off by my quick turn and didn't want to leave right away. So I'd push him away, forcefully. There was all this anger under the surface.

That Act III was an attempt to play out a scenario with Dr. Dunn, in which I would first please him and then take power over him sexually, like I had for those moments in the tub. I never had hands-on sex with him, and there was this desire to complete the act so I could win that victory over him completely. Those several moments when I stood above him with the erection he finally got out of me after four years were frozen into my memory. It really is amazing how one isolated moment in your life can hold you captive.

Yet I just couldn't get it started in praxis with these surrogates. The fantasy lived only in my head. I had no disdain for the multitude of gay men in my neighborhood, but the idea of being in a relationship with them wasn't intriguing. There wasn't much I wanted beyond that narrow re-enactment, which never came off like I had imagined.

Why would I try so hard to be gay, especially if I was so ashamed of it that I had to be drunk before going to meet someone? One reason was that I had not yet identified the real source of my shame. I figured that the erotic failures were due to a hang-up. I was simply homophobic, I reasoned, and that's why I couldn't just relax into the experience and enjoy it. This was an insidious form of self-denial, though – I fancied that I was coming out of a shell, releasing myself from shame, but in fact I was courting it, recasting it in a repeated ritual of bad sex. There was always so much nervousness leading up to the encounters with older men – butterflies in my stomach, real fear. If I had been able to get in touch with that nervousness, I would have identified it as the same kind of discomfort I had with Dr. Dunn.

The sexual misfires with guys my own age when I came to New York had different variables. There was a very specific kind of person who was intriguing to me, only one kind, someone who didn't appear or act particularly "gay" in my understanding of it, but also did not seem altogether secure in himself more generally. In an act of magical thinking I would read that as: "He is unsure about his sexuality; maybe it's kind of up for grabs as of yet." Perhaps I could capitalize on that. I was already off to the races in a fantasy, but was wrong every time – he was always straight. The attractions were narcissistic. These guys represented the younger person I had been with Dylan and others in high school, the one I hadn't grown out of emotionally. At Merrywood, my narcissistic crush on Caleb was an idealized projection of who I wanted to be. With these crushes, they were a projection of who I was ashamed of having become. The artist-outsider story had worn itself out. Yet I didn't have another one.

A few of those romantic attachments were to close friends of mine. I identified with Tonio Kröger in Mann's novella, but only to a point. I was cloying and jealous when their attention strayed from me, like Kröger was with Hans Hansen, the close friend whom he idealized and fawned over. Hans was someone he could never be – vital, confident, content. For me that would have been a buddy like Bill. Here was the key difference, though. I wasn't sexually intrigued by Bill, who was so at ease with himself and others. The guys my age who interested me had to exude some not-quite-self-confidence, because there was this underlying wish that they would be fucked up somehow, a bit broken, so I could go and fix them. That made me feel predatory with some of my own friends, which brought on more self-loathing. I hated the continuous pining. I wanted to vanquish it; I wanted to cancel it all out. That's why heroin was so appealing when I found it. It flattened out all that narcissistic, misplaced self-obsession like a steamroller.

I wanted those friends to need me, but I was the needy one. The camaraderie with them was so loaded. Whereas with the older men I was re-enacting a victory, trying to regain power, here I was simply smitten. And still there was no sex. It was a catch-22. They had to actually be straight to be interesting, yet, the moment I finally conceded that they were indeed straight, they were no longer intriguing, and I tossed them into the fantasy dustbin. I realized the dysfunction on some level, but held onto this idea that there was one just like me, if I could just find him. He was an anomaly, though. So I felt like I was an anomaly.

I spent a lot of my time those two years on Jones Street in isolation and depression. I had begun to drink like an alcoholic in earnest, beginning in the late afternoon and not stopping until bedtime after midnight. The beginning of my heroin use was fast approaching. I wasn't aware that I was unconsciously trying to medicate the trauma of what had happened with Dr. Dunn, Dylan, and Ed, and Darren's bullying. The problem wasn't some deeply embedded belief that being gay was wrong. Instead, I believed being gay was the only choice. I could win back power from an authority and get back the best friend I lost through sex, because that's what they wanted initially. That power and friendship had been taken away from me without my consent.

My inner self-hatred rested in a belief that I wasn't gay *enough* – I just couldn't seem to make it work, no matter how I tried. Meanwhile, the outward certainty that I was gay became a kind of self-fulfilling prophecy. It was so goddamned convoluted. It took years to wrap an understanding around any of that. The real answer was quite simple, and I knew it already: I was bisexual. I eventually found true acceptance of this "both/and" sexuality, but those negative experiences turned it into a "neither/nor" proposition – a conflict without resolution, for the time being.

III

Meta Blues

In which our hero discovers the lure of polemics and the folly of self-righteousness, and his resulting political awakening, through his acknowledgment of Led Zep's moral authority . . .

Throughout childhood and adolescence, I had scarcely thought about politics, but in my twenties I started to form convictions. My awareness started in a reverse manner, as I began to think about politics in the sphere of music, like a true navel-gazing artist. I was thinking about Led Zeppelin – the demiurgic predecessors to both punk and prog, the ur-river from which these agonistic steams emerged.

As I saw it, the rock'n'roll polemic I touched on earlier, the one I imagined between punk and prog, was fueled by two opposing primal urges. One was to rebel against dogmatic authority, and the other to preserve existing integrity. Great creative figures exercised authority to the extent that they influence their descendants. It was the scholar Harold Bloom who started to connect the dots like this through the centuries for me, particularly in his popular book which came out in 1994, *The Western Canon: The Books and School of the Ages*. Bloom made his case by focusing on key writers, particularly Shakespeare, and illuminating why they were canon-worthy. What would my personal musical canon look like? Was it fixed, was it open to amendment and revision? Bloom's canon was personal to the extent that he had chosen it, yet he had become an authority of sorts to others – an authority on what to read.

In *The Anxiety of Influence* and *Agon: Towards a Theory of Revisionism*, Bloom told his own story about poets and their progeny, and the agonistic relationships between them. The strong poet, he maintained, is able to avoid being *contained* by a stronger poet who had come before them. Shakespeare was for Bloom a great container. What other writers found, he had already laid claim to. He was the larger vessel in which they found themselves. It couldn't work the other way around. Bloom had fun with this idea, reversing chronology, for instance, by maintaining that Freud's analysis of Shakespeare's *Hamlet*, however interesting, is late to the game. We should better imagine a Shakespearian analysis of Freud. The character of Hamlet, after all, is proto-Freudian – his self-consciousness anticipated a modern psychological perspective.

A strong writer, however, vanquished their predecessor in paradoxical fashion, by taking over that predecessor's voice with such mastery that no one heard the influence anymore. In a twist, the strong writer's new output was even more quintessential than the original. On the face of it, this was co-opting – an act of theft that was nevertheless intelligent, bearing out the maxim that good artists copy but great artists steal.

Yet, if you stopped there, you only had the recipe, and not the reason for its success. The strong successor's voice was their own because there was also something new in it. There was an indispensable *turn* away from the predecessor – one they would not have permitted themselves. Importantly, though, the younger poet first gave themselves over to the older one completely, in what Bloom calls a "misreading": "The strong misreading," he explains in *The Anxiety of Influence*, "comes first; there must be a profound act of reading that is a kind of falling in love with a literary work . . . Poetic influence – when it involves two strong, authentic poets – always proceeds by a misreading of the prior poet, an act of creative correction that is actually and necessarily a misinterpretation." It was this process of mimicking and bastardization, combined with inspiration and imagination, and, finally, complete subsuming of that predecessor, that formed a canon through time. In all of this, Bloom was crying out against reductionism in any strain – against trying, in bad faith, to place a large figure like Shakespeare into a political, moral, or psychological vessel. He was taking issue with the literary criticism in his own academic locus, which examined literature along Marxist, feminist, or deconstructionist lines.

To the extent that he wanted to keep the canon within its own confines, Bloom was conservative. He wanted the subject of literature to be literature only. In that way, the canon would essentially determine itself. A writer's greatness was determined in equal measure by their originality and their continual engagement with their predecessors. This meant that the old dead writers were authorities, but they had become so only through that defiant turn away from previous ones: they themselves had been young upstarts at one point. Bloom celebrated the upstarts, but was nevertheless conservative because his story depended on a linear chronology in which the earlier vessel was always the larger one. Assembling this kind of canon would be mostly a process of taking stock, with little inquiry outside of these established figures. His evaluations were analogous to those of an "originalist" Supreme Court judge; Shakespeare, the King James Bible, Chaucer's *Canterbury Tales*, Milton's *Paradise Lost*, and other grounding texts were the reference point for everyone that followed. They were the original constitutional articles, and amendments were unlikely.

Have your cake and eat it too

I was particularly attracted to Bloom's description of that "turn" as an appropriation, as partial theft. It was in line with my own conviction – or, really, a wish at that point, untested – that art should be free from moral considerations. Bloom was broadening that dictum, saying that the act of inspired creation itself – the process, and not just the finished product – was also markedly amoral. This was appealing, because it redescribed my own musical creative process as transgressive. In this way, I could rewrite what I saw as the unhappier transgression that already lay within me: the experiences with Dylan, Ed, and Dr. Dunn, and being adopted. Bloom's story about writers was more fodder for my own outsider-artist story. Transgression was a mark of honor, not shame.

At the same time, Bloom's originalist chronology would always favor the past, because you found the larger vessel there, and not the other way around. That meant, though, in effect, favoring the status quo. The status quo in politics could be complicit in oppression – there could be no positive social change if things remained the way they were. In the venue of a canon though, there was nothing immediately wrong with the status quo, as much of the musical and literature I loved belonged to it. So there was no reason I saw to disavow it, whether out of instinctive rebellious spirit or moral conviction.

Bloom's celebration of the young upstarts was romantic, as he celebrated trailblazing, lone visionaries like William Blake. Yet there was an atavistic tendency. The romantic temperament, it turned out, had a conservative side, and for a time I embraced the tension in that. It sat well with a desire to have my cake and eat it too, in terms of my own identity. I wanted to be Cain, yet wanted a place in the tribe. I wanted to be a sexual free spirit, yet was plagued by insecurity and self-questioning. I was the bastard child who was given away, yet also the well-situated child in a "normal" family. I fancied that I was at turns a bohemian jazz musician running around the East Village, or a Waspy lover of the Three Bs from the Merrywood tribe. I could not reconcile all of these identities as I tried to embody them. There were always two poles, and I could never fully sit in my own skin on one side or the other. Finding an authentic political identity would play out in my *Bildung*. As with my own musical voice, it was a process of amendment, discarding, and, finally, assimilation. In the meantime, my politics were ambivalent, and blew around with the wind. Depending on who I was talking to, I would play the progressive renegade, or the conservative gadfly, from one conversation to the next. It was a work in progress.

Bloom's self-contained, self-determining canon was alluring but, I wondered, was it not another form of reductionism, like the ones he decried? A strong thinker on the other side of the fence could convincingly demonstrate that art was never free from the political structure in which it was created and received, and therefore complicit in oppression. The artist, composer, or novelist were not the creative bastard children whom Bloom described. On the contrary, they were part of the problem. It was an illusion that music and the other arts were free from ideology. Artworks, as Theodor Adorno put it, were "socially culpable."

A Marxist contemporary of Bloom's like Terry Eagleton, in *The Ideology of the Aesthetic*, maintained that the very idea that art could be free from ideology was one of the more insidious forms of ideology:

> Once artefacts become commodities in the market place, they exist for nothing and nobody in particular, and can consequently be rationalized, ideologically speaking, as existing entirely and gloriously for themselves. [. . .] It is not only, as radical thought has familiarly insisted, that art is thereby conveniently sequestered from all other social practices, to become an isolated enclave within which the dominant social order can find an idealized refuge from its own actual values of competitiveness, exploitation and material possessiveness. It is also, rather more subtly, that the idea of autonomy – of a mode of being which is entirely self-regulating and self-determining – provides the middle class with just the ideological model of subjectivity it requires for its material operations.

Subtle indeed. The insinuation was that prizing art for its autonomy – placing the transcendent power of *King Lear* in a locus that was free from the political realm in which it was written, as Bloom would have it – was just not subtle thinking. Members of the bourgeoisie – those poor drones – unwittingly perpetuated the status quo, with all its injustice, when they listened to Wagner or read Flaubert.

Bloom bet on a human subject – Shakespeare – who would contain any system of thought by essentially beating you to it, naming it for you, and letting you discover it in his plays. You want competitiveness, exploitation, or materialistic greed? Just study the characters in *Richard III* or *Macbeth*. Eagleton, by contrast, looked more to the ever-oppressive objective presence of the state; it contained everyone, including a creative light like Shakespeare. It struck me that Bloom placed so much faith on the imaginative gift of a single human artist, yet did not concern himself as much with the people reading the books he was illuminating for us. Eagleton, on the other hand, who did not count as much on the capacity for individuals to draw their own conclusions, was nevertheless thinking more about the material conditions of the people reading them. In the end, they were both staunch humanists, in very different ways.

Bloom was making the case that Shakespeare contained *our* psychological map: Hamlet's alienation was our alienation. Now, it may have been his, but was not necessarily everyone else's. If Bloom wanted to be utterly convincing, he would have had to make a "canonical" psychological map as well – one that applied to all of us. That most likely did not appeal to him, as it could very well wind up as a milky platitude about universal principles. In any case, he did not try, and that was his shortcoming. He lionized a glad-handing, reluctant hero like Falstaff in *Henry IV*, but did not consider that a woman, someone queer, or from a different racial or cultural background, might not relate to Falstaff and Prince Hal's macho bromance in the same way he did, however much humor and wisdom it conveyed. His presumption seemed unconscious on his part. The thing I enjoyed most about Bloom – his absolute self-assuredness – was also what made me uneasy about him.

Eagleton or Adorno showed how my cherished experience of an artwork was never a singular, autonomous event. It was bound up in the political structure in which I found myself. Yet it was not art's "fault" that it was created and received in a non-utopian political system. I reasoned that there was a distinction between the kind of cognitive activity that led toward a political conviction and that which led to musical expression. Both a conviction and a creative act were born out of direct experience, but you arrived at a conviction through an intellectual evaluation. That played out as a discourse between yourself and others, and one between your own ears as well. This kind of mental activity was predicative: it posited ideas, and, through induction or deduction, drew conclusions.

I knew from my own experience that creative inspiration was altogether different. To be sure, it involved that predicative thinking. You made a proposition, for instance, about why one thing was aesthetically strong and another failed, in your eyes. You needed a set of propositions to build your musical identity, which was just as much about dislikes as it was likes. Then you worked on your craft along those lines; you chose to hone in on some things and ignore others. Those "likes" themselves, though, were still mysterious. They had something to do with sense and spirit, of life experience and the way you mediated it, and not intellect. They were fluid. Likewise, the creative act itself, especially in the realm of improvisation where I operated, involved a lot of intuition. That was where the magic was, and without that magic an artwork was stillborn. To the extent that it did not arise out of premeditated evaluations, this final creative spark lit independently from politico-moral considerations. Furthermore, just as easily, history attested to the reverse order. Great music could heighten and tweak a political conviction, and perhaps even help foster one into being. It may just as well be a barbaric one as a civilizing one. Beethoven's Ninth, after all, with its poem of human brotherhood from Schiller, was used for Nazi propaganda.

Beauty and the good

So far Bloom was winning, if only by a hair. He joined a lineage that included Oscar Wilde, who famously concluded "All art is quite useless." There was a division between art and morality. Our sense of Beauty in the artwork is different from our sense of Good – good in the sense of morally upright. Knowing what is good and just implies that we should take an action to uphold the goodness. Beauty, on the other hand, was a means to its own end: it called for nothing else than our delighted contemplation. As a property we seek in art, it was useless as a moral guide.

I observed anti-Semitic writers like Ezra Pound and Louis Ferdinand Céline. Their inspired output supplied no model for their own abhorrent ideas, and vice versa. The conclusion to draw from such examples was that we wish in vain for a moral agency in art. Art operated outside of "should" and "should not." Politically engaged "rebels" against elitist canons judged a Bloomian outlook as complicit in an oppressive political establishment. Rebelling against the rebels, Bloom saw it inversely. They, with their politicized criticism, were oppressively reductive.

I fantasized that I was at turns a Bloom-like figure, knocking the wind out of some self-righteous Marxist literary critic's sails, or an Eagleton type, undermining Bloom's presumptuous pomp. It was the same kind of wish I had when I was a kid, when I wanted to ask Bush Senior, "What about the Russians?" at his campaign stop in Bedford. There was a desire to demonstrate knowledge on a subject, and now, a fantasy of vanquishing someone in an argument of ideas. Yet both were informed by some measure of intellectual insecurity. My own thoughts on the relationship between politics and art were as of yet derivative of Bloom, Eagleton, Adorno, Orwell, Isaiah Berlin, Richard Rorty, and others. That was all well and good, as I was soaking up other people's ideas. The only danger was if my political convictions *themselves* were driven by intellectual insecurity – in other words, if my only real "conviction" was to sound smart.

Yet what if this was the hidden aspiration behind any polemic, no matter how weighty it seemed? In such a polemic as the one I imagined, each figure was seeking to undermine the other one; each side was striving for a "touché" moment in the debate, when the opponent would defer, saying, "Wow, you got me!" and, humbled, would acknowledge the poverty of his own position. That moment never came though, as the two parties continually tried to contain each other, drawing ever-larger circles around the other's circles. There was always that struggle for authority, with no easy winner.

As I began to unpack the source of my political persuasions, it made sense to do the same with aesthetic ones, and I saw the extent to which they were connected. The musicians and novelists I admired exuded a legitimate, non-oppressive authority on me – one I accepted without question, welcoming it. I used their output as a model to organize and give meaning to my own thoughts, feelings, and experiences, and discerned how that authority had operated silently upon me for a long while already.

Art – particularly music and literature in my case – bore authority when it gave meaning to my life, outside of its own frame. It was an abstracted, beautiful, parental presence to which I looked for answers. My working definition for art became: that which expresses meaningful beauty. There was indeed beauty without meaning, and meaning without beauty. Art was not a mere collection of someone's scattered impressions, though, however beautiful they were. There had to be some kind of formal integrity – even if it was anti-formal anti-integrity – that linked the work with the world outside of the frame. Music could be willfully ugly, yet still proclaim: you, the recipient, may enter into my contaminated sphere, because you have already been inoculated by real beauty. Strong, worthy ugliness was always tacitly underlined by the beauty it forsook. Beauty was its First Cause. Here was the real source of authority in the music I loved. It provided the teleological *evidence* that beauty was good. That was big. It meant that beauty – the beauty that I saw in another, or the beauty that someone saw in me – was not a source of shame. It was the opposite. I was not ready to fully believe that – to sign on to it, to know it unconditionally – but music offered substantiation.

As much as I was attracted to the Romantic Bloomian camp, there was now a problem. The property of meaning in an artwork implied that mere delighted contemplation would not do. There was play and freedom, for sure, but form and order, which meant cause and effect. It played out in the seductive inevitability of a Miles Davis solo like on "So What." There was a feeling that it couldn't be any other way – that all the pieces had to align themselves together just like they did. Accordingly, that kind of formal beauty – the way the narrative seemed to write itself, or, one might say, was written already, by a godlike figure – suggested that art *could* be a moral beacon, and not just a beautiful means to its own end. Yet this was not a damning morality, enforced through threat and punishment. It was born out of that gentle, parenting, aesthetic authority I had found, one that invited me towards love and solace, but also ecstasy. Instead of saying "Don't do this, or else," the music quietly encouraged: "Do *this*, be this, embody this – and find what you seek."

A loving dogma

Coveting a distinctly *moral* upper hand, finally, was the aim of each adversary in aesthetic polemics. Why else did folks lash out at each other so vitriolically about beauty, of all things? It should have been a unifying subject. No, it was all about their sense of justice, which was deeply tied in with who they were, or, rather, who they thought they were – whether a die-hard advocate of performing baroque music only on period instruments, or a Bob Dylan fan who felt betrayed when he went electric. Ask the person why they were so strident, and you often got answers that sound alarmingly dogmatic: "It's just not *right* to approach the music that other way." "That music should only be played *this* way."

I fancied myself largely free of such musical dogma, but it was there. It had begun in high school as exposure to jazz deepened. A positive emotional reaction about some music would calcify into a fixed, broad judgment about other music. This kind of perceptual activity was unconscious. Dogma was dogma because it cloaked a reptilian impulse in an ostensibly rational evaluation, and then gave it legs. Did Bloom himself, the scholar par excellence, unwittingly betray lazy thinking, swayed by his defensive love for the literature that grabbed his imagination during his own *Bildung*? Did that thinking foster a deficient canon, one that lacked a thorough account of literature outside its gilded gates?

When dogma was thrust out of the private, navel-gazing sphere of aesthetics, its counterpart in the polis through the ages was familiarly oppressive: the theocracy of the Old Testament, which played out in cruel Levitical laws, carrying forward into the religious conservatism that repelled me in my own present day. Dogma in political discourse was a threat, or so seemed to me. It reinforced the sexual shame I felt. I did not want to sign on to any aesthetic stricture that might reflect a repellent politics. Yet, in the microcosm of musical tastes out back at Hall High, and later with the Bebop Nazis and the Goons, dogma was not threatening – it was endearing. That protective, tribal instinct was born out of love, and not hateful fear. Even when it was wedded with a bitchy dismissal of other musical genres, there was a wish for communion on the part of its spokesperson. They were less an adjudicator, and more a figure who would summon me over to share in their love.

When Coltrane walked on the peak of a mountain for fifteen minutes, improvising on "Impressions," I witnessed and experienced *freedom* as a listener, the opposite of oppression, and would aim for it in turn as an improviser. It was just that intimation of freedom, though, that laid the ground for its opposite: a dogma which stated that Coltrane, Bird, and a few others were the zenith, and that was that. Both the freedom and dogma were born out of love. This was quite different than political and religious dogma, which seemed born only out of fear – the kind of fear that led to harm.

In a locus of sacred musical play, I could give voice to the fluidity I could not accept in myself. I wanted permission to roam wide. In that way maybe I could find my truer identity. I wanted to protect and preserve that feeling. I saw that protection of personal freedoms was a hallmark of the democracy I lived in, yet it had not reached its promise, and was constantly under revision. The importance of freedom of speech and the right to privacy became personal. In my country, I observed two possible threats to that freedom: one from a foreign adversary and one, more chillingly, from the inside. That inside adversary – the one who would stamp paternalistic, censoring laws upon us all – was for me the one most threatening. If I had lived through a world war, or in a different country, it might have been the other way around.

A politics was born, first out of a self-protective instinct, the instinct of someone with heightened sensitivity who takes things to heart more than might do him good. As I gazed outwards, I realized that the greatest musical heroes of mine were marginalized in their own country, and had to live through real opression, in the form of racism. That kind of realization formed a conviction that the sanctuary I wished for myself should be available for everyone, and was not yet. The status quo would not suffice.

In utopian terms, I imagined that the freedom I experienced in jazz improvisation could play out in society. That society would be anarchic, free from any single authority. Anarchy, though, depended on a categorical imperative that each one of its citizens willingly practiced: Live and Let Live. The model was jazz. The personal was musical, and both were political, finally.

As a musician, this loving kind of dogma would need constant mediation. The danger was that I might lose the ability to find solace anywhere else outside my domain of passion. Passion – even ecstasy – was that musical *act* of love, yet to draw a line around it would impede it. Sexual passion was its carnal analogue: to achieve its climax the same way every time was deadening. I had to protect that musical anarchy, which promised no division between pleasure and love, between spirit and flesh. If the personal was political, then anarchy was an erotic act as well, played out in the music.

In the formation of my dictum, I glossed on Bloom. If I could draw passion from a sufficiently wide musical expanse – if I could find a myriad of ways to "get off" aesthetically – then I could remain charged, and continue to receive its loving ecstasy in return. Bloom's containers for English literature were limited in number, with Shakespeare hovering above all. In this he may have been dogmatic. Yet his project was to continually demonstrate the *largeness* of the container. Shakespeare contained manifold successors, from the poets and playwrights that followed him in the centuries to come, up to the present day.

Taking a cue from Bloom, I marked three qualities in the music and literature as the highest: authority, vastness, and strangeness. The way in which those qualities often contradicted each other was related to an artwork's ability to escape easy reduction. You could use the analogy of a civilization. Take the Roman Empire. Rome is great and its achievements are much more than those of the territories that it conquers. But Rome must be cruel. Its army must vanquish the Barbarian enemy or it will lose all the appealing stuff that goes with civilization.

There was a similar cruelty in the way an enduring body of work held its grip of power, as subsequent creators came along and attempted to colonize the area it already occupied. The specter of Beethoven loomed over Brahms. The ghost of John Coltrane hung over every modern jazz tenor saxophonist. The records of Led Zeppelin remained the gold standard for a certain type of hard-hitting rock that so many bands aimed for. Beethoven, Coltrane, and Led Zeppelin said to their predecessors, "Oh, you think you're just discovering this bypath, this offshoot? No – sorry, look closer; there are my footsteps there already. Yes that's right. I have trod here, and if you peruse a little further, you'll see that what you foolishly thought you had discovered, I already did, took to its logical conclusion, and then went even a little beyond where you are now. You haven't even caught up with me."

They thus cruelly reinstated their authority, and by always going further than their descendants, demonstrated that second quality: vastness. The Barbarians may have had some serious fighting skills and knew how to party, but the range of their civilization was limited: you're looking at an animal skin to sleep under if you're lucky, no eating utensils, no sewerage system. Like Rome,

Beethoven, Coltrane and Led Zep had good *infrastructure*: you could find their influence in descendants whose own oeuvres were radically different from each other. In musical terms, good infrastructure meant any number of things related to a musical craft, in addition to that creative spark: Beethoven's prowess in orchestration, Coltrane's virtuosity, Led Zeppelin's easy switches between folk-like acoustic and hard-hitting electric musical textures.

This meant that they could single-handedly spark two styles that were polemically adversarial. With Beethoven, consider how just one piece, his final Ninth Symphony, grabbed the imagination of two composers who were so different from each other: Brahms and Wagner. We hear the legacy of Beethoven's Ninth in Brahms' First Symphony in C Minor. The younger work modeled the older one's narrative shape, beginning in the trauma and chaos of its first movement and resolving in triumph and order, with an anthem-like major-keyed theme in the final movement. Brahms fulfilled the promise of Beethoven's formal innovation in music, to create music on a more epic scale than had been heard previously, but still would hold the listener's attention because of the economy of its thematic material.

Beethoven was pivotal. He consolidated the order of Classicism and presaged its fracture, pointing towards the inviting ruins of Romanticism. If Brahms was influenced by the architecture of the Ninth – by its motific constraint despite its heroic sprawl – then Wagner was led by the actual musical gestures of the work, which seem at times to oppose any constraint. He wrote music that left its listeners emotionally unbound. When he communicated joy, it could be frenzied joy – an ecstasy that plowed over everything. In "Liebestod," the great climax of *Tristan und Isolde*, there was a palpable sense of losing control. The last movement of Beethoven's Ninth, with full chorus and soloists, was a strong model for that kind of bulldozing expression that could overrun the listener.

Wagner and Brahms both unequivocally acknowledged the importance of the Ninth for their own works. Yet Beethoven's role in both their output was shaped by their divergent understandings of what it meant to be a composer. Wagner called the Ninth "music of the future," while, for Brahms, the symphony, in its unparalleled greatness, was such an imposing model that he did not complete his first symphony until 1874, aged forty-one. It represented for him the summation of a legacy. Beethoven was like a wide river and Brahms and Wagner were two diverging streams that parted from it. There was an intense polemic in their day about which of the two was the worthier heir to Beethoven. For those involved, you had to make a choice. The reasons you stood for the one were the same reasons you stood against the other.

Fuck punk

The Roman army conquers other nations, swallows them up, and they become part of the empire. They must adhere to the laws of their colonizer, but, even as they do so, they retain some of their distinctive cultural traits. Rome in turn assimilates these traits and they become part of its identity. Rome grows vaster – and stranger. Likewise, Beethoven's oeuvre is expansive, and the music in its outlying territories expresses a weirdness, at times enchanting and at times confounding, particularly in his late works. It carries his unmistakable identity, yet transmits otherness. For Bloom, that quality is part and parcel of canonical greatness. Confronting the question of what makes an author worthy of the canon, he writes:

> The answer, more often than not, has turned out to be strangeness, a mode of originality that either cannot be assimilated, or that so assimilates us that we cease to see it as strange.

In its strategy of containment, Rome had much to offer within its borders that was rich and strange, as it absorbed the varied cultures it conquered. Yet it never relinquished its role as the establishment. Beethoven and Shakespeare continually renew our sense of discovery, and, in doing so, become authorities, perhaps imposed upon us in an academic environment, or simply through our own willing submission as we absorb their output. The strangeness *becomes* the normative, which brings us back to Led Zep.

While I was chewing on all this, I was on the road on one of my first tours with Joshua Redman in 1993. I picked up some rock rag – it wasn't *Rolling Stone*, but similar, maybe *Q* or something I had picked up in the U.K. Anyhow, there was an interview with an up-and-coming punk band, talking about their experience on the road – first big tour, and so on. I can't remember their name – I didn't know them then and didn't go on to check them out. (They might be great.) What caught me was the story the front guy told the interviewer about going across the border on tour between the U.S. and Canada. I paraphrase from memory. I must have read it half a dozen times, fascinated by it:

> "We got up to the border and had to get out of the van while they checked our passports and stuff. And right then this sports car convertible pulls up next to us and this older dude gets out of the car. And I was like, no fucking way. Shit."
>
> "Who was it?" the interviewer asked.
>
> "It was fucking Robert Plant."
>
> "Wow! So what happened? Did you say hi to him?"
>
> "Yeah. . . . Well, he looked at us and saw the instruments and said something like, 'How's it going there, lads?' Some shit like that."
>
> Another guy in the band added, "Yeah, it was really a drag. There was just nothing to say. We couldn't wait to get out of there." All of the band members nodded glumly in assent.

Their anecdote ended there, vaguely, with no explanation as to why it sucked so much to see Robert Plant at the border stop. The way I read it was like this: Robert Plant for these young punkers was an authority figure – he reminded them of their neophyte status in the great game of rock'n'roll. When they ran into him on their tour, it was like your dad showing up at your high-school dance: it killed your buzz; it just bummed you out, period.

Led Zeppelin was the Beethoven/Rome of post-'60s rock'n'roll. They started out like any other scruffy young band but then rose to become a rock authority – perhaps they were setting out to do that; perhaps they weren't. Their output was so strong and righteous that bands continually drew from it. The debt was often obvious.

The band also pointed the way forward in two very different, polemically opposed directions, like Beethoven did with Wagner and Brahms: prog and punk. (I bracket out the band's unquestionable impact on metal, only to focus on the dichotomy under consideration here.) The band was proto-prog in extended songs like "No Quarter," "Ten Years Gone," or "Stairway to Heaven," initiating an urge for the epic, and making fantasy and the occult viable subject matter for rock music. "Kashmir," with its strange hemiolas, was a model for later prog, showing how you could alter the rhythmic paradigm of rock and organize your material in a fresh way, yet still rock hard. At the same time, with its raw energy, Led Zeppelin launched a punk gambit, although many old-school punkers would spit on you for saying that. None other than Johnny Ramone himself, though, said that early on he continuously woodshedded the downstroke guitar riff of Led Zep's "Communication Breakdown." If you listen to that song back to back with many from the Ramones, you hear the connection easily.

The mathematician and philosopher A.N. Whitehead stated that Western philosophy, on the whole, is "a series of footnotes to Plato," spreading Bloomian containment over a far broader timeline than the relatively short life of hard rock. A young upstart in any tradition – philosophical, artistic, scientific, theological – abhors that kind of statement. No one, unless they are self-loathing, wants to feel that they are nothing more than a footnote. Bloom's own oeuvre formed its own dramatic narrative, one about the relationship between poets and their predecessors – an Oedipal, Freudian struggle, in which the son had to vanquish his father through his own worthy poem. As he asks rhetorically in *The Anxiety of Influence*, "For what strong maker desires the realization that he has failed to create himself?"

It was Bloom's *own* story, though, and he filled it out with his own romantic speculation, imagining that Keats was conscious of Spenser before him, or Hart Crane was trying to overcome his father, Walt Whitman. The stumbling block for me was that this did not match my own experience as a young upstart. I did not experience the "agon" he described in those poets. When I heard a debt to McCoy Tyner or Red Garland in my playing, if anything, I was psyched, thinking, "Look, my shit is authentic!" Nevertheless, Bloom was onto something. The young punkers' antipathy in their encounter with a living rock god wasn't a rational kind of thing; it was on the gut level. I wondered why these guys were so dark on Robert Plant, reading the interview – what had he done to them?

It didn't seem fair. I imagined being Robert Plant, Jimmy Page or John Paul Jones, the surviving members of Led Zeppelin. You were once a young guy and you started a band in a turbulent, revolutionary time. You had a vision, you rocked hard in a new way and changed the world with your music. Other bands then go on to cop your shit but nobody can throw down like you did, because you guys instigated that voodoo – you're the keeper of the flame, so, when your drummer dies and the band breaks up, it's the end of something.

All well and good, but the next thing you know, a few decades have passed, everybody is still stealing your stuff, and nobody acknowledges it. What's more, they scorn you as part of the establishment! Punks, indeed. That's why I said to myself, re-reading the article: fuck punk, at least in spirit. Fuck mediocrity for its own sake. The reason why those guys were so down on Led Zep was plain and simple: it was resentment. Seeing Robert Plant was a reminder of everything they would never achieve, because, well, they just weren't on that level, and they weren't ever going to be. I grabbed hard onto a Bloomian outlook and applied it to everything, not just Led Zep versus lesser bands, but also any number of great/not-so-great dichotomies.

The rebel establishment

I fell under the sway of Beethoven's String Quartets my first years in New York, being especially intoxicated by the deep melancholy, loneliness, other-worldliness and ecstasy of the late ones. In the wisp of a middle section in the *Cavatina* movement of Opus 130, there was something so personal and tender that you almost wanted to look away from the music, if that was possible – it felt like something that we shouldn't even witness. That kind of expression had nothing to do with authority.

In the early nineties, I identified with German "establishment" figures like Beethoven as much as the jazz musicians I loved. My third year in New York, I spent a big chunk of my money to see the Guarneri Quartet perform all of Beethoven's String Quartets in a series of concerts at the Met. At the first one, I sat next to an older couple. The woman glared at me as soon as I took my seat, and then proceeded to talk to her husband about me as if I was not there: "Why does *he* have to sit next to us? Look at the way he's dressed . . ." I wasn't particularly underdressed, but I guess it wasn't up to snuff for her. She complained about how I smelled – I was a smoker. Fair enough.

That can happen anywhere: you get stuck next to a sour person. But, at the Guarneri concerts, it changed my perception of the classical public. They weren't, I unhappily discovered, singing along to the *Cavatina*. They were there because they wanted to wave their high-culture flag; they were there to feel elitist. This lady next to me, with her Nancy Reagan hair and pearls, needed to look down on someone, and it was me, with my wrinkled blazer and cigarette smell.

The audience at a jazz show also had its share of people who didn't particularly connect with the music, didn't listen that much to jazz, and were bored most of the time. The difference was mostly cosmetic. One crowd wanted to be elite by dressing up like the establishment; the other one wanted to be elite by coming off like hipsters. After the arrival of Wynton Marsalis, even that cosmetic difference disappeared as jazz fused into the establishment. I figured, with some satisfaction, that none of that really mattered, because none of it applied to the people who were actually getting the music.

If that didn't sound elitist, though: "the people who were actually getting the music . . ." Around that time, I was starting to play regularly with Jorge Rossy, and he and I talked about this. He articulated well for me the double-edged nature of elitism, as a term at least, explaining it this way: elitism was a charge that someone leveled against you – most likely you didn't go around wearing a T-shirt that says "I'm elitist and proud of it." Yet, at the same time, at some point you began to realize that you were one. You had won access to something exclusive and wouldn't forgo it for some contrived solidarity with the uninitiated. This elitism folded back into a political stance that was still under construction, and sat uneasily with more egalitarian sentiments. You couldn't very well be a live-and-let-live anarchist and elitist at the same time. Or could you?

When I arrived in New York, I distrusted what I saw as phony proletariat cheerleading in some of my student acquaintances. It didn't jibe with the fact that many of us were not from the proletariat at all: we were largely upper-middle-class white kids. I wanted to be a contrarian in the style of Bloom – at the age of eighteen no less. I had only one friend I knew of at the New School, Sean, who voted like me for George H.W. Bush in the 1988 presidential election against Democrat Michael Dukakis. It seemed to both of us that he was simply the better candidate. Sean and I met that first year, and our second year we became roommates in a flat on St. Mark's Place, wedged between a cruisy gay bar called B Boys and a halfway house full of junkies who were all still trying to score. There was always some kind of action on both sides when we stepped out of our front door.

Just down the street from our apartment on the corner of 3rd Avenue was the Continental Divide, which years back had been the legendary Five Spot, home to the long, fruitful residencies, immortalized on live records on the top of my canon, like Monk with John Coltrane and the Eric Dolphy/Booker Little Quintet. I heard Allen Ginsberg at the Divide, reciting his poetry for fresh-faced NYU students who had just landed in the East Village, a historical neighborhood of political rebellion. Hearing Ginsberg read his own poetry was electrifying. It was prophecy from the Bard of the Beats himself – the fire of dissent, straight from the dragon's mouth. Yet it made me uneasy. His tribe also wasn't my tribe, any more than the stiffs uptown listening to Beethoven were. My distrust of the left was a judgment, one that mirrored their own righteous indignation. A couple blocks east in Tompkins Square Park, I witnessed a "protest," where some of the people were throwing garbage bags full of rocks and urine at the police. The bags broke upon landing and the cops got washed with their piss. I just thought, fuck those people doing that.

I couldn't get behind either Bloom's conservatism or Eagleton's Marxism unconditionally, because I realized that finally they were both elitists and, however edifying it might be, elitism still smells funny, because ultimately it's divisive. It was an inconsistency in my Cain story, one that couldn't be resolved for the simple fact that I was complicit in something oppressive as much as anyone else.

As a musician in the polis, though, I finally came down with Bloom and Led Zeppelin over Eagleton and the proletariat punks. In being a Bloomian elitist, no matter how full of holes my stance was, no matter how presumptuous, I could be an eternal rebel, or at least adapt that as an ideal. I could rebel against mediocrity, and against that disingenuous kind of dissent. I could set my own standard. Maybe I would fail utterly, but my heart was in the right place, I figured, because I was rebelling against reductionism – reductionism of myself. If I would fail, it was *my* authentic failure. The romantic sentiment contained a paradox that worked for me. If a rebel is eternal, they must then be part of the establishment – call it the rebel establishment. Their weirdness and singularity are in the vanguard, perennially.

The establishment, it turned out, was the open place, not some imagined Other. As an artist, it's where I found myself drawing from most often. In the classical sphere, the establishment was obvious enough, embodied in the Three Bs. Jazz had its own establishment, though, in my reckoning. It was an authority that earned my respect through its output alone, and not through sociopolitical considerations – much like Bloom would have it. Its greatest lights were figures like Bird, Coltrane, and Miles. All the good weirdness and singularity was already there in the music itself. Fleeing from the establishment on the grounds of retaining one's supposed originality was to misunderstand what constitutes originality in the first place. Willful weirdness was boring. A creative act was not a disavowal of tradition. It was an inquiry into something much larger than myself, something that was there long before I showed up, with my shifting convictions.

Bad irony

> To complain [about the loss of tradition] and to recommend tradition as a cure is entirely useless. This contradicts the very essence of tradition. Utilitarian rationality – the consideration of how nice it would be to have a tradition in a world allegedly or actually lacking any coherence – cannot prescribe what it invalidates.
>
> Theodor Adorno, *On Tradition*

> We do not want the things in which we trust to be debunked, belittled, torn down, and we are not sure that they will be safe in the harsh light of a reflexively skeptical time. Nor can we stand the thought that they might be trivialized, brought into someone's ad campaign, movie dialogue, or self-help phrase. So we keep our best hopes safe in the dark of our own unexpressed sentiments and half-forbidden thoughts.
>
> Jedediah Purdy, *For Common Things*

In my *Bildung*, I was seeking answers to two broad questions. The first was how to become a musician, and the second was why to become one. Finding answers for the "how" question meant studying with teachers, practice, and the trial-and-error highs and lows of on-the-gig experience. The second question was more like an open inquiry: why do I want this; why should I embark on this life? The answers didn't come all at once but revealed themselves in tandem with my development.

"Why" really meant: what was the *meaning* in being a musician? I was confounded when I tried to find the answer in the music itself, because its own expression didn't employ the predicative kind of thinking that would lead to such an inquiry in the first place. It didn't need it. Music, in praxis, was the answer to its own question, or you could just as well say in inverse: in its perpetual answer, it posed a limitless question.

That was all well and good. The abstract nature of music allowed me to draw my own provisional conclusions as to why I loved making it. It mirrored my own trauma and brought redemptive beauty to it, which was a form of healing. Music didn't necessarily announce its own meaning, but it *gave* meaning to other events, ones that initially seemed to have no good reason for happening. Furthermore, in the opening exchange between myself and the listener, they might find that meaning/healing as well.

Independently of any trauma, there was the possibility of ecstasy, when, in the white heat of collective improvisation, something would fall out of all of us on the bandstand that we never could have willed, and leveled the division between the audience and the musicians, in a shared moment of grace. That was less of a seeking/finding process and more a singular event. Its impression lingered, but only like a dream that had already vanished – you had a recollection of it but couldn't ever hold it again. Still, that kind of one-off was something that made life a miracle, and not just an exercise in survival.

Here were strong answers to the "why" questions. I wondered, though, about a broader kind of "why," one that might situate the music I was making in the 1990s with my Gen-X peers. By the time we arrived, jazz had already cycled a particular course from its early origins, through swing, bebop, hard bop, modal and free jazz, and plugged-in fusion. Now we were part of a supposed Renaissance. My "why" questions included: if this is a Renaissance, why do we need it right now in the broader culture outside of jazz, if jazz was to reflect the present zeitgeist and maybe even influence it? It seemed like a designation in bad faith. The notion of a Renaissance was a wish, in as far as it sought evidence of a linear order, of something coming from something, and heading towards something else. It would be a necessary juncture, with a goal towards musical progress. For it had to have some virtue, no? Otherwise, who cared?

Yet it was one notion among others, and they were all disparate. Everything seemed to be in splinters. If there was any defining ethos in the 1990s it was one of non-specificity. "Postmodernism" was an explanation for anything and everything, but it was a term that seemed to eat itself, as it tried to account for the breakdown of linear history in linear, historical terms. In a way, it had no utility, by its own definition. Perhaps that lack of utility was embedded in its meaning, though, and the idea was to start from a place of *no* meaning. The old set of integral tools did not work. They no longer constructed anything whole. The '90s were all about coming to terms with that. In that process of reckoning, there was ultimately strong creative output from all quarters. But it took a minute.

It seemed to me that something similar was taking place in pop music, yet with less pretense. An artist like Lenny Kravitz was celebrating music he loved from the '60s and '70s in his own songs, yet he didn't need to self-consciously call it a "Renaissance." Many of the younger jazz players at the time, myself included, were paying tributes to a ten-year period – the hard bop of the second half of the '50s and the exploratory jazz of the first half of the '60s. It was as if more than twenty years had simply disappeared; as if the groundbreaking fusion of later Miles, Weather Report, Herbie Hancock's and Chick Corea's groups in the '70s, and other groups had never existed, and we were continuing from the moment right before Coltrane released *Ascension*.

There were certainly new things happening, and a lot of them went down at the Knitting Factory, a venue on Houston Street, which was altogether different than the other clubs. The music there was often truly innovative, and came from musicians from our generation, but also established ones who had been part of earlier breakthroughs. The most memorable performance I saw at the Knitting Factory during that time included players from both generations, in a band led by Dave Holland, who was the bassist on *In a Silent Way* and played on other pioneering Miles records from that period. The band was rounded out by alto saxophonist Steve Coleman, guitarist Kevin Eubanks, and drummer Marvin "Smitty" Smith – important younger players starting to make their mark. Steve Coleman was at the forefront of the M-Base scene, which included musicians like pianist Geri Allen, alto saxophonist Greg Osby, and singer Cassandra Wilson. M-Base was not so much about a style but about an ethos I wouldn't try to define. Nevertheless, it was a leap forward, and remains undoubtedly in the fiber of the music, influencing output in the present day. I was drawn in by what they were doing, and inspired by their originality. Here was something undeniably new.

Yet in the retro environment I mostly found myself in those first few years in New York, there was no discernable linear path that continued onward. We were assembled in a clearing, merely gathered. The same expressive variables that had always been there were at play, whether of bebop, hard bop, or '60s Miles or Coltrane. There were no longer discernible schools, though. Instead, there was a disparate bundle of bands: one channeled this, another channeled that. Sometimes even the front line wasn't unified within one band – the alto player played like Bird while the tenor player played like '60s Coltrane. There was no direction from or towards anything. There was undoubted love and care in much of that conjuring, and there were gigs to be had, with receptive audiences who would go along for the ride. Yet, if you were playing in the style of Coltrane's quartet, or wearing the guise of some other great ghost, there wasn't much reason you had to give beyond "It's the shit that I love the most!" Now, that was fine, but it was something quite different than the elemental *here is why* that was folded into every note the original artists played or sang. You had a "why" – but it was someone else's why. Is that what you wanted in the long run?

I sat in this group my first years in New York. We hadn't yet found our own identity. But, in order to embark on that search, there were certain factors to consider. Whatever we were going to do now, we were going to build up from this whole mass of music that came before us, the music we knew closely and loved ardently. The question became: *why* would we try to channel all that older jazz? What meaning could we give it now, that it didn't already have? If we could begin to answer those questions in the musical expression itself, then and only then could we earn the appellation of Renaissance. We couldn't just wish it and talk about it.

If we were indeed going to plant our flag in the terrain of swinging, blues-based acoustic jazz, it meant we believed there was still the possibility of fresh insight and new expression. At this point, the "why" merged with "how." How could we draw from the earlier music and not get dragged into playing a mere ritualized tribute of it? This was a more difficult kind of how. It wasn't one you could discover just by procuring information and applying discipline towards a body of work you loved, which we had already done. Just knowing the music was not enough, unless you only wanted to repeat the past. You owed it to yourself to ask why you were playing something first, because that might guide you on how to play – on what to play, and what not to play, quite literally.

Yet what an incredibly self-conscious stance for someone who called themself a jazz musician! Wasn't the improvisatory medium of jazz all about freedom from that kind of mental noise? Carrying that kind of inner chatter onto the bandstand was the last thing you wanted to do! It interrupted the flow, and missed the point completely. You were supposed to get beyond all that. Ideally, you were supposed to *start* from a place beyond all that.

Welcome to Gen X: self-questioning, often leading to one or another self-referential dead end. The big game was how to avoid the trap of repetition, or simply defeated resignation. Everywhere we turned, we were reminded of everything that had been done before, which is normal enough. Yet it was as if it had all already played itself out, and we were no longer in it. We were scratching at it, tasting it here and there. We felt like tourists, not travelers. Something had already passed by.

The fear was that we lacked authenticity. This was not unique to the jazz scene. We saw nostalgic portrayals of the previous decades in the movies we watched, and commercials that played classic rock and soul anthems from the 1960s. In its original time, a song may have been a call to racial justice, peace among nations, or some other ideal. It may have been an anguished cry to revolutionary action. And now it was being used to sell a product. "Co-opt" was a catchword. The music of an artist like Nick Drake, who embodied quiet mystery, was now used for the hard-sell in a car commercial. Someone born after 1990 might say, yeah, well, that's *always* how it's been for me. Indeed. You were born into the matrix. But, for us, we felt like the real issue had been so close to us, just a few years before we arrived. We could still almost smell it, but had just missed it, and now it was gone forever.

If we weren't careful, our irony collapsed into cynicism, as we looked to the Baby Boomers of the previous generation. They were rebelling against "The Man" in their strident youth – some authoritarian, governmental presence that would oppressively stamp them down if they didn't resist. Yet what had happened? *They* had become The Man, as far as we could see. The Man wasn't the government for us: it was the crushing authority of commodification. And they were the ones pushing the product, selling us a facsimile of their past days.

It looked to us like the generation before us had experienced something authentic in spite of their sell-out: real rupture in the form of political and social change, and large-scale participation in all that, through protest. What was our claim to fame? Things had been easy for us. Because of the relative peace and prosperity we experienced, we didn't need to gaze further than our navel. That was nothing short of blindness. The world had only recently passed through a huge geopolitical sea change with the fall of the Berlin Wall, while genocides in Bosnia and Rwanda unfolded before us. In my circle at least, at the parties I went to, in the bars I drank at with people my age, there was little talk of these events. We were untouched by their enormity. Peace and prosperity had awarded us indifference.

If pressed on problems outside of our cocoon, we answered with flimsy, passive irony. "What does it all really matter anyways?" It wasn't a coincidence that in the midst of all that easy apathy, young privileged kids like myself discovered heroin. We had lost a sense of meaning. Growing up in post-war America, we were already prone to collective solipsism. We had to be hit over the head with a tragedy that directly threatened our own national identity and sense of security, which finally came a decade later on September 11, 2001. But, in the meantime, my generation, politically speaking, was perhaps the most glibly unengaged of any in the twentieth century. That was a luxury we enjoyed without knowing we even had it. It weakened us, to a large measure – our resolve, our sense of commitment, let alone any real patriotism. The Boomers had stomped all over patriotism in their youth, we reasoned, and now tried to refry it and sell it to us in feel-good Everyman movies like *Forrest Gump*. It was not as if we all lay down and grew fat in our languor. The impulse was always there, though: instead of one towards action, there was the easy invitation to just get high and watch the movie about it.

Endgame

was bright of the ... was ... ...
and prosperity had ... ... in ...
It passed on problems onto ... our conscience ... ... with ...

If I could find no immediate sense of "why" in a generational sense, then there was one piece of good news. With no meaning at hand, there was the possibility to start from anywhere. If you could set aside the Renaissance model, there was a wide vista. This didn't mean disavowing everything from the past – that was impossible, and would have been misguided, because I loved that past.

Where to find oneself then, as an over-thinking, aspiring jazz musician? Music, in its steady abstractness, would not supply a roadmap. Literature had been the closest analogue thus far. At its best, it used language to break out of language, into something more like music. That could also work in reverse. In my musical expression I was trying to tell a story, to give a story-like cadence to the improvisation, and create not just musical phrases but sentences, paragraphs, and chapters. Novels were the model. At turns, they inspired the formal play of my compositions. Or, I found their meaning reflected in improvisation.

In *Tonio Kröger* and *Death in Venice*, Thomas Mann had helped navigate the role of the outsider artist. Perhaps I could turn to him again, in search of some broader, historically situated meaning for a young jazz musician of my epoch. In his novel *Dr. Faustus*, he offered a diagnosis if not the solution. Reading it helped me see that just about everything I was fretting about in my own so-called postmodern time, as a belated artist who arrived after something, was already in play half a century earlier.

Here, an apparition pays the composer Adrian Leverkühn an unwanted surprise visit. In a brutal monologue, he assesses the current situation, no-holds-barred:

> "What is art today? A pilgrimage on peas [. . .] Look at them, your colleagues – I know, of course, that you do not look at them, you don't look in their direction, you cherish the illusion that you are alone and want everything for yourself, all the whole curse of the time. But do look at them for your consolation, your fellow-inaugurators of the new music, I mean the honest, serious ones, who see the consequences of the situation. I speak not of the folklorists and neo-classic stylists whose modern-ness consists in their forbidding themselves a musical outbreak and in wearing with more or less dignity the style-garment of a pre-individualistic period. Persuade themselves and others that the tedious has become interesting, because the interesting has begun to grow tedious."

Pleased to meet you / Hope you guess my name . . . Leverkühn quickly realizes he has come face to face with a demonic character, his own hallucinatory version of the Mephistopheles who bargained with Goethe's Faust. This taunting presence is Leverkühn's own sickened conscience, articulating his own misgivings as a modern composer. It's Mann at his oxymoronic best: the tedious music of Leverkühn's own day hasn't really become interesting. Yet composers who wear the style-garment of the past can only hope for a certain "dignity" and little else: they have the "how" but no "why." Mephistopheles underlines that Leverkühn is not unique, even as he wants to bear the "whole curse of the time" on his own. That was instructive for me. I wasn't some special outsider artist. I was one among many, a group of undifferentiated Cains, all of us marked by our inauspiciously late arrival.

Leverkühn makes a Faustian bargain with Mephistopheles to pay for his final opus, first with his sanity and finally his life. Similar to von Aschenbach's fate, it's the Romantic credo carried to its catastrophic end – live for art's sake and, finally, die for it as well. Goethe's Young Werther would have approved. *Dr. Faustus* had even bigger ambitions, though. Mann began writing it in 1943, and Leverkühn's descent into madness was a parable for his country's moral degeneration during the Third Reich.

The atmosphere in the New York jazz scene in the early '90s was not as bleak. Mann's meditation on his nation was profound, yet it was the endgame condition he described for Leverkühn as a modern composer that resonated with me directly. I read the book mostly as a self-involved jazz musician who cloyingly loved German art music and literature, and matched Leverkühn's troubled self-consciousness to my own generational angst. We were both born into a late time, it seemed. This kind of fretting was around before I stumbled onto it, trying to find new lines to play on rhythm changes.

Alongside the tacit theme of Germany's downfall, Leverkühn personifies the worsening health of Western art music, and we are invited to ask whether there is truth in Mephistopheles' dismal assessment of Leverkühn's modernist contemporaries. Music, to the extent that it is an expression of a culture, might reflect its decline. That's bad news for everyone, but it's what you get from the logic of linear history: things are either improving or they're going to shit. I suspected that the atmosphere of political/cultural inertia in my own time indicated that a decline had already begun.

Mann turned to the critical theorist and musicologist Theodor Adorno to help him fictionally portray Schoenberg's twelve-tone technique in Leverkühn's compositions (to the real-life composer's annoyance). Schoenberg, for Adorno, was the answer to a culture industry that leveled everything, including musical expression, to a commodified exchange. With the exception of Schoenberg and his successors like Alban Berg and Anton Webern, most everything else in his own day was of no worth to him. He had scorn for listeners of "easier" classical music, even stronger contempt for American popular music, and a special hatred for jazz. That scorn was directed just as much at the listeners. He compared them to a child with a sweet tooth, or someone who always demands the same dish at a restaurant every time.

Schoenberg's music may have been difficult, but for Adorno willful difficulty was the only strong medicine that could pull us out of the stupor of late capitalism. If music had a tune you could whistle, it was worthless. This upside-down state of affairs was the dreary condition of modernism, in which the interesting had grown tedious. There was no silver lining but, if Adorno had anything, it was a strong fusion of how and why – how music should and shouldn't sound in his own time, and why that was. He wasn't blowing around in the wind with the rest of us! The decay of late capitalism was linked directly with the cultural/musical decline. Schoenberg was an outlier-hero:

> That Schoenberg, at a time in which the possibility of art itself, in its very essence, became questionable, still composed music that does not seem impotent and vain in light of the reality, confirms, in the end, what he once began.
>
> from "Toward an Understanding of Schoenberg"

Mann, though, in his portrayal of a Schoenbergian composer, confirmed none of these kinds of assessments. He effectively transmitted some of Adorno's ideas in *Dr. Faustus*, yet he poked fun at him indirectly as well, by using the quirky character of the lecturing music teacher Kretschmar as his mouthpiece. In his writing, the real Adorno often revealed a self-satisfied pleasure in his own formulations. Here, Kretschmar gets carried away in a lecture on the second final movement of Beethoven's last Piano Sonata:

> "These chains of trills!" he yelled. "These flourishes and cadenzas! Do you hear the conventions that are left in? Here – the language – is no longer – purified of the flourishes – but the flourishes – of the appearance – of their subjective–domination – the appearance – of art is thrown off – at last – *art always throws off the appearance of art . . .*"

It was Mann the ironist again, asking whether a figure like Adorno was serious, or just overblown, or a little of both. For we don't actually know whether he himself feels the kind of Adornian doom that Leverkühn's apparition was announcing. In Mann's allegorical gambit, it is not clear whether Leverkühn represents a German moral downfall or a musical one as well, especially when he mixes in humor like this. Perhaps this vagueness was what put off critics of *Dr. Faustus*. It was not the parallel between his country's debasement and Leverkühn. It was the ironizing that went along with it.

Leverkühn, in any case, is clearly not excited about the "tedious becoming interesting" in his own present day. Mann never resolves this quandary in his novel, nor does he need to. After all, Leverkühn is a mere character, and Mann the novelist has the privilege of authorial distance. Adorno, as a philosopher/commentator, does not. His duty is to tell us definitively the way things are now – the impasse, and the way forward, if there is one. In leaving the problem on the table, Mann could remain "cool and fastidious," broadcasting some of Adorno's convictions with a wink.

As with his earlier novellas, though, that wink was not an end in itself. Mann's critics had charged him of aestheticizing predatory lust in the character of Gustav von Aschenbach (most bitingly, Bertolt Brecht in his satirical sonnet "Über die Verführung von Engeln") and, here, they charged that he did the same with Germany's downfall into Nazism, through his sympathetic portrayal of Adrian Leverkühn. Mann was in danger of sanctioning moral relativism, tacitly excusing the atrocities of the Nazis.

In portraying Leverkühn's unresolvable conflict as a modern composer, though, Mann revealed just as much his own predicament as a German man of letters after the war. *Dr. Faustus* was a personal project like the earlier novellas were, and once again it was one of irony as self-redemption. Now he attempted that on a national level. If he could not "redeem" Germany itself, he could speak for the dignity of German art. Mann braced against the murderous ideology of fascist Germany in an attempt to reclaim and preserve the greatest measure of his country's cultural legacy. Once again, he was a model of sorts for me, this time for speaking one's political conscience.

Mann's novelistic irony was more viable than Adorno's damning absoluteness, because it matched my own experience as a musician with generational hang-ups, in the same way it had previously with my personal ones. That abiding, worthy, kind of irony – not the defeatist Gen-X kind – was instructive. There was a gentle but persistent voice that started to arise as I made my way, which said "The interesting is still interesting – it's on *you* to make it so." All of the overthinking was symptomatic of a perennial kind of artistic unease. It wasn't a particularly "postmodern" phenomenon.

The nail in Adorno's coffin

Perhaps the greatest disappointment in a literary figure I had admired, the greatest example of someone I had raised up in stature as an intellectual only to reveal himself as a human with warts, came when I read Adorno's essay "Perennial Fashion – Jazz." It's hard to isolate a particularly fragment, because it's all bad.

For Adorno, jazz fans are a cowardly, conformist lot:

> However much jazz-subjects . . . may play the non-conformist, in truth they are less and less themselves . . . Terrified, jazz fans identify with the society they dread for having made them what they are.

There is no real creativity in improvisation, despite what we may hear:

> Jazz fans . . . emphasize the music's improvisational features. But these are mere frills. Any precocious American teenager knows that the routine today scarcely leaves any room for improvisation, and that what appears as spontaneity is in fact carefully planned out in advance with machine-like precision . . . The so-called improvisations are actually reduced to the more or less feeble rehashing of basic formulas in which the schema shines through at every moment.

The way the schema shone through was what Adorno celebrated in a figure like Beethoven, but no matter. Reading the essay, you realize that jazz has become as a straw man for everything Adorno hates about American capitalism – about America, period. Bizarrely, jazz is equated with totalitarianism.

> The men of the Thousand Year Reichs of today look like criminals, and the perennial gesture of mass culture is that of the asocial person. The fact that of all the tricks available, syncopation should have been the one to achieve musical dictatorship over the masses recalls the usurpation that characterizes techniques, however rational they may be in themselves, when they are placed at the service of irrational totalitarian control.

Unlike elsewhere in his writing, Adorno's irony has no context. He never explains how jazz syncopation is under "irrational totalitarian control." We are left to guess what he's getting at in this kind of hysterical Freudian pronouncement:

> The aim of jazz is the mechanical reproduction of a regressive moment, a castration symbolism. "Give up your masculinity, let yourself be castrated," the eunuchlike sound of the jazz band both mocks and proclaims, "and you will be rewarded, accepted into a fraternity which shares the

mystery of impotence with you, a mystery revealed at the moment of the initiation rite."

What was going on? Why all this venom? A beginning point in understanding Adorno is that he missed the boat with jazz completely. He explained its rhythmic singularity in inverse terms:

> That fact is that what jazz has to offer rhythmically is extremely limited. The most striking traits in jazz were all independently produced, developed and surpassed by serious music since Brahms. And its "vitality" is difficult to take seriously in the face of an assembly-line procedure that is standardized down to its most minute deviations. The jazz ideologists, especially in Europe, mistakenly regard the sum of psycho-technically calculated and tested effects as the expression of an emotional state, the illusion of which jazz evokes in the listener.

Reading that almost made me not like Brahms for a moment. Brahms was indeed a rhythmic innovator, finding fresh ways to build on the tension between duple and triple meters, and the way they could rub against each other. Jazz started from that point, yet the beat itself was the opposite of an assembly line; it was constantly fluid. Brahms did a lot of things but he didn't swing, at least how I felt swing. I had heard people talk or write about how classical music could "swing." Someone would point to the relaxed rhythmic feeling and dancing quality of a particular Bach performance, comparing it to the melodic flow of Bird's lines. However well intentioned – they meant to break down a genre barrier and find a common link between Bach and Bird – it was co-opting a term. The specific *feeling* of swinging jazz, even in a mediocre offering, was non-existent in the classical music under discussion. Ease and elasticity in the beat, as well as a dancing quality, was a quality of swing, but it did not constitute swing in itself, anymore than it did polka. However much you could talk about swing – as an ever-going fluid negotiation between two and three, as a favoring the upbeat over the downbeat in a reversal of the "Western" rhythmic paradigm – it was not a European legacy, it was a African-American one. If Adorno could have grasped jazz intellectually, he might have been able to imaginatively flesh it out like he did when he talked about Beethoven. He failed intellectually as a musicologist, and imaginatively as a cultural theorist.

The essential problem wasn't intellectual or imaginative, though. It was of the *body*. In his comments on Brahms, Adorno tacitly indicated that he did not *feel* swing, and also did not feel the accent on the upbeat that was fundamental to Black music and all the American pop music he detested that came out of it. He would have been one of those people who claps or snaps on beats one and three instead of two and four, had he dared try. That kind of squareness in itself does not warrant contempt. The problem was Adorno's enmity and condescension. Since he himself couldn't experience the feeling of swing, then there must have been nothing to feel in jazz – as the "expression of an emotional state," jazz is an "illusion." What everyone else was feeling had to have been fake.

Yet he damned himself even more as a Marxist than as a musicologist. For, if a Marxist would speak for the proletariat, there was no account of the largest, most unjustly treated proletariat in America: the Black Americans who created jazz. Instead of lumping jazz in with all the other pop music he scorned, Adorno might have shown how the bourgeois was stealing from the proletariat; how white people were co-opting not just jazz but all of Black music born in America, imitating and profiting off of it far more than its original creators. As great as much of rock'n'roll is, that's it in a nutshell – Keith Richards would tell you as much. Adorno was not writing on behalf of the proletariat, to expose an injustice against them. He was ridiculing and maligning them, or, in the case of the Black Americans who created jazz, simply ignoring them.

His writing was deeply conservative, defensively confirming his own European heritage. Here, free of any self-irony, Adorno declares hierarchical cultural terminology reprehensible yet goes on to use that very terminology in his next phrase.

> The organization of culture into "levels" ... patterned after low, middle and highbrow, is reprehensible. But it cannot be overcome simply by the lowbrow sects declaring themselves to be highbrow ... Anyone who allows the growing respectability of mass culture to seduce him into equating a popular song with modern art because of a few false notes squealed by a clarinet; anyone who mistakes a triad studded with "dirty notes" for atonality, has already capitulated to barbarism. Art which has degenerated to culture pays the price of being all the more readily confused with its own waste-products as its aberrant influence grows.

In *Dialectic of the Enlightenment*, Adorno and Max Horkheimer argued that the Enlightenment had failed, opening the door to totalitarianism. Yet his descriptions of jazz as coming from the "lowbrow sects," versus his own "serious music"; of a jazz listener who has "capitulated to barbarism"; or jazz as a "waste-product" of a culture, one with an "aberrant" influence: these sound similar to the way Nazis described the music of Jewish composers. It was as if Adorno's id was rearing its head, as he valorized his own failed Enlightenment culture in the same terms of superiority with which he had previously critiqued it.

The negative experience of reading Adorno's tract had a positive outcome. My head cleared. It wasn't so much that I saw what was wrong with European art music. It was more that I saw what was *right* about jazz. It was a rightness that did not have to be measured in the terms of a European musical tradition. Whether or not Adorno was right about an endgame, I didn't want any part of it. It was the end of my infatuation with "high" culture – whatever the hell that meant. His tribe was not my tribe. I would have to find and speak culture on my own terms, in my own wandering Gen-X clan, for better or worse.

Why had I been attracted to Adorno in the first place? When I went back and read other essays of his, his unhappy snobbery was less hysterical but now was more discernible. Perhaps my initial zeal was a reaction: I was sick of the dominating conservative voice in jazz when I arrived in New York and wanted to differentiate from that strongly. Yet, instead, I had unwittingly chosen a musical philosophy that was arch-conservative, however much Adorno fellow-traveled with the Marxist left.

It didn't add up. In short, it was bullshit. So I said to myself – like I had said "Fuck the jazz stiffs" when I first arrived in New York, and then "Fuck the punks" a few years later – "Fuck Adorno." Bebop lives.

The form of freedom

I would be tickled by the rub that is: Man be my metaphor.

Dylan Thomas

Dr. Faustus had diagnosed the problem of an artist who had arrived late, giving a frame to my generational self-doubt. It was James Joyce, though, who suggested a way to creatively engage with it. Leverkühn's devil was scolding his contemporaries for their bad faith in musical styles that had exhausted themselves. To say their music was no longer original may have been true to a degree, but the problem went deeper. "Originality" was the kind of romantic notion that no longer had real currency.

In Joyce's *Ulysses*, the chapters skipped confoundingly between disparate writing styles – from the parody of staccato newsprint, to terse question-and-answer catechism, all the way to the first-person ecstasy of Molly Bloom's unpunctuated stream of consciousness. By design, Joyce mutilated a cohesive storytelling voice. As a result, language itself became a character in constant flux. In forgoing a singular, consistent narrative style, he found a way to make the tedious interesting.

This was altogether different than the exposition, development, and resolution I knew from earlier novels, which had a formal affinity to Western art music. Often, *Ulysses* read more like undulating improvisation – like Molly Bloom's famous inner monologue which forms the final chapter. For me, it resembled one of Miles's solos from the '60s quartet when Herbie would stroll, leaving him to roam with just Ron Carter and Tony Williams. In Molly's enraptured solo, all punctuation "strolled." Instead of periods, commas, apostrophes, capital letters, and the like, the word "yes" begins the chapter and appears steadily throughout it as a life-affirming trail marker, providing a more pliable formal glue in the absence of punctuation.

Mann, Joyce's contemporary, cloaked his sensual impulses in high-minded irony. He was akin to Brahms for me. I identified with both North Germans in the way they held back their own sensuality. They mirrored my own suppressed desire poignantly, but did not deliver me from it. In *Ulysses*, by contrast, the transgressive, "dirty" elements of sexuality were overt, and did not lessen the aesthetic achievement but enriched it. Rather than disavowing it, wrestling with it, or sublimating it, the word "yes" asserts the seductive power of Molly's femininity and her pleasure in wielding it. The chapter begins as she muses about her husband, Bloom, the protagonist of *Ulysses*, coming on her bottom in a recent round of sex. Her thoughts shift to how she would seduce a younger man, showing him her garters, and she contemplates whether she would do "this that and the other" with anyone from the coalman to a bishop, confirming with a repeated "yes" to herself, " yes with a bishop yes I would."

You could feel the low-grade fever of Molly's arousal, lying in bed at the end of the day. Yet this was more than just a description. Joyce sketched the way you could get yourself turned on, building a picture of sexual intrigue in your head to a randy pitch, willfully conjured in a stream of thought for the sheer pleasure of the fantasy. That all felt like "It's About That Time," the final track on Miles's *In a Silent Way*. The musicians were not so much expressing desire but *invoking* it in the steady unfolding of their ideas. Molly celebrated her sensuality similarly. This was in sharp contrast to von Aschenbach's shrouded attraction to Tadzio in *Death in Venice*. The tortured division between carnality and intellect was absent. Here, finally, was unbridled ecstasy.

It was the same kind of ecstasy as Miles's final solo on "It's About That Time" – a climax and a closure all at once, within the frame of an LP. I had found a link between two traditions I revered: a European novelistic one and a Black American musical one. Joyce was an altogether different figure than his contemporary Mann: an intellectual and a hipster all at once, like the jazz greats I held at the highest. Literature, like music, could be an experience of the body as well as the mind. The freedom of sexual ecstasy now had a formal frame, and still retained its unbound nature. This play of form and freedom fulfilled the promise of the improvised medium I worked in, and became a principle for the kind of musical expression I was beginning to develop with Larry Grenadier and Jorge Rossy – of the mind, but always of the body at its core.

Because he was free from a fixed style, though, Joyce wasn't obliged to maintain the kind of overt sensuality in Molly's monologue elsewhere in the book. He could be as cool and fastidious as Mann. At one point, Bloom masturbates, watching a young woman on the beach from a distance. As he approaches orgasm, his random interior monologue ranges from an acquaintance he met earlier in the day to how to clean his broken watch. This passage – one that caused *Ulysses* to be banned for publication initially – is still striking today not because of its subject matter but because of its humdrum description. The literality of a straightforward sexual report and nothing more would fail as art – banality itself, nothing more. There is nothing particularly exalted about Bloom's orgasm. Yet Joyce was commenting on the banality even as he was expressing it, profanely. The climax itself is rendered in one hackneyed word, "Ah!" The devil was mocking Leverkühn when he described an unhappy dictum of the modern artist – to make the tedious interesting. Here and elsewhere in *Ulysses*, Joyce had achieved just that. He had made banality humorously interesting, in the disconnect between Bloom's wandering thoughts and his orgasm.

Moreover, Bloom reminded me of myself – not as a masturbator per se but as an improviser. Perhaps the two activities had something profanely in common. I identified with Bloom's ability to reach a climax while musing in a non sequitur fashion, because, more often than I cared to admit, some of my strongest improvising was taking place in tandem with similar kinds of rambling thoughts. "Shit, I wonder if I left the coffee maker on when I left the apartment this morning . . . Will that diner still be open after the gig . . . bacon cheeseburger deluxe sounds good . . . with pizza sauce . . . black and white milkshake . . . how much does a one-way to Boston cost on the Amtrak from Penn Station? . . ." The musical ideas flowed outwards nevertheless, and they could be strong ones. Ecstasy and beauty weren't precious. They knocked around in a jumble of prosaic chatter.

Joyce could be cool and fastidious towards his characters when it pleased him, because he was that way towards style itself. This, it seemed, might be a way to approach being a jazz musician in my time. If various styles had played themselves out and the music of Bird and Trane had grown tedious in our time – not their own output, mind you, but when *we* tried to mimic them in our own present day – then perhaps I could follow Joyce's approach, which meant not holding allegiance to any pre-existing style but instead dipping into one or another as I pleased, for my own purposes.

Yet it was worth asking: what was a modernist losing by throwing away stylistic continuity? In literature, style was a narrative binder because it lent a sense of personhood to the storyteller, a sense of *someone* telling the story that was comforting to the reader. No matter how far into despair the protagonist Adrian Leverkühn journeyed, one always sensed *Dr. Faustus*'s trusty narrator Serenus Zeitblom close by, with his steady voice – a voice of concern for his friend, a voice of conscience for his country, and finally his grief in the loss of both. It was inseparable from the elegiac theme of the story itself. It was also inseparable from Thomas Mann, with his own German conscience – that same voice was there in *Tonio Kröger* and *Death in Venice*, notwithstanding their third-person perspective.

That applied to music. No matter how deep into a harmonic maelstrom Coltrane wound himself, you always heard that it was *him* and no one else – this great, daring soul that ventured into new musical territory and brought something back to share with all of us. Perhaps it was just a kind of imagining, but you felt like you knew the man – not on a personal level but on some deeper universal level that spoke to anyone who had ears. The sublime, as I had come to understand it in someone like Coltrane, always had that human recognition, even as it pointed to something transcendent. Who or what would take his place, in his absence?

If a reassuring, steady narrative voice was absent from *Ulysses*, the binding factor became form itself. *Ulysses* had a strong, unstated frame around its content. Its chapters corresponded to those of Homer's *Odyssey*, with Bloom standing in for the original protagonist, Odysseus (or Ulysses in Latin). Bloom's day in the life traces a journey through Dublin and its outskirts which eventually returns him home to Molly, just as the original hero came back to his beloved wife, Penelope. In formal terms, *Ulysses* was anything but some random hodgepodge. To have the richest experience reading it, you would have to engage with the ancient epic to a degree. Bloom's onanistic adventure, for example, corresponded to an episode that took place on the island of Phaeacia in *The Odyssey*. Odysseus has been shipwrecked there and, while the other women find him disgusting, washed up on the shore, naked and waterlogged, Princess Nausicaa takes pity on him.

Likewise, Gerty MacDowell, the dreamy young woman over whom he masturbates from a distance, knows what he is up to and offers herself to him for viewing, receiving pleasure back. Gerty's reaction to Bloom reads like pulp, describing him in hyper-romantic, chivalrous terms as "a man of inflexible honour to his fingertips" even as he voyeurs on her, masturbating. We are inhabiting Gerty's idealization – her own fantasy of what she would want in a man, projected onto him. In other words, they are using each other. There are two immediately discernible narrative voices, speaking the same text: the one of Gerty, caught up in her real passion, and one of Joyce, sardonically poking fun at it, just as he pokes fun at Bloom. Yet even Gerty's voice isn't her own at times, when it sounds like it's borrowed from another overblown, tacky source.

Joyce had easily achieved the kind of irony Mann used in his portrayal of von Aschenbach – inhabiting the erotic passion of a character, while questioning it. Yet Mann was *sincerely* questioning his character, which meant having empathy for him as he was self-destructing. He was still clearly present, fused to a degree with von Aschenbach, and I was invited to forgive him, the author, for his own affection for Tadzio. Joyce's mocking presence, on the other hand, was amorphous and impalpable. He asks us for no forgiveness because he is free from shame, an outside reporter, often in the form of trickster.

The constant stylistic flux of *Ulysses* was destabilizing but, ultimately, that flux *was* the story – a metanarrative hovering over the more immediate day-in-the-life story of Bloom. The actual subject wasn't Bloom, Gerty, Molly, or any of the other characters. The subject was storytelling itself – not just an account of literature and its varying styles but our own inner-storytelling, and how the two flowed back and forth between each other. Here was the rub. In Joyce's strategy, language did not describe characters in metaphorical terms, but, in reverse order, the characters were a composite metaphor for language.

The aesthetic effect of *Ulysses* was altogether new. A book with no firm narrative presence or style gave me, in turn, a plurality of perspectives as a reader. I was pulled in by Gerty's passion, yet, at the same time, distanced and amused by the derivative, corny description of it. This wasn't just ironic authorial distance. It was more like an erasure of any identity. I didn't really know *who* was describing Gerty's ardent feelings. Was it truly her, or only partially her, mediated through the romantic stories she had read? Was it Bloom, wishfully thinking that she would desire him back? Or was it *me* with Bloom to an extent, the two of us voyeuring her, imagining her being horny like that for our own fantasy? Or was it Joyce himself, mocking all of us? Yet what if Joyce was also taken in by his creation? Why not – he was a man with a libido as well, writing his own soft porn. The narrator was all of us in some kind of hovering Greek chorus, or it was none of us. It was, finally, the text.

If Joyce abdicated his moral responsibility as an author, it implied, at least, walking away from a moral stance as a reader. Disavowing fixed style and narrative perspective meant, to a degree, relinquishing that Mannian sincerity I valued – that desire to be good at heart, despite your own covetousness. There was an emotional adjustment to make, a certain loneliness as a reader, and, more generally, a real fear of this modern landscape, because your own sincerity – in your wish to overcome a personal struggle, and perhaps find an answer – wasn't worth a damn. No one was there to affirm it back to you. You were on your own. As an artist in turn, that leap away from moral obligation implied a broader leap away from a teleological grounding in your work. That was, after all, an obligation that hinged on a pre-existing law, something absolute that was always there before you, and in turn gave you a direction forward – something to strive for, like the striving towards God I felt in Coltrane's *A Love Supreme*. It was a sublime meeting between a finite, sincere human and a benevolent, divine presence. There was a reason to strive for good, and you would vindicate that in your creative output. In my experience as a listener, there was a key difference between Miles's fertile span of recording that began with *In a Silent Way* and continued with visionary records like *Bitches Brew*, and Coltrane's great final mature period that included *A Love Supreme*. The former celebrated carnal desire while the latter transcended it.

Was it all that simple, though: the old dichotomy of sense and spirit? This was unappealingly reductive. To say that the hipster modernism of Joyce and Miles was a descent into mere sensualism was to re-enlist a trope about the decline of art in tandem with the civilization that fosters it – exactly the dismaying modernist appraisal that Mann evoked in *Dr. Faustus*, one that ended, allegorically, in Leverkühn succumbing to his sensuality, dying in insanity from syphilis. In any case, that never calibrated with my own experience of music, because, whether it was Bach or Coltrane, music was *fusion* of flesh and spirit. Some music might be more "heady" but worthy music was *always* of the body, not in the least through its rhythmic activity. Of course, Miles wasn't only carnal any more than Coltrane was only spiritual. Yet each led to one pole in my own experience of listening to them. I began to have an aspiration for my own output: to close the gap between the divine and flesh, to reconcile sexual and spiritual ecstasy in the musical expression. Now there was this question: how might Joyce's meta-model inspire me, in musical terms?

Breadcrumbs

The fourteenth chapter of *Ulysses*, "Oxen of the Sun," tests a reader's faith in Joyce's capacity to make the tedious interesting – one might find it overly taxing to read or, indeed, simply tedious. It does describe events, obliquely – Bloom's night-time visit to a maternity hospital, followed by a boisterous drinking session with Stephen (Joyce's counterpart to Ulysses's son, Telemachus) and his friends. Yet in "Oxen of the Sun," perhaps more than anywhere else in the book, the text itself reigns supreme as the subject. In the first paragraph, Joyce has translated the text from Latin, but without adjusting the syntax for modern English. It spills out in one long, convoluted sentence, with phrases that don't discernably begin or end. If you are inclined, you can go through the chore of trying to figure out the meaning of this opening paragraph, and you can get the gist from one of the numerous commentaries on *Ulysses*. Though, if he wanted you to immediately grasp the meaning, why wouldn't Joyce have simply written it in English to begin with, or at least translated his own original Latin into readable English? What the reader has before them is more like a clue of something else that remains oblique.

On two of my first records after emerging from the *Bildung – Elegiac Cycle* and *Places – Ulysses* was never far away. Both were cyclical in design, with a theme that began the record and returned at the ending, just as Odysseus's journey was a circular one in which he eventually arrived home. Building a musical fabric like this was appealing because it promised and fulfilled emotional resolution.

The sonata-allegro form was already a strong model, epitomized in Beethoven's symphonies, chamber works, and sonatas. Within a single movement, a theme was presented, developed, and then returned at the end. It was transformative: when you arrived at the ending recapitulation, there was a gnosis gained. Beethoven could roam freely even as he wielded a strong grip and dominated the fabric of his compositions, but the constraint of such a form seemed no longer viable in the partially improvised medium I worked in. It would have been the kind of outdated "style-garment" that Mephistopheles diagnosed in *Dr. Faustus*.

Ulysses's cyclical format served as a more open-ended source of inspiration, coming from an extra-musical literary source. In writing and recording those two records, once I had my opening themes, in one way or another, I knew I had an ending already, and so there was the promise of teleological comfort. The journey was *not* arbitrary; there was meaning and order to every step. When I listen back to these early post-*Bildung* records, they sound self-conscious to a degree: I was sometimes trying to etch that order into the music, to proclaim that meaning irrefutably.

Joyce often seemed willfully difficult, and at times he might strike you as a show-off of sorts, smugly displaying his fluency in Latin in reverse fashion. T.S. Eliot was playing the same kind of game in *The Waste Land*, with its dizzying multitude of references, published the same year: 1922. Yet that willfulness was directed towards new narrative strategies, and some of those coalesced into ones I applied on *Elegiac Cycle* and *Places*. At the end of "Memory's Tricks," for example, I silently depressed the notes of its melodic motif with one hand, and with them held down, improvised other lines with the other hand, allowing the motif to peak out in the sympathetic vibrations that arose from the soundboard. It was a pianistic effect, but inspired by Joyce's erased Latin. The idea was to let meaning and order appear in relief, obliquely.

I began to think of these strategies like leaving breadcrumbs. The idea was, like Joyce, to pack your work with as many of them as occurred to you. The more the better; there was no need to worry about a surplus in the same way you usually did when trying to write or improvise with economy, because these breadcrumbs weren't overt, announced directly in the content – for instance, as a particular melodic motif – but were woven into the form in quieter ways. The listener would have to probe a bit deeper to find them. There was the hope that, the more breadcrumbs you scattered, the more you could lay out an enduring, invisible framework. Form, in my rather formless Gen-X surroundings, seemed more important than ever, and, going forward, would be, far from a constraining factor, an opening and a beginning point. Scattering these clues would admittedly be an act of vanity, as if to say to the listener, "Look what I did." Yet it would also ease my own generational self-doubt: with enough of those breadcrumbs, I could communicate formal coherence as a jazz improviser and composer, here and now.

The "art for art's sake" ethos of Harold Bloom and his romantic predecessors had a fissure at its core. In its beauty, art suggested evidence of order, even as it supposedly escaped the responsibility of issuing a specific moral directive. An author like Thomas Mann suggested otherwise: namely, that order and morality were nevertheless linked through a unified narrative voice – one with a moral conscience, however conflicted. That fulfilled, however imperfectly, the promise that the artwork's purpose was to give evidence of a greater order, and whatever moral guidance it suggested in its example was grounded in benevolence, thereby indeed conjoining beauty and the good, or at least a striving towards good, art-for-art's-sake be damned. I intuited what many had said already about the sacred music I cherished, be it from Bach or Coltrane: it was linked with God, from whichever vantage point you experienced it. Music could be an exhortation for His mercy, or it could be simple praise. Or, looked at from the other side, it could be God speaking through you the artist, guiding you as to where to leave those breadcrumbs for others to find. The music I made might dissolve the division between myself and that divine presence. The entry point was moot: it didn't matter where I ended and God began.

Ulysses established its own kind of formal order through a rigorous, exhaustive game of breadcrumbs, in a constant dialogue with a much older source from antiquity. That was Joyce's beginning point, and it wasn't the least bit banal. He recast the open question of whether or not order and morality were linked, by dispersing the storyteller into the text. If the writer had previously been akin to a godlike deity, one in whose image we recognized ourselves, God – and the sublime experience of Him – was now a pantheistic mash-up, a floating presence between author, characters, reader, and text itself. The artwork didn't affirm a moral stance through its formal logic any more than it denied one.

It was as if Joyce was saying: "So you wanted art for art's sake? Well here it is, with no apologies." Careful what you wish for, as they say. If I was to align with any part of this ethos in my own output, I would have to amend my notion of the sublime itself, with its dichotomy of fear and recognition. The former was easy to apprehend in *Ulysses*, in the novel's sheer magnitude, and in its expressive freedom that was nevertheless grounded in the invisible grid of the original Homer. But what about recognition, what about finding myself in all that, and the solace that would bring? I didn't have it all figured out yet, but found a present-day analogue to Joyce upon arriving in New York City, in what was unquestionably the most visionary, truly modern music being created at that moment.

Good irony, finally

As "Oxen of the Sun" continues, Joyce parodies various literary styles to describe the gathering in the maternity hospital. The hip-hop coming out during my first years in New York pasted a composite of earlier music into its own output as well. A classic hook from James Brown, for example, would appear abruptly, stripped from its original context. There was a marked unceremoniousness towards the material the artists used, which allowed for a new kind of expression – often humor, as with Joyce, but also a destabilizing, transformative experience for the listener. It is perhaps difficult to see in hindsight how revolutionary hip-hop sampling was in its beginning, because the act became trivialized. All pop music going forward would be touched by it, to this day, for better or worse.

Hip-hop's arrival was quite different than jazz's so-called renaissance, which still sought to preserve the integrity of the earlier body of work upon which it built itself. Irony was a big word in the '90s, often in a negative connotation. In the case of hip-hop, irony was wrapped in its very design – one would not *expect* that taking a pre-existing piece of music and looping it could lay the basis for something fresh. It would logically follow that doing so would yield a banal facsimile of the original. Yet the opposite was true.

Indeed, it was the baldness of the gesture that was so liberating. Hip-hop was free of the generational baggage and bad faith that was part of the not-quite renaissance my jazz peers and I reckoned with, which went hand in hand with a reverence that could be overbearing and pedantic. In my first three years in New York City, while groups like Public Enemy, A Tribe Called Quest, Jungle Brothers and De La Soul were making game-changing records, jazz felt like a balloon about to pop, and, looking back now, part of what helped that finally happen was the example of hip-hop. In the coming years, an artist like Robert Glasper would make good on the promise.

It was not so much the actual practice of hip-hop sampling that inspired me directly but the attitude behind it. There was something cavalier about the way the artists grabbed earlier music and chopped it up, willy-nilly. This became a feature of a '90s Gen-X ethos – I would venture to say it laid the bedrock for it, in a way that Black American music had done before, meeting the zeitgeist of an era head-on and answering it back.

If you were defeatist, you could say that Gen-Xers had no worthy commonality: no World War II to make us the Greatest Generation; no civil rights movement, Vietnam War, or sexual revolution to hang our hats on like the Boomers. Instead, our shared ground was in the network TV shows from our youth that we lovingly fetishized. The irony came in the triviality of the very thing that bound us.

Yet De La Soul found happy meaning in it in "The Magic Number," by sampling elements of Bob Dorough's original song, "Three Is a Magic Number."

It was a tune we all knew from the Saturday-morning cartoons in the 1970s, on a segment called *Schoolhouse Rock*. A song specifically made for kids to learn their multiplication tables was used as a starting point for something new. Mind you, the collection of tunes that appeared on *Schoolhouse Rock* was nothing to shake a stick at, and still holds up now— like jazz drummer and singer Grady Tate's vocal performance on "Naughty Number Nine," or Blossom Dearie's dreamy singing on "Figure Eight." De La Soul weren't just being cute, and anyways Bob Dorough's original had something enduring/ endearing, with a trippy coolness on its own terms. They had a vision of how they could use it for their own devices, and brought a new funky flow to it.

There was actually a Gen-X connection between this kind of borrowing and jazz's weightier renaissance uptown: both were driven by a curatorial urge, a passion for cherry-picking from the past. The former was ironic and irreverent while the latter was earnest and deferential. A lot of what was taking place in Wynton's neck of the woods at Lincoln Center felt like a tribute, and "The Magic Number" seemed to spring from an impulse that was more in line with bebop in its original issue. Instead of being told to remember something, you were being invited to forget about it whenever you wanted. However you felt about "Three Is a Magic Number" or "I Got Rhythm" in their first creation, it was incidental to what was taking place in the new one. Both bebop and hip-hop used their source material similarly, letting it act as a grid, "looping" it.

These hip-hop artists were the same age as us "young hopefuls," as bassist John Webber jokingly called the new arrivals to our clan, but their music was more original – it was young in spirit. It felt more like the time I was in, and brought lightness and joy to the scene just at the right time. Irony finally could circumvent itself. There was no need to get caught in it for its own sake, which was indeed a problem in the '90s, because it had a payoff: the borrowed material in "The Magic Number" added to the originality of De La Soul's creation, instead of lessening it.

The hip-hop sublime

> The book of the new school rap game
> Writers treat me like Coltrane, insane
> Yes to them, but to me I'm a different kind
> We're brothers of the same mind, unblind

Chuck D, "Don't Believe the Hype"

Public Enemy's "Fight the Power" was featured in the famous opening scene of Spike Lee's *Do the Right Thing*, with Rosie Perez dancing to it against a brick wall. It's hard to communicate what an impact that movie made when it came out in 1989. Just about everything in it was new for me. As a white person who had only recently arrived in New York, and who had never been to the Bedford–Stuyvesant neighborhood in Brooklyn where the story took place, its subject matter, the overall feeling that Spike Lee created, and Public Enemy's music were unsettling. Seeing the movie the first time in a theater was really a "Dorothy, we're not in Kansas anymore" moment. It was a reality to which I had not been privy, and a beginning point of a deeper understanding of racism in my country. At the same time – and this is surely part of why the movie is so enduring – there was this strong humanity to all the characters, because Lee rendered them all with mirthful tenderness and beauty. You missed all of them after the movie was done, even if you hated some of them at different points in watching the film. And it all took place in the city I lived in, albeit in a faraway neighborhood.

The subject wasn't emotionally cut and dried, nor could it ever be. The climactic scene in the movie came when white police officers choked the character Radio Raheem to death. It was a scene that was prescient, and has continued to play out tragically in similar acts of brutality against African-American men up to our own day. I remember the tension in the theater watching it. Black people in the audience were angry, yelling and cursing at the screen. I was angry as well, and there was a deep sadness there. At the same time, though, I felt defensiveness as a white person: "I would never condone something like that; that doesn't represent me." I came to understand that, however real my anger and sadness was, it was abstract compared to that of the Black people in the theater with me – it was based on principles, whereas theirs was felt from experience. After leaving the theater, an abstract wish for some kind of reconciliation was tempered by the knowledge as to just how hard it would be to achieve that. It wasn't as simple as saying, "We all want the same thing," and leaving it at that. The movie invited you to examine *yourself*, no matter where you stood.

In the first thirty seconds of Public Enemy's "Fight the Power," there were already three seismic shifts. The track opens with a sampled snippet of civil rights attorney Thomas "TNT" Todd:

"... Yet our best trained, best educated, best equipped, best prepared troops refuse to fight. Matter of fact it's safe to say that they would rather *switch* ... than fight ..."

Immediately following that with no segue is another sample sounding like a wind-up that will introduce a tune. Here is what caught my ears as a musician: that wind-up sounds like it's leading up to an arrival in the key of C. But moments later, when the next loop arrives, it's in D. These sudden segueless shifts were in the mix as well – the wind-up is heard in lo-fi like it's coming from a transistor radio. Then, when the real track begins, the bass explodes, and it's as if you are suddenly dropping into the ocean of a deeper groove, over-powering, relentless, yet affirming. In toggling these three settings right away at the beginning of the track, Public Enemy were renouncing a firm narrative presence in hip-hop terms, and that paradoxical feeling of destabilization and confirmation was its own sublime. There was a similar fear/recognition on tracks like "Excursions" by A Tribe Called Quest or "Straight Out the Jungle" by Jungle Brothers. It was all Dragon Music, not far at all in spirit and energy from Miles's "It's About That Time."

On 6th Avenue at the corner of 3rd Street, right next to the Blue Note, there were basketball and handball courts side by side. I would often watch the action having come up the stairs from the A train before heading back to the apartment on Jones Street. It was its own kind of sublime: there was a flow between the players, but also a quickness, and something almost violent in the way they moved around each other, sparring for the ball, cussing each other out. It was always primarily Black guys. If a white dude was bold enough to want to join in, they would audition him with a few penalty shots like everyone else – if he made two out of three, they would let him play. There was always a collective tension I felt in that act as everyone watched, but it was unnameable and silent: if you perceived animosity in it, that was you reading in.

I was listening to Public Enemy's *It Takes a Nation of Millions to Hold Us Back* every day. On the other side of 6th Avenue, there was a small shop that sold T-shirts and other band regalia. I bought a baseball cap with Public Enemy's name on it and started to wear it, in the same way I used to stitch Jimi Hendrix and Led Zeppelin patches onto my jean jacket in high school. One day I was wearing my cap, watching the players ball through the wire fence. A couple Black guys were standing close by and I noticed them size me up, looking at me. One of them snickered, and said to his buddy sardonically, "MTV Raps!"

Yo! MTV Raps was a daily segment on MTV that featured the latest hip-hop, and, the way I read it, he was making fun of me, implying that I was a white guy just catching on to Public Enemy because of their recent commercial appeal. It was another experience in the vein of the tobacco farm or the gig at Papa Gino's – feeling snubbed, made fun of, on the outside. It's no doubt I was oversensitive like I was in the earlier experiences, and I suppose I could have been imagining their scorn. Yet I also got it: when Chuck D rapped a phrase like "Death row / What a brother know" it meant something directly for those guys. I reflected on the partisan quality of the various musical cliques out back in high school. Whereas I had always tolerated their disdain of each other, I never really thought it made sense. Here, for the first time, it did.

Consolidation

When *Ulysses* appeared in 1922, classical music was up for grabs. For centuries, it had drawn primarily from German, French, and Italian sources with clear lineages, even if they borrowed from each other. In the last half of the 1800s, Russian composers took the stage, and at the end of that century American composers began to emerge. Art music, as it was called, would remain Eurocentric, but this American voice drew as well from African-American roots.

For me, it seemed like 1920, and the following two decades, would have been the most exciting time in the history of classical music to be a composer. There was a Neo-Romantic like Rachmaninoff, who was extending a pianistic tradition that began with Chopin, full of dizzying virtuosity and heart-on-your-sleeve songlike melodies in equal parts. At the same time, his countryman Prokofiev was writing in a completely different tonal language which often disavowed romantic sentiment. Prokofiev, as well as Bartok, exemplified the kind of modernism that was most appealing to me. They might write music that was squarely tonal, perhaps even simplistic, to affect an atmosphere of naivety, and then, in the next moment, follow it with dissonance upon dissonance, willfully creating discord.

Prokofiev also had an unquestionably late-Romantic side to him, and dipped into its chromatically saturated language when he wanted. It could arrive, though, in the context of acerbic discordance, like in the second *Andante coloroso* movement of his later Piano Sonata #7. The great Sviatoslav Richter, who premiered it in Moscow in 1943, said that he felt the influence of Rachmaninoff in Prokofiev's music more than the latter might have cared to admit. Here, romantic sentiment was tempered by what surrounded it – an abdication of it, something like distrust. The caustic maelstrom of the final *Precipitato* movement embodied that, in music that was no doubt colored by the war atmosphere of 1939–1942, the setting in which it was written. All these emotions existed alongside each other, and the music breathed jarring, unresolved conflict. Yet it was resolved, in a fashion, in formal terms – Prokofiev's nine Piano Sonatas join the canon, alongside his great predecessors like Beethoven, in their ability to present a unified multi-movement work which ties all the dialectical loose ends together at the finish line.

French composers Debussy and Ravel worked within the existing tonal framework yet managed to create a distinctly new harmonic palette, one that would later intersect with modal jazz. Stravinsky and Schoenberg, perhaps the most eminent figures of modernism, drew a sharp contrast. The former would work with tonality and rhythm in a such a way as to change its paradigm forever more, and thereby change the way we hear music as well. The latter would famously disavow tonality entirely, and invent a whole new system of twelve-tone composition. This was the reality of modernism, bad faith of Mephistopheles and Adorno be damned. The sky was the limit. You could call upon anything that had taken place already – thorny contrapuntal textures, perfumed chromaticism, neo-folk modal writing – or you could walk away from it all like Schoenberg.

I began to imagine the possibility of a happier parallel between the jazz milieu of the early 1990s and that earlier time. What I wanted in my own output was neither a historical catalogue nor a stylistic hodgepodge. Both approaches, in the end, were regurgitations rather than births, notwithstanding their craft. The thing about all those modernist composers is that they still sounded like themselves – just like Joyce did when he was referencing other writers. The requirement for my generation would be the same as it was for Joyce and those composers. One had to have a strong understanding of the craft, and just as strong a sense of history, because, if you were going to reference it, you had better not do it in an arbitrary, cursory manner. The how and why were as important as ever.

Park Slope and Carroll Gardens – meeting points

The first time I heard Joshua Redman's name mentioned it was most likely from Jorge. So, there was this guy Josh in Boston. He was young, my age, and already had a ton of shit together on the horn. And it was even crazier: he wasn't even in music school. He was going to Harvard – pre-law no less. Say what? And, by the way, his dad was Dewey Redman – a living legend on the tenor saxophone, the visionary who was on Keith Jarrett records I loved like *Birth*, and a member of the incomparable collective band Old And New Dreams, which featured Dewey, Don Cherry, Charlie Haden, and Ed Blackwell. What would Dewey's son sound like? My first thought was: wow, the stakes are high for this guy.

Josh was part of a large group of jazz musicians who came to New York City by way of Boston. Some of them studied at Berklee for a short time, others were at New England Conservatory. There was a thriving student scene in Boston, and it was a way to make a soft entry into New York, instead of just jumping into the fray. Jorge led the pack. He left Berklee in 1991 and came to Brooklyn with his then wife, singer María de Angelis. They found a brownstone on 11th Street in Park Slope. Once they signed the contract, everyone followed. Josh moved into the first-floor bedroom where there was also a music room that housed Maria's baby grand and Jorge's drums. Maria and Jorge shared the second floor with bassist Paul LaDuca. Between the two bedrooms was a walk-in closet where Jorge kept the drums he used to practice Paquito d'Rivera's music – he had just landed that first important gig. On the third floor there were two bedrooms. One was shared by pianist Victor Atkins and his girlfriend, and the other was tenor saxophonist Mark Turner's. I often think back to this time, when all those musicians were together under one roof, all of them just getting started on their creative paths.

In 1993, Jorge moved to Sackett Street in the Carroll Gardens neighborhood alongside Park Slope. Paul LaDuca moved over as well and now shared a floor with Charles Ruggerio, a swinging drummer I played with a lot during that time, doing some early gigs with Chris Potter, and lots of different sessions. Tenor and baritone saxophonist Chris Cheek, whom Jorge had persuaded to move to New York from Boston, took an apartment there. One floor down, Jorge and guitarist Kurt Rosenwinkel were alongside each other. Right there, in Kurt's room, they recorded Chris's Fresh Sound album, *I Wish I Knew*, with Kurt, bassist Chris Higgins and Jorge. On the floor beneath Jorge and Kurt were multi-instrumentalist Takuya Nakamura and songwriter/producer/arranger Henry Hey, who would go on to work with the likes of David Bowie. Finally, below that floor was drummer Dan Rieser, who would play in a quintessential '90s indie rock band in a few years time, Marcy Playground.

There was a rehearsal space in the basement at Sackett Street, and several different bands were born in that space. Jorge and I started having sessions there in earnest, just the two of us sometimes, working on what would later become the odd-meter trio arrangements of "I Didn't Know What Time It Was" and "It Might As Well Be Spring." Pianist Ethan Iverson and bassist Reid Anderson played there regularly with Jorge, eventually teaming up with drummer David King to form the game-changing piano trio, the Bad Plus.

Another band that hatched on Sackett Street was the Bloomdaddies. The band had a unique instrumentation, with Dan Rieser and Jorge both on drums, bassist Jesse Murphy, and a ripping two-tenor front line of Chris Cheek and Seamus Blake, who blew through an assortment of guitar pedals. Drummers Tony Mason and Kenny Wollesen subbed for Dan at different times. The Daddies were a loud band – a real contrast to the way Jorge played with Larry and me. Composer, arranger, and pianist Guillermo Klein started workshopping his big band Los Guachos at Sackett Street as well. Finally, one of the most defining, influential quartets of the '90s began there during this time, with Mark Turner, Kurt Rosenwinkel, bassist Ben Street, and Jeff Ballard on drums. Jordi Pujol at Fresh Sound Records documented all of these ensembles on a series of fruitful recordings.

Jorge's sister Mercedes was a fine jazz pianist and composer, and also arrived in NYC, by way of Berklee, a year after Jorge, moving close by in Prospect Park. Her roommate was tenor saxophonist Sam Newsome. Tragically, she passed away in 1995. She was part of a group of pianists that included Ethan Iverson and Mike Kanan, who all studied with Sophia Rosoff, a classical teacher who nevertheless took students whose primary background was jazz. None other than Barry Harris studied with her for decades. She also took non-pianists as students: Ben Street, for example.

My own teacher at the time, Fred Hersch, studied with Sophia as well, and, from what I gather, Sophia worked not just on interpretation but on generating a big sound out of the piano, by using the weight of the arms and body and not just the hands. Fred showed me some of this, in his terms, in one lesson we had, working on Brahms' Intermezzo #2, Opus 118, which I recall he played marvelously himself. We worked on sound in tandem with developing strategies for using the whole piano in the solo context, which was the main focus of our lessons. I did not internalize and apply Sophia/Fred's technique – it was too late, I suppose, to switch gears – but it got me thinking about the technique I already had, and about sound more generally.

Jorge, it should be mentioned, was always a multi-instrumentalist, and still is. Here, he describes his upbringing with siblings Mercedes and Mario:

> At home our piano was "the king." It was played by Mario Rossy senior, the patriarch, and Mercedes studied piano at the conservatory, so she had privileged access to the piano at home. This made it feel like playing the piano was a very serious and dignified affair, but with the interesting twist

that my dad played by ear, which was a looser thing but also somehow elitist (only a few chosen ones have perfect pitch, etc. . . .)

I was too lazy as a child to get involved with the piano: it felt like too much of a project and too much work after a long day at school. And it was already taken between Mercedes and my dad, so it just felt like I didn't really have that much access to it. After school I was a couch potato and would doze on the sofa every day listening to Mercedes practice (Bach, Mozart, Fauré, Chopin – LOTS of Chopin . . .).

My story of instrument choice is that one day at eleven years of age, I arrived home from school and saw Mercedes kneeling on the floor banging two cookie tins with two spoons to "A Hard Day's Night." I had never really heard the Beatles or any rock music before, at least not consciously. It was an amazing feeling. Suddenly I realized that I could just start playing music like that! No studying solfège or harmony, or practicing for hours on end! Just grab the spoons, start banging and you are right in the center of the soul of the music! I wanted to start playing right away and grabbed the spoons from Mercedes. She yelled at me, "Give me back the spoons! At least wait till I finish this song!"

I started doing it every day – I got cardboard boxes from my mum's pharmacy and got two (very Catholic) tambourines with pictures of angels and the Virgin Mary on them. The tambourines were the closest thing to cymbals or hi-hats (I didn't know what a hi-hat was at that point anyway). Finally, after one year of this daily routine, my dad got me a set of drums and I started studying classical percussion.

At fourteen, after seeing Weather Report live, I decided I was going to be a musician. Also that year, I got a set of vibes and played them for two years, more or less. The thing is that those cheap vibes didn't have the full-size bars so the dynamics were very limited and I felt they were not so satisfying in terms of expression.

At sixteen, after listening to Miles, Tom Harrell, Freddie Hubbard, and Kenny Wheeler, I totally fell in love with the trumpet. At the same time with the vibes, I felt that I was getting into a bad habit of playing very visually, moving around the shapes of the scales with an underdeveloped ear. Mario and Mercedes gave me constant shit for not having perfect pitch . . . I knew that the trumpet would force me to hear each note I played, which would be great for ear training. It also made me realize the power of playing fewer notes and well-sculpted phrases, with articulation and dynamics – the power of a beautiful sound. From then on, I played the trumpet and I also spent a lot of time playing drums because by then I was already a professional drummer, playing gigs from the age of sixteen.

In May of 1989 I went to Berklee, starting school in the summer semester. I got a scholarship as a trumpet student. When I arrived in Boston, all the cats were there: Josh Redman, Cheekus [nickname for Chris Cheek], Mark Turner, Seamus, Kurt, etc. Everyone was very sweet and encouraging: "Jorge you sound nice on trumpet! By the way, are you available to play drums on a session later?" I got the message and after eighteen months the trumpet was history . . .

I kept playing the piano regularly as a tool for musical development. But I never saw myself as a piano player. I remember one day in July of '87, after seeing Chick Corea's trio with Roy Haynes and Miroslav Vitous, and the next day Keith Jarrett's trio with Jack DeJohnette and Gary Peacock at the San Sebastian Jazz Festival, I had a very strong feeling that the piano was what I really loved the most . . . but at the time I was twenty-two or twenty-three, and I thought that I had already lost that train, maybe in my next life . . .

A couple of years after Mercedes died, I realized that I was in love with the piano and wanted to "go all the way." At that point I didn't care about a "career" as a piano player. I just wanted to play the piano all the time and enjoy the process of learning music and learning the instrument. It dawned on me that I hadn't allowed myself to feel that way while Mercedes was still alive! [Jorge began to study with Sophia Rosoff in 1997.]

I have always thought of Jorge as a musician who happened to be a drummer, versus someone who was born to play the drums only. It was part of what he brought to our trio. I'm not sure how else to describe it, but I know it was a big part of the magic.

Larry Grenadier also made a stop in Boston before making his way to New York. He tells about his beginning with music, first gigs in the Bay Area (quite a beginning!), and eventually landing in NYC:

My dad had been a trumpet player prior to having kids. He played in the army band during World War II and then after the war stayed awhile in Europe playing gigs. By the time my brothers and I were born he had given it up but instilled a deep passion for music in each of us. He taught me trumpet in fourth grade, taught me to read music, and listened to a lot of music in the house. In fifth grade, he bought me an electric bass thinking it would be an appropriate instrument to accompany my brothers who played trumpet and guitar. I went to the local music store where the teacher Ed Rod(riguez) taught me bass and also had a history managing a band of rotating young musicians called "The Juveniles." One week later my brother Steve and myself joined the group. This would have been around 1977 when I was eleven.

The jazz scene in the San Francisco Bay Area in the '70s and '80s was quite active due to some great clubs like Keystone Korner, Yoshi's, Kimball's, and an amazing group of musicians living there including Joe Henderson, Bobby Hutcherson, Eddie Henderson, George Cables, Donald Bailey, and Stan Getz, among many others. When I was around fifteen (1981), I met the piano player Larry Vuckovich who hired me to play gigs with him and introduced me to a lot of the local musicians. Through him I played the final week of the Keystone when I was sixteen with Charles McPherson, George Cables, and Donald Bailey. I remember playing a steady monthly gig with George Cables and also a weekly gig at a funky bar with Eddie Henderson. I was also part of the house band at these clubs and would play with many musicians passing through town for a week at a time.

I graduated from Stanford in 1989 where I had met Stan Getz who at the time was the artist in residence. I was also playing quite often at this

With Jorge in the
Sackett Street
apartment
Photo: Charles Ruggiero

point with Joe Henderson in various trios around SF. My friend from Santa
Cruz, [tenor saxophonist] Donny McCaslin called me one day shortly
after graduating and asked if I'd be interested in moving to Boston to play
with Gary Burton. My brother Phil had already moved to NYC and my
desire was to go there as well. I decided that moving to Boston was a good
way to head east, and in the winter of 1990 I moved to Boston to tour with
Gary. One year later, January 1991, I moved to New York City, into a loft
with Donny and Jeff Ballard.

Americana

Josh graduated from Harvard undergrad in 1991. As he recalled to me, he decided that he didn't want to go to Yale Law School where he had been accepted, and on the spur of the moment went straight to New York. Paul LaDuca gave him a ride from Boston and he moved into the apartment on Sackett Street with everyone. That fall, he won the Thelonious Monk Competition and, next, was signed to Warner Jazz by Matt Pierson, who would subsequently sign me in 1995. He recorded two records within a short time of each other. The first release was eponymously titled *Joshua Redman*, and included his peers Kevin Hays, Christian McBride, and drummer Gregory Hutchinson. *Wish*, which came out the same year, 1993, was something different. It included a dream band made up of guitarist Pat Metheny, Charlie Haden, and Billy Higgins. The ensemble alone called to mind a lot of important music: not just Ornette and Old And New Dreams, but also Pat's record *80/81*, which featured Charlie and Dewey as well. Matt Pierson recollects how he came to know Josh and eventually sign him:

> The Thelonious Monk Competition was a pretty big thing at that point, and each year my label peers and I would always attend, usually heading into battle afterward to see who could sign the winner. In '91, it was a year for saxophone, and, when I went down to DC, I had heard of Josh, but hadn't gotten to know him yet. However, when I heard his performance at the semi-finals (I think he played "Second Balcony Jump"), I was moved in a way I hadn't been by a young player prior to this time. The guy checked every box in terms of what defined a great artist in my book: depth of knowledge of the form, developing a singular sound in the lineage of his instrument, and, most important, there was a direct connection between his own personality/emotion and the sound that reached the listener. Accessible without compromise, super-intelligent, serious yet down to earth/charming, all that.

Now, for a young musician to record with older established greats was a straightforward enough Renaissance move, but to record with those guys spoke to Josh's creative aspirations. He wasn't just hearing a straight-ahead kind of sound. He was ready for something those three guys could bring specifically to the music. They all bridged a gap between so-called free jazz and a more normative swing-based tradition – Charlie and Billy Higgins, after all, were there at the beginning on Ornette Coleman's first records, and *Song X* from 1986 was a collaboration between Pat and Ornette. *Wish* opened with Ornette's blues, "Turnaround," underlining the connections.

Furthermore, both Pat and Charlie, with their Missouri roots, were exemplars of a genre/non-genre that had only been named recently: Americana. Like all those kinds of designations, Americana was a term that appeared after the music had already come into being. It was a sound you could hear already in Charlie's contribution on Keith Jarrett's 1976 ECM record *Arbour Zena*, and I got a little taste of it a few years later when I played and recorded with Charlie on his album *American Dreams* – you can hear it strongly on the opening title track. The way I would describe Americana is that whatever it reminds you of depends on music you already knew, the common link being a North American source (thus including great Canadian artists like Neil Young, most of the members of The Band, and Joni Mitchell). For me, the sound of "American Dreams" – the harmony, the spaciousness – was connected to Aaron Copland in a piece like *Appalachian Spring*.

Ironically or not, a lot of the Americana music I discovered in my *Bildung* was released by a European producer, Manfred Eicher, on his ECM label. It may have confirmed the truism that one sometimes sees what is special about a culture when looking at it from a distance. In any case, we can all thank Manfred for documenting so much great music. Another musician who influenced me greatly was Keith Jarrett, and, while I hesitate to assign genres, no matter how pliable, to any of these great figures, Keith's solo output spoke to me in a similar way. The first record I heard from him was the triple-LP set *Bremen/Lausanne*. It was a birthday gift I received from Dylan, of all people, that last summer of our tumultuous friendship, and it immediately changed my take on what was possible in music, in the same way that the Coltrane with Louis in Merrywood had the previous summer. I had heard a fair amount of jazz by that time, but this was something different.

I initially connected Keith's solo output on records like *Bremen/Lausanne*, *Staircase*, and *The Köln Concert* – and I'm not sure whether either musician would approve – with another pianist I listened to for a few years already, George Winston, and the record of his I listened to most closely was *Winter into Spring*. George Winston, in turn, reminded me of the beautiful, happy piano music from the *Peanuts* holiday TV specials, written and played by Vince Guaraldi. Vince Guaraldi led me back to another childhood idol – my first real piano idol – Billy Joel, and the way he played on an early song like "Streetlife Serenader." There were all these lines you could draw between artists who were on the face of it very different in their designs, but the thread was emotional, and the emotion was often something like nostalgia, home and hearth, melancholy at times but, under all of that, quiet, abiding joy. It was like some kind of unspoken secret they were telling me about myself, and about whom I could become as a pianist, whether it was the sturdy weaving of George Winston, the busking arpeggios of Billy Joel, the wistful boogie-woogie of Guaraldi's "Linus and Lucy," or the exalted vistas that Keith Jarrett reached.

I remember that, after I had been listening to the first side of *Bremen/Lausanne* for weeks, one evening I sat down to play on our Sohmer spinet in West Hartford, and something came out of me that was inspired by Keith's playing, something that seemed to have come from nowhere in terms of preparing for it in any way. It had that feeling of time travel I got from the fantasy and science fiction I was reading – that large, endless scope – because what Keith inaugurated in those solo recordings was improvised music on an epic scale: music from one person alone that journeyed widely in one sitting, full of turmoil, joy, and mystery. It was a powerful experience, and I would meet it again a couple decades later at the beginning of my thirties, when I began to speak my own solo voice. Solo piano for me has always been just that – *solo* – in terms of a certain courage one must have to make a solitary improvisatory journey, with no companions. That is both its romance and its challenge.

As I went along after my *Bildung*, the spirit of Americana grew in me. While it came out most easily in my solo output, eventually I found a way to play and write like that too, in a way that could draw from all that music I loved and condense it into something that was me. The writing in this vein had begun on some songs on my first solo record, *Elegiac Cycle*, and fully found its home later on two records produced by Jon Brion, *Largo* and *Highway Rider*, and a gratifying eponymous album with mandolinist and singer Chris Thile.

Pat Metheny was another musician like Keith who, on the one hand, had absorbed the jazz vocabulary and made something new with it, but whom I discovered through music he made in a wider realm. I remember the first time well. It was the same summer Dylan gave me *Bremen/Lausanne*, just a few weeks prior. That was, as I described already, a stranger and darker summer than the previous happier one at Merrywood. Ms. Hurwitz had become ill during that year, and Merrywood had closed its doors – we didn't know it then – forever. (She passed away a year later, in 1985.) My trusty cabin mate Joe, with whom I had stayed in contact, and a few other of my old campmates were going to a summer music program just down the road at Tanglewood.

I had only recently stopped lessons in West Hartford with Ms. Hurwitz in the middle of my eighth-grade school year. I remember the last few months clearly; it was an inauspicious ending to what was otherwise one of the most wonderful experiences of my young years. Ms. Hurwitz had already sent me several times to play in statewide piano competitions, and that year I was to compete as her star pupil. Only, I was slacking off: I had started cutting up with Dylan and Ed, smoking a lot of weed and really slacking on the practice. The piece I was to play was Chopin's first Ballade in G Minor – a well-worn warhorse of the piano literature, with lots of virtuoso bravura. I loved that tempestous Ballade, at turns dreamlike, noble, sentimental, and terrifying. But I never really got a handle on it or gave it its due, because by that time I was only practicing in fits and spurts. The jazz bug had bitten and, while that was a factor in my backing off from classical practice, it was more that I had begun to embark on a more libertine path, and the regimented discipline required to master a piece like the Chopin was absent in me. Classical music was put on the shelf until a re-entry during my first years in New York.

I arrived at the competition unprepared. It was a requirement that you would have the piece memorized, and I hadn't even done that. When I brought the music in with me, the three judges pointed out that I was supposed to play the piece by memory. I couldn't; and, while they let me play, I already knew I was automatically disqualified. Needless to say, that was disheartening, so I played the piece with no confidence, and the performance was full of stop/start again mistakes.

A month or so after that debacle, I auditioned for the Tanglewood summer program. Joe had told me about his audition, warning me to brush up on my scales because they had surprised him by asking him to play a few. I shrugged off his admonishment and forgot about it. When I arrived, I was ready to go with a piece I really had under my fingers – Brahms' first Rhapsody in B Minor. I was about to begin when the jury interrupted me and asked me to play the A♭ major scale, not one of the easier ones fingering-wise. I flustered and fucked it up. They condescendingly said I could proceed with the Brahms, and it was another failure like the Chopin, lacking resolve and connection to the music. I was not accepted. It was these kinds of experiences that cemented my belief that I could never have a career as a classical pianist even if I had wanted it. You need balls of steel, and my balls have always been sturdy enough on stage or in the recording studio, but more pliable, like rubber.

Nevertheless, I made a trip to Tanglewood the following summer and spent a few days with Joe there. He was hanging out with one dude who was already in college, and getting turned on to new music. We went into the guy's room and Joe said, "Play Brad some of that Pat Metheny." He pulled out *Travels*, still my favorite of all Pat's records: a double live LP on ECM. The opening track was "Are You Going With Me?" I was immediately drawn in by the pathos of the harmony, and Lyle Mays's beautiful opening solo. Suddenly, the scene shifted, and Pat broke out with a solo – *that* solo. It was a gambit I knew from one of my favorite John Coltrane Quartet performances, "Afro Blue," the opening track on *Live at Birdland*. McCoy Tyner soloed first, and the heat was already on. He built his solo up to a high pitch, and then, instead of the band dropping down the intensity to begin Coltrane's solo – the normal approach in a band, giving the next soloist a chance to start from a clean slate and tell their story – Coltrane began from there, and went even further. Pat did the same on "Are You Going With Me?" In both cases, the sublime was manifest in a superhuman surplus of power. So far, just to recap, there were four life-changing musical moments in succession, in two summers:

1. Coltrane, "My Favorite Things" bootleg, August 1982

2. A week later, "Machine Gun," Jimi Hendrix & the Band of Gypsys

3. Keith Jarrett, "Bremen Part 1," following summer, 1983

4. A week later, the Pat Metheny Group, "Are You Going With Me?"

With Pat, the sublime was just as much a physical feeling. As his solo continued, I had the sensation of something overpowering welling up in my stomach and then emanating outwards towards my heart and through my whole body. I experienced that same welling years later when our first child was born, and I was there to see it.

On that solo, Pat ran his guitar through a Roland GR-300 guitar synthesizer, and the wailing sound he got was like nothing else. It pushed its way immediately to the front of the top ten of my air-guitaring list, in a tie for first place with Hendrix's "Machine Gun." Years later, in 2006–2007, I had the great fortune to collaborate with Pat on two records, *Metheny/Mehldau* and *Metheny/Mehldau Quartet*, both released on Nonesuch Records, and tour with him and my trio with Larry Grenadier and Jeff Ballard. It was literally a dream come true, and a high point was writing a piece for Pat to solo on with the Roland GR-300, called "Secret Beach."

The next track on *Travels* was "The Fields, the Sky." I related parts of it to other Americana music that was already in my personal canon, even though there was a Brazilian spirit in the music as well. Whereas "Are You Going With Me?" connected to shredding rock'n'roll guitar from Hendrix and Alex Lifeson, "The Fields, the Sky" had a kinship with great folk-rock acoustic guitar playing on tracks like "Carry On" by Crosby, Stills, Nash & Young, or "Melissa" by the Allman Brothers, specifically near its end, when Pat strummed like only he can. Again, the idea was the same as with Keith – it took that musical locus and accompanying feeling and expanded it into a larger improvisational canvas.

Hearing Keith and Pat, I already had an unspoken conviction I would hold onto for the rest of my life and would play out when I was asked to describe some of my own records, like *Elegiac Cycle*, *Largo*, *Highway Rider*, and, more recently, *Taming the Dragon*, *Finding Gabriel*, and *Jacob's Ladder*. If you want to call this jazz, great. If you don't, great.

MoodSwing – the Joshua Redman Quartet

Josh brought something else to the table on *Wish*. There were two beautiful ballad covers on the record, one of Stevie Wonder's, "Make Sure You're Sure," and the other by Eric Clapton, "Tears in Heaven." Jazz musicians had long been using popular music as their vehicle, but it had become a fixed body of standards. Josh was at the forefront of what became a big feature of jazz in the '90s, and continues today: interpreting and improvising on more recent songs. Pat played acoustic on both of those tracks, giving them a more Americana sound. Furthermore, that night at the Vanguard, I noticed quickly that there was so much blues in Josh's playing, just like his father Dewey. He would happily stay in that zone for minutes at a time within the context of an uptempo, tricky tune in a refreshingly unselfconscious way, like on his own "The Deserving Many."

Josh may have been my Gen-X brother, but he was not constrained by any brackets the Renaissance Police may have been drawing around what influences were appropriate or not. Playing as a leader with Pat, Charlie, and Billy, multiple streams were already coming together in his approach going forward – Americana, the free jazz ethos of Ornette Coleman, an openness to covering contemporary (worthy) pop songs, and, under all that, an assimilation of the music I loved in the normative jazz tradition. This was the musician I had been waiting for from my generation – someone as connected to that tradition as I was, but open to music outside of it.

The *Wish* band went into the Vanguard in the fall of 1992. Charlie was not able to make the second half of the six-night run, so Josh hired another rhythm section. Lo and behold, it was with Leon Parker and Ugonna Okegwo, with whom I was playing regularly as a trio then. Leon put in a word for me, and I got the call! I had never played at the Vanguard, and at that time I hadn't heard Josh. Mostly I knew him as the badass guy in Boston that Jorge and others were always talking about.

I got to hear the third and last night with Pat, Charlie, and Billy. I remember that the expectation and buzz in the air was thick. Just to have those three guys with him on stage – I thought, man, Josh must just be shitting a brick. So what did he open the first set with? "Trinkle Trinkle" – one of Monk's most difficult heads. He just slayed it, with Higgins responding to his phrases, giving that Buddha smile in approval, and Charlie playing in that open, chunky way that only he could. Pat followed with his solo, and all of a sudden it was as if we, the audience, were sitting in on the session of Pat's classic trio record with Charlie and Billy, *Rejoicing*. There was a conversation between something old and something new on the bandstand.

The night had a strong impact on me – seeing some of my idols, with a guy from my generation. I had a mixture of feelings towards Josh – just a little jealousy, of him being on stage with those heavyweights, but mostly admiration for him, that he was hanging with the cats no holds barred. Most of all,

On tour with Pat, Larry, and Jeff, 2007

Photo: John Watson

I was stoked that I was going to play with him. When I did the next night, Thursday, everything came together so well. It was great to be on the stage with Leon and Ugonna as a rhythm section; we had been playing trio for a stretch, but had started out in that context, backing up Stevie D and Mark Turner, so we brought a vibe already. Comping with Josh immediately felt easy in the same way it did with Jesse – he was feeding the whole band ideas to bounce around, but also, I noticed immediately, responding to our ideas already, in turn.

That was a one-off for the time being, as Josh continued to tour with Pat, Charlie, and Billy through 1993. In the beginning of 1994, he called me to be part of a new band with Christian McBride on bass and Brian Blade on drums. We began hitting it hard, touring first in the States in the winter months. Our first gig was at Zanzibar Blue in Philadelphia. I remember meeting a polite sixteen-year-old Nate Chinen who came to the gig and wanted to talk shop after. Nate has been one of the most important writers to document our generation and subsequent musicians in the music through the years. Zanzibar was followed by the Newport Jazz Festival and Chicago Jazz Festival. It was a trial by fire on those big stages with the expectation running high, but we coalesced into a band quickly. Then we went into the studio and recorded *MoodSwing* in the early spring, having primed a lot of the material – this time all originals from Josh – and tracked at Power Station in NYC with James Farber, the master recording engineer with whom I went on to record almost all of my trio records.

The Joshua Redman Quartet with Christian, Brian, and I was a success story in terms of finding our way in the nebulous yet fertile jazz climate of the '90s. We were a band, and that meant that we achieved unity and order among the four of us, yet within that frame found a way to roam freely. The unity came from both what had come before us, and something we brought that was new, under the loose but sturdy frame of Josh's leadership, and through his compositions and arrangements. Yet I think that a big part of our success came from each of our "meta-backgrounds" – it came from the music we all carried within us in the broader sphere outside of the jazz we were playing.

I remember already being struck by that the first tour we did. The music we were listening to, often in a van or airport lounge en route to a gig, was probably only twenty per cent jazz, and that was not because we didn't love jazz but rather because we had already internalized so much of the music that most obviously informed what we were playing together – the hard bop as well as the more exploratory jazz of the '50s and '60s. You could hear that easily enough, although we never tried to simply ape it. It was a given. All of us had been absorbing that great music for a while, and it was as if a conversation had already taken place among the four of us and no further words needed to be spoken. It wasn't like we avoided talking about it, but it was not frequent. That would have been the kind of fervent conversation I might have

With Josh, London, 2016
Photo by Sisi Burn

had five years earlier when I arrived in New York, hanging out with Bill, Sam Yahel, or my St. Mark's Place roomie Sean, listening to records.

It wasn't as if we had "graduated," but we had internalized those influences to a degree, so there wasn't too much to talk about. I don't recall much parsing out and problem-solving in our rehearsals. Although some of his tunes were challenging, Josh never wrote anything for us that was difficult for the sake of being difficult, so we were able to just jump in and start playing pretty quickly. It was self-evident if I was leaning into McCoy on a solo, if Josh was channeling Sonny Rollins for a moment on a blues, if Christian was calling up Ray Brown in something he was doing, or Brian was accessing Tony Williams or Elvin Jones for a moment. I say "for a moment" to stress that Brian already had his own voice strongly. I think we all did.

The other eighty per cent of the music outside of those more identifiable sources were the things we were listening to then. Some of it was stuff we had always listened to from childhood, or it was a new romance. Christian was a certifiable James Brown freak, and was always turning us on to one or another bootleg tape he had acquired. Josh and I were both into the grunge of Alice in Chains, Nirvana, and Soundgarden, which was happening right then. Brian was heavy into roots-rock Americana from singer-songwriters like Neil Young and Joni Mitchell. I was listening to Brahms all the time.

Within all of that, there were a lot of overlaps, like Josh and I with the grunge stuff, and Brian and I with roots-rock. Sometimes there was a collective rekindling of something we may have forgotten – like when Brian put on a cassette in the van of the Spinners, that great vocal act from the '70s. I had forgotten how beautiful a song of theirs like "I'll Be Around" was, and it took me back to days in Bedford at the public swimming pool. Brian pointed out to us that some songs of theirs had a "swamp beat" – drummer Earl Young would land on the floor tom instead of the snare for the backbeat. I realized then that he was pulling that into what we were doing at times. Christian was doing the same with James Brown, I was with Brahms, and Josh was with Stevie Wonder and other classic R&B groups, in some of tunes he brought in, and his writing. Those musical streams flowed into what we were doing as much as the more obvious common ground from jazz. There was all this music from our collective childhood outside of jazz that we were bringing to the table, and we were sharing that with each other as well.

When we began to tour regularly, in our performances we would play James Brown's "I Got You" as an encore. I don't think the choice of Josh's was solely based on wanting to "get house" – to win people over by playing something that went down easy. We did get house though, every time, but it was on Josh's terms, and our own. Christian happily switched to the "porkchop" as he called it – the electric bass – and brought some of that J.B. energy into the performance. I dug in happily, channeling Herbie on records I loved like *Secrets*, trying to push the harmony outside a bit, in that funky context. It all just came together.

"Meta" was a big word in the '90s, because it seemed to offer some greater hope of order that could hover over all of the disparate postmodernist flotsam. In this regard, playing with Josh was the first time that the meta-view came into play in terms of my actual playing. I realize it only now in retrospect, writing about this period. To be a meta jazz musician meant not just to dip into various genres but to actually gain mastery over them – mastery enough, that is, to roam freely within them in an improvisational setting. I am not tooting our horn, but I do believe that this was different than what had preceded us.

The thing is: if you were on the vanguard of the jazz scene in 1963, let's say, lucky enough to play in a band like John Coltrane's Quartet or Miles Davis's Quintet, that, as I understand, was more than enough to make a legacy, which today is its own evidence. We did not inherit that legacy for ourselves, as I understand it: we received it, along with a certain bad faith at the outset of the '90s in terms of how to go forward. If we "inherited" anything, it was a charge to take from everything. Our loss was a discernible, existing stream; our gain was an ocean of possibilities. It was up to us which way to point our sails.

Smalls

In 1994, Smalls was born. It was an important place for a lot of the musicians I've written about here, where many of us got our beginnings. I relocated to Los Angeles at the end of 1995, but caught the beginning. I'll let pianist Spike Wilner describe its genesis and what the scene felt like then more generally. Some of his memories of the Village Gate and our time together overlap with the ones I've shared above. He has been the proprietor of Smalls since 2007.

It seems that our generation really got the last taste of the old, gritty New York scene. There were still so many shitty neighborhoods with real dives and bars. The music was so alive and still in the hands of the masters. You could hear Tommy Flanagan, Hank Jones, Roland Hanna any night of the week, all just down the street playing duo gigs in restaurants. Our main hangs were the Village Gate and uptown at Augie's (which is now Smoke). "The Gate", as we called it, was our Sunday-afternoon hang. Jam sessions and cats flowing in and out of the terrace. It was a real social scene. I remember well the trio that you had with Ugonna Okegwo and Leon Parker and heard you play many times at the Gate. I remember well observing your rapid transition from student to self-realized artist there – you began to find your real voice and then just exploded. That Village Gate stage was the cutting ground. I remember that stained-glass wall behind the piano and just peeping around the corner to catch the hands of whomever was playing – Mulgrew Miller or Junior Mance, someone great like that. I had a shitty apartment which I rented (with a shitty baby grand piano) that was literally right across the street from the Gate. I recall many good hangs in that pad with a roster of youngsters who are now some of today's masters – Greg Hutchinson, Eric McPherson, yourself, Sam Yahel, Peter Bernstein, and a few others hanging there crowded together, smoking some bong hits and listening to McCoy Tyner, *Live at Montreux*. Those were formative years. I have memories of spending afternoons with you practicing together on that piano, our metronome set for 96 bpm (that magic tempo for nice B♭ rhythm changes). One afternoon you set me free by making one comment on my playing – an encouraging word when I played something I thought I couldn't – and it became a catalyst for future musical and psychological growth. Sharing musical ideas at such a young age put me in a wonderful place.

When the Village Gate closed in 1994, it left a vacuum for our scene. There was a strange transitional period with no exact hang location. Then one afternoon, while hanging with our friend Grant Stewart in his East Village apartment, there was a call for a gig at a new club that was opening: Smalls Jazz Club. I made sure to be there on the opening night for the band that included you, Grant, Pete, Omer Avital, and Andy Watson and started what was to become, for me, the place I would live and work for the next twenty-eight years. Smalls was created by a sprightly and eccentric guy named Mitch Borden. Mitch was by no means a club owner. More of a philosopher, with a heart made of gold. Musicians trusted him and used him as well. He didn't seem to mind too much, or at least it seemed to me. I also started to play at Smalls at that same time but by running an after-hours jam session that started at 2 am and went to 6 am. It was brutal: I'd set my alarm clock to wake up and then get the A train (I lived in Harlem at that time) to make my gig. But the Smalls culture was wild. Mitch attracted all kind of people – invited them into the club. People that would not be welcome or able to enter anywhere else in New York City would end up at Smalls. Since he never bothered to get a liquor license, he could keep the club open 24/7 and did so. Often, he simply gave away soft drinks, rice and beans and other snacks for no charge at all. How he managed to stay in business was really due to the fact that he had virtually no overhead and an incredibly small rent ($900/month). He paid everyone in cash and some cats literally lived there. It was a hang for college-aged kids to get drunk and laid, a refuge for old burned-out junkies from the '50s and '60s, a place for madmen, witches, homeless, poets, and hangers-on. Mitch was lucky, though: he managed to hire an entire young generation of musicians to play there, musicians who later went on to become some of the most prominent in the music. Josh Redman, Sam Yahel, Brian Blade, Peter Bernstein, Greg Hutchinson, Omer Avital, Jason Lindner, Mark Turner, Norah Jones, Kurt Rosenwinkel all came to hang and do gigs. They were just kids and not famous yet. They just wanted to play. Mitch also favored the hard-core conservative bebop element, and the Barry Harris disciples who entrenched themselves at Smalls. From 1994 to 9/11/2001, Smalls was a wild, hallucinatory dream of decadence, jams, and jazz music.

IV
The Long Goodbye

The Pink Lady

Dessert after a gig with the Joshua Redman Quartet, 1994

The first time I did heroin, it was alone in my apartment on Jones Street. It spoke to me in a soft voice, caressed me and said, "Everything is going to be all right. All your troubles are gone now. All your hurt has been taken away."

It was so much better than drinking. I would drink and drink, trying to fill a hole I couldn't fill. And then I'd be a mess – loud and foul, or maudlin and self-pitying, talking shit, sometimes picking fights with people, acting like the village idiot at the bars. There was always that crap feeling the next morning: sour breath and your saliva like glue, thirst and nausea, the headaches and depression. When I started out with heroin, I would sniff just one ten-dollar bag at the beginning of the evening and then *boom* – bliss, well into the wee hours, but with none of the stupidity, none of the belligerence, only peaceful calm. Compared to a thirty-dollar bar tab, it was considerably cheaper than booze, in the beginning at least. I could stay up late in that state and when I fell asleep it was a long sleep: ten hours, sometimes twelve. None of that shitty sleep after a night of drinking when you wake up at 5:30 am and have to piss with a splitting headache, craving water and already feeling nauseous. No, you'd sleep straight through, for hours and hours. Later, I realized it was a death-like sleep – there were no dreams, there was absolutely no segue to and from a waking state. Heroin sleep is different from other sleep: it's like that part of your life disappears. It's just wiped away.

In my apartment alone after snorting that first bag of heroin, I thought: I've found it – I'm home. I've found my baby, I've found my lover, I've found my best friend, I've got everything I need now. I sat on my bed, contentedly half-conscious, for what was probably an hour or more. The time passed, nothing happened, and nothing in particular came up in my head, in a blissful stasis. It was perfect; it was just what I wanted.

I had a vision of a girl. She was young, maybe in her twenties or maybe even just a child. She was only half-real, like a cartoon, so her age remained indeterminate. She was dressed in a pink tutu skirt with white tights, and she had curly, short hair, a little like Shirley Temple's hair in the movie *Heidi*, but then it was completely white – like white powder. She held a little magic wand and would smile gently at me, waving it to and fro, not saying anything. I began to think of her as the Pink Lady. The Pink Lady was always in a room that was all red, with red velvet carpet and velvet on the walls too, an enclosed room that was warm and muted, with soft light. When I did eventually fall asleep after a night doing heroin, I was joining her in that room. The Pink Lady and the red room were solace – the Pink Lady was a mother figure who was taking me back to a red-velvet womb. She would let me nestle there, and protect me from pain.

After a while, I realized that it was no womb but a softly upholstered egg-shell of death. Death is the cessation of all suffering and pain. What is the high of heroin, what is the appeal? It's tasting death. Death for me looked like a sweet little smiling girl in a tutu with curly white locks. It could have been worse, I guess.

Yet it was an artificial death. I already knew the logic of the sublime. It was the flipside of beauty. Beauty made mortality bearable by celebrating it, whereas the sublime made it terrifying, by confirming it. The false salve of heroin was that it seemed to make death beautiful and comforting. It tamped down the fear of annihilation by dressing it up like a ballerina. If the sublime was fear of God like that of the Old Testament, then heroin was a false god. What a stupid thing to truly die for. Fuck that, I say, to anyone who thinks it's going to lead them anywhere else then a slow shitty death or a quick useless one.

You only fear God if you believe in God, and, if you play around with death, you'll need him to pull you out of its net.

Miguel

The people I ran with then were like me. When I was on the road I would find them, and we'd score together and have this kind of fleeting intimacy that broken people have: desperate, unpredictable, and then over as quickly as it began.

I remember Miguel in Madrid. I was playing at Café Central with alto saxophonist Perico Sambeat, bassist Mario Rossy, and drummer Jorge Rossy. It was a great club in those days, a good hang, always good players. Miguel and I sniffed each other out during the day, on a busy avenue close to the Prado. He had darting eyes from the street but something soft and searching under that, delicate – still just a kid like me, twenty-two, maybe younger. I only spoke a few words of pidgin Spanish but we both knew what we wanted: he wanted coke and I wanted H, and he would help me find some if I'd get him what he wanted. Deal. I had 8,000 pesetas cash from the gigs in my sock. I could get good and high and buy for a few days.

So we made this whole-day pilgrimage. We jumped the turnstile, took a train way out of the city, and when we got out I had no clue where we were. We walked through vacant lots covered in broken glass, used condoms, needles and human shit. Up ahead there were stone buildings and people milling about, all past a high fence. *Gitanos.* It was a gypsy camp. My stomach knotted. I'd heard about these places. These guys were crazy – total gangsters. Miguel was trying to give some kind of password to this big motherfucker at the entrance, and he kept on saying stuff to me under his breath – *no mira . . . chicas . . . cuchillo.* I figured out what he meant more or less: don't look at any of their women or the guy will cut you with a knife. Fuck. The whole time these girls were calling to us, moving their bodies, trying to draw our gaze their way. Some of them way too young. Tricky, tricky scene. Different laws past that fence. I bowed my head.

Then we got past the guy and were in, and the whole thing became almost civilized. There was an old gal who had fresh works for sale – wasn't that nice: 200 pesetas got you a clean rig, water, and citric acid to break down the tar. With no hassle I bought some good H – finally, not that bubblegum crap I had been getting from the African guys on the Gran Via, cut with who knows what. And it didn't smell like someone's asshole either, the way the street stuff did because every time they got swept by the narcs they'd swallow down the little plastic packs and then pick them out of their shit again later. By the time you bought it, God only knows how many turds it had passed through. Everything was out in the open out here, no police patrolling, not a one. They didn't come up this way. I thought, I could get murdered and no one would know it – I could just disappear.

Miguel got his coke easily and we found the shooting gallery. It was a broken-down big stone hut with no roof, twelve or so people in there, just up a jagged hill. I could see Madrid far away, a wrinkling mesa of stone and cars, suffused through the heat waves. Then it stopped, nothing but dust and high-ways, and then us. Would I make the gig tonight? Would I ever make it back there? I fixed up first, tying off the good vein on my right arm with my belt, pushing the brown juice in while everyone watched. Go slowly – watch out for a sting if it was cut with something dirty. No, it was good, really good; it came on strong and clean. Then there was that taste like blood in your mouth and a lurch in your stomach like you had to barf, but I had learned how to push the nausea further down into my groin and, a second later, it felt better than anything else: like right before coming and right after, all at the same time. I wanted to cry it felt so good. Miguel shot his coke next with a smaller needle into a vein in his hand. His eyes watered, his whole body reeled back and shot forward again, and he puked perfunctorily onto the ground in front of him. *Puta madre! Hombre . . .* All around, everyone shooting up, puking, bleeding, nodding out, laughing and crying all at once. And I felt like: this is home. This is where I belong, these are my people. *I'm this.*

I made it back to the city, itching and gowd out. Miguel stuck to me. I wanted to shake him. Could he come to the gig tonight? Sure, I guess. He was there at the Central only fifteen minutes and fucked it up, shooting up in the bathroom like a knucklehead, staying in there too long, getting caught. Blood on the stall, disgusted patrons, dirty looks and whispering. Jorge taking the heat from the manager, calming him down. Finally, Miguel can stay because he's my friend and we've filled the room tonight – but he can never come back again. Him sheepish, apologizing to me, jacked up on the coke, swallowing saliva, trying not to puke.

On the next break I see this older dude buying Miguel a drink at the bar. They're talking, and the older one keeps looking at me and frowning. What's his beef with me? I can see he's gay from thirty feet away. Jorge calls me over to the bar with them and introduces us. The guy looks at me and nods with a sarcastic smile like he and I have some evil pact. There's hatred in his eyes. What the fuck? Then I realize: this guy is my buddy's john – this guy pays him for sex. He thinks I'm just another john like him; he thinks we're in com-plicity, in competition. Instead of contempt for him, I feel an old fear. He's another predator – a chubby Dr. Dunn with a mustache. And for an instant I feel so bad for Miguel, who's there smiling at this fucker, trying to be nice to this malevolent queen in designer jeans that are too tight, so he can get more money for more coke and a bed for the night. After the second set they leave together.

The next day Miguel and I meet up on the street. He comes back to the hostel with me and we bang again together, him uptown me downtown. I let him take a shower. He probably hasn't washed in weeks. He comes out naked, showing me himself. He's beautiful, like a statue – all pale, but way too thin and fragile, like you could knock him over with just a little push. It's like you can see right through him, the blue of his veins. He wants to give something back for the coke I got him – his body. That's all he knows. I don't want to have sex with him. I want him to get out of there because it's too much. I'm starting to feel something, like caring for him. I want to be alone with my drugs and then just go to the gig and crawl back into the music. He's asking – please, can I spend the night? I ice him – you've got to get out of here. He gets dressed and walks out quietly, back onto the street where I met him. I'll never see him again. I shove the feelings away with more drugs. He was like me but more fucked up. He was hustling to get back the power from whoever had taken it from him, and it wasn't working. He was trying to numb out the pain with the coke. Someone stole something from him and he couldn't get it back.

[replay – Miguel:]

He comes out of the shower and dries off in front of me. I see the bruises and marks on his thin arms where he shoots his coke. "I eh-stay with you aqui, unos dias?" he asks like he had then. He looks at me, retracted and scared, shoulders hunched.

"Yeah sure." I move toward him, take the towel and help him dry off. I embrace him and he nuzzles into my neck a little bit. He holds me tight and doesn't cry but just kind of shakes a bit. "Let's just lie down," I say. "Vale." We get in the small bed. His thin body is clammy and cold. I put my hand on his chest. He was coughing the whole time I hung with him, like he had TB. Now the coughing has stopped but I feel the fast flutter of his heartbeat. I just hold him, that's all.

A couple years later, in Hamburg. Jan, a few years older than me, late twenties, but another lost lamb with sad friendly eyes, tricking by the train station. He steers me to the H. I buy him his rock. Back to my shitty hotel across from the Hauptbahnhof, the two of us. I shoot up. It's stronger than anything I've had in a while and I go out for twenty seconds, slumped down on the chair. When I come back he's crying, wet eyes full of fear, looking at me. "It's so scary to see you stick that needle in your arm, man. Do you know what you're doing?" What's he on about? He's thinner than shit with his scraggly beard and falling-down jeans, smoking that crack. Scared for me. We'd been rolling together just fine the whole afternoon, talking shit, lighting up the Reeperbahn. And now he's all touchy-feely, like he's my girlfriend. Anger, the first reaction usually – but, under it, that fear of anything like intimacy when he shows human concern. Push it away. Anger. Under anger: fear. Under fear: inconsolable sadness.

He wants to take a bath so I let him, on the nod. He calls me in there – will you get me a towel? I look at him. He's ready for sex, the question in his eyes, showing me what he's got. I ignore it, tell him I've got to get on with stuff and get ready for the gig. He dresses and leaves – we make a quick, muted goodbye. Another broken one. We were everywhere. Frozen, right at the point where everything shattered. Like wild animals – terrified of people, trying to

The Café Central and Hostal
Fernandez where I stayed
in Madrid

stick together but eventually fucking it off and walking away from each other, back out into the headlights, getting beaten down, over and over again.

I'd run into these guys, and they were looking for closeness, looking to seal a wound and heal. We were drawn to each other, not just because of the drugs. But I could never let them in any more than I did anyone else. I didn't want to get burned again like I did with Ed and Dylan. My only sanctuary besides drugs was the music, and it lasted as long as the gig. I pushed away intimacy from everyone – it frightened me.

Sarah

Sarah was beautiful to me right away when I saw her the first time: auburn hair and a few light freckles, thin with a nice slope in her ass. She had piercing eyes that were always squinting when she looked at you, asking you a wordless question, reading in. She wore mostly denim and leather, except for the nights she worked at the Blue Note, where she'd greet us in their uniform: black dress pants, white tuxedo shirt, blue suspenders and a blue bow tie. She was one of the native New Yorkers like Caleb and some of the Bebop Nazis, and had what they had: an understated, deeper radar of what was jive and what was worth your time, and a way of being jaded that I wanted for myself. I was a West Hartford neophyte and had never spent time with a girl like her.

When I first met her she was still at Columbia. Farns had befriended her at the Blue Note, and she helped them get in there without paying the cover whenever she could. She could throw down shots with the Goons, and didn't mind the jockish camaraderie around the music, or the smutty trash talk about their sexploits. She laughed all the while, more than I did. The first impression I had was that she was actually macho; even though in her demeanor she was feminine and soft in all the right ways, she had a low, gravelly voice, and could take charge when she needed to, all with that street-smart bemusement. She was not a musician herself, but understood what we were doing and had an ear in jazz, which wasn't easy to find in girls our age, or guys for that matter, outside of our circle. She gained access to the Goon tribe in her own easy way.

I started seeing her at Augie's, close by the Columbia dorms where she lived. We circled around each other for a bit but it didn't take long for us to latch together. I sensed her intelligence and liked the way she was low-key about it. She had a quietness about her and when she said something it was worth hearing. It seemed like she knew something about me that I didn't know myself right from the first time I met her. At the same time, maybe I could see something in her she couldn't see yet. As we got closer and softened into each other, I heard bits of her story and started to grasp it; there was this younger girl in there, past the skin and denim, one from high school and further back, one who had been burnt by adults she was supposed to trust. Like that often goes, we had been drawn to each other through the overlap of trauma, unconsciously.

It had been so long since I had connected with someone sexually in a meaningful way, or even in an unmeaningful, casually pleasant way. Since I had come to New York, sex was either non-existent, solitary, or a series of drunken misfires with older guys, each one a worse failure than the last. With Sarah, I was scared at first, but she slowly stripped away that unhappy panoply, through touch and gentle words. We became intimate. It felt right.

But I couldn't peel away her armor in the same way. I was too self-involved at that point, and she didn't want that anyways. She wanted to try heroin with me. I was uneasy – she had pulled me out of the inverted narcissism that had been holding me back, and I had a moment of clarity: we could have something happy together, something good and clean. But neither of us was ready. We were both just getting started on a road of penance, paying back debts, our own and other people's. So I introduced her to the Pink Lady.

There was a fragile, sweet period, though, before we got trapped in that. She shared her cultural cachet with me and I took it in. She was fluent in Spanish and we bummed around Madrid a bit when I played there, spent weekends at her mom's house in the Hamptons, and hung out with her smart, fucked-up friends from Columbia. She took me to parties in Tribeca where I'd rub up against other people in another bigger New York, one outside the insular junior-jazz scene I knew thus far. When the lease came up at Jones Street, I packed it up and Sarah and I moved in with the Goons on 2nd Avenue.

Grant had issued a strong command to us all at the bar, when we gathered there after hearing Bill had died: "I want everyone to promise that they will never do heroin again. Fuck that shit. Don't be a dumbass." It made total sense and we all agreed.

But Sarah and I didn't keep that promise. A week later I was down on 7th Street just past Tompkins Square Park, buying a couple bags for us. We snorted and walked to Save the Robots, an after-hours place full of kids like us in an upstairs room, sprawled out on cushions, all singing with the angel of death. We stayed there until the next morning and walked out into the early light, making our way back to our place on 2nd Avenue. We stumbled into a Catholic Church on 7th Street just before 1st Avenue. Morning mass was just starting. We sat down in one of the pews toward the back. The service was in Polish and we couldn't understand any of what the priest was saying. It didn't matter.

We started to weep – it came from deep inside. All the grief of losing Bill hit us right then, right as the heroin was wearing off. And it wasn't just the grief: it was the feeling that we were beginning on something that was already too late to stop. The parishioners, mostly older Polish women with beautiful faces, looked at us with pity. The priest read the liturgy, and met our gaze as he spoke, with that same sad knowing in his eyes. I looked at the picture of Mary holding baby Jesus behind the pulpit. She looked back at us with that same look. Mercy. *Come into my arms.* The Mother – the real one. The womb of life, not the eggshell of death. We cried and cried. We were lost sheep, crying for our Shepherd. He was there. We just couldn't see him yet.

Dr. Finger Fuck

> We look for light, and behold, darkness,
> and for brightness, but we walk in gloom.
> We grope for the wall like the blind,
> we grope like those who have no eyes;
> we stumble at noon as in the twilight,
> among those in full vigor we are like dead men.

Isaiah 59.9b-11

There I was on my first real dope kick. I had never tried to stop at all before that. I had been going non-stop for a long time and I had been off the road from Josh's group for a while. I kept on trying to get high but it was just getting me well. By now I was banging away ten-dime bags of heroin a day, buying $100 clips of them, burning through the cash I had just made on the road with Josh. With every subsequent kick, I would try to be medicated if at all possible, and, if I wasn't, I never made it through – I'd give up and go score. This first one I wasn't prepared for. I thought I could rough it cold turkey – what's the worst it could be, I figured, five days of hell? It blindsided me.

Less than three days later and I couldn't take it anymore. My parents took me to the emergency room in a hospital in Farmington, a neighboring town of West Hartford, because they had found out there was a detox facility there. After waiting the usual hour or so, I was taken to a small examining room and told to wait. Then this greasy fucker in medical scrubs came in and asked me a few questions about why I was there. I told him. Next thing, he tells me to drop my pants. Something about checking my glands. That's the first thing on the agenda? Bullshit. I just wanted some methadone. I did what he told because I was unable to question or protest anything at this point – I was beaten, an invalid. My dick was shrunken, almost inverse, retracting inwardly in protest like a turtle in its shell. Before I knew what was happening, the prick had a rubber glove on, whipped some lubricant on one of his fingers and stuck it up my ass. It felt miserable. Dopesick and getting your asshole probed – it was definitely a low point.

He had closed the door real quickly when he came into the room and I should have known this guy was no good. He had this evil smile as he finger-fucked me for an agonizing minute or more, looking at me intently in the eyes the whole time, trying to catch my gaze. There was that *looking* again, with no words, like Dr. Dunn. Maybe he thought I was going to get hard. It hurt more than anything. I've never been able to get inside the head of a guy who gets turned on like that. Is he gay? Or is it just about power? Those were just as much questions for myself, though, in a different light – relinquishing power, taking it back. Everyone has their own little story they build up about themselves with sex, and his was Dr. Finger Fuck. The "physical" was over then and he left abruptly, mumbling that someone would be in to see me shortly. Still no methadone.

It may seem strange but I didn't realize he was taking advantage of me until long after that. I stuffed it away immediately after it happened. It blended in with everything else that day, only slightly more horrible. When you're down and out like that, you're less able to stand up for your dignity. You're marked for the predators, and they see you limping. You let these fuckers walk all over you, and it seems almost right. My self-worth – and capacity for self-protection – had been chipped away slowly, starting with Dr. Dunn. This guy felt like a meaner version of him, and I could only just stand there and take it, hunched over on the hospital bed. It seemed normal, like another deal I had to make – first it was to graduate from high school, now it was to get some meth.

There were parts of kicking dope that felt like a kind of existential nightmare but, looking back at them, they just seem funny/sad – like all the time I spent sitting in my parents' family room on the easy chair, curled up in a ball with a wool blanket, watching cable TV. A lot of times all I could handle was Cartoon Network, because it was comforting: it took me to a place that was before everything had gone wrong, and, for moments, I could sync my being with an episode of *Jonny Quest* and feel like I was in that reality – a ten-year-old kid again. Around that time, I wrote a few short lines that caught the vibe of that period:

> The hazy rub of a day with no end –
> Time and its implications represent the needle's motor
> Purring with insidious fecality
> We run to our ruin and back again.

My buddy Simon and I had come back to West Hartford with our tails between our legs to stay at our parents' and try to get clean. We went to high school together but I didn't hang with him much then. He came to New York two years after I got there and we got tight there. We loved the same books and would talk about the Grand Inquisitor, trying to figure out what Dostoevsky really meant. Or the four of us, Simon and his girlfriend, Sarah and I, would tuck into the bars like Lucy's in the East Village and Alphabet City for long nights. When Sarah and I got strung out, Simon joined us after a while and the three of us ran together a lot.

Sarah had left New York, too. She was spending time at her mom's place on Long Island, trying to stay away from smack. She told me she needed time away from me, and didn't know for how long. It hurt. Simon and I would sit around our parents' houses all day and then make a trip into town to buy cigarettes or maybe go to a twelve-step meeting to make it look like we were trying to get clean for our parents. Then we'd go to a bar at night. Or I'd just go alone. Sometimes it was just some townie shithole with a TV in the corner, and part of me would reflect how weird it was, being back in West Hartford at age twenty-four, riding through streets I used to run down with Ricky – but now I was going into those bars, the same ones I used to pass by and see all those sad old people stumbling out of. Sometimes I wanted to cry because I was such a fuck-up and I didn't know how I had wound up where I was – defeated, already so far behind in the second inning. I felt like a ghost, like a vestige of some person I remembered only with pain. All I had now was a past that wasn't accessible, a present that wasn't worth mentioning, and a terrifying future that was pushing its way in, like a wet wind.

Simon's company took the edge off a harrowing loneliness. I missed Sarah terribly. I was desperate for her physically because my pain wasn't muted anymore; it was acute. So I just wanted to feel her warm body against me, to squeeze her and smell her, to nestle her and make love to her, but she wasn't there. There's a feeling of abundance and being fulfilled, of having your love returned. There's a feeling of neutrality and being empty, when you are alone, sending no affection towards another soul and having for the time being no expectation or longing for returned affection. And there's a feeling of absence, like a hole in your heart, when that other soul has left and yours is still reaching out its tentacles into empty space, like a blind animal.

I felt like the floor had dropped out from under me when Sarah told me we were through. I was away from her and everybody else and all of the sudden I felt everything – all the emotions that heroin had wiped away were reappearing and I would have moments of deep melancholy where I was sure I had lost everything and I knew I just had to get back in the game. So I'd make a go of it – I'd take a gig. I'd get on a bus or a plane. I'd go back to New York or Boston, and maybe I'd make it through the sets. Then I'd get that yen and I'd be downtown scoring that shit and I'd lose everything all over again. It went on like that for a long time – I tried to quit and make a clean break from the stuff for almost as long as I had been doing it, and I kept on falling, failing. I'd stumble back to West Hartford and wrap myself back into the nest of my parents' house, back into the room of my youth that still had the Pink Floyd and Rush posters, cut-out pictures of unicorns and other prog rock regalia on the walls.

My bedroom was a sanctuary but it was a graveyard: it was frozen at the moment in time right before everything shattered for me, right on the cusp of adolescence. To be in my room was like one of those dreams about my dead buddies, where I'd be with them again and take some comfort in that for a moment, but then I would remember that they were dead and realize I couldn't ever be with them again for real. Or it was like a room you enter in one of those questing video games – you kill the bad guys, collect all the treasure, and then your little elf character is supposed to go on to the next room. I didn't know where the key to the next room was, though, or maybe I had the key but just couldn't find the exit. I was stuck.

Quitting dope, then starting again. Quitting, starting – it was like that for a long time. To lose everything once is bad, but to lose it over and over again – it's pretty weird. Your whole sense of yourself diminishes – you don't really believe you're capable of pulling anything off and you marvel at what other people can do. You drag yourself to the gas station to buy cigarettes and you look at the dude behind the cash register. "Wow," you think. "That guy can work a job – he can wake up in the morning, drink his coffee, brush his teeth, suit up in his Oxford shirt and show up for *work*. How the fuck does he *do* that?" I didn't get it. I was amazed by all those working stiffs – now they seemed like the most noble, vital bunch I had ever come across. And there were so many of them – they were everywhere you went, always there, reminding me of my own lack of utility, my own weakness. How had I gotten here?

I'd get off the stuff, and I'd just be starting to feel better. The days were long. I sat around my parents' house, watching cartoons, eating Cocoa Puffs, wearing the same clothes for days in a row, wrapped in a blanket. I'd make it to the evening, and Simon and I would hit a bar in Hartford with some other friends from high school who were back in town. There were good enough times to be had if I could pull myself out of the gloom. Feeling good was temporary and you had to search for it – it was like scraping the meat off the bone. The conversation with my high-school cronies was lucid and quick. We were coming around the bend, almost halfway through our twenties, and we felt like old dogs. We didn't know that we were still young and that's exactly why we felt old – because we were trying to carry everything on our shoulders and we hadn't learned yet how to just drop stuff and leave it behind. We were good enough at diagnosing everything that was inconsistent in the people and the world around us but we didn't have an alternative. So we saw the irony in everything and laughed bitterly about it because your twenties are all about *not* coming to terms with irony, but fiddling around with it, reveling in it, imbuing it with cosmic importance; at the same time acting like it's not important to you, because nothing is important, "*anyone can see / nothing really matters / nothing really matters to me . . .*"

> . . . For youth, so rich in hidden powers, never knows what it is robbing itself of when it joins trumped-up sorrows to the pain of a real loss, as if this were necessary to impart real significance to the pain of what has been foregone.
>
> Goethe, *Wilhelm Meister's Apprenticeship*

There was a bar that was pretty hip in the South End of Hartford right near Trinity College where my dad went forty years earlier, with a jukebox that played stuff like Tom Waits's "Jersey Girl," cheap pitchers of beer, big booths, and undergraduate girls who seemed hopelessly far away and inaccessible. Simon and I would drink and drink to try and snuff out that dragon hunger, then usually just go home. But the bar was close to where you could cop heroin and coke, so sometimes we'd fuck up and be down there on Park Street in Hartford after last call, looking for a couple bags of dope, and maybe even a dime of coke for a speedball – a fast track to ecstasy. It wasn't easy and a few times we'd get beat for twenty bucks, but we usually scored something if we tried long and hard enough. Next stop was the all-night CVS to buy some needles. If they asked why we wanted them I would say that I made model airplanes with my dad as a hobby and we used the syringes to administer the glue on the small parts. Whenever you want to convince somebody to do something that goes against their better judgment (those people at the prescription counter knew we were up to no good, reading that grimacing hunger in our faces), invoke a family member in your bullshit story and that will usually get them to give you what you want. That's the kind of stuff you learn when you're a junkie – or you don't really learn it; it's more like you always had that skill, you just need to unpack it from behind a veneer of sociality. It's amazing how easy it is to lie when you really want something. Then we'd get into the car and drive around to the back of the parking lot and find a plastic spoon on the floor – all synthetic stuff on the East Coast, none of that sticky tar you had to cook up with a flame like in California or Europe. You'd mix a little water onto the powder until it dissolved, then draw up that nirvana juice into the needle, tie up with a belt, find a vein in the arm and poke around until a drop of blood circled back into the needle and you knew you had a register. Then you slowly push in, feeling first the welcome, slightly cold silent rush of a foreign liquid entering the vein. The bowels retract in anticipation, there is a strange, not unpleasant sensation of being constipated as the peristaltic movement grinds to a halt, and the impossibly sweet feeling spreads through the body, starting at the stomach, moving through the guts, all the way to the fingers, racing through the veins to all stations, bringing on utter peace and well-being. The next day I woke up in the late afternoon when the sun was already almost gone, blasted and ruined and hooked again. I'd thrown it away for that good feeling that never lasted and I was useless to the world once more. Outside, smoking the first cigarette, I would smell autumn: burning leaves, the sweet decay of the oak trees, the roasted smells. Fall was always my favorite time and those smells would bring me nostalgia and a kind of happy yen but now they just brought consternation. I panicked at the thought of feeling anything. What could I do with something like nostalgia when there was no hope to fall back onto in the present moment, when there was no light left after the happy past had flickered out like a dead match? Feelings were so wrought and heavy and they were attached to memories and other feelings and the only feeling I wanted was relief from feeling.

Looking for a moment of purity –
A window to gaze through and suspend time
or, a mirror to stare at
and feel your own transience –

Your blood darkens, but this hue
is familiar –
In fact, the act of shutting out the light
Is like a longed for
ghost-friend of suffused childhood.

There is a kindred spirit
That turns these lights off for me, then –
A most important kind of echo
That feeds and nourishes itself
with memory, that half-light
of yearning
Reflected off a spectral non-attainment.

In those wee hours,
You reached a lucid plateau
Where your stump of a body with no legs
(and no wings, yet)
squirmed along the cold floor –
Your demons bleated from your throat
involuntarily,
An invisible clammy hand
reached out to touch its own ghost.

II

That adolescent ghost still haunts.
You see he's a pale reminder of himself –
He just strings a pallid thread around old associations.

He feels stifled inside the mucus of his own failure.
Disenfranchised sold short never hit the mark –
This ghost is already an old man ghost wasted now and
permanently crippled.

(That man just spat out a tuberculocic piece of resignation.
Hey – his time is not your time. You understand? Separate
and cut off from you he is, necessarily. Watch now, he's
shielding his eyes from the sun. (Forgotten alien ghost haunt-
ing trailer parks.))

III

There is a half-light of memory that lingers. Yeah, he can recall
those nights of his ghost-youth:
The suffused-childhood nights, searching for a candycane God –
Later on, the first praline ache of lust in his groin
Idiot nights with the needle, singing with angels . . .
City nights and the hot taste of metal and blood –
and nights of impotent hope and non-attainment,
Back home one more time stringing wreaths with used-up lies
(His candycane God lingering in the air like yesterday's fart.)

(he coughs and spits again.)

(Look: He was never here really, not with us.
Alone with his dreams, first the impossible dreams
of a young man, later on, old man dreams of trailer park
heaven. Always was just a ghost, though. (That ghost
haunts me now like a dry bloody cough and the
sun shines in my eyes.))

(1/16/96)

Pleasure's checks and balances

One night, Simon and I had put together a few measly days without going down to Park Street to cop but we were still strung out – raw, achy all over, shivering – and trying for any kind of comfort besides smack. We wound up at TGI Fridays across from Westfarms Mall with Bethany, ordering lowbrow cocktails like Long Island iced teas and rum and Cokes because that's what she wanted. We went with her, plying her with the drinks, drinking ourselves, watching with weary pleasure as she got drunk.

Bethany was Hall High Class of '90 like Simon, two years younger than me, home from college for the weekend. She was a welcome sight for us: dirty blond hair, kind of tall but not too much, creamy long legs, wearing pumps and a short skirt, big smiling naughty eyes, making silly jokes, being goofy and giggling a lot, picking up on our lechery towards her, taking it on and giving us something back. In high school, she was the type of girl you'd jerk off about: glib, perky, fresh and clean, flirty in that innocent way that girls could be, when they sensed the effect they were having on you but didn't really understand what they were doing. She still had some of that energy but now she was twenty-two. As the night went on, she told us about her escapades. I never knew her back in high school except from a distance, and Simon had tried to hook up with her back then without success. And here we were now. But did either of us have any game – had we lost our hustle, being dopesick like that?

Simon's parents were out of town and the three of us made it back to his house. We sat around for a while and it became obvious that on that particular evening Bethany was more interested in me. Simon was pissed and went to bed, mumbling: "Just great – in my house, no less . . ." It was unexpected for both of us. Bethany was from his class, and he had wanted her badly already in high school. It wasn't fair for him and I felt bad, but I wanted to be with Bethany so we went into Simon's older brother's old room and he went to bed. I hadn't had any kind of sex at all with myself or anyone else for a while. Heroin puts your dick in the dirt and keeps it there as long as you're on it. But now I was several days off the stuff. Bethany and I got into the waterbed and we started to take our clothes off. She was so fresh and her body was soft. I fumbled with her bra and felt her small tits as she giggled. I could smell her breath and it was kind of sweet from the booze. There was some strawberry stuff in her hair, and her body smelled nice too, like dewy grass and a little sweat. I put my hand on her cold ass cheek and she pulled me onto her and as soon as I moved against her, I glided inside of her wetness and it felt so good, I barely had time to pull out it happened so fast. I spilled onto her belly like a fourteen-year-old, apologizing. I was demoralized. She was sweet about it. She called me her "little musician junkie," stroked my hair and said it was all right. I fell asleep for almost three hours in a row – more than I had gotten in days.

When I came with her it was almost like it hurt, because I was still dopesick. When you're sick like that, every physical sensation registers as pain to an extent because you haven't felt anything for a while – you have to get used to sensation as a phenomenon in itself again. There's a logic to opiate withdrawal. All emotions and bodily phenomena run inverse to how they ran when you were high.

High	Kicking
Euphoria	Dismay
Completely unconcerned with what the future holds	Petrified at the prospect of anything and everything coming down the pike
Totally enthusiastic about talking to people	Totally not down to talk to anyone
Also completely content being alone	Completely, utterly lonely
No pain, total relaxation, nothing hurts anywhere	Pain all over, total tension, hurts everywhere
Never feel cold	Always feel cold and shivering
No peristaltic activity	Uncontrollable wringing out of intestines
No need for sexual release; the problem is solved	Orgasm almost involuntary at times, but brings no real relief

And so on. You have to pay the piper. No high is for free. You have to tip the scales back the other direction, towards a kind of anti-pleasure.

Kevin

High school dream again. It's some kind of fundraiser for our big band. I feel some excitement to be with them, but it's dashed as I realize none of the students want to be with me. I try to get their attention but it's like they're ignoring me, or they don't hear me even though I'm close to them. A feeling of rejection begins that shoots through the whole dream: there's no way I can make them "want me there." It's that physical feeling in my gut, the old one.

A big game of tug of war starts. Huge teams are assembling on either side of the rope. There are parents of the students there and they are putting together tables of food that they have made. At this point it becomes vague: I am with the parents, assembling the food, in a function I've had at the schools of my own kids for fundraisers, etc. but I am still somehow a student from the class of 1988. This is so typical of these dreams that I am surprised I don't realize it's a dream and wake up right then. Some part of me needs to stay and see this out.

The scene shifts and expands; the tug of war area has turned into a kind of carousel. The parents are gathered on the side and the students are on the carousel, spinning around slowly. It is a gray, late afternoon. A game begins that involves Springsteen's "Blinded by the Light," used somehow as a cue for the students to spin around. I know the song and gain energy and purpose upon hearing it, in the great cover version from Manfred Mann's Earth Band that I loved to hear on the radio when I lived in Bedford. It starts to lift me up and I feel a quick wisp of joy just for a moment, remembering sunny afternoons at the public pool there where that music played, with other summer songs from Fleetwood Mac, the Steve Miller Band, and the Eagles. When I was a kid I had fun trying to learn the lyrics, always wondering what they meant. Now in the dream they make exact sense; I understand them perfectly.

Madman drummers bummers and Indians in the summer with a teen-age diplomat
In the dumps with the mumps as the adolescent pumps his way into his hat
With a boulder on my shoulder, feelin' kinda older I tripped the merry-go-round
With this very unpleasing sneezing and wheezing the calliope crashed to the ground –

I am playing this game now, which is basically to sing the song and spin around the carousel in a kind of ritual musical act. Only, I am not with the other students. Nor am I with the parents by the tables of food. I am alone, between the two groups, outside in the cold gray weather. I am now flying around in the air like you sometimes do in dreams, tracing the periphery of the carousel, and it is as if I am on a broomstick but there is no broomstick. Who is there with me? Kevin. He is there as he has been in other dreams, silent, with his quiet look. He grabs around my waist like on a motorcycle ride and we fly together, me singing "Blinded by the light . . ." loudly, desperately. I am singing the song the "best" – I know it better than all of the other students or the parents – but no one hears me, no one cares, because I am on the outside; no one except for my loyal dead friend, Kevin. But, like Bill in the other dream, he can't talk. He only stares at me, not smiling. I feel that familiar, awful fear and sadness so strongly. I want to be with him but I know I can't really be with him, that he's not going to stay. With everyone else, it's as if I'm invisible. I could scream to them, but it would be mute. That will be my hell – that is my hell: to be right alongside all of them, but ignored. I'm not invisible. I've been cast out, though, in some unspoken way, and I feel such shame.

I wake up with a hole of loneliness in my gut, feeling lost, stuck between two worlds, in neither of which I really belong.

My parents finally threw me out of the house after I repeatedly lied to them and kept using under their roof. I moved a half-mile down Main Street towards West Hartford Center and took a room with Tanya, another old high-school friend from out back – a sexy classic rock babe all the way. Her parents had moved out and left her the house she grew up in. She charged me a good rent. I moved my Baldwin upright over there and brought along Brahms' *Klavierstücke*. I would try to make a new start. I renewed contact with Kevin, who still lived with his parents just a block away from Tanya.

Kevin was my close friend in sophomore and junior year of high school. Back then, Ricky and I had drifted apart. He didn't click with the out-back crowd, and had a serious girlfriend, so he wasn't around to hang out a lot of the time. I had begun a period of sexual withdrawal during Dr. Dunn's weekly grooming, still shaken up by the stuff with Ed and Dylan. I felt ashamed and was closed off from sex, uncomfortable around anyone.

Kevin didn't bother me about that. He didn't have a girlfriend either. Kevin and I didn't have many common interests, but we clicked and just spent time doing nothing, rambling through Westmoor Park close to my house, sometimes getting high or drinking beer, sometimes not. We didn't have to say much. I had his loyalty and that was enough. Kevin never asked me to be anything different than what I was. He never expected anything of me much more than my company. Those are still my favorite kinds of friends, the kind you can sit with and say nothing and that's just fine.

We drifted apart. To my consternation, in senior year, he started latching on to Darren, the one who had piggybacked on Ed and fucked with me throughout sophomore and junior year. We stopped seeing each other, and I felt betrayed when he went over to Darren, especially since it was his loyalty I had valued. Now he was around again and we were into our twenties, hanging out with Tanya and her boyfriend Randy. Randy had been another shitkicker like Darren in high school, from Dylan's neighborhood.

I was back with these people from my past. Five years had elapsed and I had been to New York and seen some of the world; they had stayed there. I had some creative scores under my belt even if I was burning bridges, like the record with Jorge and Mario. The heroin took away all of that fear I used to have in high school, being around a guy like Randy. I didn't give a shit what he or anyone thought of me when I was loaded. Plus, Randy had grown out of being a bully and actually turned into a reasonable guy. We'd all spend time in Tanya's living room and I'd talk their ear off about anything. They'd just sit there and look at me, kind of shaking their heads – this guy is fucked up on drugs. I thought I was king of the hill.

Kevin and I started hanging out a bit again, prowling around Hartford bars, but we couldn't connect like we used to. It was me. I would tell him a bunch of stuff but wasn't really listening to what he was saying. Most of the time on drugs I wasn't really tuning into other people at all. Being an addict engenders a deeply selfish state of mind. When you are high, you feel good, but at the cost of your empathy and interest toward others. When you're not high, you're also only thinking of yourself – how you're going to get well again.

I told Kevin that I was bisexual. At that time, I would tell that to just about anyone who would listen. I thought everyone should hear about it, that it was really interesting. Really, I wanted to vent the shame I had carried and heroin was a false salve for that. I was trying to gain dominion over those negative experiences by presenting myself as a person who chose for them. One way to do that was to talk about being bisexual. I not only had the power of choice – I could choose everything all at once. It sounded good on paper, even if I couldn't actualize it.

One night Kevin and I were at a bar in Hartford and he said out of the blue, "You know what you told me, about being bi?" Yeah, sure. "I'm bi too," he said quietly. What? I didn't even hear it the first time. He had to repeat it.

It could have been a great moment to further our friendship. I could have told him what had happened with Ed and Dylan a year before I met him in high school, and why it hurt when he buddied up with Darren. He could have told me stuff too – about what that time had been like for him. Because, really, when he told me that, it was a real shocker – I didn't see that coming at all. He had walked around Hall High for four years in an AC/DC muscle shirt with a pack of Marlboro Reds folded back in the sleeve, gruff and tough. I laughed it off when he told me – no shit, man, crazy! – and that was that. I didn't honor him for making that admission to me, though. I was probably the first person he had told, and he felt like he could because of what I had told him. It had been so easy for me though, jacked up on the drugs. For him it was no doubt a big deal.

A few years later I was back in West Hartford and heard from Tanya that Kevin was dead from an overdose. I wish so much that I had really been there when he was talking to me, and I could have reached over at that bar booth and put my hand on his shoulder, and said something like: man, it's okay. And that I could have gotten to know a friend I thought I had known but never really had. But it was too late.

James

During that time in West Hartford, James, the poor overweight kid I had shoved in seventh-grade gym class, came back into my life. We had hung out intermittently my senior year of high school. He was always out back smoking, but around the periphery, kind of a loner – not a depressing Pink Floyd kind of loner but more stoic, with a sarcastic smile, weary and hardened from years of being taunted for his weight. He had some serious armor by then. We renewed contact at some point when he visited New York with his friends and I steered them towards the heroin they wanted. When I wound up down and out in West Hartford, I looked him up. We forged an intense, sad friendship.

He was still living with his parents. I had come back, but he had never left. I still remember his house clearly. It was one of the beautiful older Tudors on the west side of Prospect Avenue, which marked the border of West Hartford. On the other side of the street was Prospect Park and Hartford began there. It all fit – just across the street was the capital, the city we would drive into to buy our dope, but we were both still stuck in our suburban hometown.

The house was a bit run down, but still regal. I never met James's dad in all those years, and saw his mom only once or twice. Every time James and I entered the house through the back door that went into the kitchen, they weren't around. There were signs of them, particularly his mother: someone who loved to cook, someone who drank in the grand old Waspy manner that I knew a little from some of my parents' friends growing up. It was a 1970s lifestyle that was already frayed around the edges at that point – late-afternoon whiskey sours, big station wagons and Nantucket vacations. We would enter through the kitchen, always late at night. There was a shelf there lined with cookbooks – Julia Child, James Beard, *The Joy of Cooking*. A big range with cast-iron pans, evidence of a recently cooked roast. Liquor was always on hand with all the required equipment: mixers, glasses, steel ice trays in the freezer. James would fix us both gin and tonics in big highball glasses – mostly the booze, crushed ice and lime, with a splash of tonic water for good measure.

Then it was up the long staircase to his room. Ashtrays were assembled everywhere, always full. Often he would simply put out his cigarette on the carpet, and there were burns everywhere. When I first saw all the butts, I remembered how James and I hung out together a few times freshman year in high school at Papa Gino's where I worked that shitty job two years later. We both had a crush on Mary Brewster, who smoked like us. She was a sexy classic rock babe in the making with plenty of make-up and feathered hair, but still a tadpole freshman with Journey patches on her jean jacket. One time she was there and we and sat at the table across from her, trying to impress her, chain-smoking the whole time while we were eating our cheese pie. Mary looked at us and said, "You're not supposed to smoke and eat at the same time. That's just stupid." We put out the cigarettes in the pizza, still trying to look cool, just glad that she talked to us at all. In a way we hadn't changed, ten years later.

James had musical talent and played piano. In seventh grade we had both auditioned for the jazz band at King Philip. He had something natural, an ease at the instrument and a relaxed feel, but didn't have much training or chops. I was a schmuck and made a point of cutting him when I played in front of him and the other kids, pulling out all the stops, playing fast runs. I only remembered that much later with remorse, after he died. He could have nurtured his talent. He could have been some sort of singer-songwriter, writing broken-down songs like Tom Waits, I'm sure of it. He had wisdom, and an élan that came from his upbringing. When he talked, no matter how much liquor he had in him, he spoke in pronounced tones, with a voice that sounded a little like Orson Welles. He was the first person I knew my age who pronounced the aspirate "h" when applicable. ("Really, Brad – whhhere are you off to? We've not yet finished this bottle of Jack . . .")

James's bedroom was like his own apartment within that house. Once you entered it, you were in his world of disarray and debauchery. On one wall was a spinet piano. Several of the keys were partially melted and it was badly out of tune. He had this Jerry Lee Lewis routine where he would pour lighter fluid onto the keys, light them, and then play some crazy honky-tonk ditty while they burned. It seemed like it could have been something out of William Burroughs's biography, like a non-lethal solo version of the "game" Burroughs played with his wife Joan that led to her death, shooting apples off the top of her head until he finally shot her right in the forehead, killing her. James was Burroughs-esque – all of the writing I read from Burroughs announced an unapologetic embrace of outlawed gratification, even as it was shot through with the apprehension of something not met, something unrequited, and an underlying muted loneliness – whether in the straight prose of *Junkie* or the stranger transgressive style of his later cut-up novels. I related to that, unquestionably, and James conveyed it in his demeanor.

There were a few times James had me call an Asian escort service in West Hartford Center. It got busted in a sting a few years after that and there was a scandal, quickly hushed up. They refused his calls because he had fallen hard for one of the girls – he was in love with her, and she didn't want his business anymore. So I would call and ask for her and then was supposed to pass the phone to him just so he could just talk to her, but it never worked – they always figured it out.

We would get loaded all the time and kept each other good company. I felt close to him without knowing why. I could sense something was broken in him, too. He knew I was doing H and wanted in. He wanted to bang it with me so I tried to show him how, but he couldn't get a vein under the fat, so he'd just muscle it. Finally, one time we went together into the South End of Hartford where I always copped. We bought and then went to the shooting gallery that was in the last abandoned building of the projects there. We walked up to the second floor and there were four or five crackheads in the big room. They didn't even look up from their pipes. I shot just one dime first and it was pretty decent, hitting me strong. I mixed up less than half that amount on the spoon for him, tied up his arm with my belt, and for the first time I hit a large vein in the crook of his arm. An arabesque of blood circled back into the liquid in the needle. "Are you ready?" He nodded. I pushed half of it in to wait and see. He was out in a few seconds. I pulled the needle out and started slapping him. Nothing. I tried lighting my lighter under his finger; he didn't move. Then I'm freaking out, screaming his name, crying like a kid. I don't know how long it was, probably less than ten minutes later and there were blue lights below. The crackheads scattered like roaches as the police came up the broken staircase.

They saved his life. They pumped him up with Narcan, the EMT came and took him away in an ambulance, and they arrested us both. I spent a night in the bullpen and we got a court date. James's dad pulled some strings for us somehow and when we showed up in front of the judge two days later together, the charges were already dropped. I had never seen anything like that and was impressed. As soon as we were out of the court building, we headed back to cop at the same place. It wasn't even noon but the guy was there. He looked at us kind of funny like he remembered the other night, but took our money and we got what we wanted. This time, James promised, he was going to do it right. Since we had made a scene in the gallery the last time, we walked over to the Amtrak station close by and shot up in two stalls next to each other. Hunky-dory, no flatline, no drama. We parted ways. That was the last time I saw him. Two years later and finally clean, I was back in West Hartford for Christmas and ran into a guy at the gas station who was also his close friend. He told me James had overdosed.

I didn't process it then. I grieved for him later. When I started to put the pieces of my own puzzle together, I remembered what James told me one night, real late after a lot of booze, in a heart-to-heart conversation.

Now there was this guy Alan we knew, kind of notorious. He was older, in his twenties when we were in high school, but would hang out with all of us still, meeting us out back after school. He was thin, tall, and gangly, with a face full of acne scars. He had this hippyish act but I never felt comfortable around him; there was something off there. It took a lot to creep me out, too. I didn't get put off by people just because they looked different or didn't live by the norms. It was something else with him.

It was Kevin who formally introduced me to Alan in junior year, even though I had already seen him around, sometimes in West Hartford Center at the bowling alley or sometimes in the parking lot across from school out back, waiting for no one in particular. Alan had a connection for weed in bulk and gave us a quarter-pound, which was more than I had ever had – the vaunted "QP." Kevin and I were to sell most of it for him and could keep half-an-ounce each for ourselves. We went to meet Alan at his job and do the handoff. He worked as an undertaker at a funeral home on Farmington Avenue close to the Hartford line. It was a big, dour old brick house – they all seem to look the same – and in the back was a separate smaller building where he did his business, the size of a roofed garage. Alan came out smiling and had this sweet chemical smell that reminded me of the fetal pigs we dissected in biology. He shook hands with us bro-style even though I didn't want to, and gave us the pot, wrapped in a couple of tube socks.

Tanya knew Alan, too, and was the first one who told me that he had sex with the stiffs there. Kevin corroborated it later, saying Alan had told him. I guess he kind of bragged about it. I couldn't believe it at first, but then I did, the more I spent time with him. When we went back there a few times to give him his money and he'd come out of that building, grinning, I was repulsed, but part of me wondered: why does that turn your crank? And – how does that work exactly?

Back to that night with James, we were talking about a whole bunch of things – stuff from the past. I probably told him my shit with Ed and Dylan and Dr. Dunn. I don't remember exactly. There was some silence, as we smoked. Then James asked me, "Do you remember Alan?"

"Sure."

"He was my babysitter when I was growing up and molested me for two years straight."

Holy fuck, that was horrible. I pictured a sixteen-year-old version of creepy Alan, and James just a little kid. James told me in his patrician drawl, with no emotion. But when I thought back years later, I realized: that was his wound. And I thought, maybe that's why he got so big, already when he was young, to put a block around himself, to make sure that never happened to him again. That was the mark he carried. I thought of myself in seventh grade, shoving James in gym class, ridiculing him, the way he looked back at me then, defenseless. He had it much worse off than I ever did, already then.

And then he just died, and there was nothing I could do. There wasn't a remnant I could take and hold up and say: here's the good part. Well here it is now, James: I still miss you. I'm so sorry for what happened to you when you were a kid. You were my good friend and I dug hanging out with you. You were a swell guy, lots of fun, charming, and talented to boot. I wish I could have helped you talk to that hooker. I'm sorry I shoved you in gym class. I'm sorry I found that vein for you in the shooting gallery. And I'm sorry I wasn't a better friend.

When I looked back and thought about Kevin disclosing his sexuality the last time I saw him, after what James had told me I wondered whether Alan had gotten to him as well when he was a kid – he knew him from the neighborhood back then, too, and Alan had babysat for him. I realized that Kevin had been like me – he was closed off physically all the time I knew him. He was never with a girl the whole four years of high school. Was he "bi" like he said that night, following my cue, or was he gay? Or was he just all wound up and confused like I was, trapped inside his shell, cut off from everyone? I'll never know.

It's like you think you have a story of what your life was with the people who were close to you. Then you discover this other story, one that connected you with them in a deeper, darker way – one that you missed when they were around. There might have been some way of reuniting with them later on, one that could heal both of you, but it was too late now. That's what West Hartford was for me: one story that everyone saw, which was fucked up in a straightforward enough way; and then another story hidden under it which was more fucked up, one that led to more questions. And so there was this lone excavation, years later, to look for answers.

First Bill was gone, then Kevin and James. I wondered why it had been them and not me. I couldn't understand why I was still here. None of it made any sense. If someone tried to tell me, God had more plans for you, He kept you around, I would have said, Yeah, but still: their lives were stolen. The time that Bill gave to all of his friends, to all of us in New York those first few years before he died – we all hold it in our hearts. He shouldn't have died. That wasn't supposed to happen; it didn't need to happen, not for James or Kevin either.

I was a knucklehead in my relatively short junkie career. I was so impatient to get a vein that when I had flattened out many of them into scar tissue, I'd poke around carelessly in other spots. Eventually I had abscesses, and one got so big that my father took me to his office at night when I was back there using in their house in West Hartford, and lanced it himself in the examination room. The dirty blood from the wound oozed out for a good half hour and went onto the chair and floor; it was a big mess. I remember that I even got a little high as the junk that was lodged in there circled back through my veins. If it had been a few more days, the infection would have traveled up my arm and the arm might have had to have been amputated. Combined with the several near-overdoses where I went unconscious for a minute or more, I don't know how or why I didn't kill myself in those few years, or something maybe worse – to live with some consequence from my using that might have cut off my ability to be a musician, which was the only thing I hung onto then.

For some reason I got on the other side of drug addiction and managed to go on to have a life beyond what I could have dreamed. Being one of those who didn't get taken gives you a charge to live upright as you go on, and hopefully you walk towards that ideal. It also gives you acute insight into how precious your life and everyone else's is. But it doesn't erase the painful anomaly of loss. It's not where you find grace. Some losses are just sad and they remain that, for the duration. You don't get over them. You're not supposed to let go. You keep them close to you, you never relinquish them, and you never forget. You don't seek to be comforted. You hold some store of that grief firmly and you *don't* let go. In that not letting go, you give the person who is gone the dignity they lost, the dignity they deserved, the dignity they now can have, however delinquent that act of giving feels, however senseless their loss remains. There's your grace.

Almost done

My time in Josh's band was marred by heroin use. Did it affect the music? Yes and no. No, in the sense that I could always play when I was high, but, yes, because it tampered with everything else, and eventually made playing in the band not viable. Now there are some guys I've known who can use and keep up a modicum of professionalism. God bless them; I was not one of them. I was a drag to be around and not dependable. Josh and the guys knew what was going on, of course. The hang was marred. I was either way too chipper or I was sick, in a kind of emergency mode with no good fix, literally and figuratively.

It was a dilemma for Josh because there was no happy outcome. To fire me meant a partial fracture for a band that was playing together better than ever. Warner Jazz was giving tour support for *MoodSwing*, arranging in-store performances and the like to put the word out about the record. There was a buzz. To keep me on, though, was to enable my using, because I wasn't near ready to stop – it was only getting worse. I was visibly high on stage. If I ran out of drugs, which happened all the time, my first priority before the music was to get more of them. For the time being, Josh kept me on, with all the guys hoping I would get it together, and me not ready to take that huge step. As is often the case in a scenario where one person is using, nobody talked about what was going on, at least not with me, because my denial was thick – I acted like everything was just fine when I could, and, when it wasn't, I did what I had to do, come what may.

It got bad enough that I decided to try to stop. It was not for the right reason, which would have been to save my life, but more because I was too tired out from always trying to cop and being sick on the road. Sometimes I got lucky and could find something wherever we were, but the majority of time I couldn't. I remember once near the end flying back and forth from Chicago to New York in the middle of a week run at Jazz Showcase to get a big bundle to hold me out the rest of the week. I was beaten down from being sick. I told Josh my intention at the end of a tour to try and get clean. It would mean that I would have to miss some gigs, but he gave me his blessing, saying he supported me and it was the right thing to put all my efforts into stopping.

I had never fully tried to stop using for good, and had a whopper of a habit that first time, probably the biggest one I ever had. I had some sense that the kick would be hard but, since the time I had been physically addicted, I had never gone for more than a day or two without using. So I didn't know how bad it could get. I went back to my parents' house in West Hartford. It was hell within three days. That's when my parents took me to the facility where I met Dr. Finger Fuck. I was eventually moved upstairs and got the methadone I wanted to get over the hump. I stayed there for five days. I was introduced to the principles of recovery but none of them stuck that time, and they didn't stick for a while yet to come.

In that clinic, the staff told me about the idea of total sobriety – meaning no alcohol or any other drugs as well. That went in one ear and out the other, and, when I got out of there, I resumed drinking a lot, trying to replace the heroin high I missed. I was back home with my parents who were cautiously letting me stay there. I went to do a gig with Josh and the guys in Westchester County and got drunker than ever before the gig. I rationalized that I was not doing heroin so everything was just fine. I had never gotten drunk like that in a performance with Josh, though, and, unlike with narcotics, alcohol dismantled the motor functions I needed to perform. I played miserably that night. A few days later, Josh fired me.

I should have seen it coming and understood on some level that it was what he had to do, but I was pissed. Using, and all the havoc it wreaks, is only part of the sickness of addiction. It also cripples your ability to see the wreckage you're creating, and to care about what you're putting other people through. It's all about you. I was thinking of myself, and only saw it through that lens.

I was in a downward spiral, but still was able to play. Amidst all that, I had another fantastic, enriching musical experience, when tenor saxophonist David Sánchez invited me into his band. He introduced me to another way of feeling rhythm – through the clave. The clave is a core rhythmic feature that binds a lot of music from Cuba and other countries, and it was part of the music that David grew up with in his native Puerto Rico. Like pianist Danilo Perez, David was mentored by Dizzy Gillespie and joined his United Nations Orchestra in 1990.

Danilo was finding a way to fold the clave into his individual approach, and both he and David had made an impression on a lot of us hearing them at the Village Gate. It was something fresh and different on the scene. They had the harmonic and melodic vocabulary we were into, but rhythmically there was this whole other exciting paradigm. They weren't just repeating the kind of great Afro-Cuban hybrid Dizzy initiated years earlier. They were finding a way to fold the clave into a more pliable open-ended harmonic and formal landscape – the one that a lot of us were exploring, that post-1960s Miles Davis Quintet landscape.

Playing with David pushed me into new territory, particularly as a comper in the rhythm section. David didn't want me to really change the way I was playing, but encouraged me to think about the clave as a rhythmic grounding guide as I comped. One could call the clave a "pattern" in the same way that, on paper, the swing beat on drums is a pattern; but the idea was to get open-ended with it just like we were trying to move off the grid in a swing context. I never came close to internalizing the clave in the way David and Danilo did in the music they wrote and played, because it wasn't in me from the beginning. But it had a big effect on how I felt rhythm going forward. It was a blast playing with David. The band was rounded out by Larry Grenadier on bass,

Adam Cruz on drums and Richie Flores on congas. We toured through the States and Europe in 1995–96. David recalls that time:

> I asked you to play with the band after a few gigs at the Village Gate. I think Leon [Parker] was on some of those gigs, and he and I were already playing together. I heard that you were no longer part of Josh's band and I wanted to put together different material than what I was doing on the first recordings. Larrry [Grenadier] was already playing in the band and also had recorded on the previous recording, *Sketches of Dreams*. We were doing gigs with Danilo and I knew you guys had a thing. Also, I was keeping some of the percussion sounds which have always been part of my music, even if they're implied on the compositions themselves without a percussionist.
>
> I felt like you had a great connection with Larry and that would made things flow. Also, you both had great instincts and were into different ways of playing music and feeling rhythms. Therefore, I knew that, once I would put all the other elements together like all the percussion, including the roots traditional hand drums, you were going to flow with it and still be flexible with a sense of freedom.
>
> Coming from a Caribbean perspective, I was trying to infuse elements I experienced from early on in my life: bringing together Afro-Latin musical traditions roots music, like bomba and plena from Puerto Rico, with other musical expressions, especially the ones embedded in the heart of the African-American experienced in the U.S.
>
> I always felt like I would feel more comfortable if I would include elements from the music I grew up listening and playing. Not only with clave, but Afro-Latin ones throughout the Americas – I always felt like, even if they evolved in different ways, they had a similar cultural context, and they all shared the same lineage.

I never got to record with David, but that was by my own doing – he invited me to play on what became *Street Scenes*, the 1996 Columbia release. Because of my using, I did not make it to the date, and I regret that. Fortunately for everyone, Danilo came through in a pinch and slayed it.

To document all the subsequent rehab facilities I went to after that first one in Farmington, CT would be redundant, because the pattern was always the same: I would get out and start using soon enough. One of those was important, though, even if it failed, so I'll tell that story. It's the story of people helping me out when I wasn't helping myself, and it's also a transitionary chapter of a story that begins after this book ends – how I began again in Los Angeles.

When Josh finally let me go, I was living with Tanya in West Hartford and playing with David. One day, I got a call from someone at Warner Jazz. They said that they wanted to have a meeting with me at the office in New York. I had already recorded my first record for them, *Introducing Brad Mehldau*, with two rhythm sections: half of it with Larry and Jorge and the other half with Christian and Brian. It's a record I can stand behind even if I was using while I recorded it, and has great contributions from all the guys. It's a transition record. I was in Josh's band and had this strong connection with Christian and Brian, so I wanted to document that. At the same time, I already had something going with Larry and Jorge. What you hear is two records in one – my voice, I think, but mediated by all those great musicians who, by my lights, already had their own sound as well.

The person at Warner Bros. was vague about what would take place at the meeting, but said it was important, and that they would arrange for a limo to pick me up the next day. I thought it was kind of strange, but liked the idea in one sense: I could go to my dealer in the Lower East Side on the way there and get a couple bundles of good heroin, much better than the street stuff in the South End of Hartford. The driver arrived in the morning and we set off. As we crossed the bridge into Manhattan, I instructed him to stay on East River Drive past midtown and get off at Houston. He hesitated but complied. I went to my dealer on Delancey Street, we both fixed up together, and she sold me a few bundles. When I got back in the limo, the driver was on the walkie-talkie with someone at Warner Bros. asking where I was. By now it was afternoon.

I arrived at Warners headquarters in Rockefeller Plaza pretty loaded, was announced at the reception, and made my way up to the offices. When the elevator opened, Matt Pierson's assistant greeted me. I noticed that he was acting kind of serious. We turned a corner towards the office and, as we approached, I already saw my sister and David Sánchez seated. What the hell were they doing there? My stomach dropped. I knew it already.

It was an intervention. I entered the room, and there, sitting down at a conference table, were Matt Pierson, my parents and my sister, David, Josh Redman, and Larry Grenadier. There was a guy who looked like he was in his late forties whom I didn't know. He began speaking. "Brad, my name is Dallas Taylor. I was the drummer in Crosby, Stills, Nash & Young. I was a heroin addict for years but got clean." I was dismayed by everything that was happening, but I thought, well – it could be worse; this is the guy that laid down the groove on tracks like "Carry On" and "Woodstock." Dallas went on to explain that this was an intervention. Everyone there was done with the way things had been going. They would not support it any more. Each one of them went around and told me as much. They all spoke their truth, each in their own way: my parents and sister from the perspective of family, and the other guys as friends and bandmates. It was tough to hear. What they all said is that it was the end of the line. Matt Pierson cinched it: if I didn't go with Dallas to the rehab in Los Angeles, Warner Bros. Jazz wouldn't record me anymore. I walked out of the room and thought about it but it didn't take too long to decide – I went with Dallas to the rehab in LA.

I stayed there for three weeks but wasn't committed. Other people who care about you can point you toward recovery but, if you're not done yet, there's nothing they can do. Warner flew me back to New York City to play in the Jazz Times Convention, an annual event that presented up-and-coming acts to an audience of promoters and bookers. I did the same thing I had a few months earlier, stopping at my dealer on the way there from the airport. I played the gig with Jorge and Larry loaded, clear for everyone to see. Everyone was dismayed, needless to say, especially Matt, who was presenting me on behalf of the label, purportedly clean and fresh from rehab. Meanwhile, the Vanguard had booked me for my first trio week there. It was promptly cancelled. Everything was in place, everyone was giving me a chance, and I blew it. The limo drove me back to West Hartford where I was supposed to have a happy reunion with my parents. They saw the state I was in and threw me out the next day. My things were still at T.J.'s and I went back there.

At that gig at the Jazz Times Convention, I briefly met Fleurine, the woman who would become my wife and the mother of our three children. Eventually, I would make my way back to another rehab in LA, finally get clean, and start a life with her there.

The past, present, and future

> It is a matter of common belief . . . that when God promises to answer our prayers, He does not promise to give us exactly what we ask for. But we can always be certain that if he does not give us that, it is because He has something much better to give us instead.
>
> Thomas Merton, *The Seven Storey Mountain*
> *(An Autobiography of Faith)*

3/11/11

Taking the Amtrak train from Penn Station, New York City, to Boston. On the way to a gig at Sanders Theatre in Cambridge with a dream-team group of musicians for a piece I've written called "Rock'n'Roll Dances" which I just premiered a few days earlier as Composer in Residence at Carnegie Hall, and some additional material from other contemporary composers. It includes pianist and long-time friend Kevin Hays, pianist/ composer Timothy Andres, whose music will appear on the program, singer-songwriter Becca Stevens, and a gaggle of A-list reed players: Chris Cheek, Chris Potter, Joris Roelofs, Joshua Redman, Sam Sadigursky, and Gregory Tardy. At Penn Station in the morning before we all leave, memories are already wandering in – when I lived at the Sloane House YMCA one block from the station my first year in New York City, smoking blunts on 7th Avenue, later on wandering into Penn Station with Simon to play Centipede in the seedy video arcade that's no longer there . . . Taking the train those first years in the city to go home to my parents, remembering those train rides and the good feeling of coming home, arriving in Hartford, my dad there to pick me up, the cozy safety of home juxtaposed with midtown Manhattan.

And now I'm back at Penn Station again, going somewhere else, having the opportunity to play with all of these musicians, some that I've had relationships with for years, some I'm just getting to know. It's music that I've worked hard on and can be proud of, music that will have an audience that has grown to believe in what I do, or will at least go out on a limb with me. Gratitude – plain and simple – for all of that, for where I've come to at this point. The voice that comes in my head sometimes is there strongly: the good, clear voice that says, "This is as good as it gets. It never needs to get better than this, and I know that I'm blessed."

As we approach Boston, I decide to grab a yoga class before the gig – it's tight, but I can still fit it in. I never would have imagined that I'd be into yoga when I was coming up in New York all those years ago, smoking Old Golds with Bill, eating pizza slices with deli coffee for breakfast at noon. Funny how life changes: you trade in your old desires for new ones, and, if you play the game right, you choose healthy ones. That's how you survive for the long run. Following the directions for the studio on the Maps app, I get off one station earlier than everybody else, exiting the train at Back Bay Station.

Back Bay, Back Bay . . . I start trying to remember everything I know about Boston from the time I've spent there over the years. As soon as I come out of the station, I see a Nordstrom department store across the street and a rush of memory hits me. Now I know where I am. This is my old neighborhood – Back Bay. Shit, I didn't even remember that's what it was called. Whenever I had tried to think about my time in Boston over the years, it was all hazy – did I live in the south end of town? Was it called South Bay, South Boston? No, no – it was Back Bay. Now I see where I am, and I see myself then, walking around through the station like a lost ghost, terrified. I remember the beginning of the end for the first time in a while – I'm right here where it happened.

After Tanya threw me out, I moved to Boston from West Hartford to try to get away from heroin and make a clean break. It's what's called a "geographical," and it never works. You try to make a fresh start by going to a place that has no associations or connections with your self-destructive behavior but, invariably, you pick up where you left off after a while, plunging in even deeper. So it was for me in Boston. I had burnt my last bridge in West Hartford with Tanya. She gave me the boot because I kept shooting up in the bathroom we shared, leaving blood in the sink and on the toilet seat. "No needles in my house!" she was always telling me, and I couldn't even get it together enough to clean up after myself and cover my tracks.

I picked Boston partially because I had good memories of the place. I was chasing the past, chasing that time before everything got broken. Boston was Longy for me, with all its happy associations. It was like a dream now, but I ran to it, thinking I could maybe summon it and grab hold of it again. It's what I was always trying to do in one way or another during my *Bildung*, and here I was doing it, one last time: trying to crawl back into the dream, through fantasy, through drugs, and now through a change of residence.

So I wound up in Beantown again, more than a decade later, thinking that maybe I could find some purpose. It was the same thing that attracted me to the city when I was a kid: the feeling of the academy, the imagined coziness of old books and learning, the reassuring wonkiness of study in evidence at all the college campuses arrayed around the city and its environs. It was a world I had never occupied but always wanted to. Simon had switched gears and was in that world now – he was going to graduate school there and had a beautiful, smart new girlfriend he had met on campus. He had pretty much kicked the stuff and I figured if he could do it I could too. Maybe if I moved there I could get some of what he was getting. Yet I would remain on a fucked-up kind of periphery, a bit like that little match girl in the Hans Christian Andersen fairytale – walking through the cold streets, looking at the warm people inside.

I rented a dismal basement apartment close to Back Bay Station with no windows in an otherwise pretty nice building because it was cheap. I had barely any money and was living gig by gig. I was alone there and the blackness just followed me. That's not true – I sought it out, my old companion. The first few nights I walked around the neighborhood by myself, sniffing it out, and, in short time, I found my new old friend – I saw him on the street, standing on the corner with his hands in his pockets, and knew he was after the same thing I was. Hector.

He showed me where to score and in no time I was back to using, with no more pretext of trying to stop. Besides Simon there was no one I knew in Boston except my new pal. So I went all the way in; the whole day and night was about nothing except dope. There was practically nothing in that basement apartment except for a mattress, some clothes, a few books I had brought along, and some cutlery in the sink that I never washed. I had started to move a few boxes out of my parents' place but didn't get any further than that. Hector and I went everywhere together. One of the few other possessions I had brought with me was my stereo set, and, near the end, we brought that to the pawnshop together – he helped carry the speakers.

Sometimes we'd get some money together – almost always mine – and Hector knew where to get some better-quality H, less cut than the stuff on the street. We'd take the T out to Lynn, almost an hour trip. Then we'd walk for twenty minutes through a working-class neighborhood full of pissed-off people glaring at us hatefully and he'd leave me at a pizza place nursing a soda for an hour and finally come back with the stuff; he was already loaded and I'd be sore at him until he'd give me my cut. Then I'd go shoot up in the bathroom and everything was all right again for a little while.

Once, we made the journey with Hector's wife. They were a few years older than me, end of their twenties, and she was about five months pregnant, showing. She shot at least as much H as he did and their thing was to mix in coke whenever they could get it, or smoke rock. I was sure that baby was already dead inside her. They left me in the pizza joint and were gone for even more than hour. When they came back they were both completely gowd out. I was pissed, but mostly I was hurt. Why couldn't I have gone with them? It's because he was watching out for his lady first – it only made sense. They saw me as a chump no doubt, and probably laughed about it while they were shooting up, me sitting there sick, gnawing on a pizza crust and sucking on ice cubes like an A-class loser. I thought: I'd never hang you up to dry like that, man.

But this was the kind of friend I chose at this point in the game – a fake friend. Sure, it bothered me that I wanted dope and he was jacking me up like that. But far worse was that I actually wanted to connect with a person like that and give him loyalty. I didn't want to be with people who still loved me. They were far away now. I didn't feel like I was worth it. So I stuck with these assholes who burnt me and came back for more. I was like a house-trained dog separated from its benevolent owners, wrongly trusting the street. I could never watch out for myself as a junkie. I had no skill for self-preservation. Instinct, sure – but no chops, no edge. I was always just a little too soft. I never had that sociopathic streak in me that was required to really ice someone. So I got iced myself.

When I come out of Back Bay Station all these years later and see the department store, I realize I've walked right into my past and I remember that day – the last time I tried to score before I finally threw in the towel. I was down to my last six dollars. I had no food and no gigs and was dopesick. It was around eleven in the morning, one of those Boston January days that's impossibly sunny and yet unbearably cold – the sun beats down on your tired eyes mercilessly, making you squint and shield your gaze; at the same time the cold wind rips through your clothes, stings your ears, and goes right through your pants up your nuts. What the fuck was I doing here? I had nothing going on – I had less than nothing. Sick, tired, alone.

The day before, I had hit a real low. I had that important record date in New York City with David. I was dopesick, though, and couldn't face the prospect of going anywhere. His manager called, looking for me at the studio, and I picked up, thinking it might be Hector. She asked if Brad was there and I said no; she asked if I knew when he might be back, and I remember I said with all the phony professionalism I could muster, emphatically, "I have no idea when he'll be back."

I was blowing off this big record of David's, completely screwing him over, leaving him paying for a studio without a piano player on his biggest record yet, just as his career was ascending – it was a real low point, to just go AWOL like that on him. And for what? I had tried to score the day before and gotten beat for a ten-dollar bag and spent the whole day being sick. Now it was day number two. I had six dollars to my name. Hector was nowhere around and he wouldn't have helped me anyways. He always wanted a cut and I couldn't have offered him one now.

I ran into two girls I knew from the avenue. We had bought a few times at the same building on Tremont Street and they were always cool – Southie Irish girls who came over on the tube to cop. Acid-washed jeans, fake leather jackets, Marlboro Light Menthol 100s . . . The brunette with the feathered hair was in her middle twenties like me and the other one was a younger blonde with a mullet, probably nineteen tops, real scrappy, with a mouth – fuckin' this, fuckin' that, fuckin' everything, pronounced like "fuck-aiiiin" . . . They knew this other building where Hector went sometimes but I didn't have the password. I asked them if they wanted to go in on a bag – half a ten-dollar bag would barely even get me well but it would get me better than I was feeling. The young one took my six dollars and went into the building and I waited outside in the cold with the brunette. She was sympathetic and saw I was sick. We got along just fine. In an alternate reality we might be standing around the hors d'oeuvres table at some office party, talking about the weather. Now we were standing around a bodega waiting for some dope, talking about the weather.

I spent a fair amount of time with other addicts, chasing and using drugs, and reflected on how there was no set point at which they relinquished their civility and no clear reason why they finally did right then. For the two of us there, we may have been jonesing hard, but it didn't mean we couldn't go through the motions of sociality in our small talk. We sat there and offered information to each other. Her: "I gotta work today, she better hurry up." Me: "Wow, that's rough. I'm blowing off something big." I asked a few questions, on autopilot. It turned out she worked in a hospital as a nurse. Go figure. There was just that little bit of forced empathy, that acknowledgment of what the other one was trudging through that day, instead of standing there silently like two stupid drones. I realize now that precisely at that point near the end for me when I had lost so much and had no hope, the effort I made to engage in something like care for another person's travails, even if it was largely scripted, with one eye on the door of the apartment building to see if her friend with the mullet was coming out – just that effort was keeping me going. It was allowing me to see myself as human, as in still possessing humanity. That was important for me for some reason. Was it upbringing; was it something innate? Or was it just a desperate kind of vanity?

Staying human mattered to Brunette as well as she talked with me. Not for Mullet. She came out of the building after about ten minutes, looked at us across the street and then started walking fast the other direction. What the fuck? Brunette was as confused as I was. We walked behind her and Brunette called her, yelling. She kept walking fast, and I knew right then that she didn't want to give me my cut. Brunette knew it too, and it was awkward – she wouldn't have burned me like that. Mullet was acting on some asocial instinct; she really hadn't thought this one through because her friend was still with me. Brunette kept on calling to her, "What are you doing?" she yelled. I didn't even bother to say what we both already knew: "Your friend's trying to burn me." We followed her toward the train station. She crossed the street and headed into Nordstrom. "She's flipped her fuckin' lid," said Brunette. We entered behind her. Inside, employees lingered around at their counters, looking at us contemptuously. Mullet hopped on the escalator and we followed behind her. She turned around as we closed the gap and hissed, "Fuck off! Stop following me!" Fucking bitch, I thought. But I was too meek – if I was another kind of guy I would have walloped her right there and we would *all go to jail. She ran up to the second floor, men's clothing. We're walking around, following her – what a charade. Brunette says to her, "What are you doing this for? What's the matter with you?" Mullet turns to her and snaps back, "What's the matter with you – and your stupid boyfriend?" then looks at me with idiot hatred. I realize then, dimly, that these two are a couple, and I realize in the same moment that I'm not going to get my dope, that she'd rather spill it on the floor than give it to me, the little cunt. I slump out of the store, hollow. I couldn't have imagined that today would be worse than yesterday but now it was. And it wasn't even noon.*

The self is the conscious synthesis of infinitude and finitude that relates itself to itself, whose task is to become itself, which can be done only through the relationship to God. To become oneself is to become concrete. But to become concrete is neither to become finite nor to become infinite, for that which is to become concrete is indeed a synthesis. Consequently, the progress of the becoming must be an infinite moving away from itself in the infinitizing of the self, and an infinite coming back to itself in the finitizing process.

Kierkegaard, *The Sickness Unto Death*

It seeks its "other", knowing that therein it possesses nothing else but itself: it seeks only its own infinitude.

Hegel, *The Phenomenology of Spirit*

Dream: Dylan, Ed, and I. We have met somewhere in some kind of magical hyperreal/impossible city. Once again, I am my adult age, yet they seem to be that same age when the glass shattered. They are Peter Pans in my head, Dylan and Ed. Sadness and fear linger in the dream, and also the excitement of seeing Dylan again. It's Dylan I want to see and be close to. But I can't take him away from Ed. I put my hand on his shoulder. "Come with me," I say, pleading. Dylan says, "I can't," looking at Ed. I look at Ed, who has been urging Dylan to leave with him. Suddenly, I realize something and look at Dylan, whispering a one-word question.

"Jealous?" I say, glancing Ed's way. Dylan nods yes. Why hadn't I thought of this? Ed was jealous all those years ago, that I took Dylan away from him. That's why he initiated that rampage of hateful bullying my first year of high school – not just because he was ashamed of his homosexual feelings, no . . . it was something more at the core, more intense than shame. No, what he felt, just like I did later, was rejection, when Dylan and I became best buddies that summer and he was left on the sidelines. He had been there before me, sleeping over Dylan's house, making love to his friend. And then it was me who took his place, this kid from the other side of town who just appeared suddenly, and Dylan then gave himself to me, not him. The thing with all these dreams is that they might or might not be true: all the characters are part of me – Ed's pain of rejection, however real it might have been, is just as much my own. These kinds of realizations only come in dreams, where the various characters are just parables for my own pain and self-obsession.

The three of us are in a cabin like the ones that ski jumpers use in the Olympics. Except, instead of skis, we have dirt bikes like we used to ride as kids, and outside of the cabin are stair streets like in parts of LA or San Francisco. After Dylan nods to me, he says something quickly, like, "I'll see you later." It seems to be conspiratorial, like he is almost winking to me, signaling that he just has to get rid of Ed. But I'm filled with fear, because he is leaving, again. Ed and Dylan descend from the cabin onto a kind of track and they pedal away. Is Dylan just trying to get rid of me; is he playing me for a fool, to be with Ed?

Or is he playing Ed for a fool? Or both of us? Or, maybe, he was just confused all those years ago, when he pushed me away and it hurt so much, when he "rode away" with Ed. So he shunned me, like I shunned him earlier.

But now, in the dream, I am trying to chase him. For years, when Dylan has appeared in these dreams, there's this wish to have him back. I want to put my arm around him and give him a hug, and be there for him as a friend the way I wasn't, all those years ago. I want to tell him that everything will be all right, and comfort him. I want him to need me and love me; I want to love him back. In this way, I can be whole somehow. Is all that not just more self-obsession, though? I'm making Dylan into someone who will save me, just as I'll save him. But Dylan is just a dream in my head at this point. The real Dylan has moved on to another station – he drove away on his dirt bike decades ago. No . . . the Dylan in my head is just me – and Ed too. I want Dylan to forgive me; I want Ed to like me. But what that really means is I need to forgive myself – for everything else I broke in the years since then. In that way, I can let go of that deep fear. The fear is of something inside of me, but the love must also come from inside. Why am I afraid? Why do I still not feel whole?

Dylan and Ed ride across the track, which is thin, just wide enough for the tires of their bikes. The track is a precipice, though, and hovers over a great expanse. Below it is the city. The city is dark, kind of smoky, lonely and sad – it feels deserted. If there are people there, they are hidden. Yet I know this city from somewhere. The city is my consciousness, and Dylan and Ed ride their bikes through it. They reach the other side of the bridge and I am riding behind them, calling Dylan's name. But they don't turn around or stop. Now, they are riding up steep stairs, impossibly, at a ninety-degree angle. The stairs are on the sides of old concrete apartment buildings. As I look around the city, they make L shapes, and the whole expanse is like one of those geometrically impossible drawings from M.C. Escher.

Impossibility, impossibility. Everywhere, the feeling of impossibility, of insurmountability, writes itself onto my consciousness. This is the only set of pencils I have; this is the only drawing I can make.

Dylan and Ed ride across the horizontal part of the L shapes, and then climb up the vertical lines, traversing the sides of the buildings on their bikes. I am losing my ground. I call after Dylan in vain, still hoping that he'll come back to me. The last voice I hear, though, is Ed's. With his back towards me still, riding forward, he leads the way on his own bike, shouting to Dylan: "Ride! Ride!" In the dream, I exist in a kind of denial, and continue to chase them, thinking that they don't hear me calling. As soon as I wake up, though, I realize that Ed does hear me, and is spurring Dylan on all the more urgently, to lose me in the chase completely, to ditch me.

But if Dylan and Ed are part of my consciousness, and what I always dream of is one or another wish for self-reconciliation, this desire to be whole again, then how do I find that? In these dreams, I never achieve the union with myself – I never get that hug from Dylan; Ed never comes over to me and tousles my hair, saying, "You're all right, Brad. We're buddies again."

No, Ed says: *"Ride. Ride."*

Maybe he was talking to me, though. He meant: Ride *away*, Brad. Leave all this behind. *Leave behind the dream of repairing something broken.* Leave behind the dream of getting the love you wanted then and still crave now, so long after that rupture. Ride far away, and abandon, once and for all, that wish.

So there are two yearnings: one is to find myself again, and make myself whole. And the other is to relinquish my identity – to give up this story I've been telling myself for years once and for all, to drop an illusion that is only crippling me at this point. The story doesn't work anymore. It did for a while, but it's served its purpose.

Loving and forgiving myself; relinquishing that "self" . . . They seem to be opposite actions. That's why I feel deep ambivalence and cannot find clarity.

But maybe they're the same. Maybe they are both the place where I find God. Far, far away, away from all that self-obsession, there is an infinite Father into whom I disappear completely. And yet He rests right here within me, in all my weakness and finitude – loving, forgiving.

Carry on

My eyes are ever toward the Lord, for he will pluck my feet out of the net.

Psalm 25:15

Trout Brook still winds through West Hartford and comes to meet me when I go back to visit, soon after exiting Interstate 84, hidden behind backyards but close by the main road, driving through the center of town towards my old house. It's a stream of memories now. It murmured through Westmoor Park behind Ricky's house, its tiny tributaries wound into the woods behind Bugbee Elementary School alongside Bugbee Path, gently percolating in the summer while we made jumps on our dirt bikes, or almost silent and half-frozen in the winter, seen from that small wooden bridge full of icicles. Moving southeastward, it widened into a pond that was good for skating, before it thinned into a brook again and crossed under North Main Street. Then it flowed steadily southward along Trout Brook Drive towards Ed and Dylan's neighborhood. In some places it was wide and deep, but often it was laughably shallow, and, depending on the amount of rainfall, it was easy enough to hopscotch over some rocks to cross it. My friend Silas, who showed me the way to school on Bugbee Path that first scary day, lived one block over from me, had a backyard with a hill that sloped sharply downwards and met with the brook. On the other side was my other buddy Peter from those dirt-bike days, whose house was close to the skating pond. We played there often, the three of us.

(Vision)

It's a late January afternoon after school and the sun is already low, like a smoky blood orange in the distance. I can smell smoke – I smell the hearth of Silas's fireplace, the reassurance of those burning embers. We're playing as long as we can before Peter and I have to go home for dinner, like the three of us always did that year in sixth grade. We're making up some story about enemy troops coming up from the rear in Silas's backyard. We can hear them on the charge and in no time they'll be on the top of the hill and will start picking us off with their muskets. We've got to cross the brook! Peter goes first, stepping gingerly over the rocks. He makes it over quickly, jumping off the final stone onto the safe mossy earth on the other side. He turns around and smiles. "Your turn! Hurry up. They're coming!" We all collectively imagine the storm of footsteps and shouting, closing in on us. It was a game then but I hear the sound now in this vision and it's no fun – it's deafening; it will swallow me. The play-fear turns real. "Your turn, Brad," says Silas. Now suddenly he has a rope, and throws one end across the brook to Peter, who catches it easily. They both look at me, tightening the rope. "Use it to cross!" Peter instructs me, looking at me quizzically. "Don't be afraid, you'll make it easy." He's my friend but for a moment I don't trust him. Does he wish me well? I'm scared as I look at the brook. Now it is deeper than before, and the water darts violently over the rocks, driven by some vicious spirit.

After I got burnt by Mullet, I dragged myself back to my basement room, shattered and hollow. I was dopesick but not as bad as that first time, because I hadn't been able to use properly for a few weeks – it was touch and go. I was caught suspended in the misery between not quite sick and not quite well. There was a dry spell on the streets and it was impossible to score. The worst part, though, was the feeling of being utterly alone. Hector had disappeared somewhere with his wife. I never saw them again. Even my crappy drug buddy was gone.

I was broke anyways even if there had been some dope around to buy. The stereo was in hock. I would have sold those five or six original Coltrane Impulse sides I had with me – I just didn't know a place to do it. I wanted to use so badly because it would take away the rock in my gut instantly, if only for a short moment. I was paralyzed with fear and loneliness. I had fucked up everything: there were no gigs; I had skipped out of David's record date and left him high and dry; my parents didn't want me back there; Sarah was gone; and all my friends were far away except Simon. I didn't want to drag him into my shitty morass – he was putting his life together again, going somewhere.

If I could get high, I figured, then I could plan my next move. But there was no way to do it – no money, no dope. Maybe it was time to try to get clean again. I had been floating the thought lately. Really, it seemed like the only idea left, apart from another one. It had entered my thinking the last few days, crawling around the edges of my thoughts for the first time – to just end it, to end everything. But the idea of going through with that brought on anguish, and deeper dread.

So I found a sliver of energy. I called my dad one more time and got him on the phone. He told me about a place he had heard about in LA. It was the hardcore alternative to the other rehab I had already tried there – ninety days of inpatient boot camp. Ugh. Fuck it. – I'll try it, I croaked. I knew that if I said anything else at this point, he'd just hang up the phone right then. He said he had the number of the admissions director there and would call him and get me a bed as soon as we hung up. Then he would drive to Boston when I had the ticket, see me off, pack up the apartment, and close the lease. I wouldn't be coming back there. I hung up and called American. I still had enough miles for a free ticket and the chirpy lady on the phone got me a one-way Logan–LAX for tomorrow morning. Done.

The rest of the day was hell, but there was nothing to do but wait it out. I had only half a cheese sandwich and a couple gulps worth of fruit punch left in the fridge. I always forgot to drink water or anything when I was using so I was dehydrated and saw stars every time I got up. Practically the only thing I ever ate was those cheese sandwiches and Kit Kats when I'd get the sweet jones, washed down with the Ocean Spray fruit punch. I lay awake most of the night thinking about better days gone by from before everything got broken, imagining I could grab hold of them again. Fantasy was the only drug I had left.

> *The water is wide and deep now. I take the rope. "We'll pull on it from both sides," says Silas. I step out and begin, making my way to the middle. There is one small rock and I know it's slippery. If I can clear that one, it's easier then, with plenty of large stones. I look at Peter and Silas on either side. They're just waiting, pulling on the rope to keep it tight. But it's not enough. If I step to that small rock I know I'll slip and fall into the deep, icy cold water. I need something else – something I can lean into. It's not something Silas or Peter can give me. I don't see it yet.*

I got out of bed in the morning and packed a duffel bag with some clothes and a pocket-sized copy of Rilke's *Sonnets to Orpheus*. My dad showed up like he promised and gave me a hug. "Good luck." I watched him walk towards his car, walked into Back Bay Station and jumped the turnstile one last time, waiting for the train that would take me to the airport. I stood on the ledge, looking down at the tracks. I was in the deepest despair I had ever felt in my life. I didn't want to go on. I didn't want to get on that plane.

I couldn't turn around and go back to the empty room I'd just left. I looked at the train approaching and looked down at the tracks. One voice in my head said: "Jump." Another voice said: "Get on the train." I stood my ground and boarded the train.

From there on everything started to change. I was still sick and scared, but it was like someone was carrying me now. And every time the resolve to go on would diminish, someone's voice would say, "Go on. See it through." I made it on the plane and, when it started to take off, a new feeling I had never had before started to take hold and didn't leave. It was a feeling of lightness, of being carried. I was starting to find my God.

He's never left me since, even when I leave Him. I realized later that He had always been with me – when I was bullied every day at school, being thrown against the wall of a staircase or spat at by Ed or Darren, when I was naked in the shower stalls with Dr. Dunn, shooting up in broken buildings with Miguel and James, right up until those last days in Boston. I just hadn't known to reach out and take His hand. He took my hand now. They say that you have to extend your own hand – you have to make the first move, and then you'll come upon God. Seek and you shall find. It's true. But there have been moments in my life when He reached down and grabbed my hand. That was one of them.

I boarded the plane and it took off. The flight was long and rough but there was this feeling: everything is going to be all right. Everything *is* all right.

About an hour before landing, there was stirring from several rows behind me, some anxious voices. Suddenly the stewardess was making an announcement: was there a doctor on the plane? We all turned around. There was an Asian man in an aisle seat, probably in his mid-sixties; it looked like he was traveling alone. A nurse practitioner had made his way over there and was speaking loudly to him. "Hello there! Hello!" He asked the man if he knew his own name. "We're going to take care of you. Everything is going to be all right. Stay with me."

It's like he was talking to me. The man was having difficulty breathing. He was going in and out, he was fading. Nobody knew if he spoke English. I looked at him directly and could see him. He was looking at the registered nurse – this strong guy who spoke to him in clear tones, holding his hand firmly and keeping him from slipping away. And he was scared, but he was smiling. That guy had his hand, and he knew he would see him through to wherever it might be. He made it. The plane touched down and the medical unit took him out first on a stretcher, while we all sat silently.

There's a phenomenon where something jarring happens when you're drunk, and it instantly sobers you up – the party's over. This was kind of the same, but from the other end. I was clear-headed now; I had resolve. Somewhere in me was this conviction, strong and abiding: I want to live.

It's funny when you're scared of something: you can't look away from it. It's all you see. I am staring down into that icy, black water, because I'm afraid that if I look up I'll lose my balance and drop into it. Trout Brook – it started out a gentle stream, easy to cross, inviting even as it was mysterious, a place of discovery, a place of refuge, a place of excitement. Later, though, it became deeper, confusing, unfathomable. And now it is menacing.

I raise my eyes and see something: a branch. A large, solid branch. How did I not see this? There is this tree now, in the middle of the brook. How does it grow out of the rushing water like that; how does it stay rooted? It must have always been there and I just hadn't noticed it. The water swivels around it but it doesn't move. The January wind whips up around us, but its branches only rock steadily; they move with the wind but are not ruled by it. I raise my head slowly and now I know it's time. I drop my body towards the branch, over the icy current, letting go of the rope. There is this space, this silence as I fall through the air – a sacred moment where everything stops. Something dies, but it needs to die. What was it that poet wrote? Death cancels out everything but the truth.

My hands connect to the branch. I feel the solid wood. This tree extends deep into the earth. I sense its roots under the water. Now I am being lifted, though, lifted by that branch. The fear leaves my body. I am in the air, yet I am connected to the earth. It swings me towards the other side and my feet land firmly on the ground. Peter is there waiting for me.

"Finally!" he says, his face screwed up in a grin. "It's about time! What took you so long?"

I got off the plane at LAX and made my way to the baggage claim. There were two women there, waiting with a sign. They welcomed me with a hug. I could tell they were like me – broken. But I could see they were strong, too. "Come on, let's get you out of here," one of them said.

We got in the big Chevy van and made our way onto the 405 freeway. The windows were open, the road was wide, the warm LA air came in and the sun washed over me. The girl driving turned on the radio. Crosby, Stills Nash & Young came on – one of my favorite songs: "Carry On." It was from *Déjà Vu*, an album that Joe had turned me on to that last summer at Merrywood. I connected the feeling of that summer in 1983 – the feeling of possibility, like something was about to reveal itself and it would be like nothing I knew before – to the hope I was just starting to feel now. I had forgotten what that had felt like and it was good. Everything was coming around back again. Something was starting to heal already. I felt like I was in a dream, or maybe like I had died and was on a trip up to heaven. I was being carried now – all I had to do was let it happen. The band started to sing:

> One morning, I woke up, and I knew you were really gone
> A new day, a new way, and new eyes to see the dawn
> Go your way, I'll go mine and carry on.
>
> To sing the blues, you've got to live the dues and carry on

Epilogue

> — And we have, have we not, those priceless pages of *Wilhelm Meister*? A great poet on a great brother poet. A hesitating soul taking arms against a sea of troubles, torn by conflicting doubts, as one sees in real life.
>
> James Joyce, *Ulysses*

There were two teachers. They addressed the student.

The first one said: "To not dwell on a fixed idea of yourself – to really not know who you are, right in this moment: this is complete freedom. If you think you know who you are, you will be locked into a view which is false, because reality is fluid and always shifting. By holding onto your identity, you are holding onto all of the afflictions that inhibit you from growing and changing. Is that really what you want?"

The second one said: "Know who you are at all times and hold onto that knowledge strongly. If you never allow yourself to believe in something, you'll always be lost, walking aimlessly in a forest with no markers. Is that really what you want?"

The first teacher said: "There is not one truth. There is only what is true for you in this moment. If you think that truth is constant and never changing, you will deceive yourself and be caught in a dogma, unable to see the nature of what is in front of you right now. You will be trying to define a great variety of events in your life with a very limited set of descriptions. You will deprive yourself of the richness of intuitively experiencing anything, always having to make sure it's 'true.'"

The second teacher said: "There is only one truth. Everything around you may be shifting, but that truth never changes. You must hold fast to that truth. Otherwise you will lose yourself – you will have no ground to stand on, because truth will only be relative to you. And when truth is only relative, there is no value in the Path. There is no right or wrong then; there is no reason to struggle for anything you believe in, to face challenge – because you don't believe in anything."

The first teacher said: "When you are willing to not believe in anything, you will find yourself. Once you believe in something, you are already locked into a false perception. Truth goes beyond any idea we can assign to it. Reality cannot be frozen into an idea."

The second teacher said: "You must believe in something wholeheartedly, constantly, despite all evidence against it. You must see that truth is never relative – that through all of the claims at truth that come your way from various sources, that one truth remains. The constant flux that you observe at all times is not real – look for the non-moving truth behind all of that, and there you will find knowledge of yourself, and peace."

The student listened and thought long and hard about the two teachings. He observed that while they seemed to express opposite views, they arrived at the same conclusion. In order to find the truth, you had to move beyond your immediate perception of reality. If you were able to look deeper, you would find that "truth" of which both of them spoke. And then, in fact, whether that truth was constant or fluid wouldn't really matter anymore.

The one said that believing in something fixed was false, and the other said that believing in something shifting was false. Because the student liked both of the teachings, he decided that he would simply accept and believe both of them. As soon as he did that, he realized that they were both true, and at the same time neither of them was completely true. Neither of them could account for all of reality. He realized that the two teachings were a pair – they needed each other.

In order to arrive at a truth for oneself, the student realized he had to believe both of his teachers. He had to take both of their teachings into his heart and let them rest there. When he did that, it seemed that he knew for himself, finally, what was real. The student felt that, at this point, he wouldn't describe that knowledge as "believing" in something. It wasn't belief, now. He looked for another word, and he found it: it was faith.

Faith was indeed in something constant, but, if it was solid faith, it could allow all of the various "truths" to arise, and accept that there was something of value in every one of them. The student saw that he could learn something from what appeared to be true at one point, even if later it revealed itself as false, for, before he knew that it was false, he had to believe it was true. Faith for him meant: accepting this process of assimilating a constantly shifting truth. By allowing himself to never rest on a fixed idea of who he was, he would, indeed, over time, slowly come to know who he truly was. Yet he was only able to allow himself that fluidity because there was nevertheless some-thing constant behind it all.

At first, the student was pleased and thought he had solved a big problem. But, soon after that, something happened. He felt lost again; he felt doubt in what he had just learned. He was able to accept it intellectually, but not in his heart. He couldn't live it. He was dismayed. He realized that, as quickly as he had discovered faith, just as quickly and even more easily had he lost it. He knew then, with a new foreboding, that his faith would have to be stronger and more invincible, less contingent on whatever was coming his way in the daily strife of his life. But how to nurture that faith? This required action.

And so the real work began.

Selected Discography

Here is a discography of albums recorded during my *Bildung* specifically: that is, through 1996, several of which are discussed here in the book. It is followed by a list of several post-*Bildung* recordings I mentioned as well. The years given are the year recorded (rather than the year of release) followed by the label. For a comprehensive discography of everything I've done as a leader, co-leader and sideman, please visit the "Music" page on my website: https://www.bradmehldaumusic.com/music and scroll to the bottom.

Bildung records
Christopher Hollyday, *The Natural Moment* (RCA Novus, 1991)
Peter Bernstein, *Somethin's Burnin'* (Criss Cross Jazz, 1992)
Grant Stewart Quintet, *Downtown Sounds* (Criss Cross Jazz, 1992)
Jesse Davis, *Young at Art* (Concord Jazz, 1993)
Mehldau & Rossy Trio, *When I Fall in Love* (Fresh Sound, 1993)
Mehldau, Rossy, Rossy, Sambeat, *New York–Barcelona Crossing* Volumes 1 & 2 (Fresh Sound, 1993)
Mark Turner Quintet, *Yam Yam* (Criss Cross Jazz, 1994)
Peter Bernstein Quartet, *Signs of Life* (Criss Cross Jazz, 1994)
Joshua Redman Quartet, *MoodSwing* (Warner Bros. Jazz, 1994)
Mehldau, Turner, Bernstein, Grenadier, Parker, *Consenting Adults* (Criss Cross Jazz, 1994)
Perico Sambeat, *Ademuz* (Fresh Sound, 1995)
Warner Jams, Volume 1 (various artists) (Warner Bros. Jazz, 1995)
Introducing Brad Mehldau (Warner Bros. Jazz, 1995)
Chris Potter, *Moving In* (Concord Jazz, 1996)

Post-*Bildung* records mentioned in this book
The Art of the Trio Volume One (Warner Bros. Jazz, 1996)
Live at the Village Vanguard: The Art of the Trio Volume Two (Warner Bros. Jazz, 1997)
Songs: The Art of the Trio Volume Three (Warner Bros. Jazz, 1998)
Elegiac Cycle (Warner Bros. Jazz, 1999)
The Art of the Trio 4: Back at the Vanguard (Warner Bros. Jazz, 1999)
Places (Warner Bros. Jazz, 2000)
Progression: Art of the Trio, Volume 5 (Warner Bros. Jazz, 2000)

Largo (Warner Bros. Jazz, 2001)

Charlie Haden, *American Dreams* (Verve, 2002)

Joel Frahm and Brad Mehldau, *Don't Explain* (Palmetto Records, 2004)

Brad Mehldau and Pat Metheny, *Metheny/Mehldau* (Nonesuch, 2005)

Mehldau, Metheny, Grenadier, Ballard, *Metheny/Mehldau Quartet* (Nonesuch, 2005)

Highway Rider (Nonesuch, 2010)

Pat Zimmerli, Kevin Hays, and Brad Mehldau, *Modern Music* (Nonesuch, 2010)

Chris Thile & Brad Mehldau (Nonesuch, 2016)

Finding Gabriel (Nonesuch, 2018)

Jacob's Ladder (Nonesuch, 2020)

Acknowledgments

The author wishes to give warm thanks to those who helped shepherd this book into existence: Chris Kepner at The Kepner Agency; Alyn Shipton, Dean Bargh, Janet Joyce, and Val Hall at Equinox Publishing; Scott Southard at IMN; Melissa Cusick at Nonesuch Records; and Deborah Evans at Della Music Clearances.

More Than A Feeling
Words and Music by Tom Scholz
Copyright © 1976 UNIVERSAL MUSIC WORKS and PRIMARY WAVE BOSTON
Copyright Renewed
All Rights Administered by UNIVERSAL MUSIC WORKS
All Rights Reserved Used by Permission
Reprinted by permission of Hal Leonard LLC

Rock'n Me
Words and Music by Steve Miller
Copyright © 1976 by Sailor Music
Copyright Renewed
All Rights Reserved   Used by Permission
Reprinted by permission of Hal Leonard LLC

Carry On
Words and Music by Stephen Stills
Copyright © 1971 Gold Hill Music, Inc.
Copyright Renewed
All Rights Reserved   Used by Permission
Reprinted by permission of Hal Leonard LLC

Captain Jack
Words and Music by Billy Joel
Copyright © 1973 IMPULSIVE MUSIC
Copyright Renewed
All Rights Administered by ALMO MUSIC CORP.
All Rights Reserved   Used by Permission
Reprinted by permission of Hal Leonard LLC

Dreams
Words and Music by Stevie Nicks
Copyright © 1977 Welsh Witch Music
Copyright Renewed
All Rights Administered by Kobalt Songs Music Publishing
All Rights Reserved   Used by Permission
Reprinted by permission of Hal Leonard LLC

Don't Believe The Hype
Words and Music by Eric Sadler, James Boxley III and Carlton Ridenhour
Copyright © 1988 SONGS OF UNIVERSAL, INC., YOUR MOTHER'S MUSIC, INC., REACH GLOBAL SONGS, TERRORDOME MUSIC PUBLISHING LLC and SHOCKLEE MUSIC
All Rights for YOUR MOTHER'S MUSIC, INC. Controlled and Administered by SONGS OF UNIVERSAL, INC.
All Rights for TERRORDOME MUSIC PUBLISHING LLC and SHOCKLEE MUSIC Controlled and Administered by REACH GLOBAL SONGS
All Rights Reserved   Used by Permission
Reprinted by permission of Hal Leonard LLC

Sara
Words and Music by Stevie Nicks
Copyright © 1979 Welsh Witch Music
All Rights Administered by Kobalt Songs Music Publishing
All Rights Reserved   Used by Permission
Reprinted by permission of Hal Leonard LLC

Index

Page numbers in *italics* refer to photos.

9781800503137